THE UNIVERSITY OF WINCHESTER

Martial Rose Library
Tel: 01962 827306

To be returned on or before the day marked above, subject to recall.

Harvard East Asian Monographs 278

War Memory
and Social Politics
in Japan, 1945–2005

Franziska Seraphim

Published by the Harvard University Asia Center
Distributed by Harvard University Press
Cambridge (Massachusetts) and London 2006

Printed in the United States of America

The Harvard University Asia Center publishes a monograph series and, in coordination with the Fairbank Center for Chinese Studies, the Korea Institute, the Reischauer Institute of Japanese Studies, and other faculties and institutes, administers research projects designed to further scholarly understanding of China, Japan, Vietnam, Korea, and other Asian countries. The Center also sponsors projects addressing multidisciplinary and regional issues in Asia.

Library of Congress Cataloging-in-Publication Data

Seraphim, Franziska, 1965–
    War memory and social politics in Japan, 1945–2005 / Franziska Seraphim.
        p. cm. -- (Harvard East Asian monographs ; 278)
    Includes bibliographical references and index.
    ISBN-13: 978-0-674-02271-3 (cloth : alk. paper)   ISBN-10: 0-674-02271-8 (cloth : alk. paper)
    ISBN-13: 978-0-674-02830-2 (pbk : alk. paper)
    1. Japan--History--1945– 2. Japan--Social conditions--20th century. 3. World War, 1939–1945--Social aspects--Japan. I. Title. II. Series.
    DS889.15.S4524 2006
    952.04--dc22

                                                                    2006022961

Index by Jake Kawatski

First paperback edition 2008

Last figure below indicates year of this printing
16 15 14 13 12 11 10 09 08

For Steve West

&

Sophia and Elena

Acknowledgments

This book bears the imprint of four intellectual communities and many individuals whose advice, support, and friendship sustained me at different times and in many places. Carol Gluck saw the project through the dissertation stage at Columbia University and beyond, inspiring, guiding, and supporting it all the way. To her I owe my greatest debt. Henry Smith, Andreas Huyssen, Atina Grossman, and Jeffrey Olick set the dissertation on its course toward becoming a book. Ethan Mark, Suzanne O'Brian, Julie Rousseau, Kenneth Ruoff, Jordan Sand, Sarah Thal, and Louise Young offered helpful suggestions at various stages. In Tokyo, the Japan Foundation and the German Institute for Japanese Studies (DIJ) generously supported my research during 1994–97. Ōnuma Yasuaki of the Faculty of Law at Tokyo University and Irmela Hijiya-Kirschnereit at the DIJ facilitated this work in critical ways. Okamoto Kōichi at Waseda University was of invaluable help in pointing me to Japanese sources I would otherwise have missed, providing contacts and even accommodation during a follow-up research stay, and always lending an open ear. Special thanks go to representatives of Japanese organizations for opening their archives to me: Okayasu Shigehiro of Wadatsumikai, Yazaki Mitsuharu and Mochinaga Noriko of the Japan-China Friendship Association, Suehiro Sakae of the Association of War-bereaved Families, Tonomura Masao of the National Diet Library, who introduced me to the library of the Japan Teachers' Union, and Kamisaka Fuyuko for her introduction to the Association of Shinto Shrines archives and many illuminating conversations. Petra Buchholz,

Sebastian Conrad, and Ian Johnson in Beijing (and later in Berlin) shared their expertise with me. At Duke University, Kären Wigen and Kristina Troost gave freely of their expertise, time, and friendship as the project matured. Fond recognition also goes to David Ambaras, Miles Fletcher, Simon Partner, Catherine Phipps, and Gennifer Weisenfeld. In Boston, a postdoctoral fellowship at the Edwin O. Reischauer Institute of Japanese Studies in 2002–3 provided time and resources to revise and polish the manuscript. Research incentive and research expense grants from Boston College helped bring the book to completion. John Dower generously and graciously gave of his time, knowledge, and enthusiasm to guide the revisions both conceptually and in practical detail. Having him and Carol Gluck as mentors is an extraordinary gift. Andrew Gordon read the entire manuscript closely and helped improve the clarity of my prose immensely. Helen Hardacre, Thomas Berger, Thomas Havens, Lee Pennington, and Lori Watt shared their thoughts on various occasions. Kazuko Sakaguchi at the Documentation Center on Contemporary Japan at Harvard University and James W. Zobel at the MacArthur Memorial Library in Norfolk, VA, provided archival assistance. I am also grateful for the intellectual support of my colleagues in the History Department at Boston College and especially for Kevin Kenny's insightful reading of a chapter. Warm thanks also go to my research assistants, Chiaki Kotori, Masa Higo, Yoko Tajima, and especially Tim Henderson. Last but not least, I want to acknowledge the superb editorial guidance of William Hammell and my copy editor Jane Barry at the Harvard Asia Center, which made the production of this book not only possible but a wonderful learning experience. Responsibility for all remaining mistakes is solely mine.

My love goes to my families, those I have adopted, inherited, and made. My three "Rotary" families, the Muolos, the Truslows, and the Lewises, introduced me to life in America during my exchange student year hosted by the Sunbury, PA, Rotary Club in 1983–84. The Matsuura family of Hobara in Fukushima Prefecture, Japan, and the Kitabayashi and Sasaki families in Tokyo shepherded me through my extended stays in Japan in the mid-1980s and the mid-1990s. My family in Germany and in Canada has followed my international odyssey from afar, and no one more closely than my mother. I dedicate this book to my husband Steve, who supported and nurtured me through it all. Our daughters Sophia and Elena, emphatically convinced that writing a book is the last thing they'll ever do, have nonetheless been caught—on occasion—working hard on their own "books." I am grateful that despite such ambivalence about the merit of writing books, they never allow any doubt about what really matters in life.

Contents

Figures and Tables

Figures

Tables

War Memory

and Social Politics

in Japan, 1945–2005

INTRODUCTION

For many years following Japan's unconditional surrender to the Allied Forces, Japanese people were forced to reckon with the physical, psychological, and political consequences of war and defeat in their daily lives. Faced with a landscape of physical ruin, foreign military occupation, and their own government's feeble attempts at explaining the situation, they sought to articulate for themselves what had gone wrong and who had done wrong in the past. Many were stunned, if not outraged, when on 28 August 1945 Prince Higashikuni Naruhiko, the first postwar prime minister, called on "one hundred million to repent together" (*ichioku sōzange*).[1] Higashikuni in effect declared "the people" responsible for military defeat, exempting no one but the emperor, in whose name the war had been fought. Indeed, the concept of collective repentance was typical of Japan's wartime rhetoric, and its continued use could be—and was—interpreted as an implicit justification of the war. In sharp contrast to this attempt by the Japanese authorities to dilute responsibility among the populace, Allied occupation officials insisted on assigning individual responsibility to particular Japanese leaders, arresting and trying war criminals and purging those suspected of having supported the war.

The people responded more enthusiastically to the punishment of wartime leaders than to national repentance. The assertion of collective responsibility ran counter to their overwhelming sense of their own victimization, especially in the wake of the Tokyo air raids and the atomic bombings. But no matter how the problem was framed—as individual or collective accountability, responsibility for starting the war or for losing it—positing war responsibility immediately became a strategic instrument in the politics of reinventing Japan as a peaceful and democratic society. People from all walks of life looked back at the war years through the lens of defeat and foreign occupation in efforts to identify which aspects of Japanese society needed to be changed most urgently in order to reconstruct the social system as a whole. Many attended mass rallies and listened to academics from various disciplines, to writers and critics, to Marxists, non-Marxist progressives, and even conservatives, to war cooperators and war resisters who had been imprisoned. Depending on their field of specialization, political convictions, and war experiences, they addressed the problem of responsibility in different ways and different contexts as part of a broad public discourse.

A photograph of one of these rallies (Fig. o.1) gives a sense of the dynamism that propelled this public debate. It was taken at a "public mass meeting to discuss war responsibility" (*sensō sekinin taikai*) in Tokyo in December 1946. Facing a crowded auditorium, a panel of speakers sat against a backdrop of huge hand-painted banners, which spelled out the issues and demands put forth for discussion. Some called militarists, bureaucrats, and capitalists the plunderers and torturers of ordinary people. Others called for the punishment of war criminals and the dissolution of reactionary organizations. The banner on the left demanded the establishment of a republican government and a democratic, peaceful state. Most interestingly, the banner in the middle of the photo and to the right of the speaker read, "Pursue the war responsibility of the emperor, who deprived us of our livelihoods." They all spoke to an explicit rejection of the recent Japanese past, a sense of acute postsurrender "moral deterioration" or psychosocial dislocation, and fervent support for democratic reform, individual autonomy, and political activism. Maruyama Masao called the intellectuals who met and discussed these issues in the early years after the war a "community of contrition." The common bond, he argued, was remorse for having failed to resist fascism, accompanied by a need to make sense of the war and defeat.[2]

The second photograph (Fig. o.2) fast-forwards the discussion to December 2000. It shows a group of Filipina survivors of Japan's

Fig. 0.1 A public mass meeting on responsibility for the war, December 1946. The banner to the right of the speaker reads: "Pursue the war responsibility of the emperor." By permission of Kyōdō News Agency.

Fig. 0.2 Filipina victims of Japan's wartime "comfort women" system testify at the Women's International War Crimes Tribunal in Tokyo, December 2000. Courtesy of Violence against Women in War–Network Japan (VAWW–NET Japan).

wartime sexual slavery system, called upon as historical witnesses by an international tribunal pursuing the emperor's war responsibility. Their aged, dignified faces bespeak less the horrors of the war than the long decades since then—a time during which most of them were silent about their war experiences. The three-day event was staged in Tokyo by women's groups from all over Asia under the organizational leadership of Violence against Women in War–Network Japan (VAWW–NET Japan). An international team of prominent judges heard testimonial and historical evidence about the wartime "comfort women" system from legal teams representing the countries that once suffered under Japan's empire. Specifically, it set out to examine Emperor Hirohito's historical responsibility for such war conduct (Hirohito had passed away in 1989) as the most important omission of the Tokyo war crimes trials of the 1940s. The tribunal recommended that the state of Japan (1) fully recognize its legal, political, and moral responsibility for these wartime crimes and issue an unambiguous apology to the victims, (2) consider the establishment of a Truth and Reconciliation Commission and make available to the public all historical documents pertaining to wartime sexual slavery, (3) pay adequate compensation to survivors and establish appropriate educational tools and commemorative sites to honor them.[3] The Japanese government, not legally bound by this unofficial tribunal, paid scant attention to the event.

Japan's History of War Memory: A Framework

The two events (and their associated images) frame Japan's history of war memory. First, they suggest, correctly, that questions of war memory and postwar responsibility have been a part of public life in Japan from the end of the war into the twenty-first century. It is certainly not true that Japanese have no sense of guilt, that theirs is a culture of amnesia, or that they are politically immature. Rather, war memory developed together with—and as a part of—particular and divergent approaches to postwar democracy in the aftermath of war. Since then, the demands placed upon postwar democracy have shifted considerably, and the place of war memory in public life has shifted with them. War memory remained fragmented and contested on the political map of democracy for decades, yet it was closely woven into the political structure. At certain historical junctures—for example, Japan's independence in 1952, the normalization of relations with China in 1972, or the end of the Cold War in 1989—war memory emerged prominently as a tool of political conflict in Japan. At the beginning of the twenty-first century, the legacies of the war threatened to jeopardize international relations as Japan clashed with its Asian neighbors over territorial issues and its bid for a seat on the United Nations Security Council.

Second, even if war memory implicitly shaped the way internal political battles were contested, it rarely guided postwar politics explicitly on the state level. The events captured in the photos involved citizens who organized to debate and act upon issues of war responsibility in the face of government inertia. (In this case, both the rally in 1946 and the tribunal in 2000 took issue with the American and Japanese authorities' failure to hold the emperor responsible.) The Japanese government rarely exhibited leadership in interpreting the lessons of the war or in bringing about reconciliation with those who suffered under Japanese imperialism. Instead, successive administrations left war memory to participants in domestic political contests—to representatives of special interests, to citizens' movements, to self-proclaimed opponents of the state, all of whom used war memory to further their own aims and interests. Although there is no question that the government played a significant role in the contention over memory issues, it acted more as a foil against which particular views of the past were articulated than as a national consensus builder or ideological leader. At the same time, the Japanese people became gradually accustomed to seeing war memory argued in terms of special interests through representative politics rather than as an issue that concerned either the individual as an individual or the public as a national public. The making and negotiating of public memory took place largely on the middle level of the political process, between the individual as a political participant and the government as the articulator of public policies. This was indeed a "public sphere" occupied by groups of organized citizens communicating their interpretations of the war and the postwar to their own constituents, to the state, and to the larger public as well.

Third, even while the two events depicted here addressed Japanese *domestic* audiences, they were informed by *global* circumstances in crucial ways. In 1946 Japan was occupied by American military forces, and the power to make changes lay primarily not with the Japanese people but with the Supreme Commander of the Allied Forces (SCAP), General Douglas MacArthur. Under the occupation's demilitarization and democratization policies, SCAP imposed the war interpretation and political agenda of the victor and foreign occupier on the Japanese. That interpretation declared Japan the sole aggressor in the war. Almost immediately, SCAP set out to cleanse Japan of militarism, dismantling its war machine and eradicating the social structures of ultranationalism. The "military purge" of more than 200,000 public workers (mainly business executives, journalists, teachers, right-wing leaders, and former military personnel) in 1945–46 and SCAP's strict censorship of the public media had a profound impact on public and private lives, in some respects liberating, in others devastating.

Unwittingly but with almost uncanny accuracy, the organizers of the December 1946 rally had put their finger on the most far-reaching SCAP decision: granting the emperor immunity from legal prosecution at the International Military Tribunal for the Far East (IMTFE), which took place in Tokyo from May 1946 to November 1948. The tribunal sought to establish personal responsibility for starting and conducting an unjust war, and yet it excluded the emperor, who had been supreme commander of the military under the Meiji constitution. Instead, the emperor was installed as the symbolic center of the new constitution (promulgated in 1946 and inaugurated the following year), the cornerstone of a peaceful and democratic Japan. This effectively ended public calls for his investigation or abdication. The Tokyo trial in turn prosecuted 28 military and civilian wartime leaders and pronounced 25 sentences of death or imprisonment for crimes against peace and crimes against humanity (so-called Class A war crimes). The trials were riddled with legal, political, and procedural problems from the beginning, and many contemporary observers both among the Allies and the Japanese public understood it as an extraordinary show of power and politics that smacked of "victor's justice."[4] In addition, thousands were tried for conventional war crimes at Class B and C war crimes trials conducted all over Asia, resulting in 920 executions. Nonetheless, the Allied trials passed over some major Japanese war crimes, such as the production and use of biological weapons in Manchuria, and the government-operated "comfort women system," to which an estimated 100,000 Asian women fell victim.[5]

By investigating wartime sexual slavery and Emperor Hirohito's war responsibility, the Women's International Tribunal in 2000 self-consciously picked up where the Tokyo trial had left off. This was not the first time that the 1946–48 trial was publicly revisited; a major symposium in 1982 had brought together scholars and participants in that trial for a critical reevaluation.[6] The organization, style, and specific themes of the Women's Tribunal in 2000, however, bore the direct imprint of changed global circumstances. Rather than a Western-dominated military court wielding "victor's justice," this civilian tribunal drew upon the regional connections among citizens' groups across Asia, in particular women's groups, in a quest for belated justice and closure for war victims and victimizers alike. It built upon global experiences with different strategies for addressing historical injustices, such as South Africa's truth commissions. The aim was not only to expose Japan's responsibility but to appeal to a global public who recognized the political value of such memory work—for example, taking the issue of violence against women in war to the international human rights court in The Hague. Most important, the tribunal focused public attention not only on the war crimes themselves but on the incomplete history of their memory over more than half a century. It highlighted the gendered nature of war crimes and of war memory that had been all but invisible until the 1990s. Indeed, war memory turned out to be driven by a host of historical factors: international circumstances, domestic politics, and a shifting public culture, as well as changing divisions along generational, gender, social, and ethnic lines.

This book traces the social politics of war memory in Japan from defeat in 1945 to the beginning of the new millennium. The term "social politics" refers here to the continuing yet shifting contest over war memory among organized social groups. It draws upon the histories of five prominent civic organizations from across the political spectrum that found themselves at the forefront of this struggle: the Association of Shinto Shrines, the Association of War-bereaved Families, the Teachers' Union, the Japan-China Friendship Association, and the Memorial Society for the Student-Soldiers Killed in the War, better known as Wadatsumikai. These five organizations were established between 1946 and 1950, riding the "wave of interest group growth" that marked the immediate postwar period, and they were still active political players in

2005.[7] With the exception of Wadatsumikai, they participated in politics as recognized "pressure groups" (*atsuryoku dantai*), on the local as well as national levels, negotiating their respective social meanings of the past vis-à-vis the state and the public at large. The social politics of war memory thus operated in the interstices between "the state" and "civil society," linking the two in multiple and changing ways.[8] T. J. Pempel's observation several decades ago also applies to war memory as special interest:

Virtually any social interest that one could imagine is organized in Japan. Although many, particularly the major agricultural, business, and professional associations, retain close ties to government, most are also fiercely independent in the pursuit of their particular vision of the national interest. They organize widely, lobby lustily, endorse or oppose political candidates, and play a major role in the politics of the nation.[9]

The specific lessons and legacies ascribed to the experience of war and defeat became deeply embedded in the postwar political structure, and they were used as tools for advancing particular interests in changing contexts. All viable participants in the process of defining and redefining the postwar order accepted participatory democracy as essential, but their visions for a democratic Japan at times clashed openly.

From the 1950s to the early 1980s, this battle took place primarily between organized political interests with varying proximity to the state, even while they were gradually joined by other forms of political participation. Together, these interest groups focused war memory around a set of political issues that rarely spilled over into the international arena and only at certain moments reached beyond the framework of domestic politics to engage the public as a *national* public. This began to change over the course of the 1980s, when issues of Japanese war memory and postwar responsibility became part of a broader global culture of memory characterized by a more robust recognition of Japan as a brutal colonizer in Asia.

The first of the five organizations is the Association of Shinto Shrines (Jinja honchō), an umbrella organization that worked with representatives of the right in the Liberal Democratic Party (LDP) and the Imperial Household Agency to strengthen the ties between Shrine Shinto, the Imperial House, and the state through the use of Shinto rituals in public ceremonies. This institutional relationship had reached a peak during wartime and had therefore been dismantled by occupation policies. The Association of Shinto Shrines was crucial to keeping in public view the problem of the "emperor system," which it worked to redefine (after the end of the occupation) to better represent the essential continuity of Japanese history. Though critical of the wartime bureaucratic abuse of Shrine Shinto, the Association insisted on a hegemonic and binding definition of national identity based on the historical continuity of the emperor as the spiritual essence of all Japanese. This could be seen as an attempt to resurrect wartime ideology.

Another conservative interest group is the Japan Association of War-bereaved Families (Nihon izokukai), which lobbied LDP representatives in the Diet and in the Health and Welfare Ministry for state recognition of the military war bereaved as the nation's foremost victims of war. This prominent organization demanded that the government revive pensions for war-bereaved families and official ceremonies for the war dead at Yasukuni Shrine, both of which had been discontinued under the occupation. The Izokukai remained a major conservative pressure group in Diet politics throughout the postwar decades and fanned the enduring controversy over the appropriate commemoration of millions of military dead at Yasukuni Shrine. At the same time, precisely because of its political clout, the Izokukai elicited much public protest, which in fact revealed different war memories and postwar identities among groups of war victims and war bereaved.

On the political left, the Japan Teachers' Union (JTU) sought to diminish the power of the bureaucracy, which it saw as a continuation of wartime militarism, and opposed the Ministry of Education over its system of textbook approval, curricula decisions, and teacher employment. Indeed, school curricula and history textbooks provided material for ongoing battles over public information, interpretation, and representation of the national past in service of contemporary definitions of citizenship. The JTU's opposition to the public use of Japan's national flag and anthem, the revival of prewar national holidays, and Yasukuni Shrine as a site of national mourning for Japan's war dead made it the archenemy of right-wing organizations such as the Association of Shinto Shrines and the Japan Association of War-bereaved Families.

A progressive interest group with ties across the political divide is the Japan-China Friendship Association (Nitchū yūkō kyōkai), which worked with academic, political, trade, and peace groups to improve Japanese relations with the People's Republic of China. It continually insisted on an official acknowledgment of Japanese war atrocities against China as the necessary basis for a rapprochement. Although the U.S.-Japan alliance tended to eclipse "Asia" from public view at the height of the Cold War, unresolved legacies of the war periodically revealed contrasting memories of a shared past, within Japan as well as between Japan and its neighbors. The Japan-China Friendship Association helped in 1953–56 to administer the repatriation of thousands of Japanese left in China after the war's end, expanded trade relations with China on an informal basis, and contributed to the eventual normalization of diplomatic relations in 1972 (ratified in 1978). Throughout the postwar decades the Friendship Association publicly commemorated anniversaries of Japanese wartime aggression against China, and, especially since the 1980s, supported research into Japan's biological warfare and the comfort women system.

A small but influential peace group is the Japan Memorial Society for the Students Killed in the War, better known as Wadatsumikai. This group of intellectuals, students, and relatives of students killed during the war organized high school and university students and teachers around a pacifist critique of contemporary politics. It compiled and edited many editions of the book *Listen to the Voices from the Deep (Kike wadatsumi no koe)*,[10] a bestselling collection of letters, poems, and other writings by students who died in the war. Its members also produced important scholarship on the history and the memory of the war. Wadatsumikai evoked the tragic experiences of student-soldiers in the last years of the war and interpreted them through the lens of resistance against the state. War victimization, both physical and spiritual, translated into a popular pacifism symbolized by the atomic bombs and the ethical conflict of students experiencing the horror of war.

By the mid-1950s, the five organizations had established themselves as special interest groups dominating the political contest over the memory of war and its aftermath. They were not internally homogeneous; instead, each was continuously engaged in creating and recreating a measure of coherence and consistency in its positions over time. Yet each represented a distinctive strand of war memory along an established left-right divide in Japan's public life. The Association of

Shinto Shrines and the Association of War-bereaved Families centered their tactics on resurrecting aspects of the wartime system that occupation policies had dismantled. The Teachers' Union, Japan-China Friendship Association, and Wadatsumikai, in contrast, opposed what they regarded as the continuation of political structures that had supported militarism during the war and were incompatible with postwar democracy.

But the lines could also be drawn differently. Civic groups on the nationalist right as well as on the liberal left raised fundamentally similar concerns about the postwar democratic system, although they used different historical memories and pursued divergent contemporary goals. For example, both the Association of Shinto Shrines and Wadatsumikai targeted public structures of thought or ideology. Shrine Shintoists validated a unified, unchanging system of public values that was expressed during the war through the ritualistic reproduction of the nation centered on the emperor. Wadatsumikai activists, in contrast, insisted on a universal humanist pacifism, which was clearly incompatible with wartime nationalism and the ideology of the emperor system. Likewise, both the Association of War-bereaved Families and the Teachers' Union, two important political pressure groups directly opposed to each other, focused on the government bureaucracy as a powerful link between the war and the postwar. Representatives of the war bereaved forged close ties especially with the Health and Welfare Ministry in pursuit of their goal of restoring to military families the privileged position they had enjoyed during the war. Unionized teachers, in contrast, opposed the Ministry of Education precisely because of its pivotal role in promoting militarism during the war. Instead, it demanded the right for teachers themselves to guide educational policies. The Friendship Association, in a category of its own, made international relations its central concern. It criticized the postwar conservative government's resistance to formal relations with the People's Republic of China as a sign of lack of remorse for—and even a continuation by other means of—Japanese war atrocities against Chinese and other Asian people.

Other, not explicitly political lines of division also emerged at different moments during the postwar decades, and with varying degrees of intensity. Finely divided generational cohorts established important commonalities among people who had experienced the war at particular life stages. This was especially meaningful in early postwar Japan among those who were rebuilding the country. But the real generational conflict erupted later: between those who had experienced war as adults and the first "postwar generation," who were students in the late 1950s and 1960s. In contrast to West Germany in the latter 1960s, however, no significant change in the content and organization of war memory occurred at that time. Instead, the ideological leaders of the war generation were able to assert their perspectives on war memory within the interest groups analyzed here.

Class divisions also came into play in the social politics of memory. In the early postwar years, labor unions such as the Teachers' Union clearly looked back at the past through the lens of class struggle. Nonetheless, the emphasis on the teacher as laborer (who had not been recognized as such before and during the war) soon gave way to the more important role of the teacher as citizen. More controversial was the inherent elitism that characterized Wadatsumikai's collecting the testaments of students from Japan's top universities to the exclusion of writings by young soldiers from the working class. In the early 1960s, a debate unfolded in the intellectual journals *Shisō no kagaku* (The Science of Ideas) and *Wadatsumi no koe* (Listen to the Voices from the Deep) over the publication of a collection of testaments by farmer-soldiers (in contrast to student-soldiers), which challenged the elitist grounds on which Wadatsumikai conducted its pacifist campaign.

The gender divide entered the realm of war memory briefly in the immediate postwar years but began to be addressed in earnest only in the 1990s, propelled by the comfort women protest. In the latter 1940s, however, a "gendered memory" appeared in the conflict between war widows, who formed self-help groups early on, and war-bereaved organizations under male leadership. In the context of utter poverty on one hand and the introduction of women's rights under the new constitution on the other, some war widows joined women's political groups in an effort to define their own interests as separate from that of the state. Male-led war-bereaved groups, in contrast, were comparatively well connected in political circles and insisted on recreating the state-centered position of war widows as the honorable wives of the "departed heroes" (*eirei*). By the early 1950s, the war-bereaved had won out by successfully appropriating the plight of women in the aftermath of war. An independent, critical perspective among war widows as liberated postwar women retreated into the background. Japan's women's movement did not take up the question of war responsibility until the late 1990s, when feminist scholars began to examine the issue of war memory in light of that lacuna.

The structure of this book reflects the main phases in Japan's history of war memory. Part I describes how five of the most prominent political interest groups formed within the context of the occupation, and how they articulated their visions for postwar Japan on the basis of selective memories of the war. They represented different *strands of memory* within postwar politics and demonstrate how the political contention over memory worked in concrete cases. These organizations ranged from the far right to the radical left, and all were well-known in political and intellectual circles, although their respective political clout changed, in some cases considerably, across the decades. The end of the occupation in the early 1950s was the defining historical moment for all of these organizations, when their activities matured into interest politics.

Part II analyzes different aspects of public memory as they emerged in changing contexts and connected to specific political controversies. The social politics of war memory remained tied to issues of bureaucratic control of school curricula and textbook approval, attempts to revive official celebrations of the war dead at Yasukuni Shrine, the public use of the national flag and anthem, and the restoration of wartime public holidays. Yet these controversies also revealed the shifting parameters of the memory debate in public life, influenced by generational changes in the second postwar decade, by the volatile international context of the 1960s, and by struggles over the official custodianship of memory since the 1970s. Although the strands of memory represented by special interest groups of the kind surveyed here remained dominant throughout the postwar era, the landscape of contentious political activism changed significantly. Whereas public memory in the 1950s was closely tied to representative politics, a decade later other forms of civic activism proliferated and selectively adopted the issue of war memory as part of their respective agendas. Special interest groups were joined in the late 1960s by spontaneously organizing "citizens' movements" motivated less by a defined political ideology than by the perceived need to make underrepresented political voices heard. Anti–Vietnam War protest and environmental movements stood out among this new form of civic involvement in politics. In the 1970s, the proliferation of religious groups further qualified the place of special interest organizations as leaders in the political contention over war memory. Such groups provided the ruling conservative party with critical support seemingly "from below," and made memory issues a concern of the popular right.

Part III documents the most significant shift in Japan's history of memory. From the 1980s on, the interest-based, primarily domestic politics of negotiating the meanings of the wartime past began to engage a global, rights-based approach to memory and restitution. The mushrooming of cross-national organizations representing the interests of long-neglected war victims compromised the once-dominant position of special interest groups in the politics of memory by introducing an international dimension that could no longer be ignored in the post–Cold War era.

The First Postwar Decade, 1945–1955

It is worth pointing out that Japanese people were well acquainted with the political potential of public memory by the time the war ended. The project of modernization and empire building in the nineteenth and early twentieth centuries, as well as efforts to make sense of the conditions of modernity thereafter, readily employed strategies of defining the past. Modern wars constituted a privileged terrain. The Russo-Japanese War (1904–5), in which Japan defeated a European power for the first time, acquired an iconic place in official as well as popular discourse in the 1920s and 1930s. Not only had Japan's victory produced additional territory, but it was also evidence of Japan's international power and equality and an example of national unity.[11] It was also in the context of the Russo-Japanese War that the public commemoration of the military dead at Yasukuni Shrine and the maintenance of a network of nation-protecting shrines all over the country became both popular practice and official policy. At later stages of World War II, this cult of the war dead came to provide a prominent avenue for ultranationalist indoctrination, with profound repercussions for postwar struggles over memory. Furthermore, many Japanese found it necessary to bear witness to the political and military events they were experiencing. These testaments from the home front as well as from combat zones across Japan's empire came to constitute a valuable and prominent source of memories imbued with conflicting meanings.

August 1945, the foundational moment of the postwar era, towered over the history of Japanese memory much as the "zero hour" cliché did in postwar Germany. Defeat meant different things to different people, making it perhaps the most overdetermined point in time in Japan. In the lived reality of many, the hardships of the war, defeat, and life under foreign occupation tended to merge into each other and became almost inseparable in their personal memory. Citizens organizing around a specific political interest, however, almost by definition had to explain how the three related to each other in order to overcome this threefold trauma. It was important for this early postwar organizing that the new "peace" constitution set a legal framework for the political negotiation of war memories. It established Japan as a structural democracy that had chosen the renunciation of the right to wage war (Article 9) as its cornerstone, thereby becoming the foremost tool of the left-liberal opposition to check the powers of the state against undue encroachment on civic society. The constitution, however, guaranteed democratic civil and human rights to all Japanese people as a "gift" of the American occupiers rather than the fruit of a Japanese democratic revolution. At the time of its promulgation under occupation censorship, the foreign origins of this document did not become a subject of public debate, cloaked, as it was, in a Japanese mantle. Yet the circumstances of its origins came to figure prominently and controversially in the subsequent discourse about war memory as either the stifling of a popular democratic impulse or the loss of a putative Japanese national identity.

All five groups surveyed here have continued actively to participate in public life up to the present. Throughout this time, each group was nationally organized, with regional and local chapters, and each published one or more periodicals through which it distributed information to its members and represented its constituencies and work to the public. Each organization maintained a political agenda of its own for which it was publicly known despite shifts in focus and in method of activism. Although each operated in a distinct—though not sepa-rate—public space, addressing itself to a certain set of people, all spoke to issues of national and international concern. The public culture of memory emerged from the historical circumstances of the early postwar years, when these organizations established themselves first as popular movements and then (with the exception of Wadatsumikai) as political interest groups. In organizing, each group employed strategies to which war memory was central.

First, a new organization defined its own community. Being a Shinto priest or an elementary school teacher did not necessarily mean that one shared the same war experience or even postwar situation as other Shinto priests and elementary school teachers. The establishment of a Shinto organization or teachers' labor union involved ideological con-siderations and required an (often selective) articulation of past and present realities with which potential members could identify. Because most people lived in straitened circumstances in the immediate post-war years, much of the early organizing process was driven by a group's promise to alleviate its members' economic hardship. Economic con-siderations, however, could hardly be separated from political interests. Civic organizations began to develop their political visions by articu-lating, even inventing, collective wartime experiences for their com-munities. Explaining to themselves and the wider public the cause of the current state of ruin from their particular vantage points (for ex-ample, from the point of view of Shinto priests or elementary school teachers) not only made the current situation comprehensible, but also increased the willingness of (potential) members to engage in political activism.

Second, organizations competed for a share of public attention during the occupation years by positioning themselves as leaders of democratic change. Their initial target audience was "the people" rather than the state. But in claiming popular leadership in their country's quest for change, civic organizations automatically accepted a certain responsibil-ity for the war. J. Victor Koschmann and others have described this trope in detail with respect to left-liberal intellectuals during the immedi-ate postwar years. But intellectuals hardly stood separate from the many other social groups that formed during those years—indeed, they often helped establish them. Nor was democratic leadership an exclusive privilege of those with left-wing political views. Conservative groups, too, articulated their activities in terms of a commitment to democracy. They even shouldered a share of responsibility for the war disaster, or, more precisely, for defeat, in order to demonstrate the legitimacy of their participation in the postwar democratic process.

Third, organizations located themselves on the emerging political map of postwar Japan vis-à-vis the occupation authorities, the government, and one another. Occupation-inspired reforms, the public purge, and Allied censorship created a political and practical context within which each organization, whether left or right of center, had to adjust its activities. This was urgently true in the five organizations considered here, for all were formed in a time not propitious for their politics. The two right-wing organizations, the Japan Association of War-bereaved Families and the Association of Shinto Shrines, established themselves in the early postwar years, when the purge of military elements was at its height. The two groups with communist sympathies, the Japan-China Friendship Association and Wadatsumikai, were formed in 1950 at the beginning of the Red Purge of leftists. The teachers' union movement coalesced into one large union in 1947, just as SCAP began to crack down on Japan's militant labor unions. All of them remained legal, however, by negotiating shifts in their organizational practices and by adjusting their language to fit political circumstances under the occupation. By the early 1950s, this self-censorship stopped, and each organization's political agenda hardened considerably. But the experience of negotiating their views to accommodate the political climate continued to serve these organizations well. Indeed, those on the extreme right even opted to keep some of the self-censoring mechanisms in place for the sake of preserving their places in public politics.

Fourth, each civic group formed networks with political parties and other organizations to establish its interests in the political arena. Each benefited from the political power of larger organizations and increased its own power base by supporting a host of smaller groups. As the political system coalesced into two dominant parties in the first half of the 1950s, organizations became identified, in part through their networks, with particular stances on contemporary issues, including views of the war. Some of the more critical examinations of the wartime past—for example, the public acknowledgment of Japanese atrocities on the Asian mainland—were presented to the public as part of a communist political agenda, which rapidly lost credibility as the Cold War intensified and Stalin's crimes were internationally exposed. In other words, a group's contemporaneous political positioning largely determined the reception of, or the public willingness to confront, certain interpretations of the past. War memory, which had been so raw and omnipresent during the immediate postwar years, was largely reduced to a by-product of interest politics by the early 1950s.

The end of the occupation in 1952 constituted a particularly important moment in the history of memory, in that Japan's political options for international rehabilitation became narrowly circumscribed by its alliance with the United States in the deepening Cold War. At the same time, a whole new range of discursive possibilities concerning Japanese war memories opened up. The return of convicted war criminals to public life (and even national politics), the belated disclosure of the real horrors of the Hiroshima and Nagasaki atomic bombings, the stories of repatriates from Japan's former empire, and bestselling collections of war testaments brought a flood of memories to public prominence and provided fertile ground for liberal democrats, pacifists, and nationalists of different vintages to formulate their respective political agendas with great urgency. Three pivotal political developments in the early 1950s set the discursive framework for public memory at the end of the occupation: the San Francisco Peace Treaty, the U.S.-Japan Security Treaty, and the Korean War.

In September 1951 Prime Minister Yoshida Shigeru signed the San Francisco Peace Treaty with the United States and 47 other countries, formally ending Japan's empire and guaranteeing its national sovereignty. Although regarded as nonpunitive and nonrestrictive, the peace treaty, like the resulting liberation from foreign occupation, turned out to be at best partial: excluded from the signatories were the entire Communist bloc and most countries of Japan's former empire, in particular China and Korea. Okinawa and the Ogasawara Islands, moreover, remained American-occupied twenty years longer than the main islands—until 1972. Concurrently, Japan signed a separate alliance with the United States, the U.S.-Japan Security Treaty, which guaranteed the United States the right to station troops in Japan to protect Japan's internal and external security as part of the U.S. containment strategy in East Asia.

The two treaties combined brought Japan firmly into the deepening Cold War confrontation, leaving no option for the political neutrality demanded by the left-liberal opposition on the basis of Japan's constitutional renunciation of war. As feared by those who vehemently opposed the conservative and anti-Communist trend at the time, the "San Francisco system" established an international framework in which the official pursuit of Japanese culpability and atonement for the war was quarantined by the so-called bamboo curtain, a metaphor for the Cold War division of Northeast Asia. Unlike West German leaders, who found official apologies for Nazi crimes politically necessary in order to integrate Germany into the European Community, the Japanese government saw no political reason to make amends for its colonial past. Reconciliation with Communist China and war-shattered Korea was not called for under alliance agreements with the United States, which allowed Japanese leaders instead to focus single-mindedly on economic growth.

The peace and security treaties were negotiated against the backdrop of war in Korea, which broke out a scant five years after Japan's defeat in World War II and affected the Japanese public deeply. When hostilities commenced on the Korean peninsula, ongoing conservative efforts to curb communist influence turned into an outright purge of more than twenty thousand private and public workers following the dissolution of the Japan Communist Party (JCP) central committee. MacArthur's denunciation of the JCP on 3 May gave the so-called Red Purge legitimacy and convinced the left that the doors were closing on the possibility of a genuine democratic revolution. The proximity of war, not only in time (World War II) but now also in space (Korea), spurred an immensely visible peace movement, which proclaimed the connection between these two wars in humanitarian and political terms. The peace movement's emotional appeal rested on memories of war victimization, both as Japanese experience and as international reality. Its dynamism helped the left-liberal opposition build its political platform around protesting the conservative government's abject support of the U.S.-Japan alliance, which it saw as perpetuating, instead of renouncing, imperialist and militarist policies. Progressive scholars of Japan's history of memory have long pointed out that the manner in which the Japanese government concluded international treaties (geared primarily toward furthering U.S. military interests in the Cold War) in effect sanctioned the shelving of Japan's war responsibility issues.[12]

The Cold War politics of an increasingly conservative government at the end of the occupation period contributed to sharply defined relations between civic organizations and the state. A group's institutionalized proximity to the state—not claims of popular leadership—came to determine its political influence (although not its public visibility, as the prominence of protest politics in the later 1950s and 1960s would indicate). As organizations such as the ultraconservative Association of Shinto Shrines and the Association of War-bereaved Families successfully lobbied state institutions on behalf of their causes, left-liberal groups (in this case, the Teachers' Union, Japan-China Friendship Association, and Wadatsumikai) claimed to represent "the voice of the people" and positioned themselves in opposition to the state. War memory, insofar as it was attached to special interests, became organized along a left-right divide, which also separated the allegedly conservative state from the allegedly liberal people. Public controversies about interpretations of the war and its legacies—most notably over textbooks and national symbols—therefore tended to focus on the state as a target (of either lobbying activities or protests) and thus obscured critical issues such as the overlapping identities of victim and victimizer, as well as war responsibility toward Asia in general.

Interest-based Struggles over Memory, 1950s–1970s

It is important to recognize that the subject of the past—of both the war and the postwar—was defined eclectically and changed significantly over the decades since the end of the war. Indeed, one could speak of a "doubling" of temporalities as the historicity of the present changed over time. The wartime past, which tended to include prewar experiences and foreign occupation, doubled up with the postwar years, which in fact encompassed all three temporalities of past, present, and future as it was construed after 1945. Memories of war were the means by which visions for a democratic Japan were formulated in the immediate postwar years. But by the mid-1950s, both the war memories and the democratic visions had to contend with the realities of the preceding decade, which did not always meet the goals set in the early postwar years. At this point, memories of war (and of prewar experiences) were joined by the need to reckon with the immediate postwar past if the democratic visions were to become realities. As the postwar period continued, war memories became more and more explicitly negotiated on the terrain of the postwar past through which special interest groups legitimized their ongoing political involvement, on the right as on the left.

In 1956 the economic white papers declared Japan's "postwar" to be over as the annual GNP reached and soon surpassed prewar levels. Socially and politically, however, many legacies of war, defeat, and foreign occupation remained unresolved, from war widows' pensions and medical aid for atomic bomb victims to Japan's continued subordination to the Cold War objectives of the United States. The government lay firmly in conservative hands under the leadership of the newly consolidated Liberal Democratic Party (LDP), whose ranks included prewar and wartime politicians like Hatoyama Ichirō, Ishibashi Tanzan, and the depurged Class A war criminal Kishi Nobusuke. Moreover, the ruling LDP pushed revisions of many occupation reforms, foremost the American-imposed constitution. While attempts to revise the constitution failed, efforts to once again grant the bureaucracy power to influence the appointment of teachers and police officers met with increasing success. Predictably, the intellectual and political left were alarmed by what they saw as a swing back to the bureaucratic centralism and state coercion of the 1930s.

This social and political climate spurred the revival in 1956 of the discourse on war responsibility among progressive intellectuals, many of whom had been part of the earlier debate shortly after defeat.[13] They took issue with the apparent lack of resolution in the matter of war responsibility in contemporary political and social consciousness and ascribed this to a failure of the earlier discourse, both public and intellectual. In particular, they conceived of war responsibility as an academic pursuit. They searched for theoretical categories to approach it in a more differentiated way than had been done in the immediate postwar years and conducted historical investigations into the roots of the wartime behavior of various social groups. The debate established the term "war responsibility" (*sensō sekinin*) as the functional equivalent of what the West Germans called "overcoming the past" (*Vergangenheitsbewältigung*). This combined research into wartime conduct with a critique of postwar trends without explicitly making a distinction between the two. As such, "war responsibility" became firmly established as an issue of the left-liberal opposition, characterized by anticonservatism (based on what the left perceived as an insufficient break with the past in postwar politics), anti-Americanism (attacking the American interpretation of the war and the conduct of the Tokyo war crimes trial), and self-critique (scrutinizing intellectuals' role in society).[14]

A similar set of concerns animated the mass protest movement against the renewal of the revised U.S.-Japan Security Treaty a few years later in the spring of 1960. A broad protest coalition of the political left had formed the year before, including the Socialist and Communist parties, labor federations, women's groups, student councils, and prominent intellectuals engaged in the war responsibility debate. They came together in opposition to Prime Minister Kishi, who had staked his political career on the revised treaty. In their eyes, the treaty renewal took on an iconic meaning: it demonstrated the fragility of postwar democracy (which denied ordinary citizens an adequate political voice), the possible return to militarization and state coercion embodied by the former wartime leader and now prime minister Kishi, and the self-interest of the United States in the Cold War. Amid the escalating mass protests in front of the Diet in May and June 1960, Kishi proved the protesters' impression correct when he forced the treaty's ratification by having opposition Diet members physically removed from their seats. It cost Kishi his job, but the treaty remained in place. Postwar Japan's worst political crisis thus effectively mobilized popular war memory by invoking the continued victimization of the people by the state. But the experience also transformed it by focusing attention on the need to overcome the ghosts of the past by generating more social equity and a stronger national identity. The conservative, nationalist aspect of this message bore fruit as Japan entered its phase of high economic growth, which muted some of the political discontent and even brought to the fore positive evaluations of the war as a time of righteous national unity.[15]

The early 1970s constitute a widely acknowledged break in the history of postwar Japan, marked by the end of high economic growth, the normalization of relations with Communist China, and the reversion of Okinawa to Japan, albeit with the American military bases intact. This conjuncture of foreign-induced changes reverberated deeply in domestic politics. First, it proved Japan's viability in the world economy and as an international presence, demonstrated by the overwhelming successes of the Tokyo Olympics in 1964 and Osaka Expo '70, but also its international vulnerability in the aftermath of the 1973 oil shock. Second, restoring relations with South Korea in 1965 and China in 1972 began a process of renegotiating Japan's place in Asia that conjured up various and conflicting national memories of Japanese colonialism and war. Third, the broad-based reversion movement, which linked Okinawans with mainland Japanese for the first time since 1945, complicated the putative identity of a unified people, raising the issue of their very different wartime and postwar experiences and revealing war memory also as a local issue of social and political justice. Occupied Okinawa territorially embodied defeat, and as such the nexus between the legacies of Japan's prewar involvement in Asia and its postwar orientation toward the United States. The overwhelming national consensus on the desirability of ending the U.S. occupation there kept this issue firmly in the public eye. Moreover, the conflicting demands levied on the Japanese government, the Americans, and the Okinawans revealed ongoing political and ideological struggles over the meaning of the war in relation to the postwar.

The Vietnam War and massive antiwar protests in Japan constituted a critical context for these developments. The daily news of American military conduct against Vietnamese civilians substantiated both left-wing and right-wing critiques of American hypocrisy as self-proclaimed champions of "peace and democracy." But it also confronted many Japanese with memories of their own wartime behavior. It marked the culmination of lively citizen activism on a variety of political issues and resulted in a more critical consideration of war victimization, including questions of the Japanese people's complicity in and perpetration of war crimes. Writer and critic Oda Makoto consciously built his antiwar citizens' movement Beheiren (Citizens' Federation for Peace in Vietnam) around the notion of individual political (but nonideological) commitment and responsibility to recognize and resist state management of public life. The *Asahi shinbun* journalist Honda Katsuichi came to research the history of Japanese atrocities in China after covering the war in Vietnam, and his writings remained on the bestseller lists for years, even decades. Kinoshita Junji published a satirical and deeply (self-)critical play on the Allied war crimes trials, *Between God and Man* (*Kami to hito no aida*, 1970), set both in Tokyo and in the South Pacific, where some of the smaller Class B and C war crimes trials had been held. The first accounts of Asian military comfort women's experiences of sexual slavery appeared in the early 1970s, the emperor's war responsibility began to be systematically explored, and an outright "China boom" in the mass media explored the historical and contemporary importance of continental Asia for the Japanese.

Nonetheless, the dominant pattern of contention over both the wartime and the postwar past remained locked in a dynamic that pitted (liberal) citizens against the (conservative) state. One landmark was the beginning of the textbook trials in 1965, when Ienaga Saburō sued the Ministry of Education over the legality of textbook censorship, especially concerning historical accounts of Japanese colonial and war crimes. The outburst of students', citizens', and environmental movements against the politically constraining, socially discriminating, and physically harmful consequences of government policies also fed upon new nationalist strategies led or sanctioned by the ruling LDP in the late 1960s. The official revival in 1967 of the wartime national holiday *kigensetsu* (the birthday of the legendary first emperor, Jimmu) as *kenkoku kinen no hi* (National Foundation Day, 11 February) was followed the next year by elaborate government-sponsored events marking the centennial of the Meiji Restoration. This was postwar Japan's first large-scale public commemoration event, celebrating a century of "Japan in the world" by lightly skipping over the imperial and colonial quality of much of that history. Concurrently, the LDP supported a bill, long in preparation, to bring Yasukuni Shrine back under state management and conduct official ceremonies for the Japanese war dead there. As an important conjuncture in the history of memory, the late 1960s and early 1970s saw intensified public uses of war memory across the political spectrum and tied to various international and domestic issues.

In all these ways, the five organizations surveyed here competed with one another for public space in which to present what they considered to be essential legacies of the war. Political controversies did not engage all groups equally at all times, and such controversies are discussed in detail only to the extent that they serve to illuminate the public negotiation of memories. Overall, this study does not aim at a "complete" picture of memory in Japan, which would have to account for all that is not said or publicly visible, or even at a full chronology of Japan's history. Arguably the most blatant omission here concerns the atomic bombings of Hiroshima and Nagasaki, which have produced a memory culture unparalleled in its richness and have therefore attracted far more attention from scholars.[16] Organizations of atomic bomb victims (*hibakusha*) were deeply involved in citizen political activism from the mid-1950s on. Until the 1970s and 1980s, however, the literature of *hibakusha* groups suggested an enormous disconnect between the memory of 6 and 9 August and that of the preceding war. Since then, this strand of "victimization" memory has become subject to public criticism, so much so that in the 1980s the Hiroshima Peace Museum added a new wing dedicated to Japan's war in Asia. The important contribution of the atomic bomb experiences to the larger public culture of war memory notwithstanding, it does not add a critically new perspective to the present focus on the mechanisms by which certain interpretations were publicly formed, articulated, and negotiated as part of the political process over the five postwar decades.

Global Memory Cultures since the 1980s

The loosening of institutionalized political alliances at the end of the long conservative hegemony, and the growing interaction of local and national publics with an emerging global public culture (in part through cross-national civic organizations), focused wide attention on "memory" as both a political issue and a framework for historical analysis. Progressive intellectuals had begun writing about war responsibility as a problem of postwar history in the mid-1970s,[17] coining the term "postwar responsibility" (*sengo sekinin*), but not until the second half of the 1980s did this new discourse reach a critical volume and public audience. This discourse reflected an overwhelming concern with the people's responsibility for the unresolved legacies of Japan's colonial and war conduct in Asia and the historical and conceptual treatment of these legacies among intellectuals and in public education.[18]

Meanwhile, the Chinese and South Korean governments discovered political capital in war memory issues, which they had formerly chosen to treat lightly, and began to monitor Japanese official gestures toward endorsing an unapologetically nationalist view of the war. From 1982 on, public protests against Japanese textbooks and visits by Japanese prime ministers to Yasukuni Shrine were ignited primarily by the complaints from the Chinese and Korean governments and official media and only secondarily by domestic political contestants. In the broader context of relocating international relations in a still-undefined post–Cold War world, unresolved historical injustices became imbued with political meaning and practical utility in many parts of the world, and especially in East Asia, where regional and national divisions had for decades eclipsed the need for reconciliation, apology, and honest attention to lingering humanitarian and political legacies of the war. Memory issues became part and parcel of exploring new possibilities for a politically and economically more integrated Asian region, the new realities of economic recession in Japan in the 1990s, and the challenges of facing the United States and Asia at the same time.

Emperor Hirohito's death in 1989, which ended the Shōwa period (1926–89), the fall of the Berlin Wall in the same year, and the collapse of the long hegemony of the conservative LDP in 1993 marked a pivotal point in the history of memory in Japan, when issues of war and postwar responsibility for Japan's war conduct in Asia became tied to the politics of redefining its position in the world. This era of endings and putative new beginnings seemingly catapulted Japan's unresolved war responsibilities into the political limelight and made it an issue of broad public debate rather than a tool exclusively of political protest. The massive production of Shōwa retrospectives in the aftermath of the emperor's demise focused overwhelmingly on the war itself and was connected with a suddenly prominent investigation of the emperor's war responsibility. The feminist movements in various Asian countries began to network and succeeded in bringing the long-neglected history of Asian women's sexual slavery at the hands of the wartime Japanese government not only to national but to global public attention. In the following decade, a host of still uncompensated and often ignored victims of war, including former Korean, Taiwanese, Chinese, and Southeast Asian colonial subjects as well as atomic bomb victims, joined in a rapidly intensifying movement to press the Japanese government for individual compensation payments.

The turning point in Japan's imperial calendar found a critical political corollary with the onset of the Persian Gulf War in August 1991, the first military conflict led by the United States and its allies after the end of the Cold War. U.S. demands for Japan's active participation in the Gulf conflict confronted the Japanese government for the first time with the new challenges of the post–Cold War world as fundamentally political—rather than economic—issues. At the center stood interpretations of Japan's constitution and the legal position of the Self-Defense Forces (SDF) as participants in United Nations Peace Keeping Operations (PKO).[19] The problem of constitutional revision itself dated back to the early 1950s and was inseparable from the particular political dynamic between the conservative LDP in power and the Japan Socialist Party (JSP) in permanent opposition in which set positions, often tied to war memory, had been articulated for decades. The Gulf War brought this formerly domestic issue into the international arena, where it assumed an entirely new relevance as the only available tool with which to negotiate an unprecedented diplomatic situation. Prime Minister Kaifu's indecisive handling of the crisis, followed by furious debates in the Diet about a new "PKO bill" allowing overseas deployment of the SDF (passed in 1992), revealed two things: the inadequacy of the postwar (Cold War) political framework in the new decade and the need for a realignment of political positions and forces. These events clearly shaped the context in which the debate about war memory and postwar responsibility became a genuinely public discourse—broadly reflective of the postwar system's shortcomings and championed by new forms of political activism.

The year 1995 carried particular significance in the Japanese context, marked by the Hanshin earthquake in January, the Aum Shinrikyō sarin gas attack on the Tokyo subway system in March, and the fiftieth anniversary of the end of World War II in August. It revealed a society in flux, struggling with the demands of political reorganization, economic recession, and Asian regional integration, which had combined to engulf Japan in a genuinely public and highly contentious debate about its wartime and postwar past (in striking contrast to the seeming inability to produce viable visions for the future). Japan's response to the events of 1995 was symptomatic of significant shifts in international relations, domestic politics, and an increasingly global public culture that began in the late 1980s and continued into the twenty-first century, however differently nuanced by the demands of the Bush administration's declared global war on terrorism. While the dominant culture flows no longer bound Japan first and foremost to the United States, as had been the case in earlier postwar decades, the U.S.-Japan alliance remained central to Japan's international relations and even played into domestic conservative agendas in ways that both invoked and transcended Cold War structures.

As Laura Hein argued in a thoughtful commentary on current affairs at the end of 2003, Prime Minister Koizumi's unqualified support for the Bush administration's unilateral foreign policy decisions in the aftermath of 9/11 suggested few new or independent goals, whereas his push for the Antiterrorism Measures Special Law of 2001 fed directly into newly fervent plans to amend the constitution and allow Japan's active participation in full-scale war.[20] The U.S.-Japan security relationship and constitutional revision certainly represent two of the longest-standing issues with which war memory has been bound up since the end of the occupation in 1952. The end of the Cold War transposed these issues from the domestic terrain of political contest to the arena of international relations. In the 1990s, international relations were being reshaped by the need of nation-states to respond collectively to violent ethnic (rather than ideological) conflicts in Asia, Europe, and Africa, and at the same time by the proliferation of transnational and nongovernmental organizations performing tasks formerly reserved for national governments. It was in this changed international context that the particularity of the U.S.-Japan relationship and Japan's constitutional disavowal of engaging in military action abroad assumed unprecedented urgency, with respect not only to shaping the future, but also to reevaluating the past.

Not only Japan but much of the world faced new political challenges after the Cold War at precisely the time that the political, legal, and intellectual concern with restitution and the negotiation of historical injustices emerged as a global phenomenon. This was an unprecedented development that nevertheless presented itself with specific national inflections. Whereas in Japan the political organization of memory was once intricately linked to the representation of powerful special interests, war memory and postwar responsibility emerged in the 1990s as an issue of broad public appeal no longer predictably aligned with established strategies to preserve or undermine the postwar status quo represented by the U.S.-Japan security system and the constitution. The JSP, for example, along with the biggest labor federation, simply ended its decades-long opposition to the U.S.-Japan Security system in 1994 and even considered constitutional revision while pressing for an official apology to China and Korea for Japan's war conduct. The nationalist right emerged better organized than ever to protest against such apologies, to rewrite the constitution, and to liberate Japan from its long subjugation to American hegemony. The government, itself experimenting with various coalition arrangements, had to address questions of war memory as a matter of foreign policy but without deemphasizing its close relations with the United States. Meanwhile, a host of local and cross-national rights-based organizations have inserted themselves as viable political players in restitution cases as much as in the Iraq conflict.

The Japan-China Friendship Association, for example, once considered a radical opposition group because of its insistence on atoning for Japanese wartime aggression against Chinese victims, now appeared more in the public mainstream amid a host of civic groups demanding compensation for Asian war victims. The Teachers' Union, which had all but abandoned its antagonistic stance against the Ministry of Education by the mid-1990s, was a far less significant actor in the contention over memory than in earlier decades. Battles over the contents of textbooks were now carried out by a number of smaller, issue-oriented groups both on the left and on the right, for example, the neo-nationalist Liberal View of History Study Group (Jiyūshugi shikan kenkyūkai) led by Fujioka Nobukatsu. The Association of War-bereaved Families, for its part, celebrated a major victory in the late 1990s when its public project, Japan's first national museum of the war dedicated to the war bereaved, the Shōwa-kan (National Shōwa Memorial Museum), prevailed over much public protest and finally opened after twenty years of lobbying and preparation. Yet this project appeared driven by a fear of displacement, given the many new or newly prominent organizations of war-bereaved persons that had formed in clear opposition to the long-established Association.

Sixty years after the end of World War II in Asia, Japanese and foreign observers of Japan's "memoryscape" sensed that things had changed since 1995, though exactly how or to what effect was less clear. In April 2005 a wave of anti-Japanese mass protests across China, unprecedented in scale, brought Sino-Japanese diplomatic relations to a low point and demonstrated once again that a genuine reconciliation between Japan and its Asian neighbors remained elusive from a mainland Asian perspective. Again, Japanese nationalist textbooks and Prime Minister Koizumi's visits to Yasukuni Shrine had served as triggers for the protests. Many political commentators, however, saw larger conflicts of interest hovering in the background. Japan's active campaign to gain a permanent seat on the UN Security Council, and China's determination to block this quest, formed one specific issue of conflict. More generally, however, Japan's new muscularity in international relations—combined with Koizumi's unequivocal support for Bush's war in Iraq—pointed to a decisive rightward shift among the Japanese leadership that did not bode well for reconciliation. For the first time since the 1950s, a conservative-initiated revision of Japan's constitution, and Article 9 in particular, appeared to have become a real possibility, which could open the door to Japan's rise as a military power in East Asia.

To be sure, the LDP's proposals for constitutional revision drew sharp and extensive criticism from the Japanese public. But it is also true that for the first time, a majority of Japanese agreed that it was time to rewrite the constitution to reflect current national and global realities rather than those of the early postwar years under foreign occupation. Civic groups of all political persuasions in fact responded by drafting their own versions of revision proposals, and bookstores in Tokyo were flooded in the summer of 2005 with publications, from a variety of angles, on the issues at stake. Insofar as this newly pertinent debate focused on the conflicting and changing interpretations of war legacies over the course of the postwar period, it reflected both the concerns of and the recent patterns of conflict in the civic struggle over war memory. This time, of course, the government itself had initiated the debate, in contrast to the public furor over war memory a decade earlier, into which the government had to be dragged belatedly. It is too early to say exactly how the two debates are related. Certainly, there is much overlap among active contributors to these discussions, even if it cannot be assumed that they line up neatly along the familiar right-left divide. Like war memory in earlier decades, constitutional revision may appear to be primarily a matter of domestic politics, as J. Patrick Boyd and Richard J. Samuels have argued.[21]

The debate's global dimensions, however, weigh heavily. Not unlike the political struggle over war memory in the 1990s, the debate over constitutional revision is not Japan's alone. On the one hand, changing Article 9 is sure to affect the dynamics of Asian regionalism and therefore draw other countries into the debate; on the other, writing and amending constitutions to reflect the realities of the post–Cold War world is going on elsewhere in the world as well, most dramatically in Europe. Perhaps the most salient issue of constitutional revision in Japan in the first decade of the twenty-first century is to make the constitution amendable as a matter of regular political procedure— to make it a living and changing part of Japan's political life. Seen from this angle, the debate about constitutional revision may not so much eclipse the political contention over the meaning of the war as draw upon its long history.

PART I

War Memory and Democratic Rebuilding

CHAPTER ONE

The Politics of Essentialism:
The Association of Shinto Shrines

Japan's defeat in 1945 left enduring images of crying people prostrate on the ground, listening in disbelief to the emperor's radio announcement of surrender at noon on 15 August. In fact, reactions to defeat varied greatly among the Japanese people, most of whom were thoroughly exhausted from years of war. From the viewpoint of Shrine Shinto, the real catastrophe of war consisted of defeat and occupation by foreign powers. For some Shintoists, taking responsibility for defeat was a quick and decisive matter: along with several military leaders, the chief priest of Torigoe Shrine in Tokyo, Katsuragi Takeo, committed suicide in August 1945 to apologize to the deity for the shrine's failure to serve the *kami* truthfully—or, rather, for the fact that service to the deity had proven unsuitable to the divine will.[1] Foreign occupation, however, demanded a different set of responses. Military occupation personnel added insult to injury when they drove their jeeps directly into the inner sanctuary of Ise Shrine, where some of the sacred imperial regalia had been kept for centuries. In despair, the Shrine Board, not yet abolished, posted large signs that read "Off Limits to all Allied personnel and vehicles" in front of Shinto shrines all over the country by late September 1945.[2] The famous photographer Kimura Ihee captured this attempt to rescue some space for Shinto in the face of unconditional defeat in a September 1945 photo of Yasukuni

Fig. 1.1 Yasukuni Shrine, September 1945. The sign reads: "Off limits to all Allied personnel and vehicles." The not yet defunct Shrine Board posted such signs in front of many Shinto shrines to prevent Allied soldiers from entering shrine grounds. Photo by Kimura Ihee.

Shrine, where Japan's military dead were enshrined (Fig. 1.1).[3] Three women bow toward the shrine's gate in recognition of their country's defeat, next to an "Off Limits" sign, which had no legal backing and thus represented only a sentiment of resistance against the foreign occupiers.

Many Japanese felt liberated by the end of the war and perceived new personal and societal opportunities; others feared for their professional and social existence, particularly under the occupation's purge orders. For most, however, feelings of loss, opportunity, and new constraints overlapped in complicated ways, intensified by frequent shifts in the policies and alliances among the occupation forces, successive Japanese governments, and the emerging liberal and radical left during the first postwar decade. What did the rapid political changes mean for the professional life, social standing, religious belief, political representation, and even nationality of people living in Japan after the war? How did a person's actions and experiences during the war affect contemporary efforts to reestablish a place in society? These were pressing concerns that sparked public debates about war responsibility from a variety of viewpoints.

The combination of insecurity caused by political change, the hope engendered by the promise of democracy, and the terror (or comfort) experienced under wartime state coercion created an urgent need to define postwar democracy in terms of securing public—that is, political—representation of particular interests. Citizens' associations proliferated during this time as one response to this situation. The reconstructed left gained political strength by founding labor unions, agricultural cooperatives, and research groups, or by reviving formerly suppressed organizations. Many professional organizations that had existed during and before the war changed their names and rhetoric to conform to new circumstances. Organizations identified as militarist by occupation forces were ordered to disband but often reestablished themselves in new guises. Most of Japan's postwar interest groups formed during this time. Some embraced specific memories of the war to foster a group identity and reconstituted these memories publicly in the form of collective experiences for which personal stories were quoted as proof. As a result, memory, conceived in terms of historical lessons, came to be used politically to lend legitimacy to interest-based struggles.

Organized Shinto provided perhaps the most salient example of such reinvention under the early occupation. On 3 February 1946, less than six months after Japan's surrender, Shrine Shinto (*jinja shintō*), the most structured and representative form of Shinto, formally dissolved all institutional ties to the state and established a new umbrella organization, the Association of Shinto Shrines (Jinja honchō). The decision to reorganize as a private religious group independently of the state represented an effort by leaders of existing private Shinto groups to negotiate a new status for Shinto under the occupation's demilitarization and democratization reforms. Shrine Shinto (also known as State Shinto between 1900 and 1945) had been singled out by the Supreme Commander of the Allied Powers (SCAP) as the root of wartime militarism and ultranationalism because of its close relationship with the state.[4] Unlike Sect Shinto, which devoted itself solely to individual religious belief, Shrine Shinto governed the correct observance of shrine rituals, which celebrated the centrality of the emperor as the highest deity in Japan's national polity. During the war, when the emperor system permeated Japanese society in the service of war mobilization, Shrine Shinto maintained powerful government institutions, in particular the Shrine Board, and enjoyed tremendous prestige. By the end of 1945, SCAP had closed all State Shinto offices, declared public emperor worship illegal, and purged many Shinto leaders from office because of their involvement in the war.

Discarding the State, Embracing the Emperor

General Douglas MacArthur's politics of "demilitarization and democratization" set the stage for Shinto resistance against the occupation as well as its cooperation with it. In accordance with the Potsdam Declaration of the Allied Powers on 26 July 1945, SCAP issued a directive to the Japanese government on 4 October 1945 ordering the removal of restrictions on political, civil, and religious liberties. This directive became famous as the "Bill of Rights." On 15 December, SCAP followed up with the so-called Shinto Directive (*shintō shirei*), the Directive on the Abolition of Governmental Sponsorship, Support, Perpetuation, Control, and Dissemination of State Shinto.[5] Both directives had a decisive impact on Shrine Shinto's negotiations for a new Shinto organization. In addition, other occupation-directed events and policies provided an important context for Shrine Shinto organizing. The emperor's renunciation of his divinity on 1 January 1946 signaled the end of an era for the "shrine world," as it was often called, one that had begun with the Meiji Restoration in 1868. The purge from public office of "militarist elements" in 1946–48 (a total of 210,288 wartime military and political leaders had lost their jobs by May 1948) greatly diminished the ranks of Shinto leaders but did not prevent those purged from joining the new Association of Shinto Shrines. Further, American media censorship had a decisive impact on Shrine Shinto's self-representation in its publications, forcing overtly nationalistic opinion underground. As a result, the prosecution of Japanese war criminals at the Tokyo war crimes trial (concluded in December 1948) did not receive much coverage in the Association's publications, although it elicited harsh criticism from Shintoists after the occupation was over.

In many ways, Shrine Shinto was at the mercy of SCAP's admittedly limited understanding of Shinto in Japanese public life, which owed as much to American wartime propaganda as it did to now classic anthropological studies such as Ruth Benedict's *The Chrysanthemum and the*

Sword. In general, MacArthur saw himself as both the destroyer of militarism and the guarantor of human rights to the newly liberated Japanese. Militarism had to be rooted out before democracy could grow. On the terrain of Shrine Shinto, however, these dual goals conflicted because Shinto itself defied easy definition. As a state institution harbored in the Home Ministry since 1900, Shinto had actively promoted ultranationalist ideology in the service of war mobilization, and MacArthur was determined to abolish what had come to be known as State Shinto. But Shinto was also an indigenous religion, and prohibiting religious practice was not only undemocratic; it violated international law, according to which no occupying force could interfere with the conquered nation's religions.[6]

Insofar as Shrine Shinto remained firmly identified with militarism in MacArthur's mind, he chose to ignore Shinto's religious character and treated it as a state institution to be abolished. Once governmental Shinto offices had been closed, however, SCAP treated Shinto as a religion in order to prevent a renewed alliance between Shinto and the state under the new constitution, which was to guarantee the separation of church and state. Shinto scholars have often invoked this double standard in SCAP's policy toward Shrine Shinto as proof of Shinto's unfair treatment at the hands of occupation authorities concerned primarily with strategic convenience rather than doctrinal specifics.[7]

The problematic distinction between the political and the religious aspects of Shinto was hardly new—or even newly controversial—in 1945. At the heart of this issue lay Shrine Shinto's relationship to the state, which the Association of Shinto Shrines defined in a recent document in the following way: "People paid respect to the national spirit, and priests made sure that the rites were performed precisely. But the state did not prescribe to the people what belief their worship was founded on—whether they came to worship their ancestors, elicit special services from the deity, or seek salvation."[8] The collective celebration of national unity through ritualistic practice at Shinto shrines dated back to state-sponsored efforts of "nation building" after the Meiji Restoration. To instill a sense of national unity into the populace, the Meiji state promoted the worship of the emperor as the highest Shinto deity and direct descendant of the sun goddess Amaterasu, believed to be the mythical ancestor of all Japanese. But the exact relationship of Shinto to the state was never resolved; it remained ambiguous and controversial. In 1926, for example, the government established a Board for the Investigation of the Religious System to clarify the status of Shinto as a state institution.[9] Even during the war, Shinto's greatly increased influence in public life owed both to the state's policy of co-opting Shinto to its militarist goals and to "an increasingly closed political culture," where dissent was not allowed.[10]

It was the context, then, rather than the issues, that had changed most dramatically in 1945. In the face of occupation policy and propaganda depicting State Shinto as a major arm of militarism, Shinto leaders discovered quickly that the state had become a liability rather than an asset. But how were they to distance themselves from the state without losing control over the public? Shintoists had reason to feel threatened by the surge of anti-imperial and antinationalist sentiment unleashed by MacArthur's 1945 Bill of Rights. This directive, in Richard B. Finn's summary, "ordered the government to remove all restrictions on political, civil, and religious liberties; . . . permit unrestricted comment about the emperor and the government; and remove the minister of home affairs and all high police officials responsible for the enforcement of measures limiting freedom of thought, speech, religion, and assembly."[11] By mid-October, many prominent opposition leaders, on whose silencing much of Shinto's public influence during the war had depended, were released from prison and welcomed as icons of popular resistance against wartime militarism. Among them were the communist leaders Tokuda Kyūichi and Shiga Yoshio.

Shrine Shintoists, not yet organized in October 1945, responded in conflicting ways to the Bill of Rights. The old Shrine Board in the Home Ministry, for example, sided with the people as victims of the wartime state. In a statement on 12 October, the board urged "the government to take immediate measures to remove the anxiety-ridden restrictions on the people's freedom to practice Shinto." Another Shinto office, however, the End-of-War Liaison Office in the Foreign Ministry, set up to deal with the shrines in the colonies, was prepared to abandon State Shinto offices altogether, while retaining the emperor as the highest Shinto priest in whom the national polity rested. In its Shrine Shinto Problem Measure Bill of 14 October 1945, the Liaison Office proposed to do away with all Meiji legislation governing the state administration of shrines. Instead, it urged to "uphold the emperor's sacred relationship to the shrines, and to preserve the faith and the venerated folk customs of the people as a whole."[12]

SCAP, in essence, allowed Shrine Shinto to do just that: divorce the shrines from the state as a public agent of Shinto, but keep the emperor—not as sacred, but nonetheless as the locus of Japan's "essence." This represented a crucial continuity through 1945, deemed central by American reformers and Japanese traditionalists alike, of what made Japan "Japanese." MacArthur's insistence, against opposition both in America and in Japan, on preserving the imperial institution without the blemish of war responsibility opened a window for Shrine Shinto just as the door to public legitimacy closed.[13] It carved out a space in which the war could be remembered as the people's sacrifice for the emperor and his empire, and core questions about war responsibility and the structure of imperial ideology remained above critical investigation. For MacArthur, the emperor was the key to solving the enigma of "Japan"—of explaining both Japanese fanaticism in fighting a desperate war against all odds and the people's apparent resilience and remarkable readiness to start over after the defeat. This made sense precisely because American wartime propaganda had focused so intensely on the spiritual dimensions of the Japanese state, and SCAP found enough evidence in the contemporary Japanese media to keep up that myth.

The "Daily Intelligence Summary" coming out of GHQ's Military Intelligence Section in the fall of 1945 regularly scanned the Japanese press, including censored materials, in order to keep track of the popular image of the emperor. A report on the "Spiritual and Temporal Power of the Emperor" on 24 October claimed that "some Japanese make a distinction between the spiritual influence of the Imperial institution and the political power. . . . The emperor's political power can change overnight but the people's belief in the spiritual power of the Imperial institution will remain for many years." The evidence quoted for this assertion came from an unspecified Japanese newspaper, which celebrated the end of the war as the enlightened act of the emperor alone:

The present vital factor which we must admit is that the termination of the war, that is, the unconditional surrender of Japan, could be accomplished in the face of a doubting world, without a single untoward incident, and that this was entirely due to the Imperial Rescript. The strength and depth of our people's faith in the Emperor is fully demonstrated by this single fact. It is the religion of the people of Japan which cannot be taken from them. The great war could be brought to an end solely because of this racial religious belief.

Furthermore, the exemption of the emperor from any war responsibility was clearly rationalized in the same vein:

If the Emperor had been regarded as exercising political authority, the people might have regarded him as the man responsible for defeat and for the various forms of maladministration which culminated in defeat. The opposite was the case and once the Imperial Rescript was issued, the people gladly followed it. This heart of the people shows something more than politics.[14]

The connection between the emperor and the "national polity" (*kokutai*) was clearly taken seriously and even supported, as another report about the functioning of the national polity shows:

The announcement that the Emperor will visit the Grand Shrines of Ise on 13 Nov. to report the termination of the war is another example of the functioning of the 'national polity,' which is so much talked about and so little understood. All vernacular papers present the official announcement, in the traditional style, even the rampantly democratic members of the staff of the Yomiuri-Hōchi.[15]

Occupation officials' belief in and respect for the Japanese people's deep spiritual connection with their emperor served Shrine Shinto rather well. Shinto leaders generally agreed after the war's end that state control of Shinto institutions had been excessive and harmful to both the Shinto world and the people at large. Shrine Shinto had always had to negotiate its interests—financial, administrative, ideological—vis-à-vis the state on the one side and the Shrine community on the other. State management and financial support of Shinto shrines had varied greatly throughout modern history, and only selected shrines had benefited from them. As Yoshida Shigeru[16] told William Bunce, head of the Religious Section of the Civil Information and Education Section of SCAP, on 8 November 1945, the majority of shrines had traditionally been shrines of the people, supported and managed by them, and would probably welcome being freed from government control.[17]

With governmental Shinto offices thoroughly discredited, there was no organized resistance against the occupation. But Shrine Shinto successfully mobilized private sources capable of interpreting occupation policies and earning legitimacy in the eyes of the Allied Powers. This new leadership emerged from three private Shinto organizations, which had originally formed in response to specific needs during the 1880s and 1890s, a relatively unstable time in the history of state-Shinto relations. The Institute for the Study of Japanese Documents (Kōten kōkyūsho), founded in 1882, was an educational institute founded by Prince Arisugawa to study the national polity (*kokutai*). The Shinto Association of Great Japan (Dainihon jingikai) was founded in 1898 as the All-Japan Association of Shinto Priests in an effort to revive Shinto's privileged status, lost after the failure of the Movement for the Propagation of Great Teaching in the early Meiji period. The Association of the Devotees of Ise Shrine (Jingū hōsaikai) was a nonreligious organization that had promoted the worship at Ise Shrine since 1899.[18] Leaders of these three institutions began meeting in late October 1945 to examine SCAP's policies regarding the status of Shinto shrines, to formulate their own interpretation of what the shrines had been in the past and should become in the future, and to try and influence SCAP's decision making. These meetings paved the way for the establishment of the Association of Shinto Shrines.

The group of men working toward the establishment of the new organization included representatives of Shinto's main special interests, such as Ise Shrine, educational institutions,[19] and the shrines' public relations departments, as well as scholars of constitutional law and men with extensive careers in politics. The most vocal among them were Yoshida Shigeru, secretary general of the Institute for the Study of Japanese Documents and a high-ranking social bureaucrat before and during the war; Miyagawa Munenori, member of the Association of the Devotees of Ise Shrine and a former Tokyo municipal politician; Ashizu Uzuhiko, chairman of the Shinto Youth Organization; Miyaji Naokazu, professor of Shinto at Tokyo Imperial University; and Kishimoto Hideo, also professor at the University of Tokyo and advisor to the Civil Information and Education Staff Section (CIE).[20] Yoshida and Miyaji, along with many other influential Shintoists, were purged from public office by the occupation forces in the winter of 1945/46 and would find new careers as leaders of the Association of Shinto Shrines.

The debates among this group and their various drafts of plans for a new association prior to SCAP's Shinto Directive, issued on 15 December 1945, showed not only a range of ideas and political calculations on behalf of Shrine Shinto, but also a sense of opportunity for Shinto to rid itself of the undesirable excesses of state management experienced at the height of the war. These draft plans were communicated to the public in the fall of 1945 via the Shrine Board and the press, and more directly to SCAP in a meeting on 8 November between Yoshida and Bunce. Shinto leaders agreed that the new central organ was to be a nonpublic institution focused on fostering good relations between the shrines and their communities rather than with the state. SCAP gave them little choice in this matter. But Ashizu Uzuhiko's contention that Shrine Shinto was better off without government officials in high positions—"those incompetent, unbelieving, professional Shinto priests"— won much acclaim at the time and has, if anything, grown stronger in recent decades. Mark Teeuwen concluded in his study of the Association's policies that as long as it is financially secure and has some support from the government and the Imperial House, the shrines' freedom from bureaucratic control is rather appreciated. While critical of the wartime excesses in state management and thought control, the Association of Shinto Shrines nevertheless strove to revive the prewar status of Shinto rituals as a public expression of the spiritual unity of the people under the emperor.[21]

With the Shinto Directive of 15 December 1945, SCAP set the legal framework within which the shrines were allowed to exist and be organized. It ruled that "the sponsorship, support, perpetuation, control and dissemination of Shinto by the Japanese national, prefectural, and local governments, or by public officials . . . acting in their official capacity are prohibited," but that "private educational institutions for the investigation and dissemination of Shinto and for the training of priesthood for Shinto will be permitted and will operate with the same privileges and be subject to the same controls and restrictions as any other private educational institution having no affiliation with the government; and in no case will they propagate and disseminate militaristic and ultra-nationalistic ideology." It further explained that "the purpose of this directive is to separate religion from the state, to prevent misuse of religion for political ends, and to put all religions, faiths, and creeds upon exactly the same legal basis, entitled to precisely the same opportunities and protection."[22]

Accordingly, the Association of Shinto Shrines, founded on 3 February 1946, was a private organization, registered as a Religious Juridical Person under the Religious Corporations Ordinance of December 1945.[23] (Efforts in subsequent decades to establish Shrine Shinto once more as a public, nonreligious institution have failed.) Many practical issues regarding shrine property, educational institutions, and the status of Ise Shrine had yet to be negotiated, first among Shinto leaders, then with SCAP and in the Diet. But with prominent politicians and influential scholars in their ranks, though compromised by the purge, Shinto leaders managed to carve out a space in which to represent their interests in the public sphere, and they did so mainly through legal channels. With the establishment of the Association of Shinto Shrines, Shrine Shinto had moved from representing public to representing private interests. Devoid of state support, it now focused on the promotion of its concerns among a democratic public both free to express views critical of the state and bound by legal constraints to accept the representation of conflicting interests. Like many right-wing organizations after the war, the Association firmly embraced the overwhelmingly popular rhetoric of democracy, for only democratic guarantees to grant protection to legal minority views enabled it to rebuild Shinto in the public sphere. Indeed, "democracy" became the unifying framework— a lesson of the war all Japanese could agree on—within which fiercely political struggles about contemporary interests and views of the past were fought out. Groups on the right, especially, recognized during the first postwar decade that only genuine popular support would guarantee their legitimacy.

Shrines for the People

In 1946, however, Shinto shrines found themselves not only stripped of their status as state institutions, but also without much popular support. SCAP's propaganda depicting State Shinto as a major arm of militarism during the war had evidently molded public opinion. The sharp decrease in the number of people visiting the Meiji Shrine in Tokyo— from 350,000 in 1945 to 135,000 in 1946—indicated as much to Shrine Shintoists.[24] The widespread desperation and loss of faith among local Shinto priests bemoaned in the pages of the Association's newspaper, *Jinja shinpō (Shrine News)*, in its early years were most certainly real.

Physical and spiritual devastation loomed large over a country whose total war had ended in total defeat. But while many Japanese welcomed the Americans and embraced their values in the name of building a new Japan, Shrine Shintoists had to find a niche for themselves in a political climate largely dictated by the foreign occupiers before they could advance their own plan for a new Japan. Rebuilding their position among the populace was a matter of public outreach in the localities. It required a structure of communication among shrines as organizational units, not only individual priests, as well as a commonly agreed-upon interpretation of the past and vision for the future.[25]

This was Miyagawa Munenori's intent when he launched *Jinja shinpō* in July 1946, under the threat of occupation censorship, with a mere ten employees and few financial resources. The newspaper was to serve several purposes: to create cooperation and a sense of shared destiny between shrines nationwide, to reinterpret Shrine Shinto and traditional Japanese customs as inherently democratic and pacifist, to provide information about the Shinto Directive to priests all over the country and help alleviate their fears, and to find legal ways in which Shinto rites could be preserved and made accessible to the public. These goals hinged first and foremost on the reinterpretation of the shrines as shrines of the people. An editorial in *Jinja shinpō*'s first issue, published on 8 July 1946, clearly expressed this agenda:

After a long time under state management, Shinto has entered a new stage in its development. One may regard the ending of the special protection of the state as unfortunate. . . . But when we consider history, no one can deny the depth and beauty of the Japanese heart (*kokoro*) revealed in learning, art, virtues, and religion. If we reflect deeply upon ourselves and recognize our own depth of heart, the people will earnestly pursue the ideal of today's virtuous and peaceful Japan.

In order to search our real hearts in this way, the shrines are of the utmost importance. The Japanese religious essence is crystallized in the shrines. When the shrines failed to grow, so did the Japanese religious essence; when the shrines got distorted, so did the people's hearts. Now that the shrines are free of the political restrictions imposed by the state, we should welcome the shrines' true development into shrines of the masses.

With this advertisement of itself as an organization combining the best of the old and the best of the new Japan, the Association of Shinto

Shrines took its place among the earliest representatives of special interest on the public stage. In so doing, it participated in contemporary efforts across political lines to redefine the locus of "the public." Whereas during the war the public had been virtually synonymous with the state, the postwar project of democratization pivoted on the (re)creation of a democratic public independent of—or at least not dominated by—the state. For those who had suffered under state coercion during the war years, the need for such a critical public sphere was a main lesson of the war experience. But even the beneficiaries of the wartime state, such as Shrine Shinto, insisted on a democratic public after the war because they saw it as a chance to regain public legitimacy and visibility as representatives of special interests, apart from the state. The newspaper *Jinja shinpō* served as the foremost organ in which the organized Shinto world discussed a variety of views on current affairs as seen through the lens of Shrine Shinto's prewar and postwar experiences. In the following pages I have relied heavily on articles and editorials printed in *Jinja shinpō* as well as other publications by the Association of Shinto Shrines because they best demonstrate efforts by the central leadership to create a consensus on specific topics among its constituents and represent a distinctively "Shinto view" to the public.

In sharp contrast to progressive civic groups that formed or were revived in the early postwar years to participate in a radical break with the wartime era, Shrine Shinto based its claims of popular leadership on historical continuity across 1945. The Association of Shinto Shrines claimed that the shrines had always been the moral leaders of the people, even at the time of the shrines' "distortion" by the state. But if the shrines bore responsibility for having misled the people during the war, that responsibility was immediately qualified by the shrines' own victimization at the hands of a militaristic state. (*Jinja shinpō* staff writers reminded readers that the "shrine world," like the people, had suffered extensive losses, for many shrines had been destroyed by fire at the end of the war and, with them, their financial resources.) Indeed, Shinto leaders insisted that a reconnection with one's innermost qualities—revealed in Shinto—was necessary to reach the new ideal of democracy, surely a soothing message for those who resisted the idea that everything good should come with an American label.

As if to demonstrate Shrine Shinto's distrust of the state and its own active leadership of the people, the Association in 1947 named a "moral suasion committee" to establish a "Shinto spiritual movement" in response to the government's "Bill Outlining a Popular Movement to Build a New Japan." In a June article, *Jinja shinpō* editors staked out political ground for their organization vis-à-vis the state and the people. While agreeing with the government that a voluntary spiritual movement from among the people was needed to rebuild the country, the article criticized the government's ability to lead a popular movement and instead put its own organization forth as a more appropriate leader.

Such [spiritual] movements designed by the government tend to be unsuccessful. For us . . . it is best to choose the way of cooperation with a popular movement. In order to generate a voluntary popular movement, the appropriate fertilizer and sunlight are necessary in the same way as they are for plants, and a fire must be lit in [the people's] dormant brains. Surely [Shinto] virtues serve as a bright light to lead the way.[26]

Indeed, the Shinto world continued to insist, as it had in prewar and wartime days, on Shrine Shinto's mandate to direct the people's "spirit," which it continued to define in national terms. For even if the militaristic state had been discredited, national unity was all the more important after the war, when the country lay in ruins and the ideological superstructure of wartime unity had collapsed. Once again, Shinto proposed to provide the spiritual source of that unity, not through religious belief, which it now considered private, but through the practice of rites (service to deities at Shinto shrines and home altars) as an undeniably Japanese and historically continuous element in public life. The disastrous war resulted from the misguided appropriation of Shinto rites to the political goals of the state, argued Shinto leaders, and so the country's spiritual leadership could not again be left to the government but rightfully lay (as it always had) in the Shinto clergy itself. The Association of Shinto Shrines defined Shrine Shinto's mission as bringing national unity from "within," as opposed to learning new values from "without"—that is, the occupation and the United States.

But distrust of the state and foreign influences did not suffice to make Shrine Shinto a popular movement. A whole new structure was needed, one in which the shrines themselves, or more precisely their priests, took the lead in disseminating Shinto ideology to local people, and without state support. In fact, it appears from *Jinja shinpō*'s editorials throughout its early years that neither the government nor the people were really the focus here. Rather, the "Shinto spiritual movement" aimed at local shrines and their priests in an effort to make them into active, cooperative members of the Association. The incessant repetition of pleas for cooperation suggests that the priesthood was not easily convinced of Shinto's new organizational structure, possibly because the priests themselves held different and competing views of past and present. Statistics confirm that the problem lay first of all with individual priests, not the shrines or the parishioners. Whereas the number of shrines and adherents grew continuously after 1947, the number of priests and teachers dropped from 15,890 to 14,874 between 1947 and the end of 1949.[27]

Most *Jinja shinpō* editorials during that time addressed themselves directly to the priests, reminding them of their superior position of influence among the people, inviting them to voice their ideas and concerns, but discouraging any activities not previously cleared with the central organization. Prominent priests also contributed articles to *Jinja shinpō* alongside scholars and professional reporters. These editorials stressed that the Association did not presume to be a "power presence" but merely oversaw and coordinated activities and represented the interests of shrines as a whole:

Within the Shinto world, there is a strong sense [of today's spiritual loss] but no willpower to undertake the organizational task [of rebuilding people's spirits]. Therefore, we must first achieve unison within the Shinto world to provide organizational leadership for a spiritual movement. Because the education committee members are elected in every prefecture and are capable and spirited people, it may be difficult to unify their ideas. The Association of Shinto Shrines does not intend to take a leadership role in this. It provides the connections and the knowledge necessary for the development of lively activities based on Shinto qualities and tradition.

This is an organization that brings together the abilities of different people, a forum that the Shinto world has heretofore lacked. It is important that we build organizations in every district and that we work together as if in a research or youth group.[28]

The Association of Shinto Shrines did manage to gradually increase the number of shrines and certified priests under its aegis in the following years. It served as an umbrella organization for about 75 percent of all Shinto shrines, the rest being divided into more than 160 sects.

Memory and Shinto Restorationism

The Association's effort to expand its popular base and change Shinto's war-tainted image was a necessary step in establishing Shrine Shinto as an interest group whose political involvement transcended issues of religious practice or folk traditions. Shinto leaders accepted democratic change not as an end in itself, but as a structural framework—inevitable under the circumstances—within which Shinto's mandate could once again assume its central place in public life. Insofar as postwar reforms flatly contradicted the unchallenged centrality of Shinto rituals and public values (evident in the changed status of the emperor under the new constitution), Shinto leaders lobbied for political support in the Diet and the government to change these reforms. During the occupation years, the Association of Shinto Shrines was greatly constricted in its political activities. Under Miyagawa Munenori's leadership, however, it found ways to represent its views indirectly through the personal prestige enjoyed by its leaders and by self-censoring its publications.

Retrospectives on the Association's early years published in the 1980s provide insight into the groups' political negotiations and offer important correctives to the Association's public image in the late 1940s. One such review article challenged the common perception that the occupation forces wielded total power and forced the Japanese into complete servility toward their own government. It claimed that although Shinto leaders like the prewar Shrine Board director Yoshida Shigeru, the former Tokyo municipal official Miyagawa Munenori, and the constitutional scholar Inoue Takamaro were limited in their public work by the military purge, they were nevertheless able to build on their high personal prestige among the political elite and across political lines, owing to their prewar and wartime careers.

Indeed, Miyagawa Munenori, first administrative director of the Association (1946–53), was highly successful in building political support through personal contacts and prestige, while remaining within the legal parameters set by the occupation forces. Miyagawa had been a highly regarded Tokyo City official before and during the war. He began his career as head of Koishikawa Ward in 1927, served as assemblyman, and in 1941 became chief of the League for Asian Development's research department.[29] After the war, Miyagawa's prewar loyalties within the Tokyo City government superseded newly created party-political lines, as he helped former Diet members representing the city of Tokyo to assume leading positions in the Socialist Party, which came to power briefly in 1947 under Prime Minister Katayama Tetsu. Miyagawa was also credited with facilitating the effortless passage of the National Property Protection Bill in the Diet because of his ability to persuade Diet members across party lines.[30] During the occupation years, the Association itself remained officially neutral toward all political parties except the Japan Communist Party, which it opposed because of the JCP's radical denunciation of the *kokutai* and the emperor.

Although President Miyagawa was greatly distressed by the occupation's anti-Shinto policies, he remained committed to conducting the Association's affairs within legal limits. The Association constructed its public image by carefully selecting the issues on which its newspaper reported and by framing dissenting opinions in its reports as the views of a democratic minority. According to a recent critique, *Jinja shinpō* did not even come close to its official goal of accurately reporting "all important matters pertaining to the shrines under the Shinto Directive." It excluded from its pages all topics that were considered politically dangerous, so that "small news" was covered in detail, while the "big news" was often omitted.[31] For example, William Bunce did not tolerate the publication of articles about his meetings with government officials, yet these meetings determined much of SCAP's policy toward Shrine Shinto. Tellingly, the Tokyo war crimes trial received almost no coverage. One article in *Jinja shinpō* commented on the trial's verdict in November 1948 by reprinting excerpts from national newspapers. The excerpts were prefaced by a solemn characterization of the Japanese response to the verdict's announcement: quiet resignation before the abstract power of the law.[32]

Despite this self-censorship by omission, *Jinja shinpō* was able to "report sympathetically on the imperial family and popular spiritual traditions, respectful of people with prewar loyalties" even "in the midst of popular anger at Japan's so-called cultural traditions and disrespect toward the emperor."[33] By recent estimates, the political views expressed in *Jinja shinpō* reflected those of a small minority, about 1 percent of the public, but they were the opinions of a legal minority, and William Bunce openly regarded them as such. Articles discussing the drafting of the new constitution in 1946–47 clearly expressed dissatisfaction with the drafts—as did liberal newspapers like the *Asahi shinbun*—but just as clearly respected the majority decision in the Diet in favor of its adoption. To support their views on the emperor's status in the new constitution, *Jinja shinpō* editors quoted academic scholarship (by its own members). To argue for Shinto's recognition as a national spiritual source (above other religions), they invoked international comparisons, such as the *de facto* prevalence of one religion in all major nations— Christianity in Europe and America, Buddhism in many Asian countries.[34] But direct political attacks were carefully avoided.

The Association's membership, however, included many ultraconservatives such as Shōwa restorationists Kageyama Masaharu, Nakamura Takehiko, and Moro Kiyoteru, as well as former military and navy officers and ideologically committed and uncompromising activists like Inoue Takamaro and Ashizu Uzuhiko. Some of them found an outlet for their views in underground publications, in which several influential Shinto leaders such as Inoue and Ashizu engaged as private persons. The first such piece was entitled "Debating the History of the Beginning and End of the War's Conclusion," suggesting the potentially explosive nature of these writings. They were produced illegally and circulated among like-minded people, especially students, through hand-deliveries to private homes. Although these articles never surfaced outside this secret group of readers they have been collected separately in the Association's archives.[35] These illegal activities got *Jinja shinpō*'s editor Ashizu into trouble with the Association; he had to resign temporarily. Yet he remained one of the organization's most prominent spokesmen.

Although underground publications stopped with the end of the occupation, a measure of self-censorship continued as part of a bargain struck with government officials who feared negative publicity through association with a right-wing organization. In the early 1950s a public controversy was ignited by two articles printed in *Jinja shinpō* in which the Association gave the impression that the government was considering state subsidies for the sixtieth reconstruction of Ise Shrine, despite the unconstitutionality of such governmental aid.[36] In response to the public outcry, government officials urged the Association to refrain from making public demands on the government, as this would "confuse public opinion." It nonetheless assured its leaders that the government was supportive of the shrines and would review the Association's legal situation in return. The two articles were in fact excluded from subsequent reprint volumes. According to a 1986 retrospective, the Association thus traded in its right to publicize its views aggressively in exchange for informal support for its interests by the state.

The Association of Shinto Shrines was never entirely comfortable with special interest politics, even though it established itself as a well-connected and effective political player. Insofar as the Association proclaimed a unique "Shinto standpoint" in public debates about the political issues of the day through such periodicals as *Jinja shinpō*, it represented the "shrine world" as one among many political interests. For example, immediately after the Allied occupation had come to an end, the government sponsored a move to revise history textbooks, a backlash against the Marxist historiography of the early postwar period. Civic groups of varying political convictions became involved. The Association joined the revisionists by arguing that if Western history textbooks were written from a Christian standpoint, as some claimed, then Japanese history textbooks surely called for a correction to bring them in line with a Shinto point of view.[37] At the same time, however, its designation as a special interest fundamentally contradicted the belief that Shinto, as the only indigenous code of national ethics, ought to inform Japanese public life in general. Shinto alone, the Association argued, was capable of lending cohesiveness and continuity to the nation in the face of political divisiveness and change. Clearly, it was Shrine Shinto's "special interest" to once again establish Shinto as the essence of the national polity, which meant that Shinto was "common interest."

For Shrine Shintoists, remembering the war meant restoring to public legitimacy the status of shrines as the concrete embodiment of the idea that Japan as a national entity possessed a spiritual core, which resided in the emperor's unchanged relationship to the Japanese people throughout history. In the light of *foreign* occupation, therefore, this memory focused less on the wartime politics that had "distorted" this relationship than on the occupation's obstruction of its rightful restoration. SCAP's policies, moreover, had left enough room for Shintoists to be hopeful that this restoration could in fact be accomplished. After all, the imperial institution remained intact, the emperor was never indicted for his role in the war, Shinto rites and rituals were declared merely "religious" but otherwise not touched, and the shrines themselves remained available—or could be rebuilt. As the occupation came to an end, moreover, the "foreign factor" changed from a contemporary reality with which Shrine Shinto had to contend to a legacy that fed domestic political conflict.

While the liberal left protested against the gradual consolidation of conservative leadership, the Association of Shinto Shrines seized the moment and embarked on campaigns to demand constitutional change, the official recognition of prewar national holidays, and a more rigorous definition of Shinto ritual practice, especially as it related to shrines of the war dead. Shrine leaders moved quickly to assert their position in the final years of the occupation, above all in relation to the status of the Yasukuni and Ise shrines. By the early 1950s, writers for *Jinja shinpō* no longer stressed Shinto priests' mandate as popular spiritual leaders, but instead highlighted the importance of "nationalism"—both "imperial" and "Asian"—in their attempt to formulate a political agenda relating to the most pressing contemporary issues of national policy.

This change reflected a significant shift in the political climate, described most often as the manifestation in Japanese domestic politics of the occupation's "reverse course." The "reverse course" in U.S. foreign policy dated back to the onset of the Cold War in 1947, when occupation policy makers changed from their earlier emphasis on demilitarization and democratization to making Japan into a conservative ally of the American bloc in Asia. Japanese political groups experienced this reversal as an American turnaround from supporting progressive interests to siding with conservative and anticommunist politics. By 1951, all but a handful of the approximately 200,000 people purged in 1946 for their involvement in the war effort had been released. Some, including the eventual prime minister Kishi Nobusuke, even resumed their political careers. In turn, almost 22,000 communists or suspected communists lost their jobs in the so-called Red Purge, and the government actively censored left-wing publications. At the same time, the police force was reestablished, remilitarization openly discussed, and the bureaucracy restored to its position of power. As one writer in *Jinja shinpō* commented, "The trend to recover characteristics of the prewar social structure, from the home to public institutions, is undeniable."[38] The article about the results of the reverse course continued:

Although these are all very positive developments for the Japanese, we need to make good use of them. On the one hand, it is good that all this happens at such speed, but on the other, it is not a product of the people reflecting on the present situation and deciding to change it. Rather, the change [in the domestic political climate] is the result of changes in the international situation.

The movement to revive National Foundation Day (*kigensetsu*) as a national holiday, as well as the movement demanding state pensions for the war bereaved, are popular movements through which the people can establish the positive aspects of the reverse course, while diminishing its negative aspects, namely the power of unsympathetic bureaucrats.[39]

The Association of Shinto Shrines launched a number of such movements, directed mostly at governmental and bureaucratic institutions. On 12 February 1951, the Association inaugurated its own version of the "New Life Movement" in an effort to reestablish Shinto ritual once again as the "correct social ethic" at home and at the workplace, reform and regulate Shinto ceremonies, and promote the "spirit of respect for the national flag and anthem and loving protection of the homeland."[40] In particular, Shinto leaders asked for clarification of rituals guiding worship at shrines of the war dead in response to an announcement by the Ministry of Education in September 1951 that prefectural governors, city mayors, and village headmen could participate in memorial services. The Association's formal position in 1946 had stressed that ceremonies for the war dead should consist exclusively of memorial services without any nationalist content, accompanied instead by prayers for peace. Now it demanded—and the ministry immediately granted—that the annual enshrinement ceremonies at the spring and fall festivals be explicitly included, complete with "memorial addresses" of condolence, and "incense and flowers," by which was meant the traditional offerings of *tamagushi* (sacred *sakaki* tree branches) and *heihaku* (cloth or cut paper). A year later, the emperor and empress attended the autumn memorial service at Yasukuni Shrine for the first time since the end of the war—clearly a sign that marked Yasukuni as an official memorial for the 2.5 million war dead enshrined there.[41]

If such movements underlined the Association's politics as a special interest group, its active participation in debates about national policy from 1950 on showed its commitment to restore Shinto to its prewar place as an unchanging pillar of public life rather than merely a political interest. During the last years of the occupation period, public debate focused on the related issues of the San Francisco Peace and Security Treaty (both signed on 8 September 1951), Japan's remilitarization in the context of the Korean War, and the continuing presence of American military bases after the occupation had come to an end. While progressive groups fiercely attacked the government under Prime Minister Yoshida Shigeru for its (undemocratic) handling of these issues, the Association focused on the larger political dilemma revealed in them. The dilemma, it argued, stemmed not only from defeat in war but particularly from the misguided occupation policies of the early postwar years. Predictably, the Association of Shinto Shrines aimed its attack especially at the postwar constitution, criticizing the document itself as well as its psychological impact on the Japanese people in the context of American propaganda. The contemporary controversies surrounding suggestions of Japan's remilitarization and the ambiguous nature of Japan's independence formed the context for this attack.

"The world of politics in Japan considers remilitarization despite constitutional constraints, but the world of religion stays true to the spirit of the peace constitution even in times of danger," an editorial in *Jinja shinpō* stated in early 1951, several months into the Korean War.[42] Time and again, the paper urged religious people to concern themselves with this issue instead of leaving it to politicians. But the Association did not intend to come down in support of the peace constitution. On the contrary, it argued that the peace clause in Article 9 (renouncing war as a means for solving international conflicts) was meant to express a fundamental "view of humanity" that belonged in the realm of religion (or philosophy) and not in a political document. By placing constitutional constraints on an issue such as the role of the military, the founders of the constitution had only invited the kind of political maneuvering that could never do justice to the philosophical question at stake:

Politicians argue that in order to protect our national borders with a military force, we need to change the constitution. But because of our war experience, there is too much popular resistance against constitutional revision. Therefore, they say, we need to establish a "reserve corps" [instead of a military] in order to avoid constitutional change. It is a matter of avoiding the term "military." If we proceed in this way, we will lose the trust of both the Japanese people and our Asian neighbors.[43]

Ultimately, the Association of Shinto Shrines held that a country's basic view of humanity needed to remain above politics, a value that permeated society through religion, not a matter of political negotiation.[44] The problem was that as a result of defeat and foreign occupation, Japan had lost its spiritual basis, which Shintoists conceived of in national terms, and replaced it with crude political conflict. This loss came into sharp focus with the return of Japan's independence in 1952. Although Shrine Shinto obviously welcomed the restoration of national sovereignty, the conditions attached to independence only highlighted the extent to which Japan remained politically, economically, and spiritually dependent on the United States. This sense of betrayal permeated Japanese public life across the political spectrum in the early 1950s, although interpretations of the agent and nature of this betrayal differed widely. The Association of Shinto Shrines took up the issue of Japan's "subordinate independence" in both the national context of a deficient postwar and the international context of successful independence movements across Asia. Both lines of argument revealed an ethnic, even racial, nationalism based on principles of national cohesion, an impatience with domestic political strife, and a clear hierarchy of nations in the international arena.

Shinto nationalism differed from other brands insofar as it denied a spiritual break in 1945 and continued to place the emperor at the core of an eternal Japanese spirit that provided consistency and continuity despite political change. For Ashizu Uzuhiko, an orthodox Shintoist and editor of *Jinja shinpō*, the failure of the postwar consisted in the loss of spiritual independence. Quoting an old Shinto saying, "The heart is the house of the deity" (*kokoro wa shinmei no sumika nari*), Ashizu likened personal independence to national independence: just as a person who has the deity (*kami*) in his heart is independent, a nation that has a spiritual foundation is independent.

And what is the founding spirit of Japan? The Emperor. Japan can only become a truly independent country if the people have unanimously decided to preserve the Emperor as their country's spirit. Shrine Shinto represents that effort. But even if Shrine Shinto cannot in the present situation provide the spiritual source of national rebuilding, we Shintoists must strive to assume a spiritual role in our country. It is our task to call for and to nurture the correct spirit among the people so that we can rebuild our country.[45]

Another article in *Jinja shinpō* entitled "Japan's Future and Asian Na-tionalism" assumed a similar kind of ethnic nationalism (*minzoku shugi*) to be the driving force behind the successful independence movements in India, Indonesia, China, Vietnam, and elsewhere. Rejecting contem-porary rhetoric of "global politics" and "world citizens" (as well as Asian regionalist renderings of nationalism),[46] it insisted on ethnicity as the or-ganizing principle among peoples in the world, prior even to communist national ideology in the case of Mao Zedong's China and Ho Chi-minh's Vietnam. The correlation between nationalism and independence, past and present, appeared simple indeed. In the nineteenth and the first half of the twentieth centuries, Asian nationalism was weak and Japanese na-tionalism strong; therefore, "various Asian countries fell victim to colo-nialism while Japan alone succeeded in preserving its independence."[47] Since 1945, in contrast, Asian countries had liberated themselves thanks to a rising nationalism while Japan remained occupied. Nonetheless, the writer of this article continued, there was an important difference: Japan lost its independence in the course of military engagement, while India and Indonesia gained their independence without the use of arms. "Japan should study the nationalist movements of other Asian coun-tries," he concluded. "Tomorrow's nationalism cannot be 'scientific, using material force' . . . or, as Mencius put it, 'cannot indulge in wealth, cannot fade into poverty, cannot give in to authority and power (*fuki mo insuru atowazu, hinsen mo utsusu atowazu, ibu mo kussuru atowazu*) . . . but must rely on the highest spiritual force.[48]

The Association of Shinto Shrines advanced a view of Japan's recent past that played down the historical break of 1945 by sharply opposing politics (whether wartime or postwar) to an ethnocentric, spiritual essen-tialism. Against the inherent divisiveness and constant change of political ideology, Shrine Shinto insisted on the necessity of a unifying, unchang-ing system of public values firmly anchored in historical traditions and represented by the emperor. Only Shinto, as the sole indigenous religion, could guide the public in the correct adherence to this national essence. The Association of Shinto Shrines fought hard to erase the postwar popular perception of Shinto as militaristic. It certainly acknowledged Japan's war conduct—having "inflicted hardship" on Asian countries—but this "hardship" appeared as an unhappy side effect of laudable intentions on behalf of the Japanese nation. Likewise, Shrine leaders asserted that Shrine Shinto was wrongly appropriated to the militaristic goals of the wartime state (in particular the bureaucracy), yet insisted on its historically legitimate leadership role among the people, independent of formal state support. The designation of Shrine Shinto as "special interest" therefore fundamentally contradicted the belief that Shinto represented a non-negotiable essence relevant to all Japanese.

Nevertheless, the Association participated rather effectively in special interest politics, fostering close relations with the Imperial Household Agency as well as the right wing of the ruling Liberal Democratic Party (LDP), while refraining from any involvement in the shrines' interaction with their parishioners. The Association's politics revolved around its desire to change both its greatly diminished public status (as a result of occupation reforms) and its unpopularity, which it blamed on Allied propaganda. Indeed, the Association mourned not so much defeat as the legacies of foreign occupation, summed up in Japan's "spiritual dependence." Criticism of the Allied occupation formed the interpretive framework for Shrine Shinto's memory of the war (and Japanese modern history in general). It perpetuated crass nationalist distinctions between Japan and the rest of the world, as well as Asia and the West, and reinforced an opposition between politics (which depended on changing power relations) and an eternally constant, non-negotiable cultural essence. Such a stance could not recognize newly emerging boundaries between the state and an independent, critical public that remained central to the postwar project of democracy. From its particular vantage point, the Association of Shinto Shrines thereby influenced public memory of the war by encouraging an ethnocentric, apolitical, and ahistorical view of this international conflict while sharply discouraging any criticism of the emperor.

CHAPTER TWO

Fashioning National Heroes:
The Japan Association of War-bereaved Families

The human cost of the war fought in Asia and the Pacific was immense, and the suffering hardly ended in August 1945. Quantifying this cost is difficult, but it is generally accepted that at the time of Japan's defeat, 1.74 million Japanese servicemen and almost as many civilians were dead, 4.5 million demobilized soldiers were registered as wounded or ill, and 6.5 million military personnel and civilians had to be repatriated from every corner of Japan's collapsed empire. On the home islands, nine million Japanese were left homeless by the Allied invasion of Okinawa and the fire-bombings of 66 major cities on Honshu and Kyushu, including the atomic destruction of Hiroshima and Nagasaki.[1] Even these numbers pale when set against the tens of millions of people across Asia who died in this war, many as a direct result of Japanese aggression. As Japan itself lay in ruins, its military-industrial complex nearly destroyed, its empire gone, and occupied by a foreign power, public demands for government relief and compensation for lost lives and property all but overwhelmed the authorities. The ensuing competition for public funds among war victims pitted people with different war experiences against each other while forging alliances between others.

War-bereaved military families (*izoku*) formed just one such group of war victims. What set them apart from others, however, was the privileged position they had enjoyed during the war. Their personal losses—husbands, fathers, sons—had been treated as a special public concern throughout the war, and many had found consolation in the government's official recognition and monetary compensation for that loss. Moreover, the state's aggressive appropriation of these military dead for propaganda purposes—namely, to unite the people behind Japan's cause in fighting the war—greatly complicated the memory of the war dead. Official ceremonies of enshrining the spirits of those fallen in battle at so-called nation-protecting shrines, and again at the national Yasukuni Shrine in Tokyo, turned personal mourning into national celebration. The bereaved families were the immediate recipients of that national honor (and consolation), both symbolically and materially through government pension payments and a host of other benefits. The cult of the war dead thus combined the ideology of State Shinto (in terms of the shrines' role in ritually connecting the people with their nation's spiritual essence, the emperor) with the structures of a modern social welfare system.

After defeat, the occupation labeled the cult of the war dead and war bereaved "militaristic" and abolished both State Shinto and pensions for the war bereaved. War widows with small children were hardest hit by these measures and counted themselves lucky to find a spot in a mother-child dormitory and any kind of odd job that allowed them to earn some money (Fig. 2.1). In response, widows tended to form women's support groups, while war-bereaved self-help groups under male leadership in 1947 founded the Japan League for the Welfare of the War Bereaved (Nihon izoku kōsei renmei). In 1953 this group became Japan's foremost conservative pressure group, the Japan Association of War-bereaved Families (Nihon izokukai, hereafter Izokukai). As a private organization, the League lobbied government circles to press for new social welfare legislation aimed at reestablishing the war bereaved as a separate category in the social welfare structure and reviving government pensions for its members. Even after pensions were reinstituted at the end of the occupation, war-bereaved representatives staged hunger strikes in front of Yasukuni Shrine to press for increases (Fig. 2.2). Throughout the occupation years, these two causes—one religious, one welfare-oriented—remained separate, at least on the surface of public relations as conducted by these newly founded civic

Fig. 2.1   A war widow working with her children at the Kōtōbashi dormitory, Tokyo, May 1949. Used by permission of Mainichi Shinbunsha.

Fig. 2.2   Representatives of the war bereaved stage a hunger strike on the grounds of Yasukuni Shrine to demand more government aid, 13 January 1953. Used by permission of Mainichi Shinbunsha.

organizations. By the early 1950s, however, their links emerged once again wherever the politics of essentialism practiced by the Association of Shinto Shrines and the Izokukai's "politics of fashioning national heroes" converged around national issues focusing on the reversal of occupation reforms such as constitutional revision and the status of Yasukuni Shrine.

Creating a Community of War-bereaved Families

In postsurrender Japan under the Allied occupation, the formation of a war-bereaved movement required an ideological process in its own right. The emerging leadership faced the challenge of creating a collective mentality that provided a sense of identity among the diverse group of people who had lost relatives on the battlefield, and, perhaps more importantly, of legitimizing their concerns in the eyes of society. Their miserable living conditions were hardly unique in the early postwar years: every Japanese person's life or livelihood had been touched by Japan's war in Asia, the Pacific, and the home islands. The status and condition of the war bereaved, moreover, varied greatly depending on their proximity to the war dead, the military rank of the fallen relative, their own wartime experiences, socioeconomic conditions after the war, geographic location, and so on.[2] In addition, having lost a relative did not automatically lead a person either to glorify or to denounce the war. Rather, within the context of a vocal popular antimilitarism, war-bereaved families built a sense of community on the basis of three main shared experiences: the wartime recognition of the war bereaved as a class of their own, the denial of that recognition by the occupation authorities, and the social profile of the bereaved.

Beginning in the interwar period, official recognition and financial support for the families of the military dead and injured helped create an increasingly well-recognized and politically visible war-bereaved community. They were arguably the first to benefit measurably from the developing social welfare system in the 1920s. To qualify as war bereaved, one had to be a spouse, child, parent, or grandparent of a serviceman who had died on public duty. Three simultaneous and inter-related developments made the special treatment of the bereaved possible: social welfare legislation, which granted them pensions and a variety of other benefits; state-sponsored or supported organizations not *of* but rather *for* the war bereaved and other war victims; and the much-enhanced prominence of official enshrinement ceremonies for the spirits of the military dead at Yasukuni Shrine.

The first law stipulating pension payments to war-bereaved families was the Military Relief Law, inaugurated by the Home Ministry's Bureau of Local Affairs in 1917 as part of new legislation dealing with poor relief, veterans' assistance, children's welfare, and unemployment.[3] But not until the beginning of the war against China and the Military Aid Law of March 1937 did this support system become fully institutionalized.[4] A survey in September 1937 shows that the Military Aid Law treated the families of the war injured and war dead in one category. Payment amounts, however, were meticulously graduated according to the military rank of the injured or dead person. For example, normal pension payments for those fallen or injured in battle, the main source of income for these families, were divided into 17 different pay categories, ranging from ¥150–¥200 for regular soldiers to ¥1,867–¥2,500 for generals. Servicemen who were injured or who died in other public service capacities received smaller pension amounts and at rates that were calculated as fixed percentages of those amounts paid to the families of the war bereaved. In addition to these pensions, the families of the war injured and dead received a number of other types of welfare and benefits, depending on years of service: (1) a one-time pension payment; (2) a government acknowledgment award, which differed slightly for army and navy personnel and was close to pension amounts; (3) a special supplementary award for death by accident; (4) a government award related to death in an aircraft or submarine; (5) burial funds (four kinds); (6) free or discounted railway transportation; (7) the award of a war-bereaved badge; and (8) reduction and exemption from government and private elementary and middle-school tuition.[5] An adjustment of these welfare benefits followed in February 1942 with the inauguration of the Wartime Disaster Protection Law. The war bereaved thus received not only government pensions but a number of fringe benefits that clearly privileged them among other victims of war.

Organizationally, too, the war bereaved formed a subgroup of a larger category that included veterans, disabled servicemen, and the families of those who were injured in or had died in battle. In November

1938, three earlier support groups merged into the Imperial Gift Foundation Soldiers' Support Group (Onshi zaidan gunjin engokai), a state-supported organization designed to aid wounded soldiers, their families, and bereaved families by bolstering popular support for servicemen and veterans. The same year saw efforts by the Ministry of Welfare to establish support programs for disabled veterans and their families by creating the Wounded Soldiers' Protection Agency (Shōhei hogoin). This was expanded into the Military Protection Agency (Gunji hogoin) in July 1939, a branch of the Ministry of Welfare designed to aid servicemen, veterans, and the war bereaved.[6] The Soldiers' Support Group voluntarily dissolved itself in January 1946, whereas the Military Protection Agency was dismantled by SCAP in December 1945. The distinction between these two types of organizations—the former a social welfare aid group, the latter a government agency—was to surface again in postoccupation legislation.

Public Shinto ceremonies for the war dead commenced after Japan's military invasion of China in 1938. Apart from raising Yasukuni Shrine's profile, these ceremonies confirmed who qualified as war bereaved—namely, the relatives of the spirits enshrined in a ceremony there.[7] Around this time, the war bereaved came to be affectionately called "Kudan mama" and "Yasukuni orphan," both referring to the location of Yasukuni Shrine, on Kudan hill in Tokyo. Ceremonies of the invocation of the spirits of the war dead held at the Yasukuni Great Annual Festivals were broadcast nationally on the radio. Although popular sentiment overwhelmingly supported the soldiers and their families, voices of dissent were not altogether absent, even at the height of the war.[8] Radio announcers at ceremonies for the war dead apparently took great care to screen out voices from among the bereaved in the streets crying "Murderer" and "Give me back my child."[9] Clearly, not all the war bereaved agreed with the way the state elevated the deaths of their loved ones, but dissenting voices were few enough so that broadcasters were able to tune them out.

In the confusion that followed Japan's surrender, these enshrinement ceremonies at Yasukuni became an urgent problem for shrine authorities, who depended on the Army, Navy, and Home ministries to supply accurate information about the names of servicemen to be enshrined as well as the circumstances of their deaths. SCAP paid close attention to the resulting debate among shrine and government authorities concerning the upcoming autumn festival, which customarily included such enshrinements.[10] The *Asahi shinbun* editorialized on 18 September that a group enshrinement in October would be impossible because of the unavailability of data about the fallen soldiers, whose spirits, if enshrined without this information, would assume the identity of unknown soldiers and thus violate the sacredness of the shrine. "Naturally, in this case, Yasukuni Shrine will be a place for a memorial service and the service will bear no relation to the Yasukuni enshrinement ceremony," it concluded. On 24 October, an intelligence report coming out of GHQ reported that the decision by the Imperial Court to send a representative of the emperor rather than the monarch himself to participate in the autumn festival indicated "a public lessening of the stress on Shrine Shinto."[11] Less than two months later, on 14 December, the *Nippon Times* reported that in accordance with occupation directives and "after consultation with the families of the war-dead," Yasukuni Shrine would adopt a new name, "revert to its original non-military status," and "be placed under the supervision of a juridical person, severing all relations with the Government." Moreover, the GHQ report stated, "its operation will be directed by a council composed of members selected from among the families of the war dead."[12]

The obvious involvement of the war bereaved—and not only government and shrine authorities—in these negotiations may have confirmed, in SCAP's view, that the war bereaved as a class had actively promoted militarism and thus needed to be abolished. Accordingly, two GHQ memoranda issued in late 1945 affected the war bereaved crucially and immediately. The first was entitled "Pensions and Benefits" (SCAPIN 338), issued on 24 November 1945 and ratified by the government on 1 February the following year. The other was the Shinto Directive of 15 December 1945, which ordered the removal of all state institutions relating to Shinto, including public Shinto ceremonies for the war dead. SCAPIN 338 ordered the government to terminate all public and private annuities and other allowances or assistance money previously granted to (1) military personnel and other persons disabled because of war injuries;[13] (2) members of associations and organizations dissolved as a result of occupation orders; (3) individuals who were on the list of those to be purged for reasons of their government position or rank as a result of occupation orders; and (4) those who were detained, under arrest, or convicted of a crime.[14] SCAP justified this decision in terms of the ideological necessity and the monetary gain expected from the termination of pensions:

The pension system [for the war bereaved] is a means to perpetuate the soldiers' class by heredity, which became a significant source of Japan's aggressive policies. One important reason for the attractiveness of becoming soldiers for the Japanese people is that pensions are good. In order to receive pensions, farmers whose lives are harder than those of other classes send their sons to the military. . . .

Of course we are not opposed to appropriate humanitarian aid to people in need. We greatly recognize the need of pensions for the elderly and various kinds of social security, but the benefits and rights should be available to all Japanese, not only to a small group. A system by which the militarists, who bear most of the responsibility for today's misery and poverty, receive privileges not available to the vast majority of other victims must be stopped.[15]

From the termination of military pensions alone, GHQ expected a yearly saving of ¥1.5 billion after demobilization had been completed.[16] In response to this directive, the Military Protection Agency was abolished in December 1945, leaving veterans and the bereaved without any organizational support. On 1 February 1946, the Japanese government issued what has become known as the Sixty-Eighth Imperial Edict, effectively ending all pension payments. The compliant manner in which the Japanese government followed up on SCAP's orders was particularly infuriating to the war bereaved. The government seemed not even to have attempted to negotiate with GHQ about their special standing. Worse still, as part of a popular discourse blaming "the militarists" for the war, bereaved families had come under public attacks for their wartime pension privileges, which had robbed other needy people of their fair share. Many Japanese in fact agreed with SCAP's interpretation of the cult of the war dead at Yasukuni as having perpetuated wartime militarism. An Osaka lawyer coined the term "*eirei* cycle," to which the war bereaved had contributed in crucial ways. The "cycle" began with soldiers who had died in war, were enshrined as war dead, and publicly celebrated as departed heroes (*eirei*). Children learned about the cult of the war dead in school and were encouraged to become soldiers themselves, which in the end produced more war dead.[17] It was a self-perpetuating cycle of death, and the Yasukuni cult served as its engine.

Enshrinement required an exact record of a serviceman's name and the date and circumstances of his death, information that was written on an individual tablet and then added to the list of all enshrined war dead. So it came as a profound embarrassment when some of the spirits already enshrined at Yasukuni returned to Japan alive. On 29 November the *Nippon Times* drew attention to the case of a returning soldier who had been reported dead and had been posthumously decorated with the Sixth Order of the Golden Kite and the Seventh Order of the Rising Sun, his spirit enshrined at Yasukuni. The man insisted, however, that he had been half-unconscious because of severe malnutrition and too weak to fire even one shot in self-defense when he was captured.[18] Such mistakes were probably much more common than officially admitted; exceptional, rather, was the bravery of this soldier in telling his story to the media. Indeed, the social drama of servicemen who had long been believed dead returning to changed family circumstances was part of the general aftermath of war—so much so that in 1947 Kamei Fumio and Yamamoto Satsuo co-directed a major antiwar film, *Between War and Peace* (*Sensō to heiwa*), which centered on a war widow and young mother (played by Kishi Hatae), who had remarried to alleviate some of her hardship and was suddenly confronted with the return of her first husband from the war.[19] The film did not, however, deal with the question of what happened to people whose spirits had been wrongly enshrined, as in the case reported in the *Nippon Times*. Yasukuni Shrine officials insisted then, as they do now, that retracting an enshrined spirit out of the collectivity of spirits is an absolute impossibility.

The contradictions inherent in such wartime and postwar experiences made the memory of the war highly complex for many of the war bereaved. During the war, they had been victimized and yet for that very reason celebrated as national heroes. Under the occupation, their personal losses were ignored or regarded with suspicion (precisely because they had derived state benefits from these losses), while their material and social plight remained beyond question. Early organizations of war-bereaved families, therefore, revealed different and contentious interpretations of both the past and the present situation. The journal *Sensō giseisha* (War Victims) discussed in its inaugural issue on 1 June 1946 the political implications of considering the war dead as war *victims* (*giseisha*) or as *martyrs*, an implicit meaning of *izoku*, the term used for the war bereaved. Makino Shūji, the founder of the journal and manager of a Tokyo dormitory for war widows and their children, argued emphatically for the former and insisted on qualifying the term *izoku* with *giseisha* rather than continuing to celebrate the war bereaved as *izoku* alone, which he considered to indicate a "conservative reactionism" on the part of other war-bereaved activists.[20] Makino also explicitly rejected the notion that all Japanese were victims because Japan had lost the war— war widows, for example, suffered the personal loss of their husbands irrespective of their country's victory or defeat. Taking responsibility *for the war* meant extending aid to the victims of *war* rather than to victims of *defeat*.[21]

On 8 February 1946, one week after the Japanese government had terminated pensions, Makino appeared on the NHK radio program "Watashitachi no kotoba" (Our Language) and called for the establishment of a War Victims Bereaved Families League that would provide mutual assistance especially to war widows and their children. The response from the public was overwhelming. Local war-bereaved groups formed in every prefecture, many of them headed by war widows. In June that year, the first national organization of war bereaved was established in Tokyo's Kyōbashi district under Makino Shūji's leadership: the Federation of Bereaved War Victims (Sensō giseisha izoku dōmei). Explicitly focused on helping war widows, this group drew many local war widows' groups together and acted as a liaison organization, based in Tokyo, to help set up a national conference of widows' groups later that year.

A year later, a former staff officer of the Imperial Headquarters and general head of Yasukuni Shrine, Ōtani Fujinosuke, campaigned extensively to draw local war-bereaved groups into a rival organization committed to celebrating the war dead and their relatives, thereby (re)creating a positive identity rather than a sense of victimhood. On 17 November 1947, Ōtani and others founded the Japan League for the Welfare of the War Bereaved. The League chose Nagashima Ginzō, a former member of the House of Peers and head of a local war-bereaved group in Fukuoka, as its president. Ōtani became head of the personnel division. The League's main office was located in the Kanagawa Welfare Union, stressing the group's public image as a social welfare organization. At the same time, however, it staffed a liaison office within the precincts of Yasukuni Shrine in Tokyo, where the war dead were enshrined. Mutual assistance and welfare claims thus represented ideological and political concerns from the very beginning.[22]

In his inaugural address, President Nagashima defined the membership of the League for the Welfare of the War Bereaved as "a group of war-bereaved families who are victims of war and whose relatives died serving the public good." He, too, rejected "the principle of undistinguished equality" among war victims, but in contrast to Makino, he insisted on the special characteristics of the military war bereaved: "Compared with the general victims of homeland bombings and the repatriates, the military war bereaved are facing a situation of exceedingly cold treatment both materially and spiritually, and this organization will work to restore their honor."[23] In other words, Nagashima understood the war bereaved as victims *of defeat* rather than of war. Article 4 of the League's charter proposed to "work for mutual help among its members, promote morality through consolation assistance, cultivate character, build a peaceful Japan by stopping war and establishing permanent world peace, and contribute to the welfare of humankind."[24] Nonetheless, the main agenda was clearly to establish close ties with the Ministry of Welfare and with members of the Diet in order to counter occupation policies concerning pensions.[25]

The League's leadership did not escape the scrutiny of GHQ. The mere formation of a national organization by a group of people with close ties to soldiers and the military naturally aroused the suspicion of occupation officials, who had only two years earlier severely curbed the public role of persons involved in the wartime military. But SCAP approved the League under the following conditions: (1) apart from families whose relatives had died on the battlefield, members must include also those whose relatives had died "for the public good" in a nonmilitary capacity; (2) the group's foremost goal must be mutual help among bereaved families; and (3) the groups' officials cannot include persons currently holding public office, persons under a purge order, or former military personnel.[26] The last point was overridden even before the occupation had come to an end, when Nagashima Ginzō was elected to the Upper House by a landslide in June 1950. Since then, the League, or rather its successor the Izokukai, has been continuously represented in the Diet by one or more of its officials, and in 1996, a former Izokukai president, Hashimoto Ryūtarō, even became prime minister.

Gendered Memory: War Widows

The war had a profound and lasting impact on Japanese society. Nowhere was this as evident as in the social profile of war-bereaved families, which consisted largely of women, children, and elderly people. In many cases, women had stepped into the role of household head. Out of approximately seven to eight million war bereaved (calculated at four family members per fallen soldier),[27] a total of 564,605 women were registered as war widows by the Ministry of Welfare, according to a May 1947 survey, about 30 percent of all widows in Japan at the time. Of this total, 371,406 had lost their husbands on the battlefield; another 112,105 had been widowed by the Allied bombings, and 82,894 during repatriation after the war.[28] Most of them were in their early twenties and had small children to care for, in part because of a wartime "marriage boom" at the beginning of the China invasion, when Japan's mobilization for war had driven many young soldiers into marriage right before leaving for the front.[29] Pronatalist policies by the wartime state had greatly encouraged the birth of "healthy babies" as patriotic women's contribution to Japan's war effort. They had grown up under a militarist state ideology that celebrated them as the "wives of the honorable spirits of the war dead" (*eirei no tsuma*) and made them the beneficiaries of social welfare legislation designed to construct a collective identity of "military war bereaved."

Moreover, hundreds of thousands of women, and war widows in particular, had gained experience in public work during the war, when many participated in mobilization campaigns through patriotic women's groups. Now they also possessed new political rights as a result of the Universal Women's Suffrage Law promulgated under occupation directives in December 1945. Their "widely recognized identities as housewives, mothers, neighborhood activists, and guardians of public morality" served them well in the new "rebuilding" climate of early postwar

Japan, as they had during the war. Sheldon Garon's characterization of women activists shortly after the war's end also describes the language associated with the war widows:

Most women's organizations sought to incorporate women into the political process not simply because, as citizens, women were entitled to the same rights as men but because—they argued—wives and mothers were ultimately responsible for the stability of "daily life." The picture they presented was not of the leisured, full-time housewife but of the great mass of Japanese women, who struggled during and after the war to maintain their families while toiling in the fields, factories, and shops.[30]

At a time when the public demanded—and the Allied occupation supported—a comprehensive social welfare system[31] and women's suffrage in the name of building a new and democratic Japan, war widows became an obvious symbol for a cause championed by the war bereaved as a whole. With their families broken and their neighborhood associations under suspicion, if not dissolved, the war bereaved represented a pool of people numbering in the millions who had an obvious claim for comprehensive social welfare.[32] The new language of equality and citizens' rights introduced in the constitution fit this cause well and rang true at a time when the word *demokurashii* (democracy) was on everyone's lips.

War widows faced particular circumstances *as women* and as single mothers that some understood as separate from their wartime identity as *wives* of fallen soldiers. As widows they were of course bereaved, but not all the bereaved recognized what it meant to survive the war and the early postwar years as *women* deprived of their family and social networks, not to speak of their government pensions. In response to the general disregard for the challenges war widows faced in making a living for themselves and their children, many formed support groups for women in their local communities. Some widows' groups were sponsored by influential male leaders in local industry and social welfare agencies, such as Tsubokawa Shin'ichi and Dr. Wadatsuki Shin'ichi, who put their energy into establishing training centers to help rural and urban widows get back on their feet. In Tokyo, Makino Shūji's Musashino Dormitory for war widows and their children became the center for public campaigns to alleviate the particularly hard living situation of

war widows and spurred the establishment of the Federation of Bereaved War Victims, which was generally recognized as the beginning
of the war-bereaved movement as a whole.[33]

But other war widows' groups organized independently, managing
practical programs to promote better living conditions and educating
women about political reforms that affected them as women. In particular, some stressed women's liberation from the wartime militarism
that had considered them solely as wives of the spirits of the military
dead, and instead encouraged them to think critically about the war and
the transition to postwar democracy.[34] Women's magazines such as
Shufu no tomo (The Housewife's Companion) and *Fujin kōron* (Woman's
Review) took up this topic regularly in the early postwar years, sponsoring roundtable discussions and other debates on what it meant to
survive as a war widow and especially whether or not to remarry. In
the February 1947 issue of *Shufu no tomo*, the lawyer Miyake Shōtarō
addressed the "war widow problem" as an urgent social question in
Japan and called for widows to remarry. In sharp contrast to the rhetoric of remaining loyal to the spirits of the war dead (championed by
war-bereaved groups under male leadership), Miyake urged widows to
take their new constitutional rights seriously in order to overcome their
hardships in a society that was unsympathetic to their plight.[35] Remar-
riage as a personal choice was a step in the right direction—namely,
away from a wartime ideology of sacrifice to the nation.

Women's consciousness of their status as war widows was certainly
not uniform but rather varied according to whether the husband had
been a career soldier or had been drafted into the war, whether he had
died during the war or afterward (from injuries or during repatriation),
and whether the widow herself was living in the city or in the country.[36]
Urban women had many more opportunities to become active in newly
founded political organizations for women, such as the Women's Democratic Club (Fujin minshu kurabu) or the New Japan Women's League
(Shin Nihon fujin dōmei), which was headed by the leading suffragist
Ichikawa Fuase.[37] But this tended to put widows' groups in tension
with local war-bereaved leaders, who all too easily accused widows of
involvement with left-wing, communist-led movements. Although such
an explicit politicization may not have been common among widows'
groups, it does seem clear that war-widow and war-bereaved groups

tended to approach their respective memories of the war and visions for the future from an explicitly gendered point of view in the early postwar years.

As a counterpart to war widows' groups, local war-bereaved groups usually formed around fathers who had lost sons to the war and were joined by veterans and local officials. The gender division thus was reinforced by a generation gap: young women in their twenties or thirties staffed the widows' groups, while older men in their fifties and sixties led the war-bereaved organizations. Although this difference did not translate into two neatly distinct political views of the war and the postwar, of course, it appears that some of the young widows began to understand the gender politics of wartime militarism and its cult of the war dead.[38] By the same token, such personal and public contexts mattered enormously to the male leaders of war-bereaved groups as well. Many of the League's officials had the critical advantage of professional careers before and during the war, through which they had built political connections that proved invaluable to their postwar quest of restoring both the social welfare benefits and the national recognition of military families.

Occupation officials recognized that some form of welfare for widows and their dependents was necessary after the elimination of pensions. But instead of supporting widows as women and mothers, they subordinated a consideration of gender-specific needs to the established—if nonetheless suspect—category of bereaved military families. GHQ Welfare Division Chief Nelson B. Neff and CI&E's Women's Information Officer Ethel B. Weed encouraged local war-bereaved groups under male leadership to establish women's sections within their organizations to support women and children. Many local war widows' groups did indeed join the newly established League for the Welfare of the War Bereaved in late 1947, and it quickly came to depend on women as a liaison between its male leaders and GHQ.[39] By mid-1948 a "Widows' League" had formed to press for the establishment of "women's sections" (*fujinbu*) in each local chapter of the League. At the same time, the general (male) leadership approached both houses of the Diet with petitions for reviving war-bereaved pensions by foregrounding the special situation of war widows. This strategy worked well: in May 1949 Diet members from both houses formed the Mother-Child Welfare Measures

League, and two months later the women's section was officially established under the leadership of four women representatives.

The League's successful incorporation of war-bereaved women effectively ended all independent national organizing of war widows and instead clearly subordinated gender to the social category of war bereavement. Makino Shūji's Federation of Bereaved War Victims, essentially a war widows' organization, disbanded in 1949, and only small, local widows' groups remained. This clearly hindered the development of a gendered war memory that was sufficiently critical of the view of war widows as honorable *wives* of the war dead. As part of the League, widows no doubt made a convincing case for its goals as a social welfare organization as well as for its ideological agenda. They acted as a link between the war dead of the old Japan (by remembering their husbands) and the new generation of a peaceful Japan (by raising their children). The elderly received some attention in the context of pressure for a comprehensive social welfare system, and the orphans (*iji*) moved into the spotlight in the second postwar decade, when the new generation acquired a public voice.[40] But the early movement of the war bereaved focused on the widows.

An opinion poll of war widows taken by the *Tōkyō shinbun* newspaper found war widows struggling to make a living for themselves and their children yet gratefully taking on life's challenges on their own—without thoughts of remarrying—in hopes of a better future.[41] Such stories of impoverished war-bereaved families depicted war widows as weak in a material sense, for they had lost their livelihoods, but strong in a spiritual sense, and the country's best asset for rebuilding because of their personal stake in redeeming their husbands' sacrifice. The "Widows' Resolution" of the Saga Prefecture chapter of the League for the Welfare of the War Bereaved stated clearly that bereavement constituted these women's primary identity; that is, they were the wives of the honorable spirits of the war dead rather than women with new political rights.

1. We will always see ourselves foremost as members of the war bereaved and will never be ashamed of the spirits of our fallen husbands.
2. We will always keep our husbands' hearts in ours and raise our children well, thereby building a peaceful Japan.
3. Let us work all the harder at our jobs.
4. We will always live correct lives.[42]

Social Welfare Measures

From its inception, the League focused on two interrelated goals: broadly, creating a consciousness of a "war-bereaved problem" in society, and, more narrowly, pressing concrete issues of special interest to all or parts of its membership through political channels. Clearly, public awareness of the war bereaved as a social (and political) category was needed in order for the Diet to consider specific measures geared toward them. The League "called out to society" by stressing members' particularly woeful living conditions, emphasizing their unique contribution to building a new Japan, and calling the state to its responsibility:

The war bereaved have lost their families because of this war. No experience is as terrifying as war. The war bereaved are stronger than others, working to ensure the eternal continuation of peace. It was their fate to lose their family members and loved ones. It is their wish to build a new and peaceful Japan on the basis of this experience. . . . We must therefore address such issues as education for orphans, housing, employment opportunities, and various other welfare services.[43]

Central to this process was the publication of the newsletter *Nihon izoku kōsei renmei kaihō* (hereafter *Kaihō* or League News). It served to coordinate activities among local chapters all over the country, and to communicate national petitions and legislation concerning the bereaved, thus helping to give them a public voice. *Kaihō* began as an eight-page monthly newsletter on 10 February 1949, some two years after the League's foundation. After nine issues, it was renamed *Nihon izoku tsūshin* (Japan War Bereaved Newsletter, hereafter *Tsūshin*), reduced to four pages per issue, and published first monthly and later bi-weekly.[44] In the early years, each issue typically had at least two lead articles, one by President Nagashima Ginzō, addressed to League members, one by a Diet politician or Health and Welfare Ministry official and addressed to the bereaved as a whole, and often an article describing a current petition or a recent piece of legislation. Each prefectural association had some space to report on local activities, and the first several issues printed lists of their addresses and the names of their leaders. The League's central office in turn communicated requests to the localities for particular activities, announced deadlines, and printed examples of forms to be used for petitions. From the beginning, Yasukuni Shrine officials contributed at least one article to every issue. There was also advertising space for companies supportive of the League's cause.[45]

In line with promoting the condition of the war bereaved as a broad social issue, the paper also discussed bereavement as an international phenomenon. In 1950, a short debate appeared in the pages of *Tsūshin* about the universal versus the particular meanings of this problem. The initial article, entitled "International Aspects of the War-bereaved Problem," quite remarkably accused the war bereaved themselves of bearing responsibility for the war because of their support for Japan's wartime leaders. It questioned the commonly held idea that the state owed the war bereaved compensation because it had lured their relatives into fighting a losing war, silencing their concerns and concealing the aggressive nature of the war. The anonymous author challenged the reader to consider this argument from the viewpoint of American mothers who had lost their sons, or Chinese wives who had lost their husbands. "Do these women accept that their loved ones died because we Japanese elected people who led our country into a reckless war?" he asked rhetorically. "Insisting on our ignorance [during the war] does not obtain for us the acquittal of international society."[46]

A rebuttal was close at hand, for such arguments had the potential to dig uncomfortably into questions of war responsibility. Ikeda Heiji wrote in the next issue (15 June) that caring for one's own country's war bereaved was a natural act of real human love independent of victory or defeat in war. Victorious countries treated their bereaved kindly, praising them for a job well done, he asserted, but woe to the vanquished who were so subhuman as to treat coldly those who had given their lives for their country. As for having supported politicians who led the country into a reckless war, the war bereaved carried that burden as much as, but no more than, the rest of the Japanese people.[47] Although evidently not all the war bereaved shared this narrowly construed view, in effect it prevailed and came to inform their interest politics as a whole. As issues of social welfare and the community of the war bereaved gradually retreated into the background, demands for the revival of a state-sponsored cult of the war dead—which by no means enjoyed the support of all the war bereaved—came to the fore. In time, mourning for the war dead was replaced by celebrating their heroism. Whereas the former could and did connect the various peoples involved in the war, the latter reproduced the same nationalist divisions that had once guided wartime leaders.

The broad political changes associated with the "reverse course" in Japanese domestic politics around 1947 facilitated the emergence of the war bereaved as a political interest group in ways similar to the experience of the Association of Shinto Shrines. Leaders of the League took advantage of the increasingly conservative political climate by actively lobbying government institutions. First they applied for "foundational juridical person" status (*zaidan hōjin*), which granted organizations tax-exemption as incorporated foundations. This was not in fact granted until 1953, when the League dissolved and reestablished itself as the Japan Association of War-bereaved Families. Second, beginning in 1948, the League petitioned the Diet and the Welfare Ministry, against GHQ policies, to consider reviving pension payments to the war bereaved, to find permanent employment for the bereaved, especially widows, to provide aid for the education of orphans, and to allocate rural land lost in the land reforms to guarantee the livelihood of its constituents. This led to the passing of a Resolution Relating to the Support of War-bereaved Families in both the Lower (14 May 1949) and the Upper House (16 May).[48]

But much more lobbying was necessary before these resolutions were formally taken up in a cabinet decision by the government on 16 January 1952. President Nagashima Ginzō's landslide election to the Upper House in June 1950 certainly marked an important step along the way. But the leaders of the war bereaved turned out to be feisty negotiators: shortly after the January 1952 cabinet decision, which guaranteed payments of only half the minimum amount demanded by the League (¥ 50,000 per person), five busloads of League members arrived in front of Prime Minister Yoshida's private residence in Kanagawa, demanding an audience. When this was not granted, between 28 and 35 representatives, including ten women, proceeded to spend the entire night in front of Yoshida's house, protesting against his refusal to give them an interview.[49] Yoshida eventually agreed to meet with League representatives, and the first postwar piece of legislation concerning Japan's war victims, the War-injured and War-bereaved Families Support Act (abbreviated as *Izoku nado engo hō*), went into effect on 30 April 1952.

This law regarded the war bereaved explicitly as *victims of war* and constituted the basis on which the government awarded a one-time condolence payment and, beginning in August 1953, annual pensions. Eligibility was no longer calculated by military rank, but distinctions were made between enlisted servicemen (*gunjin*), civilian employees of the military (*gunzoku*), and civilians mobilized for the war effort (*jun-gunzoku*). Originally no special provisions were made for war widows. Aggressive campaigns by leaders of the war bereaved resulted in four revisions to this law (1953, 1955, 1971, and 1974), each of which significantly enlarged eligibility and payments. Additional laws followed, aiding war widows (1963) and war-bereaved parents (1967), and providing special condolence money for bereaved families (1965).[50]

Whereas the War-injured and War-bereaved Families Support Act fit squarely into the category of social welfare, the second piece of legislation, the Military Pension Law (*onkyū hō*), introduced in August 1953, represented an explicit *revival* of wartime pensions and thus bore the distinct flavor of wartime state ideology. Tanaka Nobumasa and other critics have argued that the revival of war-bereaved pension payments represented an important continuation of wartime practices that *rewarded* military families for their public service (celebratory), rather than *compensating* them for their losses (apologetic).[51] The pension law was revised 56 times between 1953 and 1995, most importantly in 1955, when the families of convicted war criminals became eligible and executions of war criminals were officially treated as "deaths incurred in the line of duty." This provision established the grounds on which Yasukuni Shrine enshrined Class B and C criminals, based on a list of names compiled and made available to the shrine in 1966. And it served as the basis on which fourteen Class A war criminals were enshrined—secretly—during the Yasukuni fall festival in 1978. A total of 911 Class A, B, and C war criminals are currently enshrined at Yasukuni.[52] Moreover, soldiers' overseas imprisonment was added to the service time for calculating pensions in 1970, further expanding the categories of eligibility. Predictably, pension amounts also increased over the years.[53] Figure 2.3 presents the revival of pensions for the war-bereaved in the context of other laws pertaining to war victims relief measures in the postwar period.

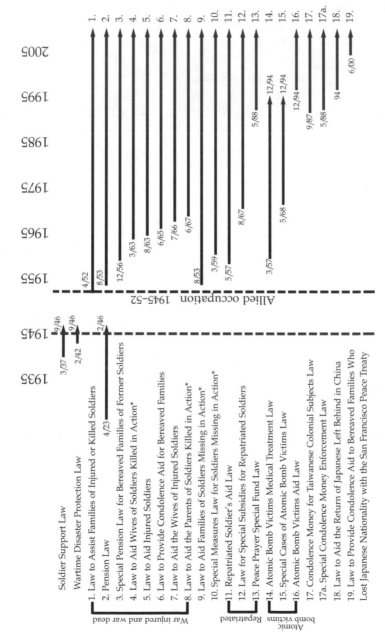

Fig. 2.3 The development of war victims' aid legislation. Items marked with an asterisk (*) are restricted to Japanese citizens. Items 14–16 include Japanese and non-Japanese. Adapted and updated from Tanaka Hiroshi et al., *Izoku to sengo* (Iwanami shoten, 1995), p. 133.

Bereavement and Nationalism

The revival of military pensions for war-bereaved families after the end of the occupation was accompanied by a surge in nationalist ideology and power politics on behalf of the war-bereaved movement. The struggle for social welfare benefits had always been accompanied by vague calls for "spiritual" assistance, which now became a political tool in its own right. Izokukai leaders had previously argued that the war bereaved also suffered spiritually at the hands of a state that "treated them coldly," a state that recognized neither its historical responsibility (the war dead had fallen in service to the state) nor its contemporary responsibility as a democratic nation concerned with the welfare of all its citizens. It was this dual neglect by the state that they invoked when characterizing the war bereaved as the "utmost victims of the war," as they did customarily when addressing their own membership. However, in negotiations with state officials, who clearly referred to the war bereaved as one group of war victims among many, their leaders simply claimed equal status with other victims.

At this time of rapid political gains, the League's representatives held national conferences beginning in February 1951, each of which produced a revised declaration of the organization's basic goals and assumptions. With the Second National Conference on 22 November 1951, the meaning of "war dead" evolved from the loose phrase "those who fell in public service" to a more explicitly nation-state-centered "those who fell for the state and the people." At an executive meeting preceding the Fourth National Conference held on 10–11 June 1952, the League's policy further changed so as to allow families of executed war criminals to join. It called for "the spirits of executed war criminals, students and heroic countrymen" to be "enshrined at Yasukuni or in local shrines for the defense of the fatherland," and even proposed the establishment of a national "people's day of thanksgiving for the war dead."[54]

These various organizational changes and adjustments culminated in the League's official reestablishment as the Japan Association of War-bereaved Families on 11 March 1953, with ample political representation in both houses of the Diet as well as the Health and Welfare Ministry. Concurrently, the new organization acquired legal status as a tax-exempt foundation (*zaidan hōjin*) and was entitled to rent-free use of the Kudan kaikan, the old wartime Soldiers' Hall in downtown Tokyo, which is national property. The significant ideological changes that accompanied this institutional restructuring became obvious in an amendment to the Association's new charter in October 1953, which redefined its political interests in terms other than social welfare. Gone were broad, inclusive phrases that had been central to the original foundation charter, such as "stop war," "establish eternal world peace," and "promote the welfare of humankind." Instead, the Association's goals, as stated in Article 2, focused exclusively on a wartime term, "manifestation of the spirits of the departed heroes" (*eirei no kenshō*), which became critical to its subsequent political agenda.

Eirei no kenshō referred to "the enshrinement and worship at Yasukuni Shrine and through state memorial services for soldiers and military families who died in war as honorable victims, sacrificing their bodies when the state was in crisis."[55] The term *eirei* had been widely used from 1911 on, when it appeared for the first time in the inaugural issue of Yasukuni Shrine's journal *Yasukuni jinja shi* (Yasukuni Shrine Records), and it became official terminology during World War II.[56] With the Association's charter amendment of 1953, campaigns to make *eirei no kenshō* a reality moved to the forefront of its agenda, replacing the earlier emphasis on social welfare with matters of political ideology. This goal came to define the Association's special interest and resulted in sustained campaigns in government circles to restore Yasukuni Shrine to its wartime status as a place where the state conducted national ceremonies honoring the war dead.

In the context of establishing a popular movement to demand state management of Yasukuni Shrine, leaders of the Association felt it necessary to define how the term *eirei* was to be understood in the context of contemporary patriotism. In 1960, therefore, the board of directors called upon a "basic problem investigation section" to research and publish in the following year a pamphlet entitled "What Is the Spirit of the Glorious War Dead?" after consultations with experts in history, social thought, education, youth problems, and international affairs. In this pamphlet, patriotism was characterized as a natural and universal desire for the security, peace, and prosperity of one's country, a feeling contingent on historical circumstance and thus subject to change over time. But patriotism also related the past to the present insofar as contemporary love for one's country was grounded in the correct recognition of the historical circumstances and sentiments that provided the context for patriotic action in the past. *Nihon izoku tsūshin* editorialized, for example, that wartime Japan

faced grave difficulties never before encountered, and the people living under such circumstances naturally sacrificed themselves for the peace and security of their homeland. It should be a matter of course that we continue across the change of times [i.e., 1945] to express our gratitude to them as a manifestation of our patriotism. The spirit of the honorable war dead is rooted in this sentiment [of giving thanks and loving the nation], and it stands at the center of our patriotism.[57]

The call to remember the war dead by empathizing with their sense of crisis rather than judging them with the benefit of hindsight was hardly unique to the Association of War-bereaved Families, and it may account for its popular appeal. Nonetheless, the centrality of this phrase effectively preempted historical interpretations of World War II and the role of soldiers and other military personnel. It left no space for critical evaluations of cooperation in the war effort, because all military involvement was deemed "good" or at least non-negotiable. Although that interpretation did not produce a "good war," it endorsed military activities carried out in the name of the nation and settled any questions of responsibility concerning those involved in them. The war dead in effect became an abstraction, celebrated uniformly as heroes (although most had arguably died unheroic deaths) without consideration of their individual deeds. This may also explain the logic behind the inclusion of convicted war criminals among the ranks of heroes to be worshiped.

Indeed, the war-bereaved community itself split over the issue of Yasukuni Shrine in the mid-1960s, spinning off various smaller groups, including the Association of Christian War Bereaved, which opposed the enshrinement of the war dead at Yasukuni. The most sustained challenge to the Association's attempts at justifying the war came in 1986 with the founding of the Association of War-bereaved Families for Peace (Heiwa izokukai zenkoku renkakukai). Despite this, as a powerful organization with a clear political mission, whether interpreted as propelling ultraconservative politics in the Diet or as voicing a simple popular wish to remember the dead, the Izokukai seized a major role in the process of creating public memory of the war in Japan.

Although the obvious ideological implications of the Association's policy concerning *eirei no kenshō* appealed to a wide stratum of conservatives in Japan, it remained controversial and earned the Association at least as many fierce opponents as it did supporters. At the same time, many Japanese had little interest in the Association's politics on the state level. Being a local member did not necessarily entail support for, or even insight into, the kind of war memory the Izokukai represented through its political activities. Indeed, much of the Association's popular appeal derived from what may be called organized assistance for personal remembrance. For example, local branches organized annual group tours to Tokyo to visit Yasukuni Shrine and pray for a family member who had died in the war. For many Japanese, belonging to a local Izokukai chapter was part of an established social network, often handed down from one generation in a household to the next. And yet this seemingly nonpolitical relationship had political implications. It helped perpetuate a sense among many Japanese of an uncritical, indeed "natural" relationship to the wartime past, a desire to validate the deaths of relatives in a way that did not require a rethinking of the war. Other civic organizations demanded much more of a commitment to a certain goal or view, such as the decision to practice Shinto or to work for the improvement of Japanese-Chinese relations. The Izokukai greatly benefited from a large pool of supporters who remained politically uninvolved and yet unwittingly helped to anchor the Association's particular version of the noble war among the wider public.

When the first post-LDP prime minister Hosokawa Morihiro stated in an interview upon his inauguration in 1993 that in his opinion Japan had fought an aggressive war in World War II, the Japan Association of War-bereaved Families was among the most vehement public protesters. In a declaration issued on 1 October 1993, the Izokukai proclaimed that "the Greater East Asian War was a war of self-defense for the protection of the life and fortune of the state and the people."[58] Clearly, both the Association of War-bereaved Families and the Association of Shinto Shrines affirmed Japan's role in the war as a legitimate effort to assert its national interests against foreign countries in the context of international power relations. Both assumed a unified national community in which the people were bound to the nation-state in an organic relationship of mutual responsibilities. But whereas Shrine Shinto sought to recover the spiritual essence of the *nation* based on the unbroken imperial line, the Izokukai focused on the primacy of the modern *nation-state* in public life, which represented a clear continuity with prewar and wartime ideology. Shrine Shinto nationalism centered on the emperor through a vague cultural or spiritual ethnocentrism; the nationalism of the Association of War-bereaved Families imagined the state as a concrete political formation, which alone was capable of expressing national interests and for which their relatives had sacrificed their lives heroically. If the Association of Shinto Shrines could be described as a reluctant interest group, the Association of War-bereaved Families enthusiastically embraced special interest politics in the public sphere of negotiating memory of the war.

Organizationally, too, the two groups remained on separate planes. Shrine Shinto was much more severely constrained by the constitution, which effectively prevented a renewed affiliation of Shinto with the state. Moreover, its constituency was inherently limited to a smaller sector of society—namely, Shintoists. The Association of War-bereaved Families, however, was able to compete equally with other interest groups for state support, and it directly benefited from the long conservative hegemony that prevailed during most of the postwar period. Its constituency included people from all walks of life, whether ideologically committed to the Association's goals or not. From their separate positions within Japanese postwar society, however, these two ultraconservative groups pursued similar politics of celebrating national unity and national strength as exemplified by the Meiji state, while affirming the wartime state's intentions even though they acknowledged their disastrous results. To the limited extent that "war responsibility" became an issue, it concerned only the relationship between the state and the people within a strictly national context.

CHAPTER THREE

Forging Political Subjectivity:
The Japan Teachers' Union

The eagerness of Shintoists and war-bereaved families to organize on a national scale paled in comparison with the enthusiasm and alacrity with which teachers (especially elementary school teachers) created their own unions in the early postwar years. Leaders of Shinto and the war bereaved struggled to undo defeat—that is, to regain some of the political, social, and economic ground their constituencies had lost because of the collapse of the wartime regime and the subsequent occupation reforms. Leaders of the Japan Teachers' Union (Nikkyōso, henceforth JTU), in contrast, threw themselves into undoing the war itself, picking up the pieces left by the union movement of the 1920s and vowing to complete Japan's democratic revolution. Amid the rubble, chaos, and promise of democratic reforms in the fall of 1945, veterans of the interwar teachers' unions, joined by intellectuals and figures of the Japanese resistance, saw an opportunity to liberate teachers from the state and return them to the people—to transform teachers from passive agents of a militarist state into active agents of democratic change.

May Day demonstrations served as one prominent avenue for mass protest against government policies, from "Food May Day" in 1946 to "Bloody May Day" in 1952 and beyond. In the early 1950s, a broad coalition of opposition groups on the progressive left vehemently protested against the terms of the San Francisco Peace Treaty and the U.S.-

Fig. 3.1   May Day demonstration against remilitarization, Tokyo 1953. The slogan of the Japan Teachers' Union appears on the two foremost banners: "Never send our students to the battlefield again." Tōkyōto kyōshokuin kumiai, *Tokyōso jūnenshi*, 1958. Used by permission of the Tokyo Teachers' Union.

Japan Security Treaty as "remilitarizing" Japan because they allowed the United States to maintain its military bases there and set the stage for the rebuilding of Japan's own military. Teachers' unionists joined this struggle with the slogan "Never send our students to the battlefield again!" (*oshiego o futatabi senjō ni okuruna*). The slogan was coined by a teacher from Kochi at the eighteenth central committee meeting in January 1951 and adopted by the Union as representing teachers' moral self-reflection and ethical commitment to peace and democracy. It appears prominently in a photograph of a JTU demonstration in Tokyo (Fig. 3.1)—on two banners also decorated with skull and crossbones. Other banners protest against "remilitarization" or announce the many union chapters participating in this rally.

The meteoric rise of the teachers' union movement in the early postwar years was indeed an integral part of what J. Victor Koschmann has called "the politics of democratic revolution." This revolution was conditioned by occupation-sponsored reforms, urged by a general economic collapse, and fired by the political viability and intellectual fervor of the newly resurrected and broadly inclusive left. It began at a time when the term "war responsibility" (*sensō sekinin*) appeared widely in public debates on the political issues of the day. It suggested a broad consensus among the liberal left that the catastrophe of war had structural roots in the wartime "system"—usually labeled either "feudal" or "fascist"—and that a radical transformation of society was necessary to achieve a complete break with wartime thought and practice. For educators at the forefront of the teachers' union movement, war responsibility was a sociopolitical issue at a time when democratization embodied everybody's hopes for a new and greatly changed society. It was also a moral issue dictated by the war experience and postwar devastation, and it sometimes became an intellectual issue as teachers joined academics, writers, and critics in their debates about the correct approach to this complex problem.

One of the explicit goals of the Teachers' Union after its establishment in June 1947 was to promote core democratic values such as individual autonomy and political consciousness and participation. Teachers connected this to the Japanese prewar experimentation with liberalism, socialism, Marxism, and movements for democracy. Thus two otherwise separate issues—the location of responsibility in the wartime period and the intense concern with the postwar project—became virtually inseparable. The intellectual left in general, and unionizing teachers in particular, represented this juncture of past and present in that they saw themselves as a social class (and as a profession) bearing responsibility for the present and also for their acknowledged impotence in the past.

Between the founding of the first two postwar unions in December 1945 and the establishment of a single, federated organization on 8 June 1947, more than 80 percent of all teachers and 95 percent of all elementary school teachers unionized.[1] Although the early groups of elementary and secondary teachers fought for bread-and-butter issues, the unified JTU had by the early 1950s matured into a radical political interest group exerting pressure on the government in regard not only to education but also to domestic and foreign policy problems. Perhaps the single most important factor in the Union's growth was its leadership's insistence that educators were political subjects with economic as well as academic interests. At the same time—and herein lay a fundamental contradiction—the Teachers' Union claimed to spearhead genuinely popular opposition to postwar bureaucratic rule as a dangerous continuity with the wartime past. The Union never limited its activities to promoting the economic welfare of its members, although negotiations for higher wages, job security, and benefits constituted its first and most successful campaigns. Rather, in aspiring to make education the springboard from which to launch postwar democratization, the Teachers' Union affirmed the centrality of education to the ideological process but insisted on the need to ensure its independence from the state. Union leaders continuously invoked the prewar and wartime education system as the antithesis to the postwar project and warned against its reproduction in the present.

Riding the Wave of Democratic Change

Of crucial importance to the emergence of the teachers' union movement in the fall of 1945 was the mutual tolerance, even support, of the newly reconstructed Japan Communist Party (JCP) and the occupation authorities. In order to establish civil liberties, SCAP's Bill of Rights of October 1945 ordered the removal of all restrictions against formerly outlawed political parties and organizations and called for the release from prison of prewar socialists and communists. In immediate response, the JCP issued its "Appeal to the People" on 4 October, declaring its willingness to cooperate with the Allied occupation in the pursuit of a common goal—namely, the exposition of core democratic values such as individual autonomy, political consciousness, and participation in politics. The majority of schoolteachers fervently supported and promoted the national effort to transform and rebuild Japanese society as a democracy. At a time when public opinion despised militarism and celebrated those who had resisted the wartime regime, these newly liberated forces quickly won tremendous prestige as leaders of democratic change. They included prewar teachers' unionists, Communist Party members, and left-wing intellectuals, and the leaders of the budding postwar teachers' union movement came from their ranks. They shared the occupation's emphasis on education reform as key to weeding out ultranationalist ideology and building democracy.

As part of its demilitarization and democratization policies, between 1946 and 1949 SCAP ordered, and the Ministry of Education carried out, the screening and purge of teachers and educational administrators who had supported militarism and ultranationalism during the war. In fact the initiative for this purge came from educators themselves. As early as September 1945, teachers, professors, and students demanded—through strikes and petitions to the Ministry of Education—the resignation of educators and school administrators who had promoted militarist doctrines.[2] Moreover, the vast majority of educators who resigned did so before SCAP's purge order, presumably under pressure from their colleagues: 115,778 teachers and educational officials resigned even before official screening began, and an additional 3,151 persons were purged as a result of the screening by the end of April 1949.[3] At the same time, general purge orders removed 186,000 central government employees by the summer of 1946 and about 7,000 persons in local government by the general election of April 1947.[4] The purge facilitated the unionization of teachers insofar as it decreased opposition from the far right among teachers and thus indirectly endorsed the generally socialist or communist union leadership.[5] In addition, the voluntary and involuntary purge encouraged turnover among the school principals and local educational officials whom union members saw as their most immediate enemies.

Throughout the fall of 1945, SCAP issued increasingly specific directives on educational reform ranging from school lunch programs to the national school system and a reorganization of the Ministry of Education itself. The first educational directive, Administration of the Educational System of Japan (issued on 22 October 1945), ordered the dissolution of the wartime Bureau of Moral and School Education, the Institute of Research in Racial Characteristics, and the Seminary of Moral Training. In addition, a Bureau of Social Education and a Bureau of Textbooks were created along with new bureaus to aid decentralization.[6] MacArthur's memorandum to the Japanese government on the Suspension of Courses in Morals, Japanese History, and Geography, issued on 31 December, had an immediate impact on school life and on unionizing teachers in particular. It directed the Ministry of Education to suspend "all courses in morals, Japanese history, and geography in all educational institutions . . . for which textbooks and teachers' manuals have been published or sanctioned by the Ministry of Education." But it also enlisted the ministry to "collect all textbooks and teachers' manuals" used for these courses, to "prepare and submit to this Headquarters a plan for the introduction of substitute programs," and to "prepare and submit to this Headquarters a plan for revising textbooks to be used in Morals, Japanese History, and Geography" classes.[7]

These early reform initiatives matched many of the demands of the early teachers' unions concerning the organization and content of education, demands that dated back to the small and short-lived unions of the 1920s. Decentralization of the educational system, equal opportunity for education, reeducation for teachers, revision of the curricula, and revision of textbooks had all been outlined by independent teachers' organizations such as the Japan Teachers' Union Association for Enlightenment (Keimeikai) in 1920 or the Japan Educational Workers' Union (Nihon kyōiku rōdōsha kumiai or Nikkyōrōso) in 1931.[8] But SCAP's manner of implementing some of these reforms hardly satisfied the expectations of the union movement, for no attempt had been made to replace the old bureaucratic power structure with a new system that would have guaranteed teachers active participation in decision making. The teachers' union movement, dominated in the first postwar years by JCP members such as Hani Gorō, Inagaki Masanobu, and Iwama Masao, demanded time and again the right of teachers—through the unions—to control the schools in place of the Ministry of Education. Although union leaders agreed on the need to radically curb the ministry's power, they did not speak with one voice on the extent to which they were willing to push this agenda. In fact, the establishment in early December 1945 of two competing national teachers' unions, the dominant Zenkyō (Zen Nihon kyōin kumiai or All-Japan Teachers' Union) and the much smaller Nikkyō (Nihon kyōikusha kumiai or Japan Educators' Union), was a result of the significant differences in terms of both ideology and political tactics that consumed the early union movement (Fig. 3.2).

The teachers' union movement also benefited from early postwar labor union legislation in important ways. In the fall of 1945, MacArthur actively promoted the growth of labor unions to ensure that workers could protect their economic interests against their employers. In accordance with occupation policies, the Welfare Ministry drafted Japan's first postwar piece of union legislation, the Trade Union Law (enacted on 22 December 1945), which guaranteed the right to organize, bargain

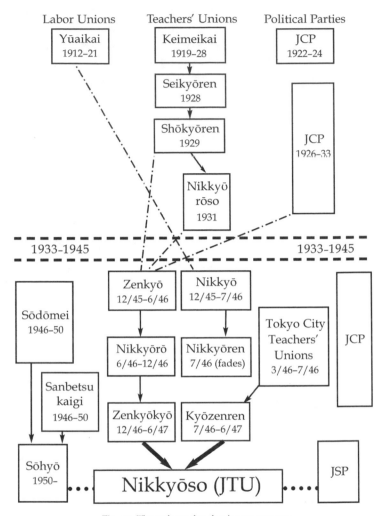

Fig. 3.2 The early teachers' union movement.

Prewar organizations: Keimeikai (Japan Teachers' Union for Enlightenment), Seikyōren (Young Educators' League), Shōkyōren (League of Elementary School Teachers), Nikkyōrōso (Japan Educational Workers' Union, Yūaikai (Friendly Society), JCP (Japan Communist Party).

Postwar organizations: Zenkyō (All Japan Teachers' Union), Nikkyō (Japan Educators' Union), Nikkyōrō (Japan Educational Labor Union), Nikkyōren (Japan Teachers' Union League), Zenkyōkyō (Council of All-Japan Teachers' Unions), Nikkyōso (Japan Teachers' Union), Kyōzenren (All-Japan Teachers' Unions League), Sōdōmei (General Federation of Labor), Sanbetsu kaigi (Congress of Industrial Unions), Sōhyō (General Council of Trade Unions), JSP (Japan Socialist Party).

Adapted from Donald Thurston, *Teachers and Politics in Japan* (Princeton: Princeton University Press, 1973), p. 60, Table 1.

collectively, and strike. This applied to the private and public sectors alike. The Labor Standards Law, enacted in April 1947, set minimum standards for hours, wages, insurance, injury compensation, and unemployment benefits.[9] Yet this set of laws was designed to permit only a controlled and decidedly nonpoliticized labor movement. As Sheldon Garon has argued, the principle guiding these laws had essentially not changed from that of the union laws in the 1920s: it aimed at "preventing industrial breakdown and the emergence of a radical labor movement."[10] Nonetheless, in the midst of a genuine economic breakdown in 1946–47, the labor movement turned instead into a radical political force under JCP leadership. In response to the massive strikes staged in protest against government policies, SCAP encouraged the Japanese government to amend the National Public Service Law in July 1948, thus revoking the right of public employees (including teachers) to strike and bargain collectively. Despite this setback, the JTU in subsequent decades successfully conducted a huge annual wage struggle against the Ministry of Education, and remained an affiliate of the General Council of Trade Unions (Nihon rōdō kumiai sōhyōgikai or Sōhyō, founded in 1950).[11]

Conceiving of teachers as part of the working class offered a concrete means to relieve the acute economic distress teachers as a whole experienced after the surrender. They were able to unite across political lines relatively quickly and easily in part because they were all starving. They took to the streets alongside trade unions in the food riots on May Day in 1946 and otherwise tried to present a united front with the labor movement against the government. According to a study by the Operations Division of SCAP's Civil Intelligence Section, a teacher's salary on average covered barely one-third of his family's expenses in February 1946.[12] Amid rampant inflation, elementary school teachers and those in the countryside were particularly hard hit. Students were made to work to increase food production, schools and universities suspended classes, and signs of malnutrition appeared in pupils as well as in teachers. If the general preoccupation with food led to political apathy in some local elections, it nevertheless heightened the political activism of teachers as a professional group.[13] Barely three weeks after the establishment of Zenkyō and Nikkyō in December 1945, teachers presented the following demands to the Education, Home, and Finance ministries: (1) a 500 percent increase in pay; (2) allocation of personal work materials such as clothes and bicycles; (3) provision of housing; (4) equal opportunity for promotion of teachers of all grades according to ability and experience; (5) salaries paid by the state; and (6) continuing education for employed teachers.[14]

The need to be able to bargain for higher wages and benefits most clearly defined the teachers' union as a special interest group. Unionization required the collective consciousness of teachers as laborers willing to take on bureaucrats and capitalists in order to improve their livelihoods and workplaces. Gone were the days, union leaders hoped, when the teaching profession was regarded as a "heavenly calling," which implied living "a life of noble poverty."[15] When the main teachers' unions decided to come together and form the Japan Teachers' Union in June 1947, their primary goal was to define the economic, social, and political status of teachers as a professional group (Article 1 of the JTU's founding document), followed by "the promotion of the democratization of education and freedom of research," and, third, "the establishment of a democratic state that respects peace and liberty."[16] The official declaration of the same day also stressed the role of the teacher as laborer: "With the collective strength of 500,000 teachers just joined together, we work toward the rational improvement of the way we are treated [by the state] and our social and political standing. We reach out to join hands with the workers and farmers of all Japan and the whole world, and together we vow to fight the evil bureaucracy, destroy it, and advance the establishment of a flourishing democratic education and culture."[17] Furthermore, the editors of the JTU's journal *Atarashii kyōiku to bunka* (New Education and Culture) clearly stated in its first issue that "new education and culture do not originate from the teachers' spiritual love for education and culture but from a correct understanding of the Union's economic and democratic struggle, which is bound up with love for education and culture by the hands of the teacher-laborers themselves."[18]

If the making of the postwar teacher remained a heavily ideological enterprise on the national level of the JTU, it became much more direct and personal on the Union's prefectural level. In 1949, Naka Torata, head of the JTU Culture Section in Kumamoto Prefecture, wrote of the empowerment many teachers had come to feel as Union members.

Less than two years after its establishment, the JTU had already improved teachers' personal and professional lives in various ways. The coordination of teachers within the Union had fostered a strong sense of togetherness. Indeed, the old, prewar teacher had ceased to exist, according to Naka. "An entirely new type of teacher has emerged, one for whom teaching is not just a heavenly calling but whose social, economic, and political standing has improved, who is his students' leader and teacher, . . . who has risen in the world." Teachers had gained self-confidence by their own efforts, because they had liberated themselves from the prefectural board, the education section chief, the principal, and the parents. They now valued their own freedom of speech and action and were able to voice their opinions even regarding the principal. Lastly, teachers now experienced democratic methods first-hand by organizing and managing the Union.[19] (Thurston's findings in the late 1960s tended to support this enthusiastic view. In his careful study of the JTU, based on extensive polls, he determined that about 97 percent of JTU members—about 95 percent of all teachers were Union members—felt strongly about the Union as protector of their livelihoods.)[20]

The Struggle against State Coercion

Participation in the labor movement not only helped define the JTU's interests as a professional organization but also raised teachers' consciousness of themselves as agents of democratic change. The abortive general strike of 1 February 1947, when the JCP tried and failed to win control over the labor movement, marked an important turning point. After that date the emphasis on the "teacher as laborer" lost steam while the "teacher as citizen" gradually moved to center stage. The failure of the strike, compounded a year and a half later with the loss of the right to strike and bargain collectively, complicated the assumption that teachers qualified as revolutionary subjects simply by virtue of their status as laborers. The Union in response began to represent itself to the public as the voice of "the people" in opposition to the government and the bureaucracy in particular, and less as a so-called special interest group. Hani Gorō, a Marxist historian, popular speaker, and prominent member of the JTU, perceived the greatest danger to postwar democratic change in the continued hegemony of the bureaucracy, with its links to the emperor system. "Japanese bureaucratism will obstruct Japan's democracy to the end," Hani had written in October 1946. "Modern bureaucratism is the product of absolute imperial rule. Even today Japan's bureaucrats refuse to take responsibility for having sacrificed so many lives [during the war] and instead perpetuate their rule over the people."[21]

In tandem with social scientists and literary critics debating "war responsibility," teachers active in the Union discussed the political and ideological nature of the wartime social structure and dismissed it as being typical of a premodern system—or, conversely, of "fascism." Whether "feudal" or "fascist," such a system lacked the notion of individual responsibility, consistently seeking to suppress individuality and coerce it into the state structure. Maruyama Masao eloquently spoke to this critique in his analysis of the Japanese spiritual structure as lacking the notion of individual self-consciousness. In his 1946 essay "Theory and Psychology of Ultra-Nationalism," Maruyama found in the diffusion of power and the externalization of moral values the reason for both the system of coercion during the war and the contemporary low level of moral and political consciousness.[22] In light of the contemporary task of building a society that was immune to fascism, the philosopher Mashita Shin'ichi pointed to the intellectuals' relationship to politics as part of the reason for the rise of fascism. Like many teachers active in the JTU, he saw the problem in the fascist totality, which had aimed at the complete nullification of culture by politics. By cooperating, intellectuals had allowed politics to rob them of their individuality.[23]

While artists, filmmakers, and literary figures debated "subjectivity" (*shutaisei*) in relation to their own role in society,[24] leaders of the teachers' union movement styled "the teacher" (both as an individual and as a profession) as the subject and agent of Japan's imminent bourgeois-democratic revolution. Yet this was a subject still in the making; in the past, the teacher had been merely an object of a (militarist) education system. The Union thus urged teachers to discard their political apathy and develop a political consciousness of themselves and their profession. First, teachers needed to understand that they had been made into puppets of the state through educational policies originating in the Meiji period. Second, they had to become aware of themselves as members of the working class. Third, they needed to gain control over educational policies. Fourth, teachers could teach democratic citizen-ship to the next generation only by being active citizens themselves. Such citizenship, moreover, required critical reflection on the past.

Like Shrine Shintoists, unionized teachers tended to affirm the great importance that the prewar state had placed on their respective con-stituencies from Meiji right through the end of the war. Laying claim to that importance for postwar reconstruction, however, required the denunciation of the wartime state's distortion (of Shinto) and outright abuse (of education) for militarist purposes. The Teachers' Union stressed that the crippling and eventual destruction of education was "the result of the bureaucrats' evil policies" (exemplified by the 1890 Imperial Rescript on Education) that had made resistance against the war a near impossibility and thus forced educators into political apathy. The locus of responsibility seemed clear enough. Teachers had been deprived of their political rights by those who eventually led Japan into war and defeat—namely, bureaucrats, militarists, and capitalists. Build-ing a democracy meant that teachers had to realize and exercise their political rights as workers and as educators. Therefore, the JTU focused first on fostering awareness among teachers of their present position at the bottom of the educational power pyramid as historically and politi-cally conditioned.

Educators have a poor sense of politics, and politicians a poor sense of educa-tion. . . . While the poor sense of education among politicians is nothing new, the poor sense of politics among educators is not a tradition but the result of politicians' evil policies. That has to be remedied at once. . . . Education and politics cannot be separated. Above all, educators must develop a deep interest in politics, otherwise we will not be able to build a democratic state. We must treat educational problems as political problems, we must have representatives, and they should be treated fairly and democratically.[25]

More specifically, in looking to the past, the JTU created for itself a stereotype of the prewar elementary teacher whose postwar re-creation it worked hard to prevent. Donald Thurston summarized this image pre-cisely: the role of the prewar teacher had been to disseminate statist ide-ology (especially the emperor system) under increasing pressure from above and as a participant in a "sacred occupation," without concern for individual livelihood. The prewar teacher was noncreative because he was not allowed to design courses or select textbooks; subservient to his principal; indoctrinated instead of educated in normal school; and politically impotent vis-à-vis the government.[26] Consequently, no effective antiwar movement took root in the 1930s. Such a characterization entirely overlooked the dynamics of the state's efforts (finally successful in the 1930s) to co-opt teachers, who, in this picture, resisted co-optation almost instinctively.[27] It drew attention away from questions of teachers' deep implication in the war effort through their participation, willing or unwilling, in planting the wartime state's ultranationalist ideology into young minds. Issues of war responsibility, individual or collective, retreated behind efforts to analyze the prewar social and political structures that had made teachers into apolitical puppets of the state, instruments in the service of militarism. Ironically, the purge of many war-supporters appears to have muted the issue of individual responsibility for the Union as a whole, enabling its leaders to focus on the prewar and wartime victimization of teachers as a systemic problem.

When Union leaders spoke of the "rehabilitation" of education at the time of the JTU's establishment in June 1947, they meant the removal of prewar and wartime policies that had distorted education, not the return to a pristine past. The Potsdam Declaration had similarly stated in Paragraph 10: "The Japanese Government shall remove all obstacles to the revival and strengthening of democratic tendencies among the Japanese people." Conservatives, however, had a different kind of revival in mind. The first postwar minister of education, Maeda Tamon, insisted in a Diet deliberation in January 1946 that the Imperial Rescript on Education still represented the foundation of Japanese education and only needed to be stripped of "unfortunate misinterpretations" by wartime militarists.[28] Moreover, by 1952 the phrase "restoration and revival of education" had been firmly adopted by the Ministry of Education in its campaign for the reinstallation of ethics classes in schools. Writing in the Union's journal, renamed *Kyōiku hyōron* (Critical Education Review) in 1951, Katsuta Shūichi, a well-known scholar and promoter of people's education, denounced such efforts as necessarily undemocratic because Japan had possessed no democratic morals ethos in the past.[29]

Permanent and principled opposition to the Ministry of Education defined JTU politics from then on, while earlier rhetoric of staging a socialist revolution became politically less viable. In part this was the outcome of compromise between different factions within the Union (stemming from the 1947 merger) which differed considerably on the desired degree of opposition to the bureaucracy.[30] Previously organized as the Japan Educators' Union (Nikkyō), a group of mainly secondary school teachers and university professors, it was politically oriented around the right wing of the Socialist Party. After Nikkyō merged with the more militant Zenkyō to form Nikkyōso (i.e., the JTU) in 1947, its members became a minority within that group, while former Zenkyō members formed the leadership. Nevertheless, because of the moderate faction's influence, the JTU established itself as an affiliate of the Japan Socialist Party (JSP) and not the JCP, and settled into a legitimate space of oppositional politics in all matters of educational policy.

The struggle against the state bureaucracy had thus become not only a matter of political fact but one of principle. It bespoke a commitment to organized resistance against the state, rooted in a memory that equated war with the victimization of citizens through state coercion. The Union's organizational structure reflected this principle of resistance on every level, matching the government's power structure rather than seeking to destroy it. Donald Thurston found intriguing correspondences between the JTU's headquarters in Tokyo, with its national leaders and elected representatives in the Diet, and the capital's educational bureaucracy. This desire of JTU leaders to establish their organization as the counterpart to the Ministry was further evident at the prefectural and local levels, where local branches of the JTU placed themselves in opposition to prefectural and local boards of education, and union chairmen spoke directly to governors and superintendents.[31]

The principle of resistance often took precedence over issues of substance. For example, local boards of education and textbooks became weapons in this decidedly uneven, and yet remarkably vigilant, struggle. The Ministry of Education resisted the establishment of elective school boards on the prefectural, city, town, and village levels from 1947 on, because this development was meant to diminish the ministry's central power. When the JTU won the right of teachers to run for seats on these school boards, promising the Union a means to influence educational policy, the ministry stepped up its opposition to local school boards. But it soon became apparent that the local boards failed to ensure decentralization because of a lack of funding and administrative talent, so that inexperienced board members routinely looked to central authorities for guidance. In response, the Education Ministry and the JTU in effect switched sides on this issue. When the Union realized that local boards represented a liability rather than an asset, it focused on making the prefectural boards fully elective. The ministry, on the other hand, saw its chance to reconvert local school boards into appointive bodies (cast into law in 1956) and thus place its officials in a position from which it could control Union activities.[32]

Control over the editing and authorization of textbooks was the terrain on which the Union received perhaps the most significant public support in its struggle against the Ministry. This controversy commenced in the early postwar years and grew fiercer in subsequent decades, spilling over national boundaries in the early 1980s and crossing political lines in the 1990s. Until recently, however, issues of textbook content, particularly interpretations of the war in Asia and the Pacific, functioned merely as a banner under which a large percentage of Japanese protested against what they saw as excessive state control in public affairs. Questions concerning the nature of Japan's invasion of China, for example, retreated behind a more central war memory—namely, the danger to democracy of bureaucratic rule. Writings about the war in the Union's journal *Kyōiku to bunka* (Education and Culture) almost always focused on Japanese "fascism" at home, denouncing the wartime government's intrusion into the public and private lives of professionals. This was a view of the war that recognized teachers as victims of a system that denied them their professionalism, their identity as workers, and their humanity, for these were the qualities that postwar teachers needed to acquire in order to become political subjects. The ways in which teachers had understood their professional and personal lives as integral parts of the wartime system were largely left unexamined.

One powerful way in which the JTU carved out a public space for its interpretation of democratic revolution—bound up with its understanding of the (undemocratic) past—was to foster an ongoing debate about it through its representatives in the Diet, in schools, and through publications and public campaigns. The prominence of a wide, left-dominated public discourse in early postwar Japan provided the intellectual context in which the leaders of prewar teachers' unions applied and adjusted their ideas about the socioeconomic reconfiguration of teachers as a professional group. From their vantage point as educators, they participated in the larger Communist Party–led project of mapping out Japan's social revolution based on prewar Marxist debates over the course of modern Japanese history. Even as the JTU stressed the working-class character of its membership, it also capitalized on its own intellectual resources. Many prominent intellectuals assumed leadership positions in the Union, and important topics were routinely addressed in roundtable discussions with famous Marxist scholars, then in their heyday of intellectual influence. In turn, the Union became an avenue for left-wing scholars to articulate their concerns to a wide public audience as the public prestige of intellectuals began to diminish after the passing of the immediate postwar years.

The exclusion of the JTU from direct access to political power in the late 1940s increased the need to raise awareness of educational problems. While demonstrations and other pressure tactics alienated many, Union publications maintained a public audience through information about and analysis of contemporary political issues. The Union published far more books, periodicals, and pamphlets than, for example, the Japan Association of War-bereaved Families or most other political interest groups. It supplied schools with materials, such as collections of documents on political issues, notably its own struggles.[33] After the Union had lost important legal rights in 1948, the need to negotiate its role in the world of education came into sharp focus.

Although Diet members and public opinion leaders recognized the Union as a political interest group by the summer of 1948, expectations about its contribution to society differed. That year, Union leaders called on socialist politicians, university professors, critics, and other public men and women to share their views on "what to expect from the Teachers' Union." Some wanted the Union to focus on non-academic issues (such as teachers' salaries); others saw it as a "cultural enlightenment group" that could break down the residual conservatism in local schools, particularly among authoritarian principals. Still others hoped it would take the lead in educating the general public, entering into classrooms and homes through children's magazines and the like.[34] Union leaders themselves were keenly aware of the need to involve the public at large in its struggle for democratic change and of the teacher's central role in this endeavor. In 1949 Kawada Hisashi, director of the

Tokyo Municipal Labor Committee, wrote in an article discussing the Teachers' Union:

> It is through . . . education that we can begin to raise the social independence of students, enrich individuals, and install in them a heretofore nonexistent modern citizenship. The role of principals is great, but so are the ability and personal influence of teachers. . . . Educators' self-consciousness and self-confidence comes not only from working for a living, but from loving their profession. Through the education of their students, teachers rediscover their own lives all the time and realize what their profession is all about.[35]

If teachers' political consciousness of themselves as laborers aided unionization, it was ultimately their public role as educators and citizens that qualified them as subjects of a democratic revolution. The "teacher as citizen" quickly gained prominence on both the individual and collective levels in the context of the early 1950s and further radicalized the Union's platform and tactics. The purge of communist teachers in 1950 was seen as a major blow to the ability of teachers to act as role-models for active citizenship, because it deprived them of the right to choose their individual political affiliation and activities.[36] Furthermore, opposition to the San Francisco Peace Treaty, the U.S.-Japan Security Treaty, and rearmament broadened the scope of the JTU's political activism and made it a leading voice of public protest in foreign and domestic policy issues.

Never Send Our Students to the Battlefield Again!

Especially from 1950 on, when peace treaty negotiations came to a head, the JTU's emphasis on establishing systemic channels for popular criticism of state policy found a powerful corollary in collaborative protest activities with other antigovernment organizations, especially opposition parties, labor unions, student groups, and women's organizations. Indeed, the mass protest against what was termed a "partial" peace treaty (championed by the United States and limited to the noncommunist world) and the demand for a comprehensive treaty that would include all Asian nations, catapulted the JTU to center stage of national politics. By then it was clear that the principle of resistance had to extend from domestic power structures to the international hegemony of the United States if peace was to be preserved. This connection between domestic and international politics emerged clearly when the United States demanded Japan's remilitarization and the continuation of U.S. military bases after Japan's formal independence. The Chinese Communist Revolution in October 1949, followed by the outbreak of war on the Korean peninsula in June 1950, filled such demands—and popular protest against them—with great urgency, which was captured by the opposition in terms of a stark juxtaposition of "war promoters" and "peace defenders."

Joining a broad opposition movement, the JTU protested against the "San Francisco system" as a so-called separate peace because it excluded Communist China, Korea, and the Soviet Union and firmly incorporated Japan into the *Pax Americana*. The opposition demanded instead a peace treaty based on four "peace principles": no rearmament, no U.S. military forces stationed in Japan, a comprehensive rather than "separate" peace, and permanent neutrality in the Cold War.[37] Prime Minister Yoshida's rejection of these principles signaled to the Union (as it did to the left in general) the failure of the government to embody Japan's constitutional promise by adhering to peace and democracy within and without.[38] In this context, the liberal left understood resistance against the government and the treaty negotiations as the duty of a democratic citizenry, while the radical left looked directly to Communist China as an example of a successful socialist revolution in Asia.[39]

Unionists were able to draw conceptually upon the public statements of a group of prominent intellectuals around Maruyama Masao and Tokyo University President Nanbara Shigeru who had formed the Peace Problems Discussion Group (Heiwa mondai danwakai) in August 1948. Opposition mass organizations were quick to adopt their peace principles.[40] The "Statement on War and Peace by Japanese Social Scientists" (December 1948) laid out the need for a comprehensive peace treaty by considering Japanese independence in light of relations with China and other Asian countries; it clearly stated that Japanese remilitarization and American military bases on Japanese territory amounted to a violation of the constitution's Article 9. In early 1951 the JSP adopted its famous "Three Peace Principles," calling for (1) a comprehensive peace treaty, (2) neutrality, and (3) opposition to military bases. The General Council of Labor Unions added a fourth principle: opposition to remilitarization. The movement for a comprehensive peace treaty, which had begun in 1948, thus joined hands with the peace movement, which exploded onto the political scene in 1950, when war broke out in neighboring Korea.

The Teachers' Union located itself at the intersection of these two movements and used its extensive national, prefectural, and local presence in education as a means to mobilize popular pacifism through so-called peace education. It combined the insistence on organized resistance to the state with a substantive call for antimilitarism, which extended from school environments and textbooks to parental responsibilities and toys. (Union leaders stressed the importance of teachers working with parents—for example, to raise peace-loving children, a process that included restricting the use of war-simulating toys, even if their manufacture had become Japan's first export-oriented industry.) The Union's slogan "Never send our students to the battlefield again!" quickly became the rallying cry of "peace education," combining reflection on the war with commitment to a vision of a world at peace. Its spirit was explicitly international, extending to humanity in general, and immediately caught the imagination of the liberal left.[41] The Socialist Party adopted the slogan and introduced it into the Diet; the Women's Democratic Club mirrored it with its own slogan, "Let's not send our husbands and children to war!" Other peace groups adapted and expanded it to fit their own particular constituencies (as in Wadatsumi-kai's triple slogan addressed to youth, mothers, and workers).

Among the many public peace demonstrations in Tokyo in the early 1950s, perhaps the most prominent was organized by the General Council of Labor Unions and the JCP on the grounds of Yasukuni Shrine on 1 September 1951, certainly an unusual choice from today's perspective. (An image of this public peace demonstration is reproduced on the cover of this book.) It suggests that the early peace movement was very much driven by the memory of the war, which had, after all, ended only half a decade before and was fresh in people's minds. It also implies that Yasukuni Shrine as a site of memory had a real potential to be imbued with meanings other than militarism and worship of the war dead. Most intriguing perhaps are certain overlaps in the meaning of *the war and of postwar developments* for peace protesters and Yasukuni Shrine officials, in terms of both an overwhelming feeling of victimization and nationalist sentiment. Soldiers as well as teachers and workers had been victims of wartime state coercion on the one hand and had actively participated in implementing such state policies on the other. Furthermore, by the early 1950s, all felt betrayed by the postwar state of affairs under foreign occupation, if for different reasons. This tended to translate into a thinly veiled ethnic nationalism not only among Shintoists, who wanted Japan's imperial "essence" properly restored, but also among left-wing activists, whose anti-Americanism and "Asian" nationalism were sometimes reminiscent of wartime sentiments. Still, the substantial ideological divisions between the political right and the left as they developed in the early 1950s prevailed, and war memory, however slippery, became increasingly identified with represented special interests.

For the JTU, as for many organizations committed to liberal opposition politics at the time, Marxism and modernism remained the ideological tools with which to translate war memory into political practice, and they contained their own biases and blindness. Maruyama Masao once described the modernist project as a "condition of ongoing struggle against the forces of a corrupt and oppressive tradition," a struggle centered on "individual self-determination."[42] For Maruyama and other progressive intellectuals, Japan's "corrupt and oppressive tradition" was being actively revived throughout the 1950s by a succession of conservative governments determined to undermine the postwar (modernist) project. These public intellectuals saw the departure of the postwar from prewar and wartime society as consisting precisely in popular monitoring of the state and resistance to its attempts to assert itself over public opinion. In other words, the political function of a newly recreated public sphere was at stake. The JTU, like other interest groups, negotiated between providing a forum for a *critical* public discourse and competing for access to state institutions through its representatives in the Diet and local governmental bodies. If these two roles contradicted each other in Habermas's theory of the public sphere in the modern welfare state, the Teachers' Union and interest groups on the opposition left in general found them complementary.[43] Representing "the people" against the state assured the Union both its popular appeal and its legitimacy as an interest group affiliated with the opposition Socialist Party.

In the early postwar years, the JTU held, the sense of political subjectivity necessary to end this system of bureaucratic control was not allowed to permeate all of Japanese society but was instead confined to certain civic groups. Although the Union worked tirelessly to democratize such a sense of political agency on behalf of the people, it succeeded primarily in keeping the public eye fixed on the state. Undoubtedly it is to the Union's credit that official attempts to conceal Japan's wartime crimes became issues of public debate at various times. By focusing on the state's prewar hegemony and coercion, however, the Union occluded the question of popular war responsibility from the plane of progressive opposition, much as Shrine Shinto did on the plane of conservative national identity. When the Union asked teachers to examine their own conduct, it implied individual responsibility for postwar efforts and the failure to complete the democratic revolution, similar to the debate about war responsibility among intellectuals in 1956–57. Yet this did not lead to an examination of teachers' cooperation in the war effort. Maruyama, too, refused to acknowledge and investigate war responsibility from the angle of individual consciousness, precisely because wartime society had been characterized, in his words, by a "system of irresponsibility."[44] Similarly, the JTU continued to insist that the prewar teacher was a puppet even while beginning to call on the postwar teacher as an individual and citizen.

The JTU's history of massive popular support stemmed at least in part from its criticism of the bureaucracy (wartime and postwar), a criticism that was shared to an extent by people as politically far removed from labor unionists as Shrine Shintoists were. For even if the Teachers' Union and the Association of Shinto Shrines appeared diametrically opposed to each other on issues like the emperor system, they shared a similar view of the wartime bureaucracy as excessively controlling and harmful to their interests. The Association of War-bereaved Families, in contrast, campaigned for the revival of wartime bureaucratic support of its constituents. Teachers and Shrine Shintoists found it easier to hark back to an earlier history and distance themselves from the war, while the war bereaved could not, because their presence as a political constituency was rooted in the wartime bureaucracy. Nonetheless, because of Shrine Shinto's relative loss of public influence and radical disconnection from the bureaucracy under occupation policies, Shrine Shinto actively lobbied the government for support, whereas the Union steadfastly opposed governmental involvement in education. For much of the postwar period, the antagonistic relationship between the Ministry of Education and the JTU provided the framework for left-driven political conflict over war memories, just as the cozy relationship between the Association of War-bereaved Families and the bureaucracy set the stage for right-driven conflict.

The politics of memory advanced by the Teachers' Union complemented that of its archrival, the Japan Association of War-bereaved Families, insofar as both focused on the nation-state as the critical unit of memory formation. But whereas the war-bereaved families validated an organic relationship between the state and its citizens characterized by mutual obligations, the JTU attacked the state for perpetuating irresponsibility by ruling *over* instead of *through* the people. Especially on the national organizational level, the Union practiced a politics of resistance against the state informed by a self-created political subjectivity, which, it argued, had been forcibly prevented from developing under the prewar and wartime regimes. For the Teachers' Union, the war appeared as a domestic problem only, a matter of state-society relations that in Marxist vocabulary was usually characterized as "fascist." To blame the state was to rescue the nation. Just as the Tokyo war crimes trial and much of public opinion held "the militarists" responsible for the war, the Union blamed "the bureaucrats" and emphasized the continuities between the prewar and wartime state that had yet to be broken in the postwar by the people (teachers) themselves.

CHAPTER FOUR

People's Diplomacy:
The Japan-China Friendship Association

The peace treaty negotiations in the last years of the occupation and Japan's independence in April 1952 galvanized the progressive and radical left in opposition to the conservative Yoshida government and its American supporters. They inspired mass protest movements of unprecedented scale and focused interest politics on issues of the war and its aftermath that had not been adequately addressed under the Allied occupation. One such issue was Japan's relationship with China after the Communist Revolution and the establishment of the People's Republic of China (PRC) under Mao Zedong in October 1949. The United States' deliberate exclusion of China and other communist countries from the peace treaty and the growing enmity between the two during the Korean War (1950–53) alarmed many Japanese intellectuals, businessmen, and socialist and even conservative politicians, some of whom had been so-called China hands before and during the war.

An eclectic group of people with personal and professional ties to China now formed a movement to "set the grand stage of Japanese-Chinese friendship" by promoting cultural and economic exchanges "between the two peace-loving peoples" based on remembering and atoning for Japanese war crimes against Chinese people, especially Chinese forced laborers in Japan.[1] One of the first collaborative projects of atonement was the retelling of an uprising at the Hanaoka mine

Fig. 4.1 Excerpts from *Hanaoka monogatari*, a 1951 collection of woodcuts depicting the June 1945 massacre of Chinese forced laborers in Hanaoka, Akita Prefecture, and its postwar commemoration. Used by permission of Nitchū yūkō kyōkai.

through a long series of woodcuts (Fig. 4.1). These were originally presented as a slide show at local storytelling events. Prepared under the guidance of a local artist, Nii Hiroharu, and published in 1951

in book form as *Hanaoka Story* (*Hanaoka monogatari*), these woodcuts
adapted a Chinese tradition of political protest art that had become
very popular in China before and during the war. The series depicted
in graphic detail the conditions of Chinese (and Korean) forced laborers in the camp at Hanaoka, their brutal treatment at the hands of Japanese supervisors, the laborers' uprising, and the Japanese authorities'
bloody crackdown in June 1945, which left 418 Chinese dead. The last
panels showed the commemoration of the massacre: the collection of
the victims' remains and the (Buddhist) ceremonial return of their ashes
to China in white boxes. Reprinted in 1981 by Mumyōsha shuppan
in Akita, the book remains in print today after more than 50 years
and serves not only as a record of the Hanaoka massacre but also as
a powerful reminder of Japanese brutality and aggression against Chinese, Korean, and other Asian laborers, especially during the last years
of the war.

This sentiment of remorse and atonement for specific Japanese war
crimes was central to the establishment of the Japan-China Friendship
Association (Nitchū yūkō kyōkai) on 1 October 1950, the first anniversary of the Communist Revolution. The Friendship Association held
that without a peace treaty and the normalization of official relations
with the PRC, the state of war between the two countries continued to
victimize both peoples—if not with bullets, then by preventing the set-
tlement of humanitarian issues and economic recovery through trade.
In the group's first statement, leaders blamed "American imperialism"
for causing a revival of "Japanese militarism" by pressuring the government into a U.S.-Japan alliance that required remilitarization, thereby
implicitly threatening Chinese national security. But it was the Japanese
government that, against the will of its own people, refused to forge
amicable relations with Communist China and furthermore failed to
acknowledge its wartime crimes. In sharp contrast, China, which had
suffered under Japanese militarism, was successfully building a people's
state on the principles of peace and national independence and extending a "hand of friendship" to its neighbor.[2]

Although the Japan-China Friendship Association did not have a
direct prewar or wartime organizational predecessor to salvage or re-
connect with (unlike the Association of Shinto Shrines, the Association
of War-bereaved Families, and the Teachers' Union), the careers and

personal lives of its leading members were deeply intertwined with mainland China and the Japanese presence there in the first half of the twentieth century. The Friendship Association's first president from 1950 to 1953 was Uchiyama Kanzō (1885–1959), who had spent half his life in Shanghai, where he ran a Japanese bookstore from 1917 right through the end of the war. Uchiyama had learned to walk a thin line there, taking advantage of the Japanese army's protection of Japanese civilians in Shanghai during the 1930s, while offering his bookstore as a secret meeting place for Japanese and Chinese literary figures, some of whom were clearly resisters to Japanese imperialism in China. Known in the early 1930s as the Japanese-Chinese Culture Salon, Uchiyama's bookstore was a refuge for the famous Chinese writer Lu Xun before his death in 1936 and one of several Shanghai liaison centers for Japanese communists like Ozaki Hotsumi, an *Asahi shinbun* reporter later involved in the Richard Sorge spy ring. Uchiyama conceived of his role in Shanghai in cultural and personal rather than in political terms, to the extent that it was possible to do so at that time.[3] He remained there until 1947, when he returned to Japan and reopened his bookstore in the Kanda district of Tokyo, this time specializing in Chinese books.

Itō Takeo (1895–1984), another founding member of the Japan-China Friendship Association, had an illustrious prewar and wartime career in the research section of the South Manchurian Railway Company (SMR). As the director of the company's Shanghai office, he had been "quite friendly" with "the ablest China hand in the navy, Tsuda Shizue," while also maintaining close relationships with left-wing intellectuals critical of Japan's war in China, including Ozaki Hotsumi. The discovery of the Sorge-Ozaki spy ring in Tokyo and the execution of Ozaki led to a series of arrests of scientists working for the SMR Research Department in Shanghai in 1942–43. Itō was sent to prisons in remote areas of northern China in June 1943 but released the following year. In his memoirs, he traced the *de facto* dissolution of the Research Department to these arrests and asserted that the "real significance of the SMR Incident lay in the fascist assault and repression by the military of our scientific work."[4] A number of Itō's Research Department colleagues remained in China after 1945 to oversee the dismantling of the SMR and help transfer to the Chinese the fruits of their labor (for example, technological advances in extracting Manchurian energy re-

sources).[5] Others found positions in the academy and built up the field
of postwar East Asian Studies at Japanese universities.

The Japan-China friendship movement also relied heavily on politicians with prewar careers in social activism. Its second director was
the JSP politician Matsumoto Jiichirō (1887–1966), the founder in 1922
and chairman of the Leveling Society (Suiheisha), an organization for
the restoration of the *burakumin* (outcast class) to full social privileges.
Elected to the Diet in 1936, Matsumoto continued his activism on behalf of the outcast class until his arrest in 1942. In 1946, he founded
the National Committee for Buraku Emancipation (Buraku kaihō zenkoku iinkai), which developed into a mass organization after 1950,
backed by many left-wing groups. Another prewar social activist and
postwar Socialist politician was Ōyama Ikuo (1880–1955), who had been
a prominent Marxist economist and spent the war years in exile in the
United States. Returning to Japan in 1947, he became a member of the
Lower House of the Diet and a leading member of several peace organizations. Instrumental in the Friendship Association's quest for the
revival of trade with mainland China was the active participation of
Hoashi Kei (1905–89), a postwar Socialist politician and Diet member
(of both Upper and Lower Houses), who was reelected seven times
from 1947 on. Hoashi had been director of the Heavy Industry Council
in the prewar period and a consultant to the Ministry of Commerce and
Industry under Tōjō in the early 1940s. He concluded agreements on
Japanese-Chinese trade in the 1950s and 1960s and was also on the
board of directors for the Japan–Soviet Union Friendship Association
(Nisso kyōkai) and the Association for the Return of Koreans Living
in Japan (Zainichi Chōsenjin kikoku kyōryokukai).[6]

When the Friendship Association was established, one-third of the
78 founding members were intellectuals and China specialists. Another
third came from the business world, half of them representatives of
Chinese overseas businesses, and the rest were JSP politicians, labor
union representatives, and social movement activists, including the
mayors of Kyoto and Yokohama. The professional eclecticism of this
organization helped in creating a mass movement in the 1950s around
the notion that Chinese-Japanese relations, rather than the U.S.-
Japanese alliance, should serve as the basis of postwar peace. It is safe
to say, however, that the core of the friendship movement consisted

of people like Itō Takeo and Uchiyama Kanzō, who brought to this movement a wealth of personal experience living and working in China before and during the war, and a deep commitment to righting the wrongs of the Japanese imperialist presence there.

Responsibility Evaded:
Reparations and an "Incomplete" Peace

Japan's defeat in 1945 did not immediately erase its deep, multilevel entanglement with developments on the Chinese mainland. As the examples above show, many Japanese had made successful careers in China before as well as during the war, and the line between participating in the government's militarist ventures and nurturing an anti-imperialist attitude deeply sympathetic to the Chinese people tended to be blurred in real life. Some Japanese were more courageous than others in recognizing and resisting Japanese imperialist ventures in China, but most simply played their own small parts in Japan's vast and multifaceted presence there, which extended far beyond military combat. The legacies of this complicated history, however, were largely buried in new Cold War enmities as perceived by Washington and implemented by the occupation forces in Japan. GHQ dealt directly with two main issues concerning Japanese-Chinese relations: the repatriation of Japanese from the Chinese mainland, and reparations. Repatriation was an ongoing humanitarian problem that spilled over into the 1950s and required the engagement of private organizations such as the Red Cross and the Japan-China Friendship Association. The return of Chinese and Koreans living in Japan at the end of the war, many of them forced laborers, was another matter. The loss of their status as Japanese nationals after the war, as well as the contemporary conditions of civil war in both China and Korea, made this reverse repatriation difficult and in some cases impossible.[7]

The reparations issue, however, was even more directly bound up with Cold War politics and the interests of the United States in particular. Both the United States and the Chinese Nationalist government had drawn up their own reparations programs well before the end of the war. In the course of negotiations between the two in the deteriorating Cold War environment of the late 1940s, however, the reparations program formulated by the U.S. State Department steadily shrank until its virtual renunciation in the San Francisco Peace Treaty against concerted Chinese opposition. As Okamoto Kōichi has argued, this represented the loss of a major opportunity to rebuild Japanese-Chinese relations on a fundamentally new basis of Japanese contrition and apology.[8] The Japanese government had no independent foreign policy and thus no official say in this matter, of course, but it nonetheless made clear that it regarded the reparations program as a way to build up East Asian trade and thus aid economic recovery rather than as compensation for the damages it had inflicted on its neighbors during the war.[9] This was the "evasion" of responsibility, if not outright hostility, toward China that activists in the Japan-China friendship movement were reacting to when they formed their organization in 1950.

The U.S. government had always approached Japan's reparations as an issue of economic policy rather than of punishment and restitution. It quoted the "lesson of World War I" in Europe—the argument that the economically crippling indemnities imposed on Germany after World War I had indirectly led to Hitler's rise to power as a justification for this stance. The Chinese, in contrast, remembered not World War I but the first Sino-Japanese War (1894–95) and the enormous reparations payments forced upon them by a victorious Japan. Meiji Japan had used Chinese indemnities to modernize; China, in the aftermath of World War II, demanded that Japan transfer its assets and industrial infrastructure to rebuild the shattered Chinese economy and compensate for the huge public and private losses that it had inflicted in the course of the war. The latter part of this demand was to fall by the wayside, ignored by the United States as early as the Cairo Conference of November 1943, and rejected outright under the so-called reverse course, when occupation policy focused fully on Japanese economic recovery rather than on continuing to build "peace and democracy."[10]

The Communist Revolution and the establishment of the PRC in October 1949 sealed the fate of U.S.-Chinese negotiations over Japanese reparations. The United States declared Communist China an enemy and brought Japan fully into its own orbit of strategic and economic interests in the region. The resulting mass protests in Japan against the exclusion of China and other Communist countries from the peace treaty and the demand for a "full peace agreement," however, virtually ignored the abandonment of the reparations program. Indeed, major leaders of the protests, such as the Teachers' Union, explicitly stated their desire to have reparations waived and instead to rebuild East Asian trade relations so that Japan would not remain dependent on the United States.[11] In contrast, organizations specifically focusing on Japanese-Chinese relations were formed at this time to demand the resurrection of trade between the two countries on the basis of atonement for Japan's wartime aggression. The Chinese Revolution demonstrated to them that China had in fact thrown off the shackles of the past and was building a peaceful society on new principles, while the Japanese government had failed to make a clean break with its imperialist past by showing remorse for its war conduct. Whereas most on the liberal left saw that break with the past embodied in the commitment to "democracy," participants in the Japan-China friendship movement staked their hopes on a fundamentally altered relationship with China, which required a full acknowledgment of Japan's unilateral responsibility for its aggressive war in Asia.

Critical to the unity of this eclectic movement was the belief that the breakdown in relations with China was due to Japan alone. This reflected not only a moral and intellectual standpoint but also a political stance toward the contemporary situation, informed by a particular view of the prewar and wartime past. Essentially, the group held that Japan's century-long practice of imperialistic and militaristic policies toward China, paired with a popular attitude of contempt for its "backwards" neighbor, was now being revived through Japan's support of American imperialism in Asia. As early as January 1950, a statement of goals for the proposed Friendship Association hinted at this belief:

The first step toward rebuilding a democratic Japan is to dispose of our self-satisfied island-nation mentality and to become an international people willing to preserve peace in all directions. It is therefore necessary that not only the Pacific but also the Japan Sea and the East China Sea become "free waterways." It is an old truth that "Japan will not prosper if China does not prosper." We should recognize this, but in a way that corrects the old view of China.[12]

In the early 1950s, the Friendship Association accused the Japanese government of failing in at least three ways to "correct the old view of China." First, the government both covered up and evaded practical responsibility for Japanese war crimes committed against Chinese people in both China and Japan. One specific example heavily publicized by the Friendship Association in its first years was the Hanaoka massacre of 30 June 1945. Second, neither the Japanese government nor the people correctly understood the significance of the Communist Revolution. It was in China, not Japan, that people had succeeded in throwing off the shackles of the imperialist past and were building a free society of "new men" based on the principles of independence, equality, and peace. Third, by following the United States in recognizing the Taiwan Nationalist regime as the legitimate representative of China, Japan once again used China's internal affairs for its own self-serving political purposes instead of accepting reality. (This last point became increasingly controversial as members disagreed on how to interpret events in China, especially the Cultural Revolution of 1965–66. The Japan-China Friendship Association would split in 1967 over this issue.)

Specialists on contemporary China, including scholars and critics in the humanities and social sciences, served as the Association's main resource in its endeavor to articulate a responsible memory of Japan's war in China. The Japan-China friendship movement attracted members of the intellectual community who had professional or personal ties to mainland China, enthusiasm for the Communist Revolution from an ideological standpoint, and a political understanding of culture. Takeuchi Yoshimi, perhaps the best-known postwar scholar of modern Chinese literature, held views that mirrored those of the Friendship Association but never actually joined the movement and refused several invitations to visit China as a member of a cultural delegation. Although Takeuchi became a political activist for a short time at the height of the 1960 movement against the renewal of the U.S.-Japan Security Treaty (Anpo), his understanding of revolution was theoretical rather than practical, and he steadfastly refused to get involved in politics.

Nevertheless, Takeuchi's vision of Chinese resistance to foreign and domestic exploitation as a "model" for Japanese society had great intellectual influence on those active in the Japanese-Chinese friendship movement. It resonated powerfully among those who contrasted the success of China's Communist Revolution with the dearth of revolutionary promise in Japan in the early 1950s. Takeuchi's China, in Lawrence Olson's words, "served a vitally affirming purpose as an object of aspiration and an abstract good."[13] Intellectuals working in the friendship movement, however, devoted themselves to making China the subject of political discourse and popular knowledge in Japan. They accepted the PRC as a "qualitatively different kind of civilization peopled by 'new men.'"[14] As a first step toward changing the Japanese people's poor understanding of China, the Association printed an article denouncing the Japanese term *Shina* as imperialist and promoting the use of *Chūgoku* as the correct name for the People's Republic of China.

According to Arai Shiroichi, [*Shina*] came into use with the beginning of Meiji as a measure for promoting the elites' aggressive policies towards China. It was used for various policies and has for a long time elicited bad connotations for the Chinese people. It is originally a European and American term, borrowed by Japan only at one particular time in history, and the Chinese have never used it for themselves. As a step in our reflection on ourselves, we must stop using the term *Shina* immediately, because it casts the terrible shadow of the past on our relationship with China.[15]

In fact, intellectuals writing in *Nihon to Chūgoku* not only demanded atonement for Japanese wrong-doing in the past but clung to the political and moral notion of a new reality. If Japan had led Asia into war, China was now the leader in building peace and prosperity for all in Asia. Indeed, a 1953 article entitled "The New China and Japan" took issue with every criticism of the new regime in China in the contemporary media and turned it around to demonstrate the PRC's competence and good intentions. Politically, China presented no threat to its neighbors because its strength rested neither on dictatorship nor on monopoly capitalism. With the people taking the lead, "why should a country that has reformed itself, that knows the way to develop on its own . . . be a threat to its neighbors?" Militarily, the Korea conflict had shown that China sent the People's Liberation Army abroad only to support, not to dominate. It had consulted with the Korean government before dispatching its troops and had been the first to withdraw. Economically, the Chinese Revolution had contributed to building peace because it rested on the economic empowerment of the people. "Japan's history has shown that Japanese colonialism in China and Korea was based on the absence of domestic economic growth.

The people were losing their freedom with every day, while the capitalists increased their power. This is the path to invasion, and China is on
the opposite path now." In fact, China represented an economic asset
to Japan in as much as relations could now be formed on the basis of
independence and equality instead of colonialism.[16]

These arguments lined up all too well with sentiments expressed in
Zhou Enlai's speeches and in *People's Daily* editorials. They also overlapped with a wider anti-American, pro-Asian nationalism espoused by
many prominent intellectuals on the liberal left, including Maruyama
Masao and Shimizu Ikutarō. Opposition to the San Francisco Peace
and Security Treaty, which excluded the PRC and guaranteed the
United States military bases in Japan, represented a common starting
point for action among pacifists of different ideological convictions
and formed the core of the Friendship Association's campaign for the
restoration of formal Sino-Japanese relations. The Asia-Pacific Peace
Conference, held in Beijing in the fall of 1952 with participants from
40 countries, provided an internationally visible opportunity for "people's diplomacy" through cultural exchange. Until the last minute, the
Foreign Ministry withheld permission for the Japanese delegation of
fourteen peace activists (including representatives of the Friendship
Association) to travel to Beijing. Preparatory meetings in Tokyo as well
as in Beijing attracted wide participation and media coverage. A resolution regarding the "Japan Question," one of eleven official statements
issued over the course of the twelve-day conference, demanded a complete peace treaty with Japan, expressed the Japanese people's desire
to "promote the establishment of an independent, democratic, free
and peaceful new Japan by stopping the revival of Japanese militarism,"
and called for the complete withdrawal of foreign troops from Japanese
soil.[17]

The belief among friendship movement activists that peace in Asia
would originate in China once American imperialism was overcome
appeared to have been powerfully reaffirmed in the Five Peace Principles that Zhou Enlai and Jawaharlal Nehru announced at their summit
in June 1954: mutual respect for territorial sovereignty; nonintervention;
nonaggression; equality and reciprocity; and peaceful coexistence despite rival ideologies. This held enormous significance for the intellectual left as an attempt to apply democratic principles directly to interna-

tional relations rather than to domestic affairs alone. Moreover, the left regarded this extension of democracy as having originated in Asia and not the West. It gave intellectuals involved in "cultural diplomacy" a sense of triumph over America and Europe in the realm of political ethics. Shimizu Ikutarō expressed this sense when he wrote:

If we think about the significance of these five principles, it must be seen as only natural that these principles, differing from the great principles and theories to date, were created not in Washington, Paris or Moscow, but in a corner of Asia. That is not in the company of power, but rather in opposition to power. . . . The life of democracy is, through the hands of the peoples of Asia and Africa, being reborn.[18]

The movement to change the basis of international relations in Asia from the U.S.-Japan security alliance to Sino-Japanese friendship rested in part on a new ethnic nationalism centering on Asia. It was a reactionary nationalism in the sense that it was born out of resistance particularly against the United States (and the Cold War system), and thus in some ways resembled the Greater Asianist thought of the Meiji period.[19] But in defining a shared Asian identity and destiny, perceptions of cultural and racial commonality retreated behind a belief in historical progress. For it was in Asia that a new system of international peace, independence, and democracy promised to replace the old capitalist nationalism that had caused World War II and was still championed by the United States.

Grassroots Diplomacy

Within the contemporary political environment and from the standpoint of resistance against the state, the Japan-China Friendship Association adopted "people's diplomacy" as its *modus vivendi*.[20] This term, *kokumin gaikō* in Japanese, was adapted from the Chinese *renmin waijiao*, coined by the PRC's first premier, Zhou Enlai.[21] However, the Chinese term *renmin* (*jinmin* in Japanese) means "the people" in communist terminology, whereas *kokumin*, the Japanese appropriation, implies the people of a nation rather than a proletariat. The Friendship Association did not simply adopt communist language but adjusted it to reflect the political realities of Japan. Conceptually, "people's diplomacy" shifted the agency in foreign relations from states (which conducted wars) to "the people" (who created peace). Practically, the term was used to describe the informal relations between the Chinese "people's" state and Japanese civic organizations like the Friendship Association. The Friendship Association thereby insisted on the putative unity between the Chinese people and their (communist) state on the one hand, while simultaneously stressing the diametric opposition between the Japanese people and their government on the other.

At best ambiguous in theory, people's diplomacy was clearly compromised in practice. Never intended to be more than a temporary arrangement in Japanese-Chinese relations, this "people's diplomacy" actually coexisted rather easily with official policy. Its success in managing Sino-Japanese relations in fact depended on the tacit consent of the government: the Friendship Association persistently lobbied the same state institutions it protested against, so as to ensure its position in brokering relations with the PRC. To be sure, the Association deserved credit for creating and maintaining important channels of communication with the PRC from which official relations, once they were normalized (in 1972) and formally restored (in 1978), could easily be institutionalized. Nevertheless, until then its activities also helped to perpetuate the political arrangement by which relations with China remained outside the political mainstream, while official policy focused on relations with the United States. This political arrangement created the framework in which the Friendship Association's memory of the war commanded public attention. Acknowledgment of and atonement for Japan's wartime aggression had its legitimate place in postwar public life—namely, as part of special interest politics. But insofar as this interest remained outside the political mainstream, it did not sufficiently challenge official policy, which marginalized China and ignored war responsibility because it was politically expedient to do so in a Cold War context in which the United States was for Japan the hegemonic power.

Although the Japan-China Friendship Association established itself within a few years as a political interest group connected with the opposition Socialist Party and recognized on the highest bureaucratic level, it styled itself as a "people's movement." At its inaugural meeting on 1 October 1950, the founding members identified four main areas of public life toward which their group would direct its activities: public opinion, cultural exchange, trade, and foreign policy:

1. The Association will reflect deeply on the Japanese people's mistaken view of China and work hard to correct it.

2. The Association will put great effort into cultural exchange between the two countries in order to deepen the two peoples' mutual understanding and cooperation.

3. The Association will make great efforts to promote Japanese-Chinese trade in order to assist the economic recovery of the two countries as well as the living standards of the two peoples.

4. Based on the friendly cooperation of the Japanese and Chinese people, the Association will seek mutual security and peace by contributing to world peace.[22]

Accordingly, the Friendship Association's activities ranged from setting up Chinese cooking and language classes to facilitating trade agreements and negotiating the repatriation of Japanese left in China after the war's end.

One of the Association's efforts to bring together people from all walks of life and establish relations with Chinese people involved a letter-writing campaign on the occasion of the fourteenth anniversary of the Marco Polo Bridge incident—the military clash between Chinese and Japanese troops on 7 July 1937 that marked the beginning of the Sino-Japanese War. Between 1 July and 15 August 1951, the Association called on individuals and groups from political, economic, cultural, scholarly, labor, and housewives' circles to send greetings to Chinese individuals and groups on the mainland and on Taiwan. An article in *Nihon to Chūgoku* entitled "Considering August 15th: Let Us Send Greetings to China!" invited people to write down their "heartfelt thoughts and wishes for the Chinese people" and send these letters to the Friendship Association to be mailed to Chinese newspapers (and ultimately collected and published in a single volume). The letters urged readers to remember the human misery set in motion by the Marco Polo Bridge incident, not only for the Chinese but also for the Japanese, who "were driven into such an aggressive war," and for the whole world. Moreover, current circumstances threatened to revive the horrors of that war:

In the past two to three years, as the crisis in Korea poisoned both the international climate and that in our own country, our hopes for peace—acquired at the highest sacrifice—are fading, and the sound of shells and smell of gun-powder have returned. Given Japan's precarious past, we have to establish friendly relations with our neighbor China. We cannot allow hostile relations to develop nor can we tolerate them. Cooperation between the Chinese and the Japanese is our heart's desire, . . . and we commemorate this year's anniversary of 7 July as the most straightforward step toward mutual understanding between our two peoples.[23]

The letters reprinted in subsequent issues of *Nihon to Chūgoku*, typically written by presidents of labor unions and other organizations, echoed the sentiments expressed in this passage. They emphasized the unity between the Chinese and Japanese peoples by stressing their common victimization at the hands of Japanese militarists in the past and the conservative Japanese government in the present.

This characterization of Japanese attitudes toward China closely matched the Chinese Communist Party's official criticism of Japan and exposed the Japan-China Friendship Association to accusations of acting as the CCP's mouthpiece. The precise nature of relations between the Friendship Association and the CCP is difficult to know, but strong ties obviously existed between the two via the Japanese Communist Party, which was under heavy Chinese influence in the first half of the 1950s.[24] According to some accounts, the CCP used the Friendship Association outright as a vehicle to infiltrate Japan on a popular level in order to alienate Japan from the United States and demand Japan's neutrality in Asia.[25] The Association strongly denied this, and the fact that it was able to establish itself at the height of the Red Purge suggests that direct ties to the PRC or even the JCP could not be proven. The *Mainichi shinbun* carried an article on 17 July 1950, even before the Association's official establishment, branding the movement's leaders "a group of spies" carrying out subversive activities against the U.S. military without the knowledge of the majority of its would-be members. An official statement by the Association on 21 July rejecting these claims settled the controversy only temporarily.[26] Throughout the months leading up to the signing of the peace treaty in September 1951, the PRC mobilized youth groups, student organizations, and the councils of every major city in China to send messages to "the Japanese people" encouraging them to protest the treaty. Statements opposing a "partial peace" by the Chinese National Association of Social Scientists and the Association of Natural Scientists dovetailed neatly with the peace appeals issued earlier by Japanese scientists and the Peace Problems Discussion Group around Maruyama Masao and Nanbara Shigeru. Friendship movement activists in Japan translated and distributed all these messages.[27]

Conversely, the Friendship Association accused the Japanese government of using anticommunist ideology to avoid facing the new political realities in Asia and escape responsibility for Japan's wartime aggression. During the peace treaty negotiations, this was an especially heated argument voiced by much of the opposition on the left. A public controversy unfolded when it became known that Prime Minister Yoshida had secretly written to John Foster Dulles on 10 February 1952 agreeing to conclude a peace treaty with the Nationalist regime on Taiwan without having formally brought this matter before the Diet. An article in *Nihon to Chūgoku* denounced the "Yoshida letter" in moral terms, as a continuation of the utter disrespect for China that had caused the war in the first place—and a denial of responsibility for the war against the Chinese people: "If Prime Minister Yoshida felt even an inch of remorse for Japanese militarist undertakings in China, why would he refuse to recognize the government which represents all of China at the present time and instead conclude a "peace treaty" with a government exiled to Taiwan?"[28]

To highlight Japan's past and present practice of construing the political reality in China in its own interest, the statement quoted wartime prime minister Konoe Fumimaro. Konoe had insisted, in 1938, that "we will not deal with Chiang Kai-shek" at a time when Chiang did in fact represent China while Japan supported a puppet regime in Nanjing. Now that Chiang was exiled, the argument continued, the Japanese government insisted on recognizing him, this time in order to bolster its alliance with the United States. The authors of the statement also pointed to the February 1947 massacre in Taipei of Taiwanese resisting the Chiang regime. They stressed that by recognizing Taipei instead of Beijing, Japan had again allied itself with an aggressor rather than with the communist liberator. Indeed, it was the Association's view that establishment politics in Japan had not fundamentally changed since the war.

Building a people's movement, however, entailed specific organizational strategies in addition to community work. By 1953 the Japan-

China Friendship Association had secured a wide net of political affiliates. Six smaller organizations had joined as members, all offering specialized services in one or another aspect of Chinese culture.[29] In addition, two Japan-China trade organizations, two academic research institutes, and two organizations facilitating repatriation of Japanese from China became close affiliates. But the largest, if least structured, reservoir of recognition came from so-called mass organizations across the political spectrum: seventeen labor unions, eighteen peace groups, the six main political parties,[30] and even the five most powerful bureaucratic agencies: the cabinet, the Foreign Ministry, the Health and Welfare Ministry, the Labor Ministry, and the Agency for Assistance to Returnees.[31] Although labor unions and peace activists collaborated closely with the Friendship Association on many occasions, the same cannot be said of governmental and bureaucratic institutions. Their inclusion in this list of affiliates nevertheless indicated that the establishment, too, acknowledged the Association's legitimate niche within special interest politics. The Japan-China Friendship Association in turn facilitated the establishment of other China-related organizations such as the Committee to Commemorate Chinese Prisoner of War Martyrs (Chūgokujin furyo junnansha irei jikkō iinkai) in 1953, the Japan-China Association for Cultural Exchange (Nihon Chūgoku bunka kōryū kyōkai) in 1956, and the Liaison Society for Returnees from China (Chūgoku kikansha renrakukai), also in 1956.

People's diplomacy enjoyed almost immediate public visibility and success in relation to the issue of restarting efforts to repatriate Japanese nationals left in China at war's end. After the initial wave of 1,492,397 returnees from China through 1946, the numbers plummeted to 3,758 in 1947 and to 92 in 1951, owing in large part to the confusion of civil war on the Chinese mainland. Adhering to its refusal to restore formal diplomatic relations with the PRC after 1951, the Japanese government declined to take the initiative in resolving this issue. Instead, the Beijing government announced on 1 December 1952 that about 30,000 Japanese still residing in China enjoyed the protection of the Chinese government, lived happy lives, and even sent money back to their families in Japan. It asserted that those who chose to return to their homeland would receive assistance from the Chinese government, but since China could not provide enough ships, it asked for the help of Japanese citizens' groups under the leadership of the Chinese Red Cross Society.[32] The Japanese Red Cross, the Japan-China Friendship Association, and the Peace Liaison Society (Heiwa renrakukai)[33] became the liaison partners on the Japanese side. The Friendship Association immediately contacted some of the Japanese living in China through their newspaper *Minshū shinbun* (People's Newspaper) as well as their families in Japan. The first ship of Japanese returnees arrived in Japan on 23 March 1953, and the number of repatriates reached 26,051 by the end of the year. The Japanese government had provided the ships but offered few services to help the newcomers relocate in Japan.

The successful repatriation efforts offered the Association an opportunity to convince the public that the Japanese government not only took little responsibility for its militarist past but in fact continued it. In sharp contrast, the Chinese government appeared willing both to lay the past to rest and build an amicable relationship with Japan and also to share its peaceful progress with Japanese individuals who could now transmit their positive experiences to their compatriots at home. Even before their return, the Japanese left in China had become one of the Friendship Association's constituencies. The Association gave them a voice in Japan by printing their letters in its periodicals and provided mediation services for their return, but also clearly used them to support the Association's political goals.

When the first ship arrived, the Friendship Association's vice-president, Hirano Yoshitarō, personally welcomed the one thousand returnees as "victims of Japan's aggressive war who return not defeated but with important gains from the new China." He expressed regret at the lack of government measures to help relocate them, which demonstrated the state's unwillingness to assume responsibility for its own citizens as well as for the Chinese killed by Japan during the war. Most of all, Hirano urged the returnees to become ambassadors of China through their personal lives and experiences there: "We believe that you are the people who can connect our two countries because you have first-hand knowledge of the new China. The Japanese people are thrilled to have you home, so please use this opportunity and teach them about the new China and deepen their interest and commitment to friendship with China."[34]

Japanese war criminals tried and convicted at Chinese Class B/C war criminals received special attention upon their return to Japan in 1956. They had received comparatively light sentences so as not to harm Sino-Japanese friendship, as a Chinese official statement explained,[35] and had undergone significant reeducation during their eleven-year residence in China. Once in Japan, some of them spoke publicly at town meetings and various local committees about their experiences in China and put on amateur performances of Chinese arts.[36] But they also brought the issue of war responsibility into sharper focus than earlier returnees had done. The Friendship Association reminded its readers that the punishment of these war criminals did not absolve the rest of the Japanese of their responsibility for the war. In a sense, the war criminals were also victims of Japan's militaristic policies. But unlike the majority of Japanese living in Japan after the war, they had deeply reflected on their crimes during their stay in China.[37]

While the repatriation issue struck a humanitarian chord and thus received public attention, the trade issue played a significant role in the confrontation between the Japanese government and the PRC-backed opposition. Trade with China actually enjoyed support that crossed political lines. Insofar as the particular political arrangement in which the revival of trade with China took place in the 1950s revealed competing goals, the China trade was an obviously charged issue in both foreign policy and domestic politics. The ruling LDP did its best to keep the China trade outside Japan's international relations framework, which was guided by the U.S.-Japan Security Treaty. The JSP, however, sought to use the China trade to attack and eventually alter Japan's international position as a principal ally of the United States. In a speech to the Japan-China Friendship Committee on 13 July 1950, Katsumata Seiichi, head of the Socialist Party's Policy Research Committee, highlighted the connections between economics and foreign policy. He argued that American economic aid artificially propped up the Japanese economy instead of allowing it to develop the self-sufficiency that was vital for true national independence. Even though MacArthur insisted on the purely economic nature of American aid, the advent of the Korean War had exposed underlying political considerations. "Instead of remaining dependent upon the United States economically, we need to develop trade with China which can then serve as the basis for economic recovery."[38]

But as long as the focus remained on mutual economic benefits, the restoration of trade relations was marked by successful cooperation because it was desired by all sides, if for different reasons and in different forms. No conservative cabinet—from that of Yoshida's to Kishi's and beyond—wanted to sacrifice the China market, even if the Friendship Association accused them of deliberately hindering the people's "natural" aspirations to trade with the Chinese. The conservatives in turn regarded communism in China as "unnatural" and probably short-lived, and were prepared to wait until the reestablishment of diplomatic relations with the PRC would no longer demand Japan's abrogation of the San Francisco Peace and Security Treaty. Yoshida Shigeru hoped to speed up this process by "Europeanizing" China through the promotion of trade relations.[39] He argued in 1951—in defense of his decision to conclude a peace treaty with Taiwan—that formal relations with the nationalist regime on Taiwan did not preclude informal trade relations with the PRC.

In fact, Yoshida Shigeru's "separation of politics and economics" (*seikei bunri*) and Zhou Enlai's "people's diplomacy" dovetailed rather nicely on the issue of trade. The Chinese insistence until the mid-1950s on dealing with the Japanese people but not their government only reinforced Japan's policy of treating trade and official diplomacy as separate matters, informally consenting to the former while officially refusing the latter. It also drew the support of influential LDP politicians and businessmen sympathetic to the Japanese-Chinese friendship movement. Murata Shōzō, president of the Japan International Trade Promotion Society (Nihon kokusai bōeki sokushinkai) and a member of élite financial circles, worked closely with the Japan-China Friendship Association and traveled to Beijing numerous times to negotiate and sign trade agreements with the Chinese. He considered diplomatic relations with the PRC to be premature, given the international situation in the 1950s, and insisted that the establishment of economic relations precede the restoration of diplomatic relations. Murata thus supported the government's position while taking the lead in ensuring the success of people's diplomacy.[40]

And yet, people's diplomacy was in fact able to challenge, and even undermine, the official separation of politics and economics by working toward closing the perceived gap between "the people" and "govern-

ment." M. Y. Cho observed a gradual politicization of successive informal trade agreements with China, originating from pro-China organizations and even extending to the cabinet itself.[41] Whereas the first
trade agreement of 1 June 1952 was decidedly apolitical, the third
agreement of 4 May 1955 clearly outlined the establishment of mutual
and permanent trade representation missions in each country, with personnel to be granted the same status as official diplomats. Moreover,
their responsibilities were to include political lobbying within their respective governments for normalization of official diplomatic relations.
In this way, pro-China organizations in Japan not only benefited from
the increased power vested in them because of the government's *seikei
bunri* policy, but in turn used their success in promoting trade relations
to advance a broader agenda vis-à-vis the conservative establishment.
There were nonetheless significant setbacks, for example the Kishi
cabinet's refusal to sign the fourth trade agreement in 1958, after the
PRC had openly demanded that Japan commit itself to China's three
political principles—"no hostilities against the PRC, no involvement
in the two-China conspiracy, no hindering the normalization of Sino-
Japanese relations." Despite this temporary failure of people's diplomacy, informal mechanisms remained in place for the quick revival
and expansion of economic relations with China in the early 1960s,
eventually leading up to Sino-Japanese rapprochement in 1972.

Clearly, the Friendship Association aimed to shelter a wide range
of affiliations and constituencies under the umbrella term "people's
movement." Its commitment to further its aims through people's
diplomacy thus acquired different forms and meanings in different settings. Socialist and Communist Party politicians representing the Association's interests in the Diet presented themselves as the "voices of
the people" vis-à-vis the conservative establishment. Business people
who depended on trade with China and their political representatives
drew on the contemporary flow of private trade on a regional and busi-
ness-centered basis, as well as on the desire in financial circles to
reestablish China as a principal market for Japanese goods. Japanese
repatriates from China as well as Chinese residents in Japan could act
as the most direct ambassadors for Sino-Japanese friendship, precisely
because they personally bore the marks of Japanese hostility against
China. Perhaps most importantly, intellectuals and scholars, for whom

intellectual freedom was a concern, practiced a more direct form of people's diplomacy. As authorities on Chinese affairs, they were able to give the Japanese public an alternative view of contemporary China through lectures and the collection and distribution of documents that were otherwise unavailable. These four constituencies show one aspect of the Friendship Association's interest politics in relation to war memory in the postwar political arena.

Remembering Japanese Aggression

The Japan-China Friendship Association never failed to emphasize the centrality of cultural exchange in the process of building good relations between the two countries. These cultural activities nevertheless had clear political implications, not only because of the Association's favorable treatment of Chinese communism, but because of the prominence of cultural policy generally in diplomatic relations among countries all over the world. As Akira Iriye has shown, cultural internationalism became an urgent matter in the aftermath of World War II, reflected, for example, in the establishment of the United Nations Educational, Scientific, and Cultural Organization (UNESCO), whose 1945 constitution declared that "since wars begin in the minds of men, it is in the minds of men that the defences of peace must be constructed."[42] So widespread was the belief in the importance of cultural contact for the preservation of peace—perhaps especially among countries that had suffered defeat in war—that a West German Press and Information Bureau release could express perfectly the general aspirations of the Japan-China Friendship Association: "Through alliance policies, you win allies, through trade policies, business partners, through cultural policies, friends."[43] This could equally well have been the motto of the Japan-China friendship movement. The preface to a joint statement of 51 intellectuals in support of friendly cooperation with China in March 1952 defined "friendship" as "a question of civilization that becomes concrete through the introduction of cultures and the exchange of documents, literature, and ideas."[44]

From the early 1950s on, the Friendship Association collected Chinese printed and visual materials, including newspapers, magazines, research documents, photographs, art, and movies, and distributed them to publishing companies, schools, and its own members. Until March 2005 copies of these materials were collected in the Japan-China Friendship library, located in the Nitchū yūkō kaikan in Tokyo. Unlike the Association's political work, which was handled mainly by the central office in Tokyo, cultural activities were carried out predominantly on the prefectural and local levels. Local chapters were heavily involved in community work, creating public awareness about the PRC through lectures, movies, photo and art exhibitions, publications of war memoirs, and the distribution of Chinese-language books and magazines.

Much of this cultural activity took place under the rubric of the "movement never again to allow war between Japan and China" (*Nitchū fusaisen undō*) and focused on the commemoration of Japanese wartime aggression against Chinese people. This included observance of the anniversaries of the main war events on the Chinese mainland, in particular the Manchurian incident (1931) and the Marco Polo Bridge incident (1937), which were studiously ignored in the national press until decades later. Most of the war crimes memorialized by local Friendship Association chapters had taken place in Japan proper, however, and involved Chinese forced laborers and prisoners of war. These local organizations coordinated research into wartime incidents at mines, factories, or farms in 135 locations all over Japan, with the heaviest concentration in Hokkaido, and compiled exact data on the Chinese laborers who had worked and died there.[45] They began by collecting the remains of the Chinese dead and conducting Buddhist ceremonies to honor them before returning them to China in white boxes. The Japanese government apparently did not involve itself in such basic humanitarian work and left the bodies of these Chinese dead scattered in the fields near their workplaces. A gruesome photo of piles of skulls and bones near the Hanaoka mine in Akita Prefecture taken in November 1945 attests to this.[46] In addition to many small, local ceremonies, large commemorations were held in bigger cities. The first of these took place in April 1953 at the Honganji temple in Asakusa, Tokyo. In February of that year, the Chinese Victims Commemoration Committee had been set up to coordinate these activities. These were Buddhist ceremonies, whose rites were shared by Japanese and Chinese alike, at least in principle. As such, they formed an important contrast to the Shinto ceremonies usually employed for the commemoration of the

Japanese war dead. Later ceremonies, such as a commemoration held in Fukuoka in March 1971, included Korean and Japanese victims of wartime mining incidents as well.

Throughout the postwar decades, but especially from the 1960s through the 1980s, local Friendship Association chapters erected stone monuments all over Japan to commemorate Chinese victims of Japanese wartime aggression, to reflect on Japan's war responsibility, and to remind subsequent generations of the lessons of that war and the abuse of human rights in the name of imperialism and militarism. Many of these monuments seem to blend harmoniously into their park environs, bearing the characters for "Never again war between Japan and China" (*Nitchū fusaisen*) in front and a more detailed inscription in the back or on the sides. Some of these monuments stand out for their abstract designs. A five-meter-tall stone pillar commemorating the Hanaoka massacre was erected near the mine in 1966 and bears the characters for "growing tradition of friendship" (*hatten dentō yūgi*) on one side and "against aggressive war" (*hantai shinryaku sensō*) on the other, using Chinese, rather than Japanese, word order. On the back the inscription reads:

With the support of caring people from both Japan and China, we have erected this monument to friendship and never again to allow war between Japan and China. In 1944–1945, 993 Chinese, who had been brought here illegally under Japanese militarism, lived here in the Chūsan Dormitory at the foot of this mud-filled dam, abused and forbidden to speak their native language. On 30 June 1945, these laborers as well as those who wanted to protect the honor of their fatherland rose up as a group to at last oppose Japanese imperialism heroically. Here lie the remains of 418 people who gave their lives patriotically to this cause. We will forever remember this incident, our prayers never again to allow war between Japan and China chiseled into stone for the grandchildren of both countries.[47]

Although this inscription clearly places the responsibility for this human rights abuse on Japan and "Japanese militarism," it avoided an opposition between the Japanese and the Chinese people by including Japanese resisters to militarism among the "patriotic" victims murdered here.

The Friendship Association attracted the sometimes violent attention of those who interpreted their activities as politically motivated and in fact dictated by the PRC. Indeed, the American occupation forces themselves lashed out at the group in 1951 (the so-called *People's Daily* Distribution Suppression incident), when it arrested several members for distributing "communist propaganda." In the Nagasaki incident in May 1958, right-wingers burned the Chinese flag that had been displayed at a local conference to promote Japanese-Chinese trade and cultural exchange. Monument inscriptions that referred to Japan's war in Asia as unambiguously "aggressive" also invited vandalism. After a wave of popular protests against Japan swept China (and to a lesser extent Korea) in the spring of 2005, the Japan-China Friendship Association received threats from right-wing groups in Japan that made it cancel the annual meeting scheduled for late May in Awara, Fukui Prefecture, and switch to a new venue in Tokyo in November. According to the *China Daily*, managing director Yazaki Mitsuharu said in an official announcement that the Association could not guarantee the participants' and local residents' safety in the face of these threats.[48] This did not keep the Association from issuing a formal letter on 2 August urging Prime Minister Koizumi not to visit Yasukuni Shrine on the occasion of the sixtieth anniversary of the war's end out of respect for Chinese suffering at the hands of Japanese militarism during the war.

Unlike the Association of Shinto Shrines, the Japan Association of War-bereaved Families, and even the Japan Teachers' Union, the Japan-China Friendship Association made memory of Japanese wartime aggression a prominent part of its mission. It stood committed to the acknowledgment of Japanese war crimes against Asia and China in particular. What set the Friendship Association apart from other organizations concerned with war memory, however, was above all its shift in focus from the national to the international level and its belief in regional cooperation as the only way to a peaceful future. This regional focus was supported from various angles, including geographic proximity, economic necessity, cultural affinity, and ideological commitment. The Friendship Association regarded the Cold War split of Asia as reproducing the deeper and longer split separating Japan and China throughout modern history. At the same time, it recognized the displacement of this historically problematic relationship by the Cold War system and protested it as Japan's "second guilt," to borrow a phrase Ralph Giordano coined for postwar Germany (the first guilt being Japan's condescending attitude and military conduct toward China during the war).[49]

For at least three decades, Cold War divisions continued to define both Japanese and world politics, effectively marginalizing voices such as that of the Friendship Association. And yet the Friendship Association's view of Japan's war and postwar enjoyed an informal, unofficial public visibility that paralleled its political position in managing informal Japanese-Chinese relations. War memory that acknowledged and probed into Japan's war responsibility toward Asia was neither absent from Japanese public life nor actively silenced by a dominant, official narrative. If silencing mechanisms were in place, they did not appear to hinder the Association's extensive public activities—lecturing in schools, maintaining archives open to the public, or erecting memorials to Chinese victims of Japanese aggression. Rather, the Friendship Association's attempt to shift the parameters of public discourse from a national or trans-Pacific understanding of the war and the postwar to one centering on Northeast Asia did not muster the kind of political expediency necessary to challenge official policy under the Cold War system. Because so much of the Association's work appeared to be an advertising campaign for the PRC at a time when the majority of Japanese held deep suspicions of communism, the Friendship Association's work (and its rendition of war memory) had limited appeal. When the Cold War context gradually dissolved in the 1980s, Chinese-Japanese relations "naturally" took center stage, and the acknowledgment of Japanese war crimes in Asia found increasing public support.

Even though leaders of the Friendship Association stressed the grass-roots nature of their activities, they left no doubt that they aspired to positive governmental involvement. The goal, after all, was to change the government's foreign policy and restore official diplomatic relations with China. The phrase "people's diplomacy," as used by both the PRC and the Friendship Association, identified the Chinese people with their government but diametrically opposed the Japanese people to theirs. In other words, the Chinese people, adequately represented by their government, built friendly relations not with the Japanese government but rather with the Japanese people, who were represented (for the time being) by nongovernmental organizations such as the Friendship Association. Although the Friendship Association worked to close the perceived gap between the government and the people, it did so through democratic channels rather than by attempting a socialist revolution. Within the first few years after its establishment, it became a legitimate political pressure group officially affiliated with the Socialist rather than the Communist Party, and several members won election to the Diet. Moreover, it received support even from conservative financial circles for warning the government of the economic risks of losing the China market.

CHAPTER FIVE

Commemorative Pacifism:
The Japan Memorial Society for the Students
Killed in the War

In the fall of 1949, a student group at the Tokyo University Cooperative Press published a collection of testimonies by elite university students who had been killed in the war. Entitled *Listen to the Voices from the Deep* (*Kike Wadatsumi no koe*), the book became a bestseller that winter and a canonical text of Japanese pacifism in subsequent decades. It represented efforts by students returning from the war to inaugurate a student-run academic press independent of political parties and "progressive" in outlook. They shared a deep sense of nostalgia for learning nurtured by their experiences at the front and a feeling of personal guilt toward their peers who had not returned from the war. This sentiment was aptly expressed in a poem by the French philosopher Jean Tardieu (published in 1943), a call for an intellectual and moral pursuit of war memory from the point of view of the survivors: "Since the dead are not returning, / What are the survivors to understand? / Since for the dead there is no way to lament, / About whom and what should the survivors lament? / Since those who died cannot but keep silent, / Should the survivors do the same?"[1] The poem struck a chord: first used as the epigraph for the book, it also appeared in the opening shots of a 1950 antiwar movie based on the dead students' words (also entitled *Kike*

Fig. 5.1 Wadatsumi statue, Ritsumeikan University, Kyoto, 1953.
Used by permission of Mainichi Shinbunsha.

Wadatsumi no koe), and today it graces the homepage of a website dedicated to this brand of pacifist war memory.

The organization behind this activism, the Japan Memorial Society for the Students Killed in the War (Nihon senbotsu gakusei kinenkai, better known as Wadatsumikai), was established by intellectuals, students, and relatives of the war dead who came from Japan's elite universities, especially the imperial universities of Tokyo and Kyoto. It was born on 8 April 1950, following the commercial success of the book and in the broader context of Japan's coalescing peace movement and the outbreak of war in Korea. Wadatsumikai resolved to work for peace by keeping alive the memory of Japanese university students drafted into the war in December 1943, "whose priceless youth and lives were wasted and buried by war, who were robbed of their hopes and wishes by death."[2] This sentiment was symbolized by the "Wadatsumi statue" (Fig. 5.1), a bronze sculpture made in 1950 by the renowned artist Hongō Arata, a founding member of Wadatsumikai. The over-lifesized statue (2.24 meters high) represented a student-soldier, a young male nude in the style of Michelangelo—that is, with a clearly Caucasian physique. One fist is lifted as if ready to fight; the other hand is raised to his chin in a contemplative gesture, and his expression is quiet and

Fig. 5.2 Poster for the film *Listen to the Voices from the Deep* (*Kike Wadatsumi no koe*), 1950. Cover of
the booklet "Kike Wadatsumi no Koe" (1986). Courtesy of Wadatsumikai.

sad. This muscular figure conveyed health and youth as well as thoughtful sensitivity, all of which was wasted in war.[3] The statue was to represent the contradiction between fighting and studying, war and peace.
The head and face, however, were clearly aligned with the peace gesture, suggesting that even if the *wadatsumi* student-soldiers had lent their
bodies to war, their minds had remained pacifist.

A narrow cohort of people formed this so-called *wadatsumi* generation:
male students from Japan's elite academic institutions, who had been
around twenty years of age in 1943, thoroughly unprepared for life at
the front and unscrupulously used for Japan's last, and largely suicidal,
strikes against the Allies. The term *wadatsumi* was adapted from a phrase
in Saitō Mokichi's collection of classic poetry *Man'yō shūka*, much be-
loved by students during the war. Originally a hybrid of Korean and
classical Japanese,[4] the word *wadatsumi* referred to the spirits that appeared in different forms in the universe: the mountains, sea, water,
earth, fire, wind, and food.[5] After the war, *wadatsumi*, written in the *kana*
phonetic script and not in Chinese characters, came to mean specifically
the student war dead whose anguished spirits inhabited the air, sea,
and mountains and admonished the living to work for peace. To the

founders of Wadatsumikai—the teachers, surviving colleagues, and relatives who felt personal responsibility toward this generation of students—the *wadatsumi* student-soldiers represented the unspeakable suffering of war, the unforgivable waste of human life and potential by the militaristic state, and the inherent pacifism of the people.

This particular strand of memory resonated deeply with ordinary Japanese in the early postwar years. John Dower described their feelings in a chapter entitled "What Do You Tell the Dead When You Lose?"[6] The memory of the war dead, Dower wrote, was greatly complicated by the experience of defeat. "Defeat left the meaning of these war deaths—kin, acquaintances, one's compatriots in general—raw and open."[7] In the political fervor of the postsurrender era, individual and collective attempts to explain these deaths contributed significantly to the definition of emerging political platforms because widespread feelings of guilt and responsibility toward the dead could be appropriated in different ways. Shintoists and the war bereaved who felt alienated by the early occupation forces continued to justify these deaths in the name of the emperor and a national struggle against foreign imperialism. But many more embraced the postwar mantra of peace and democracy and reinterpreted their losses as giving birth to a new and different Japan. This was the tenor of Nanbara Shigeru's speeches as president of Tokyo University: he consoled the departed souls of fallen students by resolving to work for peace through academic knowledge to ensure that they had not died in vain. In founding Wadatsumikai as a *commemorative* peace organization, its leaders wanted to preserve the "purity" of this human urge to atone for lost lives (as opposed to a political ideology) as the basis for peace. To perpetuate this sense of personal atonement as a social value and reinterpret it within contemporary discourses became Wadatsumikai's political mission in the decades to follow.

In contrast to other political organizations, Wadatsumikai framed its vision for a democratic Japan in explicitly internationalist terms and resisted direct affiliations with political parties or large interest groups. Rooted in student unions and initially supported by the JCP-affiliated student organization Zengakuren,[8] Wadatsumikai used its personal connections to the war bereaved as well as its intellectual prominence to help launch Japan's peace movement. Yet it was not a union, a war-bereaved organization, or an academic study group but an institutional hybrid physically located on university and high school campuses and deeply concerned with the political aspects of student life. Although it drew strength principally from a tight community of academics from Japan's elite universities, Wadatsumikai nonetheless aspired to be part of a mass movement. Its ongoing search for an appropriate position in public life reflected both the changing public appeal of the pacifist-humanist strand of war memory and the changing patterns of popular participation in politics throughout the postwar decades. Wadatsumi-kai's reorganization in 1959 and reorientation in 1970 both coincided with major popular and student protests, although its leaders refrained both times from active involvement in the radical student movement. Organizationally and philosophically, Wadatsumikai embodied the communication and conflict between different generations, defined with respect to personal war experience and receiving their specific inflections from contemporary political issues and power constellations. Neither membership numbers (which never exceeded several hundred) nor representatives in the Diet but cultural productions for mass consumption paved Wadatsumikai's way to public visibility: books, films, plays, and other works of art. The group's intellectual leaders, well-acquainted with European and especially Marxist theory, developed more sensitivity to the capitalist market than to critiques of the "culture industry" such as Adorno and Horkheimer's. For them, the politics and the economics of pacifism were closely intertwined. By enthusiastically participating in the production and consumption of culture, they shaped and also reflected popular receptiveness to ideas about war memory and responsibility. Rather than a marginal or counter-memory, the history of Wadatsumikai commercially and intellectually anchored a progressive political agenda in postwar public life.

The Dead and the Living

I have unlimited love for my fatherland.
But I don't have a fatherland worth loving.
Like a ghost who has seen the abyss.[9]

The idea of organizing a peace preservation movement originated in—and remained closely tied to—the collection and editing of letters and testimonies by students killed in the war. *Listen to the Voices from the Deep,* the most successful of these books, had been preceded, in 1947, by a collection of writings by Tokyo University students entitled *In Distant Mountains and Rivers* (*Haruka naru sanga ni*), which went through three editions within the first year of its publication.[10] Nakamura Katsurō, a member of the student council at the university's medical school, had read an announcement in the university newspaper urging students to come forward with records of peers killed in action and, beginning with his own brother's testimony, decided to collect more. He was joined by his colleague Bekki Tatsuo, who had been deeply impressed by his encounters with other student-soldiers on board a ship from the Philippines to Singapore, on their way to different Southeast Asian battlefields. Together with other students, Nakamura and Bekki formed the Tokyo University Student-Soldier Memoirs Editorial Committee (Tōdai senbotsu gakusei shuki henshū iinkai) in the spring of 1947, with Nakamura as head, and heavily advertised their project on campus and on the radio in their hometowns throughout the summer. With the help of their professors, who contributed articles to make the text appropriate for classroom use, and assistance from several progressive publishing houses such as Ōtsuki shoten and San'ichi shobō, *In Distant Mountains and Rivers* appeared before the end of the year.[11]

Despite the volume's almost instant popularity, it generated controversies both among the editors and among readers. The book was meant as an antiwar statement and an antidote to any emerging nostalgia for wartime independence and heroism in the context of the Allied occupation. In his preface, Watanabe Kazuo, a professor of French literature at Tokyo University, had made it clear that even a hint of affirmative disposition toward the war would be detrimental in the context of Allied censorship. But others, especially younger students, expressed ethical concerns about the selectivity of the testimonies, the editing out of patriotic songs and statements supporting the war, the willingness to self-censor in light of American preferences, just as one had done during the war in fear of the Home Ministry. Looking back on the production of *In Distant Mountains and Rivers* in 1966, Yasuda Isamu and Odagiri Hideo recalled a roundtable discussion in the journal *Nihon hyōron* (Japan Review) shortly after the book's publication. Yasuda remembered how shocked he felt when all the students present claimed to have resisted the war. Instead of talking honestly about their war experiences, they simply voiced an opinion that had become "correct" after the war. Yasuda perceived this first collection of testimonies as an opportunistic, even slightly hypocritical, attempt to create an antiwar consensus after defeat, rather than an effort to bear witness based on "deep honest feeling." Odagiri Hideo, who was not himself involved in the production of the book but attended the discussion, had a different experience. At Hōsei University during the war, most students (himself included) had done their best to avoid the draft, but without open resistance to the imperial police unit (*kenpeitai*). The war experience substantiated their doubts, and in the aftermath of defeat they were able to formulate a critique through such publications as *In Distant Mountains and Rivers*.[12]

Criticism from a larger audience concerned mostly the exclusiveness of the collection, which featured only the testimonies of Tokyo University students, the top tier among Japan's educational elite. Nakamura Katsurō recalled that contributions from students at other universities were immediately stigmatized as second-class. A wish to remedy this problem while building on the book's popular appeal was behind the publication of *Listen to the Voices from the Deep*, which far exceeded the first volume in popularity and longevity. Although this project, too, was anchored at Tokyo University, the new editorial team included professors and students from different élite institutions who selected letters, poems, and other writings by student-soldiers enrolled in universities around the country. These records were not primarily meant as archival documents, preserving knowledge about life during the war or bearing witness to extraordinary events. Rather, they testified to the spiritual transformation of young men interpreting the world of war with the intellectual tools they had acquired at the university during times of peace. Their model had been a collection of letters by German student-soldiers in World War I, translated, published, and then blacklisted in Japan during the war, yet popular among students at the time.

In other words, rather than wrestling with the limits of the ability to communicate and represent wartime experiences for which there existed no intellectual framework, Japanese student testimony concerned itself precisely with "that older language of moral concern, that of civic humanism,"[13] and borrowed generously from European ideas, ancient and modern. The universalism of the *wadatsumi* voices, moreover, appeared to the editors extremely useful in attacking the specificity of Japanese militarism as a political and social structure of coercion. The testimony pitted (abstract) freedom of scholarship, idealized as bound neither by time nor by place, against the (concrete) horrors of physical battle. December 1943, when the government ordered thousands of university students to drop their pens and take up arms, marked for the student-soldiers the decisive moment when "peace" turned into "war," freedom—however compromised—into slavery. Rather than examining, as the Teachers' Union did, the political uses of education for militarist goals, the editors of *Listen to the Voices from the Deep* wanted to highlight the possibility, or rather imperative, of individual and collective resistance on the basis of learning, which, in its humanistic essence, was pacifist. The volume, then, sought to ground in popular consciousness the right to resist the call to arms as a fundamental element of a democracy.

By October 1949, when the book appeared in bookstores all over the country, the notion of pacifist resistance had acquired an immediate urgency thanks to a dramatically changing political situation. The optimism of the earlier collection, *In Distant Mountains and Rivers*, which occluded the existence of any pro-war sentiments, had turned into a gloomy pessimism, which saw Japan once again on the road to war in the context of Cold War rearmament. Both Professor Watanabe in his preface and Odagiri Hideo in his postscript pleaded with readers never to allow the human catastrophe of war to happen again. "The blood that was shed can never be atoned for except by ensuring that such blood is never shed again," Odagiri wrote.[14] As John Dower concluded from his reading of *Listen to the Voices from the Deep*, "there could be little doubt that it was primarily the Americans whom the compilers had in mind when they spoke of 'those who once again plot war.' Essentially, the pure and noble dead were being recruited anew to stand against America."[15]

Indeed, the enormous popularity of this second collection of student-soldiers' writings owed less to a new editorial vision than it did to the growing sense among the liberal left that Japan's democracy project was being abandoned in favor of a Cold War military buildup. The beginning of the Red Purge brought the emerging danger close to home, as many at the Tōdai student union were Communist Party members or sympathizers. The negotiation of a "partial" peace treaty with the United States and its allies to the exclusion of the Soviet Union and China fired much popular protest, particularly on university campuses by student activists and liberal scholars. The intensifying threat of an armed conflict on the Korean peninsula and pressures from the occupation authorities to build up Japan's police force made war once again seem an imminent possibility.

Within this political environment and encouraged by the commercial success of *Listen to the Voices from the Deep*, the editorial committee of the student union met with colleagues, students, and relatives of the student war dead on the Tokyo University campus on 8 April 1950 to establish their commemorative society for peace, Wadatsumikai. Peace groups were being organized all around them: the Peace Problems Discussion Group (Heiwa mondai danwakai) around Maruyama Masao was founded in January, and the Society to Preserve Peace (Heiwa o mamoru kai) in February. The latter would be reorganized into the Japan Committee to Protect Peace (Heiwa yōgo Nihon iinkai) in August. They all shared a sense of anxiety, even desperation over the political developments in 1950, expressed clearly in Wadatsumikai's prospectus of 11 March:

Today, again, we stand at the crossroad of war and peace as we hear talk about anticipating war day in and day out. We are reminded of the terrible killing fields [of World War II] and it has become the hope of the bereaved to preserve the feelings of the student-soldiers in every form. . . . With the publication of *Wadatsumi no koe*, the Tōdai cooperative union has laid the cornerstone of our commemorative society for the preservation of our humanity and the desire to actively contribute to the preservation of peace.[16]

The prospectus further established the responsibility of the living to the dead through historical inquiry and correct application of that knowledge in the present:

The dead are not far. We survivors know that well, and in order not to let [war] happen a second time, we must call for reflection. It is our wish to preserve peace on the basis of a deep understanding of, concern with, and courage to face the real terror of the war, transmitted to us by the bones of the dead scattered in the fields. We need to reckon with the reality of what exactly Japan's imperialistic war was before the Pacific War began. We need to confront the fact that people who understood the situation and informed others were silenced, while others closed their mouths voluntarily. That's the reality we have to learn about in order to make a commitment to peace.[17]

The proximity of war strengthened but also politicized the spiritual bond that the group of students and professors at the Tōdai student union had felt so strongly after defeat. Students were now clearly in the minority (14 out of the 65 organizers), followed by bereaved relatives of student war dead (21). The majority of the founding members were well-known scholars (all 30 were listed by name in the document), and most belonged to the same generation. Born around the turn of the century, many of them had been involved in prewar opposition movements,[18] studied abroad (in the United States, Western Europe, and even the Soviet Union), and moved into prominent academic or public positions after the war.[19] Almost all had graduated from Tokyo Imperial University in the humanities rather than the social sciences and ranged in their intellectual approach from Marxism to modernism. The historian Hani Gorō, the poet Nakano Shigeharu, the philosopher Ide Takashi, the novelist Sata Ineko, the sociologist Ōyama Ikuo, and the writer Miyamoto Yuriko (wife of JCP leader Miyamoto Kenji) actively worked for the JCP. Odagiri Hideo, Nakano Shigeharu, and Miyamoto Yuriko founded the Marxist literary society New Japanese Literature Society (Shin Nihon bungakukai). Hani Gorō and Mashita Shin'ichi were active members of the Teachers' Union; Hirano Yoshitarō and Ōyama Ikuo helped establish the Japan-China Friendship Association; Yoshino Genzaburō organized the Peace Problem Discussion Group (Heiwa mondai danwakai); and several others participated in other peace groups. They elected as president Yanagida Kenjūrō (1893–1983), a graduate of Kyoto Imperial University and philosophy professor at Taihoku University, who based his interest in historical materialism on a critical reflection on the war.

Clearly, at the time of Wadatsumikai's establishment, many of its active members were well-placed within the progressive intellectual and political community and even divided their time among several organizations. But perhaps the most important factor, generationally and professionally speaking, was that their students were sent to war and died while they themselves carried on their research at home. Wadatsumikai was founded on the basis of this shared sense of personal responsibility for the student war dead and the strong academic and political connections of its members. Its leaders rightly calculated that the latter were needed to gain a measure of public prominence for the former. And yet the vagueness of its pacifist humanism, the elitism of its claim to lead the masses, the changing politics on the left, and the lack of political representation in the Diet created organizational difficulties that forced Wadatsumikai to redefine itself several times.

Packaging the Wadatsumi *Voices*

Despite the prominence of social science language, whether Marxist or modernist, a simpler, more fundamental concept informed Wadatsumikai's message: the importance of communication. The phrase "voices of the student war dead" (*wadatsumi no koe*) served as the group's motto throughout the postwar decades, whether the emphasis lay on the voices themselves, their silencing during the war, listening to them in the present, or answering them from a contemporary standpoint. The "voices" were not limited to the Japanese war dead but could include those of Asians who had suffered Japan's wartime aggression, as in the admonition "Listen to the voices from Asia" (*kike Ajia no koe*).[20] In fact, continuous efforts at defining the *wadatsumi* generation by age, education, academic affiliation, social background, personal sentiment, writing ability, nationality, and recently even gender showed shifting and expanding meanings of war memory in changing political contexts. But the most immediate concern for Wadatsumikai remained the construction of an identification of contemporary youth with the *wadatsumi* student-soldiers, essentially a recreation of the sentiment that guided Nakamura Katsurō and his colleagues at the Tōdai student union in 1947.

At a time when the meaning of democracy was closely related to the massification of society and most political organizations strove to evolve into mass movements, cultural productions for mass consumption seemed to be the key to reaching public audiences. Accordingly, Wadatsumikai poured its energies into commemorative services for the fallen student-soldiers, the production of a movie about them, a play to be performed by students first in Tokyo and then around the country from mid-July 1950 on, and a musical composition that would "appeal to a nationwide public audience to raise the consciousness of all Japanese." The musical never materialized, and the proposed student peace commemoration hall, which was intended to promote Wadatsumikai and establish it as a corporation, still awaits realization after more than

60 years. By far the most successful publicity measure was the inauguration, in October 1950, of the newspaper *Wadatsumi no koe* (hereafter
Koe). The original idea had been to open the newspaper up "beyond
students' voices for peace and to include those of war widows, orphans,
workers, and representatives of all Japanese."[21] As it turned out, the
newspaper came to serve as Wadatsumikai's most important mouthpiece, while the collection of letters and the film became part of an
antiwar repertoire that generations of Japanese high school students
would grow up with.

In the spring of 1950, the Tokyo Student Theater Circle commis-
sioned a play based on the 1949 collection of letters, first performed in
December 1950. Concurrently, the Tōyoko film company made a film
based on the same materials, which was released in June (Fig. 5.2). Both
scripts were published in the summer of 1950 and attracted much publicity, paired with some criticism. To be sure, fitting such disparate and
deeply personal records into one storyline required a level of simpli-
fication and manipulation that rendered the film "idealistic, formalistic,
stereotypical, and unoriginal," in the words of the screenplay critic
Gosho Heinosuke, who otherwise welcomed the movie and its message.[22] Partly this was the result of a difficult compromise between
Tōyoko's producer, Sekikawa Hideo, who insisted on making a film that
could mobilize the masses at a time when war in Korea was imminent,
and Wadatsumikai's wish to bring out the philosophical aspect of honoring the dead students as war resisters.[23] More importantly, no one intended the film to be a serious work of art but instead a loud and clear
political statement—timeless in its basic ethics, yet timely given that the
Korean War began only days after its release. The message was not simply that war kills people, but that a fascist and militarist society sacrifices
its best and brightest by refusing to treat them as human beings. Taking
responsibility for oneself and one's fellow citizens meant resisting the
call to arms, futile under the war regime but all the more necessary in
the present. The preciousness of life and the imperative to defend it at
all costs was the lesson these students learned through their deaths on
the battlefield. Their experience admonished the survivors never again
to allow a political system that made resistance to war impossible.[24]

While the stage play focused on students' experiences at home and
the contradiction between their pacifist upbringing, their studies, and

the realities of everyday life,[25] the movie depicted Japanese troops—including several students and a Tokyo University professor—wasting away in the Burmese jungle toward the end of the war. The professor, a young scholar of French literature, is consistently humiliated, ridiculed, and maltreated by the cruel and thoroughly uncivilized commander of the troops but finds comfort in the company of one of the privates, who turns out to have studied with him. Together they reminisce about their lives at Tokyo University, their doubts about the war, and their goodbyes to loved ones. Although everyone suffers, physically and spiritually, their dialogues spell out the meaning of war and peace. Their specific kind of suffering, the pain of knowing that war was ethically wrong without being able to prevent it, defined a specific sense of war responsibility that in the summer of 1950 succeeded in firing a popular pacifism.

Yet apart from the film's extraordinary timing, its strategy—the foregrounding of the intellectuals' war experience against the uniform, repellant, and overly drawn-out depiction of the soldiers' utterly pathetic misery—did not necessarily allow easy identification with the student-soldiers. If, at the moment of death, most of the soldiers simply cried, "*Okaasan!*" ("Mama!"), the French literature professor lectured to himself and his student about the deeper meaning of the philosophy of Montaigne. Not surprisingly, much of the criticism centered on the audience's presumed personal identification with these Tokyo University intellectuals. One of the actors felt that, reading the screenplay, one could not readily empathize with the students without having oneself experienced such a war situation. Another wondered about the experiences of so many others who had not left written records and thus remained unrecognized. "Who was this war for anyway?" he asked.[26] Indeed, the movie did not make the slightest effort to place the war in any historical context and completely effaced the enemy against whom the troops were supposedly fighting. This gave it an unrealistic quality, but it also forced the viewer to consider the enemy within—the military itself—and the meaning of war and peace in terms of political repression and liberty.

Hongō Arata's monument to the student war dead, the "Wadatsumi statue," also created some controversy. The idea of creating a peace monument to the student war dead stemmed from a fascination with the European modernist and Soviet realist war monuments that had been erected mainly in the wake of World War I. An advertisement for the monument placed a picture of the Wadatsumi statue in the midst of a collage of photos depicting war memorials in Berlin and France, as well as one at the University of Vienna specifically commemorating its fallen students.[27] Surrounded by these different monuments, the Wadatsumi statue looked like a cross between Käthe Kollwitz's sculpture of a mourning mother and the triumphant East Berlin monument to Soviet soldiers proclaiming victory over Nazism. But another, Buddhist-inspired notion lay behind the statue. The student war dead needed a home to which their spirits could return, and since they were students, this place was to be a university campus, preferably Tokyo University.[28]

Wadatsumikai had planned to place the statue permanently in front of the Tokyo University library, a prominent spot indeed, but the university administration rejected the proposal. The administration argued that it was inappropriate to erect on campus grounds a statue that was directed to "the masses nationwide," since only objects directly related to education or the university itself had a place there.[29] Shortly thereafter, one official called Nakamura and explained that the university was trying to attract more women and that the representation of a nude male body was therefore inappropriate.[30] Worse, university president Nanbara Shigeru, who himself had honored the fallen student-soldiers, commented that "the statue would serve its aim better in Kudan," the site of Yasukuni Shrine, implying that the students belonged with the "honorable war dead" whom the Izokukai celebrated as national heroes. To be associated with the Izokukai added insult to injury for Wadatsumikai, for the student-soldiers represented the polar opposite of the Izokukai's departed heroes (*eirei*). "The student war dead are no *eirei*," Wadatsumikai countered, "they remained students to the very end . . . and they did not wish to die for their fatherland."[31] The real reason for the university's refusal to place the statue on its grounds lay in the administration's fear that it would become the symbol for the increasingly radical student movement, led by Zengakuren, with which Wadatsumikai was affiliated.[32]

The statue remained in Hongō Arata's atelier until it was transported to Kyoto in the fall of 1953 and formally unveiled at Ritsumeikan University on 8 December 1953, the tenth anniversary of the first student-soldiers' departure to the front. Ritsumeikan president Suekawa Hiroshi, a scholar of civil law who had himself seen students sent to the front in 1943, had personally asked for the statue to be placed on his campus and praised it as a reminder to the younger generation to preserve peace.[33] Less concerned about the politics of the student movement than his counterpart at Tokyo University, Suekawa had his own reasons for requesting the statue. Ritsumeikan University had been known for its rather enthusiastic cooperation in the war effort and, to avoid being closed by the occupation authorities, had to remake itself into an institution promoting democracy. Suekawa, who had a record of wartime resistance, was elected in 1945 to preside over the transformation and found the Wadatsumi statue as a symbol of peace useful indeed in promoting the university's new image. The statue remained at Ritsumeikan until its destruction at the hands of rioting students in May 1969; today, a replica is on display at the Setagaya Museum in Tokyo.

The Politics of Pacifism

In the context of the early 1950s, when many political organizations consolidated, radicalized, and became institutionalized within or outside the conservative establishment, Wadatsumikai quickly grew into a highly politicized peace group protesting against the draft and U.S. military bases and advocating self-government for students. This stormy first phase in its history, however, ended with the group's dissolution in 1958. Because of its members' strong ties to academic institutions, Wadatsumikai located itself at the intersection of the student and the peace movements. Both movements developed under JCP leadership and reflected the party's internal conflicts as well as tensions resulting from the JCP's changing position within a broad left-liberal coalition. But Wadatsumikai's leaders deliberately kept relations with the JCP loose and refrained from endorsing the party at election times.[34] Instead, they sought to create a mass movement both inside and outside the opposition mainstream, making use of the organizational energies of left-wing politics without being consumed by them. Given their multiple loyalties—to the academy, to students, to the war bereaved, and to JCP subgroups in constant flux—this approach produced more internal tensions than the group could withstand. Organizationally, Wadatsumikai straddled a generational, social, and ideological divide that appeared productive in 1950 but proved destructive eight years later. Nonetheless, in the early years, its mix of prewar and postwar generations, professors and students, intellectuals and workers promised to generate the kind of broad dialogue needed to let the voices of the war dead resonate with the concerns of contemporary youth. The success of its huge signature campaign opposing the military draft, participation at international peace conferences, and the easing of international conflicts in Asia around 1953 suggested that the politics of pacifism were working.

One overarching theme defined Wadatsumikai's activism in the 1950s: opposition to remilitarization as a national and international phenomenon. The Korean War amply testified to the danger of international military buildup and called to mind the specter of a World War III. The U.S. military bases, the consolidation of the Self-Defense Forces, and official attempts to reintroduce the military draft called for popular resistance to a government bent on repeating the mistakes of the past. Moreover, in the mid-1950s, Japanese fishermen were exposed to intense radiation during U.S. atomic tests on the Bikini atoll. This accident jumpstarted the antinuclear movement, which refocused Japanese pacifism around Hiroshima and opposition specifically to nuclear weapons. But especially in the early years, Wadatsumikai was more inclined to use these issues as a backdrop against which to mobilize a popular pacifist consciousness than to analyze the politics behind them. The experience of the *wadatsumi* student-soldiers called for a social mechanism that ensured a broad commitment to resist the decision to go to war, irrespective of the specific circumstances. Under the heading "War is not unavoidable," President Yanagida invoked the double fear of "losing one's son, husband, brother, relative, teacher, or loved one, and the fear of having to kill one's counterpart in a neighboring country." Only if students and youth were able to unite and lead a popular movement against war could this fate be avoided, not only for the sake of Japan's future but ultimately for world peace.[35] In sharp contrast to the Association of War-bereaved Families, Wadatsumikai attributed war not to a conflict of interest between nations or races, but to the oppression of the (pacifist) people by the (militarist) state. Likewise, the people themselves had the responsibility to resist the call to arms and refuse to participate in any way. The front page of *Koe*'s special issue on the general elections in the spring of 1951 featured a large socialist-realist image of a group of people throwing themselves against a cannon to hold it back. Below appeared three slogans in extra-large print: "Young people, don't take up arms! / Mothers, don't send your children to the battlefield! / Workers, don't make weapons!"[36]

To facilitate genuine cooperation among workers, students, intellectuals, and the general public, Wadatsumikai inaugurated its own "Peace Discussion Group" on 7 February 1951.[37] This group focused on international peace issues as well as national educational problems. At a time when Japan's remilitarization was a matter of intense public debate, Wadatsumikai especially targeted high school students, the next potential *wadatsumi* victims. Soon high schools became the core of Wadatsumikai's activism, with chapters at more than 200 high schools around the country. The newspaper *Koe* set aside space specifically for high school students' concerns and in turn informed its young audience about student peace activities in Japan and around the world. Short articles, an abundance of images, as well as advertisements for new books made the newspaper interesting and readable. Quotations and essays from famous pacifists in Europe made the Japanese quest for peace appear timely and fashionable—the Danish Nobel Prize winner Nils Bohr publicly denounced nuclear weapons, the French head of the International Peace Assembly organized worldwide peace activities, and the theologian Karl Barth of Basel University warned the German people not to comply with remilitarization. *Koe* reported from international peace conferences and youth peace festivals, printed photos of peace demonstrations in other countries ("We are young—let us live," "Remilitarisierung—ohne uns"), and borrowed freely from socialist-realist images of confident young women and men ready to stand up against oppression and to break their own shackles.[38] Slogans spoke directly to young people in a language that they could easily adopt and identify with:

Make the voices of all young people heard! Insist on your demands! / Then unite and fight to make them reality! / Fight for the right to live in peace![39]

I oppose the military draft and do not want to become a soldier! / I will not let a relative or loved one become a soldier! / I will regard a person who enforces the draft as an enemy of peace![40]

In the context of the Korean War, the conclusion of a peace treaty that excluded the Soviet Union and China, and the high-profile Asia-

Pacific Peace Conference in Beijing in the fall of 1952, the evocation of "Asia" became an appeal to conscience similar to the voices of the *wadatsumi* student-soldiers themselves. In June 1951, one year into the Korean War, Wadatsumikai campaigned for Japanese support of Indian prime minister Nehru's peace proposal by appealing to a sense of guilt for Japan's prewar and wartime conduct in Korea. "The Japanese people (*Nihon minzoku*) once oppressed the Korean people, and in order to atone for this crime, we must stand for peace and happiness for our neighboring brethren; but above all, shouldn't we set everything else aside and thoroughly embrace [the peace] proposal?"[41] The same issue of *Koe* reprinted excerpts from testimonies about the horrors of air bombardment from Korean POWs and civilians as well as a letter to an American soldier who had died early in the war. The following issue featured a long letter by a Chinese junior high school student recalling the subhuman brutality of Japanese soldiers against Chinese civilians toward the end of World War II (he was eight years old at the time).[42]

As with the *wadatsumi* students, voices of conscience and of admonition made themselves heard through letters and testimonies and told of personal tragedy and individual reckoning with those experiences. While the victims' voices were concrete and immediate, the victimizers (the Japanese "militarists" and American "imperialists") remained remote and faceless. Testimonies from war, past and present, were meant less to inform readers about the atrocities of war than to recreate for young people the emotional outrage and urge to "work for peace" that had inspired the *wadatsumi* survivors to found their movement. They focused on generating a kind of public-personal engagement through identification with the victims. But this approach suffered, one might say, from too much memory and too little history. The conflation of victims and perpetrators, the neglect of political in favor of purely military war aims, and the absence of a sustained critique of popular cooperation in the war effort deprived the *wadatsumi* strand of memory of an adequate historical foundation. In their eagerness to reach "the masses," the Wadatsumikai intellectuals relied on the viability of the political moment rather than the increase of knowledge.

After 1953, when military conflicts in various parts of Asia neared their conclusion, the *wadatsumi* message gradually lost its distinctiveness and became subsumed by the emerging antinuclear movement and escalating student demands for self-government. In addition to national student organizations, Wadatsumikai supported and cooperated more actively with large interest groups, such as the General Council of Trade Unions (Sōhyō), the Teachers' Union, and others, judging from the increasing number of high-profile articles by the presidents of these organizations in *Koe*. The Japan-China Friendship Association co-sponsored an event in November 1954 in which a Chinese antiwar activist at Ritsumeikan University discussed the Wadatsumi statue explicitly in light of Japanese war atrocities in China and the need for Japanese-Chinese friendship. A two-page feature on Premier Zhou Enlai and an article on a recent semi-official mission to China followed in the same issue, touting the Friendship Association's slogan "Japanese-Chinese friendship is the guarantee for peace in Asia."[43] By the mid-1950s, however, the issue of constitutional revision began to form the center of Wadatsumikai activism as reflected in *Koe*, supported by the student and antinuclear movements, the group's organizational legs. Government attempts to override the education reforms of the occupation era and to amend Article 9, the peace clause, brought into sharper focus the situation of the students facing the draft in December 1943. Lacking the immediate context of war, Wadatsumikai leaders gradually withdrew from large-scale demonstrative pacifist activities, held more frequent member conferences, and began to reflect more critically on the parallels between wartime and postwar "fascism" and their own place relative to the past and the future.[44]

In sum, the first phase of Wadatsumikai's history saw a failed attempt to create a mass movement through special interest politics. Born out of the Cold War divisions of 1950, it was ultimately consumed by them. The students and professors at the Tōdai student union who saw an opportunity to convey their brand of commemorative pacifism to the public within the charged political atmosphere of the early 1950s would later find that the subsequent institutionalization of left-wing politics contradicted the humanist basis of their message. Reflecting back on this first phase of their organization in the early 1990s, Wadatsumikai leaders criticized the "vicious circle" Cold War logic of being forced to pledge allegiance to one of two opposing sides. This "easy left-wing peace-movement stereotyping" did not allow for a pacifism based on critical war memory but instead made it a tool of leftwing politics. But the main problem, from a 1990s perspective, concerned the lack of real historical reflection and criticism of the war, of Japanese colonialism and aggression, and especially of the role of the student-soldiers as active participants (that is, perpetrators) in the invasion of Asian countries.[45] Indeed, the term "war responsibility" did not appear in *Koe* until the founding of the second Wadatsumikai in 1959, when the group began systematically to explore the history and culture of wartime society that had produced a war spirit that very few could escape. In their eagerness to show wartime resistance based on an inherent pacifist disposition, they circumvented their own war responsibility, that of the intellectuals. In their zeal for internationalism and universal values, they missed an interpretive opportunity to critically consider nationalism, ethnic inequalities, and gender differences.

Nonetheless, Wadatsumikai was instrumental in building Japan's postwar peace movement, which has continued to command an impressive political presence. The group located itself where the peace and the student movements overlapped and participated in politics through public statements of protest, signature campaigns, and its influential journal. But it did not establish itself as a political interest group negotiating affiliations and sending representatives to the Diet. Instead, Wadatsumikai became Japan's foremost organization specifically dedicated to the intellectual pursuit of war memory and postwar responsibility. Committed to keeping *Kike wadatsumi no koe* on the reading list of high school students generation after generation, a special committee continued to revise the collection and publish new editions with large commercial publishing houses. (The most recent one appeared in 1995, of which an English translation is now available.)[46] Nationally and locally organized symposia and seminars on contemporary and historical topics brought scholars, students, and activists together on a regular basis and often resulted in monographs. And the periodical *Koe* became a scholarly journal that is widely read and respected in intellectual circles to the present day.

Wadatsumikai offered an important counterpoint to the anchoring of the war bereaved as a social group in right-wing politics, represented by the Izokukai. It delivered the most comprehensive critique of the emperor system in the 1970s, when the Association of Shinto Shrines campaigned for the revival of prewar aspects of the imperial institution.

It remained deeply involved in educational issues alongside the Teachers' Union but separated itself from the JTU's political strategies. Finally, Japan's problematic relations with other Asian countries slowly emerged as an important issue in Wadatsumikai's activism. Overall and irrespective of the specific issues discussed, however, the discourse on war memory and responsibility that unfolded in the pages of *Koe* showed a particular interest in Germany, especially the postwar German left. Because Wadatsumikai's pacifism rested on philosophical exploration as well as on a politics of personal identification, Germany—as a "nation of thinkers" with a history of extraordinary wartime crimes—offered important parallels. The use of Germany in the Japanese debate as a way of drawing attention to the problem of war responsibility became very popular in the 1980s but had to a large degree already been anticipated in *Koe* decades earlier. In various ways, Wadatsumikai designed its political agenda around the interpretation of contemporary political issues explicitly in light of the memory of and responsibility for Japanese militarism.

PART II

The Political Dynamics of War Memory

CHAPTER SIX

War Memory and Generational Change:

Refashioning Special Interests

Changes in the generational makeup of interest groups' constituents represented perhaps the first perceived challenge to the way memory operated in politics in the second postwar decade, roughly from the mid-1950s to the mid-1960s. Particular memories of the war, which civic organizations had defined for their respective constituencies during the Allied occupation, needed to be appropriately transmitted—or newly justified—to a younger cohort of members without personal war experience. Herein lies a critical link between the early history of the five organizations discussed in Part I and the subsequent decades, when these groups positioned themselves at the forefront of struggles involving war memory *directly* and *publicly* within a diversifying landscape of civic political activism.

The impact of generational change and conflict in the construction and transmission of war memory was perceived especially strongly by organizations of the war bereaved, which tended to articulate their special interests on the basis of personal relationships to the wartime past. The Izokukai in 1960 established a youth section for war orphans (*iji*), who were put in charge of trips to World War II battlefields in Okinawa and the Asia-Pacific region to collect the remains of the war dead and perform commemorative ceremonies for their "divine spirits." An independent youth organization, the Japan Youth Group to Collect

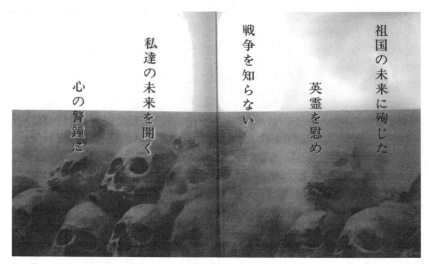

心
の
警
鐘
に

私
達
の
未
来
を
開
く

戦
争
を
知
ら
な
い

英
霊
を
慰
め

祖
国
の
未
来
に
殉
じ
た

Fig. 6.1 Motto of the Japan Youth Memorial Association, 1967. JYMA, *Ima, nani o kataran*. Courtesy of the Japan Youth Memorial Association.

War-Dead Remains (Nihon seinen ikotsu shūshūdan) was formed seven years later explicitly to recruit university students to collect war remains everywhere in Asia; it worked closely with both the Izokukai and the Health and Welfare Ministry. Renamed the Japan Youth Memorial Association (JYMA), it published detailed annual reports on its activities. The inside cover page of these annual reports bore an image of smoking skulls with a poem that captured the sentiment behind this memory work (Fig. 6.1): "Consoling the divine spirits of the war dead / who gave their lives for the future of the fatherland— / Let us ring a bell in our hearts / to open the future for us, who don't know war." In sharp contrast, the pacifist group Wadatsumikai, which embodied cross-generational discourse on war memory, experienced the turmoil of generational conflict in the late 1950s and again a decade later, when its own student members destroyed the group's symbol, the Wadatsumi statue at Ritsumeikan University (Fig. 6.2).

The Changing Temporality of the Past

This chapter shows how responses to perceived political and social changes in the late 1950s and early 1960s anticipated the diversification of public memory activists from the late 1960s on, even as leaders of

Fig. 6.2 Student riots in May 1969 left the Wadatsumi statue smashed (right) and group leaders struggling to assert the original purpose of their organization. Used by permission of Mainichi Shinbunsha.

established groups aggressively reasserted their own original agendas. Much of the memory debate at that time took place *within* these organizations rather than *between* them. It revealed two critical aspects of the memory process: the ever-changing demands of the contemporary present upon interpretations of the past, and the increasing diversity of each organization's custodians. Indeed, this was a "refashioning" of special interests, now in response to both the changing temporality of the past and the changing social reality of the present.

It is well known that Japanese society underwent tremendous changes in the first postwar decades, especially with the onset of high economic growth. For postwar memory in particular, not only was the present changing, but the past itself changed with it. The definition of the past grew more complex as time passed, layering evaluations of Japan's postwar developments on top of memories of the war years. In the process, war memory and postwar responsibility became closely intertwined in the imagination of those who were critically invested in Japan's postwar democratic project. It was precisely because the stakes had been so high in the years of democratic rebuilding following wartime defeat that changes over time mattered so much. And because interest groups had constructed a specific war memory for their respective constituents in the early postwar context, this memory was in need of an update once the context had changed sufficiently.

This dynamic subsequently became an integral and ongoing part of how memory functioned in postwar politics. In the late 1950s, however, when the leaders of civic organizations first became aware of the profound changes in public culture, it hit them as a new challenge that demanded a substantive response. Discursively, judging from the groups' periodical publications as well as the mass media, the troubling complexity of postwar Japan's rapidly changing society was captured in phrases such as "generational change," which could be embraced, and "generational conflict," which had to be preempted or, later, reckoned with. Structurally, some civic groups attempted to incorporate—and domesticate—these rapid contextual changes by creating subdivisions within their organizations. Others saw no solution other than to dissolve the original group and rebuild it along different lines.

Group leaders perceived the changing temporality of the past and the present in terms of numerous challenges that they felt compelled to deal with. One important change was political. Within the constitutional and international boundaries set by the Allied occupation and the peace and security treaties of 1952, Japan's political system had yet to congeal on its own terms. But regained independence and national sovereignty also opened up the terrain for critical reevaluations of various occupation reforms and defined consolidating political platforms in important ways. Conservative bureaucrats and politicians, many of whom had built their careers during the war, returned to political prominence in the early 1950s and promoted policies designed to reduce what they perceived as too radical a break with wartime structures. The intellectual and political left, decimated by the Red Purge, was, if anything, intent on widening the break with the wartime past. This dynamic gave structure to a political polarization in which war memory played an intrinsic and important role.

By the mid-1950s, constitutional revision, especially proposals to abolish the "peace clause" (Article 9) and raise the status of the emperor, had become the single most divisive issue in Japanese politics under Prime Minister Hatoyama Ichirō (1954–56). This was the context in which postwar Japan's so-called two-party system (also known as the "1955 system") emerged. Early in 1955, Socialist Party factions reunited to form the Japan Socialist Party (JSP), followed shortly thereafter by a similar merger of two conservative parties—the Liberals and Democrats—into the Liberal Democratic Party (LDP). This institutionalization of conservative hegemony and socialist opposition came to characterize the postwar political landscape in important and lasting ways, a legacy not exactly of war but of postwar struggles over the meaning of war, defeat, and foreign occupation.

Well-established interest groups on the left, such as the Teachers' Union (JTU) and the Japan-China Friendship Association, pushed into permanent opposition, began to revise their political strategies especially vis-à-vis the Communist Party (JCP). For the JTU, this led to the emergence in 1958 of a moderate faction, the so-called Miyanohara Line. It eventually won the leadership in 1962, moved the Teachers' Union away from overt political struggles, and restructured it around an emphasis on its members' economic well-being. The Japan-China Friendship Association responded to political changes not only in Japan but also in China. The PRC's first successful nuclear bomb test on 16 October 1964 greatly complicated the Association's assertions that the Japanese government alone was to blame for the rift in Sino-Japanese relations, and that the PRC had fully embraced peace and anti-imperialism as a legacy of World War II. Still, the Friendship Association was able to issue a statement just eleven days later essentially endorsing the PRC's argument that it needed nuclear weapons to defend itself against the United States, a situation that lent particular urgency to a speedy rapprochement between China and Japan.[1]

Organizations on the right, such as the Association of Shinto Shrines and the Izokukai, found that their increasing proximity to the conservative power center certainly gave them a competitive edge in the LDP's pork-barrel politics, yet it did not smoothly translate into the kind of state sponsorship of their interests that they sought. Their search for greater political effectiveness in turn revealed divisions among their own constituents, which group leaders met, largely successfully, with a mixture of organizational strategies and renewed ideological fervor. It was during the second postwar decade that a variety of "postwar resolution" measures (*sengo shori*)—primarily related to the belated compensation and welfare of Japanese victims of the war—made their way onto political platforms and into legislative chambers, further highlighting the "special interest" nature of war memory. The Yoshida cabinet had reinstated government aid to wounded veterans and war-bereaved families as soon as the occupation ended in April 1952, and it resumed pension payments the following August. The subsequent push for compensation legislation, however, was led by groups such as war widows and war orphans, repatriates from former Japanese colonies, dispossessed land-lords, and especially atomic bomb victims, who demanded *special* state recognition not only for their wartime suffering but also for their post-war contributions to rebuilding.[2]

In part, war victims' groups competed with one another over the enlarged pot of social welfare funding made available by the economic growth of the 1960s. The greatest number of postwar compensation laws were in fact passed during this time. But the intense lobbying of organizations such as the Association of Shinto Shrines and Izokukai in the late 1950s and 1960s is perhaps better understood as part of an ideological project that their particular memory of the war called for: the restoration of the type of state sponsorship that they had enjoyed during the war but lost in the sweep of early postwar democratic re-forms. If status as a special interest group was necessary to survive the Allied occupation in the case of the Shintoists and war-bereaved fami-lies, the time had come a decade later to merge these interests once again with those of "the state."

Another important change was demographic. Social scientists have produced a host of statistical profiles and ethnographic portraits that attest to the dramatic impact of postwar recovery (and later high eco-nomic growth) on population movement and social group formation in the 1950s and 1960s. Likewise, civic organizations that had formed in response to defeat and the need to mediate specific aspects of social and political dislocation, wrestled with demographic changes, geograph-ic as well as generational. For example, the Izokukai had originally formed as a self-help organization for the war bereaved, especially war widows. A decade later, both the urgency that had informed this pur-pose and the social cohesion of local war-bereaved groups had greatly diminished. The Izokukai leaders' decision at the end of the occupation to reorient the main organization toward state lobbying for highly po-litical and ideological purposes only heightened the effects of this trend by widening the gap between the central leadership and the prefectural and local constituencies. By the latter 1950s, then, Izokukai leaders had introduced a new "social welfare" component to their campaigns, this time focused not on the war widows but on the orphans. This can be read as an attempt to reconstitute a particular strand of memory endowed with social, political, and ideological messages that spoke to changed circumstances.

Perhaps the most complex change lay in the social consequences of economic high growth and material affluence. When these were compounded by government efforts to deflect political conflict in the aftermath of high-profile struggles over the U.S.-Japan Treaty and a bitter coal strike, civic groups on the political left as on the right sensed an increasing public indifference to special interests formulated around particular war memories. Yoshida Yutaka and others have long argued that the economic miracle eclipsed the discourse on war responsibility in the 1960s.[3] More accurately, high growth *transformed* public memory of the war. Civic groups whose special interests lay in reproducing a specific link between past and present tended to respond to this challenge actively. On the one hand, leaders turned their attention inward, toward fostering unity around war memory; on the other hand they targeted the state directly (both the governing LDP and the bureaucracies) in an aggressive pursuit of their political interests. This removed debates on war memory and responsibility one step further from the wider public and only reinforced the thoroughly political nature of this issue.

Mirroring conservative responses to social change in both West Germany and the United States at the time, these groups offered their critiques of the present political situation as an obvious outcome of the preceding postwar developments, which had failed—from various points of view—to generate meaningful lessons of war and defeat. The Association of Shinto Shrines, for example, in 1961 blamed a "JTU–dominated" education system for the generation gap that had produced not only left-wing student riots, but also right-wing terrorism, as seen in the assassination of Asanuma Inejirō, chairman of the JSP, by a seventeen-year-old rightist in 1960. These twenty-year-olds, claimed an article in *Jinja shinpō* (the newspaper of the Association of Shinto Shrines), had grown up without developing a set of core values focused on Japan's national essence—a base that only the public practice of Shinto could provide.[4]

Paradoxically, accusations of youthful indifference to the wartime past overlapped with a much-discussed "history boom" in the second postwar decade, which reached a climax in 1968 with the Meiji centennial. The unprecedented output of war memoirs beginning in the latter 1950s, as well as a spate of popular films about World War II, suggested that the entertainment value of war history threatened to displace debates about the political "lessons" learned from the war and represented by interest politics. Although the commercialization of memory was not exactly new at the time, such uses of war memory appeared to take on a life of their own, posing further challenges to the political organization of war memory.[5] The history boom, according to an editorial in the August 1965 *Asahi shinbun*, revealed the Japanese public's desire to discover its ethnic distinctiveness within the universal trajectory of modernity.[6] These personal histories reached popular audiences searching for positive identities, not serious inquiries into war history and responsibility, or historical critiques in the Marxist or modernist tradition. To be sure, interest groups could draw on such popular productions of memory insofar as they illustrated some of their concerns. But more often than not, the popular media of memory ignored rather than promoted special political interests.

Finally, the political, demographic, and social changes that civic organizations felt compelled to address in the second postwar decade were not Japan's alone but contributed to a broader change in public culture that followed similar trajectories in Western Europe and America. From the mass-mediated celebration of domestic life and private memories in the 1950s to the politics of the student and counterculture movements that seemed to grip Paris, Berlin, Berkeley, and Tokyo all at once in the late 1960s, individual as well as organized participation in public life took on different forms, which themselves became objects of contestation, and on a global scale. In terms of memories of World War II, this change in public culture has conventionally been characterized as a shift from "silence" in the 1950s (an "inability to mourn," as the title of a famous psychological study by Alexander and Margarete Mitscherlich proclaimed)[7] to bold critiques as part of a violent generational conflict in the latter 1960s. While this may be too stark a contrast, the public language in which people cast their memories of the war took on a very different coloring. Personal remembering was more widely and more deliberately invoked for public and political purposes, just as international and domestic political changes brought different memories into public view.

The shifting discursive presence of memory in turn was reflected in the great proliferation of citizens' groups involving themselves in political activism in a rather spontaneous, eclectic, and largely nonideological manner, and in the public consciousness of a real or at least potential global reach for such activism. In Japan as elsewhere, these broader changes in public culture were most often conceived in generational terms. Yet long before the "younger" generation discovered war memory as a language of protest, the older generation of civic leaders, those of the established organizations surveyed here, seized upon what they termed the "correct" transmission of (their own) war memory in an effort to maximize their continued public presence.

The Emergence of "Generational Memory"

Against this background of a changing present and past, organizations—especially those of the war bereaved—invoked "generations" as largely imagined communities through which to grasp, and control, new challenges. The concept of generational cohorts was perhaps most widely used to capture competing views of past and present in the context of demographic change, both by the war memory organizations and in the wider public discourse.[8] As early as 1945, writing in the literary journal *Kindai bungaku*, Honda Shūgo distinguished between three generational cohorts whose experiences of war and ultranationalism differed significantly. Of the three, it was the Shōwa "single-digit" generation (those born between 1926 and 1934) who were to enter public discourse as a benchmark against which subsequent generations were measured, for they came to represent the human bedrock of postwar reinvention and recovery.

Indeed, the interest groups' use of "generation" as a tool to understand the transmission of memory over time was as pervasive as it was undifferentiated. With little variation, discussions simply pitted the "war generation" (*senchūha*) against the "postwar generation" (*sengoha*)—that is, those with personal war experience against those without. The "prewar generation" (*senzenha*) received much less attention, except in the context of determining legal responsibility. This generational discourse was about agency in the production and consumption of memory, not about concrete war experience. For by the late 1950s, not only had the audience changed, so to speak, but the producers were a more diverse lot, bringing potentially different perspectives to bear on the rearticulation of the explicit links between the past and the present. Quite concretely, this had much to do with the necessities of organizational life, such as maintaining a viable membership, training new leaders, and formulating new visions to adjust to changing times.

Two groups in particular, the conservative Izokukai and the liberal-intellectual Wadatsumikai, confronted the question of intergenerational transmission of memory directly in the second postwar decade. As organizations whose constituencies included relatives of the war dead, they had formed "communities in mourning" in the immediate postwar years, albeit from different standpoints. Izokukai leaders founded their organization on bereavement as a "social condition," whereas Wadatsumikai based its activism on grief as a "state of mind," to replicate a distinction Jay Winter made in the context of collective mourning in Europe in the wake of World War I.[9] This difference largely determined the manner in which each organization approached the dynamics of memory as a collective enterprise. The former treated the condition of bereavement as an organic link connecting the living with the dead in a way that affirmed both as part of the same continuous social whole. The latter, in contrast, embraced grief for the fallen students as a subjective sentiment of the historical witness—the students' contemporaries—and used it to cultivate a collective commitment to political change. Both organizations thus combined specific political goals with their desire to reproduce themselves as organizations of the war bereaved whose memberships and messages were in danger of erosion with changing generations.

For all their political and structural differences, they also had much in common. First, by the late 1950s, both groups had come to articulate the organizational challenges they faced primarily in terms of generational change, and both defined generational cohorts as communities centered on particular social, intellectual, or political experiences. Second, against the background of the unfolding Security Treaty revision crisis of 1960, they emphasized the "correct" transmission of war memories in an effort to define their organizational and ideological structures in new ways. Third, both Izokukai and Wadatsumikai sought to close the generation gap by defining their own special interests as important criteria of citizenship and nationhood.

If war memory served special interests in the early postwar years, when many of these organizations were formed, its reproduction became an ideological project in the following decade. At the center of this project stood real and imagined generational communities, even when "the state" was increasingly targeted as the locus of public memory. At the end of the occupation, when Japan regained its sovereignty yet the proximity to the war was still a reality of everyday life, the "young generation" embodied the promise and hardship of the "new Japan." In 1951 Izokukai's bi-weekly newsletter *Izoku tsūshin* reported that Prime Minister Yoshida had honored a seventeen-year-old country girl who had lost her parents to the war and struggled to make ends meet and get an education for herself and her three younger siblings. "You are our hope," Yoshida told her, indicating that young people who had not been directly involved in the war would rebuild Japan.[10] Similarly, the monthly journal *Wadatsumi no koe* (named after the collection of student-soldiers' letters) in 1952 called on its readers to "listen to the young students," who knew better than to follow their wartime counterparts' example, and to resist Japan's remilitarization.

By the late 1950s, however, the once-promising young generation presented a "social problem" to the Izokukai, and Wadatsumikai even broke up over the politics of the student movement. In both cases, a putative "postwar generation" embodied the changing temporality of the past as it was perceived by organization leaders, who began to define organizational interests in terms of their memory of the first postwar decade and not only the war itself. Izokukai President Takahashi Ryūtarō introduced a "war orphan policy" in November 1958 to rectify the institutional neglect of the "young generation," who had grown up at a time of great turmoil after the war, and to ensure that they would "inherit correctly" the spirit of the main organization. Welfare issues concerning the children of bereaved families had until then been handled exclusively by local chapters under the auspices of the women's section, and had been limited to the establishment of a scholarship fund in 1952. While education remained on the agenda, finding employment for youths coming of age in the late 1950s gained urgency, as did their integration into the political life of the organization. The fundamental spirit of this venture, Takahashi explained, was that "we come together as an organization to think about the various obstacles the war orphans must confront as students and as members of society, and to make space within our organization for communication between the old and the new generations. This is critically important to Izoku-kai's future."[11]

Tanaka Tadao, a reporter for the literary magazine *Bungei shunjū* writing in *Izoku tsūshin* in June 1959, explained "today's youth problem" in terms of a loss of "traditional authority" after the war, by which he meant quite concretely the absence of fathers in war-bereaved families and more generally the weakening of state authority under postwar democracy. As a result, young people had grown up without real authority figures either in the home or in society. Moreover, Tanaka projected the generational divide he perceived in 1959 back onto political divisions revealed in early postwar debates about building the "new" Japan. "Adults were able to keep cool heads and think deeply about the situation of defeat, while young people flung themselves into the turmoil without listening to the reasoning of the adults." Far from faulting the younger generation, however, Tanaka argued that this lack of adult guidance stemmed as much from the difficult circumstances under which war widows had had to raise their children, who therefore "had grown up deprived of maternal attention and love," as it did from postwar education, which rendered the war dead not honorable but meaningless.[12]

As a remedy, Tanaka recommended frequent visits to Yasukuni Shrine to instill into these troubled youths a positive sense of their fathers' accomplishments, despite their deaths and Japan's defeat. Rather than trying to make youngsters intellectually understand the logic of the wartime regime (i.e., the Greater East Asian Co-Prosperity Sphere)—and run the risk that they would criticize it—he suggested passing on memories through what Paul Connerton called "habitual bodily practices": namely, commemorative rituals at Yasukuni. "The most important way we can work for our people (*minzoku*) is to make it a custom to report to the spirits of the dead in our families. This spirit of connecting with the war dead is not something our children should understand intellectually; instead, it is important to pass it on from body to body, to make it a physical practice."[13]

Certainly more appealing, if not more effective, than this type of top-down admonition were the social profiles of prototypical war orphans, usually girls, which proliferated in the column called "Young People's Window" (*Wakōdo no mado*) on the back page of *Izoku tsūshin* at that time. For example, a fifteen-year-old junior high school student from Iwate Prefecture seemingly came to represent the experiences and aspirations of a whole generation of war-bereaved children in her auto-biographical piece "For a Peaceful World without War." She had been born as the youngest of four children right before her father was killed in action. Never having actually known his face, she built up a beautiful image in her dreams based on the stories her mother had told. She felt deeply grateful to her mother, who had raised her and her siblings alone grieving for her lost husband. Until the middle of sixth grade, she thought that her father must surely be alive somewhere on earth, but now she understood that he had sacrificed himself for the country and the people. She was enraged to live in a society that did not care about what it meant that her father died in service to the country. "Friends comment on how great it is to have a father killed in action because you get money from the state. Even adults consider me lucky compared to those whose fathers had died of illness and did not receive pensions." She, on the contrary, was convinced that her father had been a strong person who—like all the other war-dead fathers—had really wanted to live but "died for peace." "We need to quickly build a great society in which my father's wish is realized [i.e., a peaceful world without wars] and my mother gets a little happiness," she concluded, and setting up networks of communication and cooperation among the "one million war orphans" was a step in the right direction.[14] Both Izokukai leaders and student members thus participated in the deliberate construction of a new and allegedly shared social identity particular to the war orphans coming of age in the late 1950s.

For Wadatsumikai, by contrast, the generational division centered instead on the political and intellectual identity of the cohort who had lived through the war and found their own memory interests usurped by the politics of the student movement. Students had been prominently involved in Wadatsumikai's campus-based chapters from the start. At that time, a common interest in remembering the student war dead and resisting the military draft had minimized generational and political differences among faculty, the war bereaved, students, and campus administrators. Over the course of the decade, however, as the war grew more distant and domestic political struggle took on more institutionalized forms, differences in interests and style of political protest between the group's constituencies became harder to reconcile. The peace and student movements shifted their activism in ways that paid lip service to the memory of the war but focused exclusively on the failures of postwar democracy. Wadatsumikai's original message of commemoration and mourning became all but irrelevant to students mobilizing against administrative hierarchies and even to the antinuclear movement, which came to life in the aftermath of the Bikini fishing boat incident on 1 March 1954. Clearly, in the second half of the 1950s, memory of the student war dead and the politics of pacifism were no longer the ambitious pair they had been, and the resulting gap among activists, political interests, and styles of public protest increasingly became articulated in generational terms.

Tokyo University's forced closing of Wadatsumikai's head office on its campus in February 1955 marked this development conspicuously. The move was designed to weaken student organizations opposing the administration; instead, it effectively eclipsed Wadatsumikai's leadership, several of them Tokyo University professors.[15] As a result, many founding members and intellectual leaders of the group turned away from public activism and instead debated—in closed academic circles— the problem of their own *postwar* responsibility as intellectuals. Mashita Shin'ichi and others joined progressive social scientists, philosophers, and critics around the Science of Thought Research Group (Shisō no kagaku kenkyūkai) to address and resolve the problem of war responsibility at a time when this appeared no longer to be a public concern. Meanwhile, students active in various local chapters took over the publication of the newspaper *Wadatsumi no koe* and turned it into a voice of the student movement, campaigning against nuclear war, military bases, constitutional revision, and education policy, with few, if any, references to World War II and the *wadatsumi* student-soldiers.

One perceptive article by a *wadatsumi* study group at Hiroshima University, however, captured Wadatsumikai's "uniqueness" among left-wing groups in terms of its inherent tension between the memory of those who had lived through the war and the memory of contemporary students who had not. In commemorating the student war dead, the article argued, the "war generation" (the founders of Wadatsumikai) relived their own personal experiences, while the new generation of students had initially been "swept along by the sincerity of the intelligentsia's passionate love for the lives and the knowledge of the student war dead and for the responsibility that this entailed in the present." Yet the young students experienced the fate of the student war dead as an unfortunate burden, even a threat to their future, and took away from it no more than a commitment to resistance and accusation. Now that the memory of the war was disappearing fast and student interest in the war dead was waning, the article concluded, it was all the more important that Wadatsumikai not confine itself to the student movement but actively engage those who had lived through the war.[16]

The generation gap alluded to in this contribution from a local chapter became the fundamental guideline for Wadatsumikai's reorganization in 1958–59 around members of the *wadatsumi* generation (i.e., contemporaries of the student war dead), notably Yamashita Hajime (1920–), Yasuda Takeshi (1922–86), and Hashikawa Bunzō (1923–83). In a handwritten message officially closing its newspaper in October 1958, the standing committee attributed the group's difficulties to student politics that had usurped *Koe*'s original purpose as an organ of remembrance.[17] A year later, in his preface to the new edition of *Listen to the Voices from the Deep*, Odagiri Hideo rendered the generational war-memory gap as a broad social phenomenon, laden with imminent dangers but also unique opportunities:

During the course of the past decade, Japan experienced a very real transformation, especially with regard to the lives of the younger generation. The readers [of *Listen to the Voices from the Deep*] ten years ago were young students whose memories of the war were still vividly engraved in their hearts and indeed on their bodies. . . . But today's younger generation, which grows larger every year, remembers the war only in fragments or has faint recollections from childhood. We interact with increasingly large numbers of young people who do not have realistic images of the war, a real feel for the pain and cruel destruction it caused, or a sense of the sheer human breakdown that the war brought about.[18]

Rather than simply lamenting this lack of understanding on the part of the younger people, Odagiri drew upon it to recreate—within the context of the antinuclear movement and the impending Anpo crisis—the sense of urgency that had pervaded Wadatsumikai's establishment in 1950. "So far, nobody has thoroughly analyzed the recent war or has shown evidence of really understanding its relevance, for that matter. Rather than merely dealing with each individual's personal memories, we urgently need to excavate the whole nation's general experience of the war. That way, the memory of the war can transcend any so-called generation gap and become something truly societal." Most importantly, Odagiri imbued the young with an opportunity, even a calling, to contribute to a politically responsible memory precisely because of their distance from the war. "Precisely because they have no personal wartime experience, today's younger generation has a unique opportunity to raise the war experience to the level of an ideology—and is indeed required to do so. Our job is to examine many individual experiences of the war closely without being personally overwhelmed by them."[19]

The discursive focus on generational change served as a catalyst for recontextualizing war memories as organized political interests in the late 1950s, when those interests had acquired a (postwar) history of their own. It is important to recognize, however, that this entailed neither an actual generational change among organization leaders nor a substantial reassessment of war memories themselves. Rather, both Wadatsumikai's and Izokukai's efforts at reorganization to address the coming-of-age of the "postwar generation" suggest the changing *function* of war memory in public life. No longer purely in the service of building a better future, particular memories of the war now served to critique the *postwar* past. The concern with the transmission of memory to a younger generation in effect reasserted the continued validity of earlier memory interests and the original leaders' prerogative to define the "correct" lessons and legacies for their respective constituencies.

The Anti–Security Treaty Crisis

The call by organizations such as Izokukai and Wadatsumikai for recentering war memory in postwar politics found an almost uncanny and certainly dramatic counterpart on a national scale in the extraordinary events of the anti–Security Treaty (Anpo) crisis in the spring of 1960, when Prime Minister Kishi Nobusuke forced the renewal of Japan's treaty with the United States through the Diet despite massive opposition. This treaty, originally signed in 1951 in conjunction with the San

Francisco Peace Treaty, bound Japan to the United States in a Cold War military alliance and guaranteed the latter the use of military bases in Japan, thereby effectively qualifying Japan's independence with respect to its foreign policy in the region. The issue of revision and renewal of the treaty, however, became almost synonymous with Prime Minister Kishi, whose authoritarian leadership style—and personal history as an accused war criminal—compounded public distrust of his larger political agenda.

The spectacle of mass protest demonstrations against the treaty's renewal in front of the Diet building in Tokyo and in large cities around the country suggested, to many, the fragile and contradictory nature of postwar democracy. Indeed, the Anpo crisis was understood not primarily as an issue of foreign policy but instead in terms of domestic power relations. Generally ignoring the historical condition of foreign occupation as an essential catalyst for the development of postwar democracy in Japan, protesters rallied against the LDP's autocratic governing style as a dangerous continuity from the wartime past. This was a crucial aspect of the political relocation of war memory at this time. Veteran leaders of early postwar movements on the liberal left, who had organized around political interests based on particular war experiences in the late 1940s, were able to mobilize an impressively large sector of the Japanese public around the problem of Japan's wartime past, however schematically conceived. Their experiences of heightened political activism had engaged—indeed bridged—two very different historical contexts: whereas the earlier discourse on war responsibility had unfolded in the midst of material devastation and under foreign military occupation, the 1960 demonstrations took place against the background of economic growth and relative material comfort under a domestic democratic government. According to Wesley Sasaki-Uemura, "The Anpo generation comprised people who had direct experience of the war . . . saw the sudden transformation of their leaders into 'democrats' with the coming of the occupation after the defeat," and then witnessed "many of the same prewar government figures . . . return to power."[20]

The protests became massive, however, precisely because they caught the imagination of students and young people, who had no war experience but great concerns about contemporary society. Prominent among the organizers were members of the radical student organization Zengakuren. For a few weeks in May and June 1960, generational, class, and gender divisions appeared negligible as "the people" rose *en masse* against "the state" in an effort to take "democracy" into their own hands. Despite their efforts, the revised Security Treaty was signed and ratified, and even though Kishi Nobusuke was forced to resign shortly afterward, the government remained firmly in conservative hands. Moreover, the broadly public engagement with memories of the war and their relevance in contemporary politics dissipated as quickly as it had formed, seemingly usurped by a drive toward economic high growth under Ikeda Hayato's new leadership. For the leaders of the Anpo generation, however, the experiences of both successful mass mobilization and political failure called for a reexamination of their own place in postwar politics, which focused their attention once again on the problem of war memory and generational change.

There is no doubt that the historical memories of the so-called war generation played a significant role in the anti–Security Treaty movement, in terms of both mobilizing politically entrenched opposition groups (such as the JSP and the trade union group Sōhyō) and inspiring spontaneous citizen activism (for example, Tsurumi Shunsuke's Voiceless Voices, or Koe naki koe no kai).[21] How, then, did the crisis, as it unfolded in May and June 1960, affect civic organizations that had long been at the forefront of negotiating particular war memories on the terrain of postwar Japanese politics, and on opposite ends of the political spectrum? Neither Izokukai nor Wadatsumikai participated in the movement in an official way, although some of their members did as individuals, particularly in the case of Wadatsumikai.[22] Both groups experienced the crisis as a particular challenge for their respective organizations— coinciding as it did with their own efforts at restructuring—and both related it to perceived generational divisions among their constituencies. While Izokukai leaders remained almost entirely silent on the anti–Security Treaty movement, focusing steadfastly on the establishment of their youth section, Wadatsumikai embraced the struggle (and its aftermath) as the terrain on which to construct an organization that would assume intellectual leadership in making the Japanese public politically responsible with regard to its wartime past.

To be sure, Wadatsumikai emphatically supported the Anpo protesters' resistance to a treaty that implicated Japan in the United States' military objectives in East Asia. Moreover, the group certainly embraced the principle of active popular resistance to government authoritarianism precisely because of the fateful absence of such opposition in wartime Japan. The anti–Security Treaty struggle, like the Korean War ten years earlier, provided exactly the kind of crisis context in which Wadatsumikai's message of memory and antiwar commitment had an immediate public resonance. In 1960, however, the core issue for Wadatsumikai as an organization related less to its particular brand of commemorative pacifism than to its mode of public engagement in the context of a national crisis. At stake was not only the memory of the war experience but also the memory of Wadatsumikai's antiwar activism during the previous decade, which had rendered unsatisfactory results. According to Yamashita Hajime, the new Wadatsumikai no longer saw itself as an activist group of antiwar protesters allied with the student peace movement but strove to be an independent, nonaligned group of individuals, mainly intellectuals and students, tied together by a desire to define, analyze, and transmit the lessons learned from the *wadatsumi* tragedy, or, in Ueda Yūji's words, the *wadatsumi Idee*.[23] Within the context of the anti–Security Treaty crisis, this meant that Wadatsumikai refrained from participating in the People's Alliance, which employed highly confrontational tactics at demonstrations in front of the Diet and elsewhere.

Instead, leading members held a symposium (as they would annually in mid-August for the following nine years)[24] on "An Intellectual Pursuit of the War Experience" (*sensō taiken no shisōka*), which sought to link the Anpo and war experiences within the same historical continuum. The intellectual historian Yamada Munemutsu carefully laid out the agenda for this symposium as an attempt to frame Wadatsumikai's particular standpoint on war memory in terms of "how the Japanese live and think at the crossroads of the fifteen-year war and the fifteen years of postwar development."[25] The inherent tension between "thought" and "experience" gave this approach to memory its creative edge, according to Yamada, for it validated one's subjective experience of the war as a product of a particular ideological framework, which could then be analyzed (and criticized) as a historical phenomenon from an "Anpo"—that is, postwar—point of view. In many ways, this line of inquiry picked up and refocused the 1956–57 debate about war responsibility, which had centered

on the intellectual task of establishing analytical categories for an investigation of "war responsibility" and ended with a plea for more rigorous
historical research into actual wartime conduct as a means to critique
postwar trends.[26] Not surprisingly, key participants in this debate, including Maruyama Masao (1914–96), Hidaka Rokurō (1917–), and Tsurumi
Shunsuke (1922–), had experienced the war as young adults and were
prominent leaders in the Anpo movement; Hidaka and Tsurumi were
instrumental in shaping Wadatsumikai in the 1960s and beyond.

The emphasis on intellectual pursuit (*shisōka*) and experience (*taiken*),
which were to preoccupy Wadatsumikai's discourse for some time after
the Anpo crisis, brought the issue of generational memory to center
stage. The topic itself was the brainchild of the new Wadatsumikai leadership around Hashikawa Bunzō, Yamada Munemutsu, Yasuda Takeshi,
and Sugi Toshio—all established intellectuals who belonged to the so-
called *wadatsumi* generation, contemporaries of the student war dead.
Their desire to excavate the ideological structures within which they
themselves had experienced (or failed to resist) the war effort, as well
as the experiences that later led them wholeheartedly to oppose it, was
driven by a phenomenological sense of the past—namely, their own
self-consciousness (or subjectivity) as historical witnesses. Although
"intellectual pursuit of the war experience" defied clear definition even
among the participants, the topic was surely premised on the idea that
responsible war memory was anchored in individual, existential experience of the war and was meant to enlighten others who lacked such
experience. This emphasis on witness history provided an obvious link
to the events of spring 1960. The Anpo struggle validated the highly
affective—even "bodily"—experience of witnessing history in the making and prominently included students in this community of witnesses.
For example, mourning the Tokyo University student Kanba Michiko,
who died in a clash with riot police on 15 June, gave renewed meaning
to the testaments of the elite student-soldiers collected in *Kike Wadatsumi no koe*.[27] Hosaka Masayasu, in his 50-year history of *Kike Wadatsumi no koe*, judged the collection to have "biblical" status among protesting students in 1960.

It soon became clear, however, that the intellectual discourse envisioned and promoted by the Wadatsumikai leaders included younger
members as *students,* not colleagues, consistently identifying them as lack-

ing in experience rather than offering valuable perspectives of their own. Koyama Hiromitsu, a student member reflecting on the anti–Security Treaty movement, was struck by the generation gap that had opened up within Wadatsumikai between the "war generation," who used the struggle to promote their own "complacent insider" discourse about the war experience, and the "postwar generation," who tried to learn about the wartime past in order to make sense of their Anpo experiences.[28] The student members wanted to break up the older "community of contrition"[29] in order to open up the question of war responsibility both conceptually and practically to a broader audience. At Wadatsumikai's fifth student conference on 30 June 1960, they called for clarification of the "postwar generation's war responsibility" as a logical consequence of belonging to the same ethnic or national community—as opposed to having experienced the war "in one's own body and soul."[30] "National responsibility" (*minzoku sekinin*) did eventually become an important topic, but in the context of Anpo, "generation" emerged as a central aspect of Wadatsumikai's philosophy of war memory, not simply as a sign of the change in times. All participants in this debate were clear about that, however different their standpoints.

Organizations on the political right such as the Izokukai tended to keep a lower profile during the anti–Security Treaty crisis than those affiliated with the opposition. The few comments on the Anpo struggle that did appear in the pages of *Izoku tsūshin* suggested that the leadership regarded the Security Treaty renewal as a necessary evil, the student protests as a genuine threat to democracy, and Kishi's handling of the situation as inept and unfortunate.[31] Instead of getting involved, they looked to foster favorable relations with the incoming Ikeda cabinet. Nonetheless, like the Wadatsumikai students, Izokukai youth articulated a pervasive perception gap between the generations as they worked to secure a measure of control over their own youth organization, then under construction. This division was potentially more threatening to the overall political goals of Izokukai as an interest group than was Wadatsumikai's generational conflict because the war orphans questioned some of their organization's core ideological principles. On the eve of the Anpo crisis, in August 1959, 131 youth leaders from across the country convened for three days to debate their aspirations for a youth organization and voiced an astonishing degree of intellectual independence, perhaps bordering on heresy in the eyes of those committed to wartime nationalist ideology.

Izokukai youth leaders, not unlike their Wadatsumikai counterparts, insisted on the validity of their own standpoint on matters such as "patriotism" and "peace" and found the central leadership's take on these issues "surprisingly ignorant." In an open letter to Izokukai vice-president and Lower House member Aizawa Hiroshi, they attacked the leadership's vision for the new youth section's role within the organization—especially Aizawa's stated goal of organizing the youth section around "the spirit of patriotic martyrdom" (as stated in the Izokukai's 1952 charter). The war orphans felt pressured, the letter asserted, into simply adopting such loaded concepts; officials made no attempt to re-examine their meaning from a contemporary perspective. At the August convention, youth leaders generally agreed that their overall goal was to work for peace in a way that negated prewar aspirations and instead thoroughly reflected postwar sensibilities, to make Izokukai a full-fledged peace group working to "preserve eternal peace among humanity" and on this basis to connect with peace organizations worldwide. They ranked "peace" above "patriotism," which turned out to mean different things to different people and represented the greatest source of friction between officials and youth leaders. A 24-year-old public employee said: "'Patriotism' and the 'spirit of our honorable war dead' (*eirei*) are dead words for our generation. They have no appeal. . . . How does one think about the subject of patriotism? Fathers who lost their children and children who lost their fathers think differently. Does the country exist for our benefit or do we exist for the country's benefit?"[32]

Echoing such doubts, a twenty-year-old company employee asserted, "Today, patriotism and morals are considered reactionary, as if they were acts of opposition. . . . But my type of patriotism is in sync with our present times and is not the same as the patriotism of the 'Great Imperial Japan.'" A twenty-year-old student then linked this rethinking of patriotism with the overall goal of world peace: "The highest form of patriotism is one that extends from the individual to the nation (*minzoku*), from the nation to humanity, and from national peace to peace in the world. For that, one needs to have an independent sense of self and to value the spirit of the honorable war dead from the standpoint of humanity."[33]

These voices bespeak a desire to take memory of the war dead beyond the confines of organic relationships of bereavement and allow those who grew up after the war to formulate new and politically more relevant interpretations for themselves. Although this cannot be directly attributed to the Anpo movement *per se*, the context of mass political protests and the prominent place of students in them had an impact both on the self-consciousness of Izokukai youth leaders and the central leadership, who immediately stipulated "no political involvement" (in national politics) for the youth section charter. Such rare surfacing of dissent in *Tsūshin*—first on the eve of the Anpo crisis and later when the Vietnam War intensified—draws attention to the politics of internal control and the need for monitoring the changing dimensions of war memory with regard to contemporary political interests.

The national crisis surrounding the renewal of the U.S.-Japan Security Treaty in 1960 not only brought back memories of war and the inadequacy of postwar reforms; it also revealed competing views along generational (and not only political) lines about the function of such memories in public life. In the wake of Anpo, those in leadership positions opted to protect their established memory interests rather than renegotiate them on a volatile political terrain. The successful reorientation of popular energies away from political protest and toward economic high growth in the aftermath of the Anpo struggle—easily the crowning accomplishment of the Ikeda administration—tended to conceal the essentially conservative efforts of organizations such as Izokukai and even Wadatsumikai to manage the "correct" transmission of memory along special interest lines.

Managing the Transmission of Memory

After more than two years of deliberation, it was clear that the main leadership of the Izokukai had succeeded in establishing the youth section in its image. The opening declaration on 4 December 1960 reflected a sense of great instability—even historic change—that more likely described those who had built up the organization since 1947 than those coming of age in 1960. It also reproduced, phrase by phrase, the key points of the 1952 Izokukai charter: to promote "peace, prosperity, and love for their fatherland" by upholding "unwavering reverence to the spirits of the two million war dead" and vowing "to honor peace as the last wish of our fallen fathers."[34] Organizationally and financially, the youth section and its various local chapters depended on the Izoku-kai headquarters in Tokyo, which stipulated that the youth section "advance the main organization's goals and cooperate with its activities as young people preparing to become the next generation of Izokukai leaders." Accordingly, the youth section committed itself to "honoring the spirits of the glorious war dead," which meant above all active participation in the campaign to bring Yasukuni Shrine under state management.

Nothing illuminated the place of the new youth section within Izo-kukai as well as their main practical task, inaugurated in April 1961: leading expeditions to Okinawan battlefields in order to collect the remains of fallen soldiers and conduct commemoration services. These trips had been going on for ten years already, coordinated by the Health and Welfare Ministry, but now youth section representatives from each prefecture were put in charge of this emotional ritual of remembering the war dead—their fathers. For several years, the youth column in *Tsūshin* featured countless reports from Okinawa with titles such as "I found my father's bones!" (*chichi no ikotsu ga atta*). The youth section's commemorative activities in Okinawa began with the inauguration on 30 April 1961 of a peace monument to soldiers who died there, attended by young leaders from all prefectures. Later that year, on 23 June, the sixteenth anniversary of the end of the Battle of Okinawa, Okinawa Prefecture officially announced an annual observance of a prefecture-wide holiday to console the dead and pray for peace.[35]

Leading up to the twentieth anniversary of the war's end, the Association's youth section celebrated its fifth year with a motorcade "parade" that lasted seventeen days (22 July to 7 August) and spanned the whole country. One motorcade left from the north (Hokkaido) and another from the south (Kagoshima), carrying banners with the message "Never make war orphans again!" (*futatabi iji o tsukuru na*) through towns and villages until they met up in Tokyo. (The slogan clearly resonated with the JTU's "Never send our students to the battlefield again" and the Japan-China Friendship Association's "Never again war between Japan and China.") The purpose of the parade was officially "to praise the divine spirits of the war dead as the cornerstone of contemporary Japan's prosperity, and to appeal broadly to the people to build a peaceful Japan and strengthen the youth section organization." In general, the Izokukai youth section was much more explicitly engaged in peace activities than its mother organization, and it actively sought to nurture connections with Asian and international youth groups.[36]

In June 1967, the Japan Youth Group to Collect the Remains of the War Dead formed to work in tandem with the Izokukai youth section and the Health and Welfare Ministry. Their first trip was to Peleliu, Palau, in 1968, followed by other Pacific island chains and Southeast Asian countries, especially Burma, and in the 1990s Siberia and Mongolia.[37] They edited large photo collections showing the preparations for these trips (including anatomy lessons), excavation sites, and piles upon piles of burning skulls and bones as commemoration services were performed, with a Japanese flag in the background. There was also ample evidence of adventure and leisure for these students as well as friendly interaction with and humanitarian aid for local people. Indeed, the many pictures of Japanese posing with local residents created the impression that these young people were not only engaged in patriotic activities in faraway places but also working to further international goodwill and provide clean water and basic health services. Given the extraordinary geographic space that the Japan Youth Group (now known as JYMA) covered, one is tempted to think of a re-creation of the Greater East Asia Co-Prosperity Sphere on a semi- or non-governmental level.[38]

The central leadership of the Izokukai, however, also sought to shape an ideological consensus across the generational divide with a heavier hand. As part of the fifteenth anniversary of the Izokukai's establishment, the central office published two monographs "for the enlightenment of future generations" in 1962: a volume documenting the fifteen-year history of the organization and an edited collection of first-person writings by its members entitled *Ishizue* (Foundation).[39] The latter is a fascinating document illuminating the construction of a collective social memory of the war bereaved from many private memories of individual suffering. Tellingly, it is centered on women—the war widows and mothers of the young generation coming of age in the 1960s. President Kaya Okinori (1889–1977) wrote in the preface to the book:

It is indeed impossible to read without tears the dramatic, graphic autobiographies of the bereaved, who have gone through such unimaginably difficult times over the past fifteen years since they lost their relatives—the war dead, who bravely sacrificed their lives in the hopes of achieving eternal peace for our country. . . . We hope that . . . this publication will make a positive contribution to the betterment of the social and spiritual lives of the war bereaved and the future of this country at large and please the spirits of the honorable war dead.[40]

A committee of ten Izokukai officers (six from the women's section, three from the youth section, and a standing director of the central Izokukai as chair) selected 84 essays, 5 poems, 47 songs, and 8 haiku out of some four hundred entries for this project. The selections had to satisfy the following criteria: vivid descriptions of the human qualities of the war bereaved and their pride as relatives of the war dead; a beautiful sense of their loyalty to their country, memories of the dead, and profound respect for their spirits; and detailed accounts of the difficulties of life after the war and their financial, social, and emotional recovery.[41] The result was an exceedingly sentimental book of memories that celebrated the organic bond between the war dead and the war bereaved as a cycle of self-sacrifice and reciprocal gratitude: if the war dead had sacrificed themselves for those who survived, surviving mothers had sacrificed themselves for their children, who then owed gratitude "all the way down." *Ishizue* illustrated compellingly the values at stake in the cult of the war dead.

At the fifty-fifth meeting of the board of directors in February 1960, the central leadership also sponsored a committee to investigate questions about these values raised by youth leaders. The resulting report, published about the same time as *Ishizue*, set down clear ideological guidelines, defining patriotism, the "ethos of the honorable war dead" as it informed the conduct of the war bereaved, the country's contemporary situation, and the need for a new postwar order.[42] According to this report, patriotism manifested itself in the individual sacrifice (including giving one's life) necessary to keep the country safe and at peace, and in the country's (and its citizens') grateful response to that sacrifice. The "ethos of the honorable war dead" as the philosophical and ritual link between sacrifice and gratitude therefore stood at the center of patriotism.

The report then addressed political change over time as illustrated by the different (alien?) political ideology introduced by the occupation.

"Patriotism" in this context provided stability, the core value through which to understand and adjust to changed circumstances without having to start from scratch each time. Distinguishing between prewar patriotism and postwar patriotism therefore made little sense; instead, it was important to be aware of what connected the two across 1945: the "manifestation of the departed war heroes" (*eirei no kenshō*).[43] The committee report addressed "measures toward war-bereaved youth" specifically in this context and urged them to "take seriously their special task of understanding the meaning of the military dead through the memory of their own fathers, to come to a consensus on this, and to build a new order in which their knowledge fits the present times." For this purpose, the youth section needed to be an integral part of the main organization and realize its responsibility to understand, substantiate, and promote the goals and activities of the main Izokukai.[44]

The appointment of Kaya Okinori as president of Izokukai in August 1962 further consolidated the power of ideological hardliners within the main organization, which grew into a full-fledged political pressure group under his leadership. Kaya's illustrious career in public service straddled the 1945 divide in particularly conspicuous ways. A graduate of Tokyo Imperial University, he served as finance minister in the first Konoe cabinet (1937–39) and under Tōjō (1941–44), and became directly involved in military affairs as president of the North China Development Company and as officer for the war bereaved in the Military Protection Agency. Under the occupation, Kaya was put on trial as a Class A war criminal, found guilty on five counts of overall conspiracy and waging war against China, the United States, the British Commonwealth, and the Netherlands, and sentenced to life in prison. Along with almost all surviving Class A war criminals serving prison sentences, Kaya was released in 1955 and resumed his political career three years later as an LDP member of the Lower House of the Diet. Reelected five times, he also served as minister of justice in the second and third Ikeda cabinets.

During Kaya's fifteen-year term as president of Izokukai, the Association led an aggressive political campaign to bring Yasukuni Shrine under state management. Though ultimately unsuccessful, this campaign united the women's and the youth sections around common goals, and the generation issue apparently faded as a point of controversy. Nonetheless, debates about restructuring the youth section to prepare it for future leadership positions surfaced in 1965 and especially in 1968, when Kaya and the women's section president, Nakai Sumiko, called on the war orphans to model what it meant to be "healthy citizens of Japan"— in contrast to the student radicalism on display at Sasebo and Haneda airport.[45] There can be little doubt that the central Izokukai leadership employed measures of ideological coercion in its effort to address the inevitable generational change among its own constituents. Molding new leaders in the image of those who first established the Izokukai was clearly the objective. This strategy evidently worked well in securing the organization a highly influential position on the political right.

Wadatsumikai, as an intellectual group on the opposition left, found itself in a very different position. Managing the "correct" transmission of war memory to a younger generation presented challenges of a different nature insofar as the epistemological problem of generational memory was embedded in its discourse about war experience and postwar responsibility. The old group leaders' insistence on an intellectual history of the war experience hardly solved the "generation gap" so evident to all. But the participation of those without direct war experience certainly added a conceptually important dimension to the discourse on memory—namely, the medium of narration in the understanding of "experience." Student groups at various universities focused intensely on the testaments collected in *Kike Wadatsumi no koe* and proved to be more sensitive to the mediating quality of these texts as texts than were the contemporaries of the fallen student-soldiers, who could not get over the tragic nature of these deaths and thus perpetuated an overall sense of victimization.[46]

The problem of generational identity in the construction of a pacifist memory of the war only grew over the course of the decade, for it was intertwined with at least three separate issues: the status of the war bereaved in the group, the intellectual challenge of conveying life experiences to those too young to appreciate them, and student demands for a politically more committed and socially less exclusive organization. These concerns attest to the uneasy coexistence of openness to the conceptual problem of generational memory on the one hand, and privileging the consciousness (or subjectivity) of the historical witness over contemporary political activists on the other. The Wadatsumikai leadership was certainly not oblivious to the diverse opinions of its members concerning new directions for the organization's activism after the Anpo crisis had subsided, as a detailed survey conducted in January 1961 suggests.[47] In his analysis of the questionnaire, Hashikawa Bunzō frankly admitted that the leadership's insistence on refraining from political involvement in a situation as threatening and intense as the anti–Security Treaty struggle was simply inadequate.[48] Subsequent political crises such as the Vietnam War would elicit a more explicit political engagement.

Ultimately, however, in the context of the student movement at the end of the decade, the generational fault lines tore Wadatsumikai apart once more. In May 1969, rioting student members destroyed the Wadatsumi statue, which had made its home on the Ritsumeikan University campus in Kyoto, after a falling out with the leadership over its refusal to support them in their battle against university administrations.[49] If the *wadatsumi* student-soldiers could not be invoked against repressive university policies, the student section protested to Wadatsumikai's leaders, how did their deaths differ from traffic casualties? "If the central Wadatsumikai aspires to be a mass movement, it cannot treat the masses as fools but must expose the aggressiveness of the Japanese economy."[50] According to Odagiri Hideo, a prominent leader of both the first and the second Wadatsumikai, the students considered the statue to be "theirs" because it represented the group's original endorsement of radical political activism, for which they realized they had longed in vain. Needless to say, the Wadatsumikai leaders, most of whom had helped found the movement in 1950 as well as reestablish it in 1959, understood this as the failure of their vision for the second phase of the organization and voiced exasperation over the generation gap that separated them from contemporary students. If anything, the students' action only confirmed the founders' stance against this type of political engagement. They nonetheless reorganized for what became known as Wadatsumikai's "third phase," which focused throughout the 1970s on a critique of the prewar and postwar emperor system and produced some pioneering scholarly work.[51]

The smashing of the Wadatsumi statue sent a minor shockwave through the progressive public via the mass media. Regardless of its specific impact on Wadatsumikai as an organization, the spectacle of university students toppling "their" symbol of pacifism and resistance against co-optation by the state became itself symbolic of deep generational divisions in postwar Japanese identity. A 61-year-old contributor to a writing contest on the topic "Father and Child: Can the War and Postwar Experience be Passed On as an Inheritance?" published in the general-interest magazine *Sekai* in August 1969, interpreted the students' action as the "end of the postwar": the collapse of a popular pacifist consensus that had guided people's postwar aspirations. Among the twenty-year-old writers in this collection, all of whom were preoccupied with the smashed statue, the negative juxtaposition between those with war experience and those without came in for severe criticism. Even though these student writers hardly condoned their peers' violence and saw it as indicative of an embarrassing historical ignorance, they interpreted it as the smashing not of pacifist sentiment but of the war generation's self-referential grip on war memory as the basis of postwar identity. Precisely because contemporary students had not themselves lived through the war years, they could not absorb their elders' "inheritance" but needed to construct memory anew based on their own postwar experience, from Anpo to the Vietnam War. "How do you expect to pass on [the experience of war]? Build Wadatsumi statues everywhere? Keep publishing collections of testaments? No matter how many statues we see and how many testaments we read, we'll just perpetuate the same feelings [of the older generation]. No, we won't even have the same feelings."[52]

By the end of the 1960s, however, the generational discourse on memory had largely run its course. Even though students incorporated issues of war and postwar memory into their wider attacks on university administrations and state authority, no explicitly "postwar" conceptualization of memory independent of direct war experience gained significant currency at this time. The political and intellectual climate of the second half of the 1960s favored a different and newly prominent aspect of memory—namely, Japan's *national* memory of a *world* war whose history it shared with most of Asia, not only with the United States. Efforts to refocus war memory away from the obvious fragmentation of domestic politics and generational diversity and toward an imagined national unity conceived in cultural and ethnic terms and juxtaposed to other nations expanded the parameters of "memory" in important ways. They did not, however, change the location of war memory within special interest politics as framed by the enduring conservative hegemony in government and the bureaucracy.

CHAPTER SEVEN

Memory between Special and National Interests:

Japan and Asia

The idea that each nation involved in World War II produced its own specific national memory of that shared history emerged in the course of the 1960s. To be sure, competition for national recognition abounded at any time as particular war memories continuously demanded national space. A national memory of the war was certainly "imagined" in the sense that it was constructed discursively—and usually negatively—according to one's political standpoint. The liberal left equated national memory with state efforts to revive prewar nationalism by negating Japanese war crimes and elevating national values. The conservative right, in contrast, defined national memory as a series of masochistic reiterations of Japanese failures at the hands of foreign imperialists. By the mid-1960s, the legacies of Japan's involvement in Asia as well as with the United States had certainly begun to shape public discourses of national identity as well as foreign policy.

Normalization of relations with South Korea in 1965 and with the People's Republic of China in 1972 signified two important markers of this development, which depended heavily on international circumstances, primarily America's military involvement in Vietnam. At the height of the Cold War in 1965, public protest against the negotiation of the Japan–South Korea Peace Treaty between Satō Eisaku and Park Chung Hee ran high in both countries, in part because no apology or

Fig. 7.1 Public protest against the Japan–South Korea Peace Treaty and the Vietnam War in Shimizudani Park, Tokyo, 3 October 1965. Used by permission of Kyōdō News Agency.

compensation for Japan's colonization of Korea was included in the deal. At an October demonstration in Shimizudani Park in Tokyo, banners by various anti-government groups demonstrated a clear link between the demand to stop the Japan–South Korea treaty and the demand to end the war in Vietnam (Fig. 7.1). Both were seen as "obstructions to peace and prosperity." Seven years later, the overwhelming majority of Japanese people welcomed Tanaka Kakuei's successful trip to Beijing and the opening of official friendly relations between the two countries. On that occasion, Tanaka recognized the immense damage Japan had caused China during the war, an acknowledgment perhaps underlined by his low bow to Zhou Enlai (Fig. 7.2). Zhou accepted this gesture as a representation of the contrition of the Japanese people, who had also been victimized by their wartime militarist leaders. These two contrasting encounters with different national memories of the war in the course of intra-Asian diplomacy illustrated Japan's own struggle over national memory and identity in a changing political environment.

Fig. 7.2 Tanaka Kakuei (left) bowing low toward Zhou Enlai (center) at a banquet in honor of the normalization of relations between Japan and China, Beijing, 29 September 1972. Used by permission of Mainichi Shinbunsha.

Just as the discourse on the intergenerational transmission of memory had emerged in the second postwar decade, important contextual changes facilitated the new focus on the contours of a "national memory" in the third postwar decade. To put it broadly, Japan's place in the international community came into much sharper focus than it had since the end of the occupation. Tokyo's hosting of the 1964 Summer Olympic Games perhaps best embodied the embrace of this new internationalism, for it at once symbolized Japan's commitment to international peace and friendship and demonstrated its possession of financial, logistical, and technological capabilities on par with those of any modern industrial nation. The film director Ichikawa Kon captured this historical moment movingly in his documentary *Tokyo Olympiad* (1964), which began with a long shot of a blazing red sun deep over the horizon, followed by a very brief and contrasting glimpse of a building being destroyed. The rest of the prelude lingered in a leisurely, even loving, manner on the Olympic torch as it made its way from Greece through Asia Minor, India, and Southeast Asia to Okinawa, Hiroshima, and finally Tokyo. The camera focused on people's faces and their different emotional re sponses to this international ritual connecting far-away (ancient) Greece with modern Japan and sites of the utmost war destruction (Okinawa and Hiroshima) with the pinnacle of postwar achievement: a thoroughly rebuilt, clean, efficient Tokyo awash in international flags.

Next, Ichikawa used scenes of foreign teams arriving at Haneda Airport to reflect on the real divisions structuring the contemporary world—between nations, as is customary at the Olympics, but also between races, and most tellingly between the so-called First, Second, and Third Worlds. The American team arrived first in the film, in an aggressive closeup of the wheels of a PanAm jet touching down on the runway, followed by a frontal shot of mostly blond, smiling, young American athletes disembarking. The Russian team arrived separately, on a private jet, captured in group shots rather than through individual portraits. Perhaps the most sympathetic coverage was reserved for the tiny (and highly "exotic" looking) teams of newly founded nations in Africa and Pacific Asia, who were participating in the Olympics for the first time. As the commentator pointed out, they represented "youth" not only as individuals but as nations being welcomed into the international community, and as independent, de-colonized countries making a fresh start. Not surprisingly, the "Japan" featured in *Tokyo Olympiad* was rather more complex. As the camera followed the Japanese torch-bearer—an atomic bomb survivor—up a long set of stairs to light the Olympic flame, middle-aged women and men looked on with serene expressions while children cheered. At the end of the opening ceremony, spectators united in a gesture of peace, the release of thousands of doves into the sky, which ironically startled and confused many athletes in the stadium.

The film's quiet meditation on generational change, ethnic and racial diversity, and world-political divisions simultaneously celebrated Japan's postwar achievements and foreshadowed fierce conflicts over the *national* responsibilities engendered by Japan's past and present alike. The changing needs of American Cold War policy in Asia, conditioned by the prolonged and exceedingly ugly war in Indochina, affected international relations in the region profoundly. The PRC contributed to changes in the balance of Cold War relations by exploding its own nuclear bomb in October 1964. For Japan, new opportunities for clarifying its national integrity and viability in the region opened up, only to be circumscribed by its implicit role in the Vietnam War as a U.S. ally, which colored the long-overdue diplomatic negotiations in East and Southeast Asia at that time. Japanese Prime Minister Satō Eisaku, in office from November 1964 to July 1972, became known for his forceful foreign political agenda, which centered on bringing the highly controversial peace treaty with South Korea to a conclusion and negotiating the reversion to Japan of the Ogasawara and Ryukyu islands, then still under U.S. occupation.

Satō's goal of improving Japan's international profile, however, began at home and took full advantage of such symbolic events as the Meiji centennial in 1968, for which the Japanese government sponsored the most elaborate commemoration ceremonies since 1945, celebrating Japan's first modern—that is, international—century. Within this context, Japan's recently achieved status of economic giant but political dwarf in the international community struck Japanese and non-Japanese alike as a phenomenon that called for a host of historical and cultural explanations. Historians and social scientists, pundits and critics in Japan as well as in the United States took on this task with great enthusiasm.[1] Meanwhile, established political organizations that had built their special interests on particular interpretations of the war and postwar developments adjusted their agendas to fit a "national" framework.

Civic groups whose interests had always focused explicitly on national dimensions of public life, such as the Association of Shinto Shrines and its concern with Japan's national "essence," were important voices in the quest for a national identity. When diplomatic relations with Korea and Communist China became politically viable, the Japan-China Friendship Association gained public prominence with its insistence that Japan officially recognize its national responsibility for war atrocities. The Japan Teachers' Union (JTU), among many others, found that its special interests resonated powerfully in the nationwide movement for Okinawa's reversion to Japan. It revealed the enormous complexity of a "Japanese" national memory if it was to include Okinawa's very different wartime and postwar experiences and exemplified precisely the *lack* of so-called postwar democratic accomplishments.

The new focus on the national contours of war memory introduced important temporal and spatial shifts in the presence of the past without, however, significantly altering the political organization of memory in terms of competing interests. These shifts in public memory emerged with regard to different yet overlapping political developments that preoccupied public life in Japan in the latter 1960s and into the 1970s.

First, a vibrant discourse unfolded across the political spectrum about the concept of a national community and how it might be framed historically.[2] It focused on the ethnic collectivity of the Japanese bound by a shared history, rather than on the subjectivity or authenticity of the historical witness, which had been central to memory as war "experience." Second, divergent memories of the war as part of different national histories—and indeed contemporary "nationalisms"—surfaced as an issue in foreign policy and diplomacy with respect to the United States, South Korea, and the PRC. The ongoing war in Vietnam, and mass protests against the war in Japan, formed a critical and indeed explosive context here. Third, the movement to end the U.S. occupation of Okinawa and reintegrate the Ryukyu Islands into Japanese territory (achieved in 1972) raised important questions about the unevenness and inequality inherent in "national" conceptualizations of war memory that assumed ethnic or territorial unity. Even though there was a broad public consensus about Okinawa's reversion as a matter of Japan's national interest, mainland Japanese support for the movement stemmed from divergent and often incompatible special interests. Fourth, the search for explicitly national parameters of memory at the same time produced the articulation of "counter-memories" in the form of individual action opposed to collective ideology. This was the *raison d'être* of spontaneously organizing citizen activists spearheaded by the Citizens' Federation for Peace in Vietnam (Beheiren), which significantly altered, yet did not break up, the landscape of organized special interests as the leading custodians of public memory. Together, these four zones of political discourse made up the larger arena in which the public contest over Japan's national war memory in the latter 1960s was most visibly carried out.

Framing National Memories of War

The 1960s were very much colored by the experience—for many the trauma—of the Anpo movement. In its aftermath, the political climate changed markedly, on both the intellectual and the popular levels of public discourse. Andrew Barshay identified a strongly revisionist, if not reactionary, nationalist turn among Japanese thinkers in the context of a broader public "transvaluation" of the meanings of democracy into the economic realm.[3] His reading of thinkers, critics, and literary figures such as Hayashi Fusao, Mishima Yukio, Etō Jun, and Kōsaka Masaaki clearly suggests a search for new frameworks in which Japan's recent past acquired positive meanings, an effort to put an end to the plainly interest-driven, contentious nature of memory in postwar politics. Analyzing public discourse on a popular level, Yoshikuni Igarashi interpreted contemporary renderings of the Tokyo Olympic Games in 1964 as an attempt to overcome not only the bitter political conflict of Anpo four years earlier but Japan's postwar struggles as a whole.

The juxtaposition of 1945 and 1964 in the Tokyo Olympic games encouraged spectators to make a short circuit from the destruction of 1945 to the reconstruction of 1964, leaving out the historical process of the nineteen years between. . . . It was not the destruction of war itself, but postwar Japan's struggle to deal with the destruction, that the success of the Olympics assisted in masking.[4]

If "peace and democracy" had not fashioned a national consensus on the relationship between the war and the postwar, perhaps new urban-scapes and flawlessly orchestrated cultural events for international consumption would accomplish this. This logic undoubtedly had appeal, for it was replicated in different guises in the decades to come, markedly in the urban renewal projects of Hiroshima that Lisa Yoneyama analyzed.[5]

War memory, however, remained firmly anchored in the postwar project, however differently invested and presented. Of importance here was the idea that the domestic political struggles over the meaning of the past could be contained by shifting public attention toward the more properly *collective* concerns of a national community, whether in the form of "heritage" for identity purposes or "legacies" informing policy. In part, this was also an attempt to overcome the perceived generation gap opening up in society and endangering the cohesion even of organized particular memory interests. As Barshay pointed out, Hayashi Fusao's famous polemic "In Affirmation of the Greater East Asia War," first serialized in 1963, endorsed themes presented by the conservative philosopher Ueyama Shunpei (in "The Meaning of the Greater East Asia War in Intellectual History," 1961) but rejected their generation-specific perspective. Ueyama Shunpei (1921–) wrote as a member of the so-called *wadatsumi* generation, who had experienced the war as young adults and tried to find meaning in the deaths of so many of their contemporaries (albeit without endorsing the politics of Wadatsumikai). In contrast, Hayashi, a generation older, argued that the war must instead be seen as part of a much longer (indeed, a 100-year-long) historical trajectory marked by Japan's struggle against Western domination, and thus as the historical legacy for all Japanese.

Hayashi was guided less by matters of history than by concerns about memory. He was angered not by generation gaps but by a politics of memory that he, rightly or wrongly, interpreted as dancing to foreign tunes. Although he insisted that Japan's "century-long war against the West definitely ended in 1945," he surely perceived it to have continued by other means—that is, memory. For even if the war had ended, Hayashi argued, the Japanese still had not formulated a fully independent view of it, letting themselves instead be guided by various interpretations specific to the political aspirations of foreign powers. Ueyama had already laid out this disturbingly "pluralistic" field of war memory in terms of three competing interpretations circulating in postwar Japan: the U.S.-inspired view of the "Pacific War," defined as one between democracy and fascism; the Soviet-centric view of an "imperialist war" that had pitted the U.S./British and the Japanese/German varieties of imperialism against each other; and the Communist Chinese view of a "war of resistance" against Japanese imperialist aggression. Hayashi then proposed to answer Ueyama's call to overcome this foreign-induced multiplicity of interpretations with a single interpretation based on the Japanese people's "unique experience." He called it the "historical view of the Greater East Asia War" and was quick to point out that this term did not refer to the wartime ideology that had informed policies such as "eight corners under one roof" but instead offered the Japanese people a much longer historical perspective from which to reflect on their history on their own terms.[6]

The significance of Hayashi's text did not lie in his outrageous pairing of "Greater East Asia War" (the official wartime term for Japan's military operations in East and Southeast Asia) and "affirmation"—other than as a successful attention-getter—for his choice of language never produced the kind of national consensus he had in mind. After all, most Japanese found it difficult to "affirm" any war, much less one that had ended in defeat and whose dead they still mourned. Rather, Hayashi attempted to move the political contention over the memory of the war from domestic to international politics by portraying the competing interests in Japan's postwar project as mere puppets on strings controlled by foreign hands. He popularized a specific political agenda of the nationalist right, which sought to deny the special interest status of war memory in domestic politics, especially the legitimacy of progressive concerns with war responsibility, and challenged the government to renegotiate Japan's international relations. This strategy clearly resonated at a time when Japan's economic success on world markets had begun to contrast sharply with its continued political subordination to the strategic interests of the superpowers in Asia. Hayashi, in other words, claimed war memory as a national interest.

Other attempts at framing a Japanese national memory within an explicitly international context included a more clearly comparative approach stressing the specificity (and independence) of different national experiences as part of a shared post–World War II condition. The pacifist intellectual group Wadatsumikai, too, moved from concerns with "generation" to an exploration of "nation" as an alternative framework for war memory, but with strikingly different results. In August 1964, Wadatsumikai held its fifth symposium, on "Ethnicity and War Experience: World War II and Various Peoples," which explored war memory in the Soviet Union, West Germany, France, and China in comparison to Japan. This analytical strategy sought to delineate broad lessons learned from the war, based on historical explanations currently dominant in these countries, looking at each nation first on its own terms and then in relation to Japan. It consciously moved away from the group's earlier focus on the subjective experience of the historical witness, which had, like Ueyama Shunpei, placed too much weight on generation-specific memory. In contrast to Hayashi Fusao's search for older and more authentic legacies to help the Japanese reclaim their past from the dominance of foreign "teachers," however, the participants of the Wadatsumikai symposium were interested in facilitating a collective sense of war responsibility specific to the Japanese as victims (*higaisha*) as well as victimizers (*kagaisha*) in the war. The juxtaposition of these two identities, or rather their simultaneity, was to preoccupy Wadatsumikai for some time to come, and it also formed the basis on which comparisons with Germany became interesting in the 1960s.

The symposium's broadly comparative study of five countries (including Japan) came to the astonishing conclusion that only Japan appeared to have learned from the war. Area specialists and others presented their analyses, the gist of which may be summarized as follows. The Soviet Union's ideology of state totalitarianism required people to identify with the regime and willingly give their lives to protect the fatherland. France upheld the view that its own involvement in the war pivoted on its heroic resistance movement. In West Germany, three different and equally useless interpretations circulated: first, the damage done to German national pride in World War I had led to World War II; second, World War II was a struggle between freedom and totalitarianism, and freedom won thanks to the United States— an argument sanctioned by the anti-Communist, pro-remilitarization Christian Democratic Union (CDU); and third, the criminality of the Nazis had forever shattered the continuity of German history and created a black hole devoid of positive historical lessons. The panelists concluded that Germany had nothing to offer Japan with respect to substantive ideas on the issue of war responsibility, because Germans were not even concerned with the central question of lessons learned from the war. China's experience, on the other hand, was entirely different from Japan's; even the past from which legacies were drawn was different. What mattered in the Chinese case was the Communist Revolution of 1949—a logical consequence of China's wartime liberation struggle and much more significant than the war itself. This had important (and clearly unfortunate) consequences for postwar Japan, for it had rendered Japan's war against China invisible in public memory, just as China had been inconsequential to Japan's postwar reconstruction.

As crude and schematic as this brief survey may seem to the contemporary reader familiar with the whole body of literature equating historical memory with national narratives, it is important to keep in mind that "memory" had not yet emerged as an independent subject of inquiry, in Japan or elsewhere. Equally striking about this symposium is the degree to which Wadatsumikai's exploration of the ways in which war memory informed postwar politics in various national settings was so obviously guided by its own politics of memory: the insistence that the one basic lesson to be learned from the war was never to allow it to be repeated. Although the panelists recognized a diversity of opinions in each country, even the existence of generation gaps, they clearly left no space for competing lessons, national or otherwise, that did not accept its own basic principle of pacifist humanism.

In effect, both Hayashi's and Wadatsumikai's versions of framing a Japanese national memory extended the power-political dimension of war memory from the domestic to the international realm. This entailed a telling reversal of roles between the political right and left. In the context of international "memory," the "nationalists" claimed Japan's victimization at the hands of other nations, which they used skillfully to drum up popular national sentiments, while the "pacifists" claimed the moral high ground for the Japanese people, who had learned the right lesson from the war experience. Although recognizing this common ground in no way diminished the intensity of the political contention over war memory in the postwar system, one can see how both a Hayashi style nationalism and a Wadatsumikai-style pacifism coexisted quite comfortably in Japanese public memory. In the 1960s, in particular, both had tremendous popular appeal depending on the crisis context favored in public discourse at any given time.

This concern with national lessons and legacies intersected powerfully with the debate on national identity that colored the intellectual and cultural world of 1960s Japan. It seemed as if "politics" was to be replaced with "culture," and "war" with "modernization," in efforts to define a collective (and more positive) understanding of the relationship between Japan's multilayered past (encompassing prewar, war, and postwar) and its present. Tessa Morris-Suzuki analyzed in some detail the various ways in which older concepts of Japanese "culture," "civilization," "race," and "ethnicity" reappeared to explain "Japan" both to itself and to the international community at that time.[7] Of particular relevance for the reframing of memory in national terms, however, was the contextualization of the war as part of a longer historical trajectory of "modernity" (*kindaika*). This did not necessarily lessen the centrality of "1945," but it clearly distracted from the concreteness of the war "experience" in favor of broader national narratives, which sought to excavate a national identity based not on the legacy of World War II, but on Meiji as national heritage.

The public infatuation with Meiji as the cradle of Japanese modernity brought the emperor back into view, the "ghost at the historical feast"[8] whose symbolic status under the postwar constitution simultaneously discouraged critical public discussion and encouraged an all the more passionate embrace by representatives of the far right and the far left for different political purposes. The revolution of 1868 had "restored" the imperial institution to political power in the name of bringing Japan into the modern age, which, by the end of the nineteenth century, included the acquisition of colonies and an empire abroad. Furthermore, the Meiji Constitution of 1889, which established the emperor as sovereign, had set the political framework for both the liberal developments of the Taisho era and the militarism and ultranationalism of the 1930s and early 1940s. The decision of the occupation authorities in 1945 to strip the emperor of his political powers—without, however, abolishing the imperial institution or putting Hirohito on trial—left both the believers in and the opponents of the imperial system deeply dissatisfied. After many years of lobbying, the Association of Shinto Shrines in 1967 claimed a first victory in its quest to bolster the public significance of the imperial institution. That year, the government officially reinstalled the most prominent wartime holiday, *kigensetsu* (the birthday of the mythical Emperor Jimmu, celebrated on 11 February and abolished by the occupation authorities) as *kenkoku kinen no hi* (National Foundation Day).

Shrine Shintoists enthusiastically participated in the debate about the meaning of Japan's modern national identity. Its deepest expression, they insisted, lay in Shrine Shinto, with the emperor as its highest custodian. They celebrated Meiji as the time when the shrines acquired their proper status as public institutions but wrestled with the "corrupting" consequences of state bureaucratization during the war years. Above all, Shrine Shintoists insisted on the spiritual continuity between the 80 years following the Meiji Restoration and the 20 postwar years, without which there could be no Japanese identity.[9] This identity in fact had been on the verge of extinction after Japan's collapse in August 1945, according to the chief Shinto priest Sakamoto Ken'ichi. It was only thanks to Emperor Hirohito's speech of 1 January 1946 that this danger had gradually faded and given way to a direct relationship between the emperor and the people, one based on mutual respect, love, and trust instead of the myth and fiction built up by the wartime bureaucracy. What had remained unresolved after the war and thus required the continuous efforts of the Association of Shinto Shrines was the reestablishment of the shrines according to the restoration ideal so they could serve as the spiritual basis of the state.[10]

On the opposite end of the political spectrum, Wadatsumikai came to define its first long-term scholarly project in terms of an in-depth critique of the emperor system (*tennōsei*), whose survival in 1945 it interpreted as the most serious flaw in Japan's postwar democracy. Beginning in 1970, under the charismatic leadership of Watanabe Kiyoshi, a high school teacher, this project looked into the precarious topic of the emperor's responsibility for the war. Many special journal issues as well as several monographs resulted from this cooperative work. *Tennōsei* (as in *tennōsei fashizumu* or "emperor system fascism") had of course been a prominent term of historical critique among Japanese Marxists in the early postwar decades, but it was Wadatsumikai's explicit turn to memory as personal responsibility that brought Hirohito's role into the center of this academic inquiry.

Clearly, there was a desire to establish a national framework for locating contemporary Japan vis-à-vis other countries and vis-à-vis its own past. In the context of the public controversy surrounding the Meiji Centennial, John Whitney Hall observed, "I suspect that the present conflict over the significance of Meiji is not simply a product of politically motivated, antiestablishment interests or of men still troubled by memories of wartime excesses or of occupation humiliations; it emerges from deep intellectual uncertainties in Japan's continuing search for historical identity and the desire to safeguard newly won political freedoms."[11] Hall put his finger on a critical point, for the problems of historical identity, war memory, and interest politics were in fact intricately linked.

Postwar "Settlements" with South Korea

The Japanese government became directly involved in debates about national memory and responsibility for war legacies when new opportunities arose to normalize relations and settle outstanding war debts with the two neighboring countries that had suffered the most under Japanese wartime imperialism: Korea and China. These opportunities, however, proved extraordinarily complex. American strategic interests in East Asia, and later the war in Vietnam, required a greater political, economic, and preferably even military role for Japan in the region, which immediately conjured up memories of the war and galvanized domestic opposition around Article 9. In the early 1960s, U.S. efforts focused on enlisting Japan to assume responsibility for stabilizing South Korea, which was almost entirely dependent on American economic aid. But the authoritarian and repressive regime under the new military dictator, Park Chung Hee, who had come to power through a military *coup d'état* in May 1961, not only quelled hopes for a more liberal regime in South Korea but also raised serious questions in Japan about the political implications of supporting such a regime. Japanese politicians, and indeed the LDP itself, were as deeply divided about relations with South Korea as they were about relations with Communist China, and the two issues were clearly linked. The business community, however, had strong interests in both countries and responded much more positively to American pressure.[12]

"Settling the past," with its expectation of compensation, apology, and reconciliation, was therefore enormously complicated by a host of contemporary political, strategic, and economic factors rooted as much in the respective domestic situations in Korea and China as in the contentious politics within Japan and its alliance with the United States. These complications came to a head during the Ikeda (1960–64) and Satō (1964–71) administrations, and the decisive context was America's war in Vietnam. By early 1963, President Kennedy had stepped up his campaign to convince Ikeda and Park to normalize relations between their countries, drawing on both leaders' anticommunist convictions and mutual economic interests in order to ease American commitments on the Korean peninsula and redirect them toward Indochina. In John Welfield's judgment, Japanese economic assistance to Korea under the Basic Treaty, which was finally concluded in 1965, "indirectly . . . created the conditions that enabled Park to dispatch a total of 312,000 troops to assist the United States in Vietnam."[13] Nonetheless, incoming Prime Minister Satō also drew clear lines in response to American pressure: he assured the Japanese people that insofar as U.S. containment policies aimed at building a NATO-type military pact linking Japan with the Republic of Korea, Taiwan, and the Philippines in a "multilateral Far Eastern security organization," military involvement outside of Japan's borders was simply not an option under Japan's postwar constitution.[14]

America's strategic objectives in the region, South Korea's dire need for economic assistance, and Japan's political desire to define its national interests by overcoming the constraints of the past (or at least to contain the domestic struggle over their meaning) formed a complex terrain on which war-related questions about Korean property claims, fishing rights, and compensation of forced laborers were negotiated. These diplomatic negotiations also produced Japan's first official apology to South Korea, delivered by Ikeda's foreign minister, Shiina Etsusaburō, when he arrived at Kimpo Airport in Seoul in February 1965. In it, Shiina said:

We feel great regret and deep remorse over the unhappy phase in the long history of relations between the two countries. Now I believe that, with our eyes to the future, it is our mutual desire this year to establish everlasting friendship between Japan and South Korea, based on the thousand-year-long history of our bilateral ties, and also to form a new historical starting point from which our two nations can join forces to prosper together."[15]

The admittedly vague wording and the calculated manner in which this speech was drafted, as well as the fact that Japan did not send Yoshida Shigeru, as Korea had requested, but the foreign minister, may not suggest great sincerity, but Koreans evidently appreciated it and saw in Shiina a man who was "different from the typical Japanese politician."[16]

In the Basic Treaty signed on 22 June 1965, Japan declared void all treaties with Korea before its annexation in August 1910 and agreed to pay South Korea $300 million in grants in the form of goods and services, $200 million in government low-interest loans to promote economic development, and $300 million in private commercial credits.[17] South Korea in turn renounced its right to demand reparations and refrained from pressing for a formal apology for Japanese atrocities during the colonial period. The treaty itself contained not a hint of remorse on the Japanese side; in fact, Japan insisted that the grants and loans be regarded as "economic cooperation" rather than as compensation. Korean government records, which were not declassified until January 2005, show, however, that the Japanese government offered—and Park Chung Hee rejected—direct compensation payments to individual forced laborers. No doubt this represented an attempt to settle Japan's war debt without boosting the undemocratic Park regime, which deeply troubled Japanese conservatives and opposition leaders alike. But Park insisted on receiving the grants as a lump sum, which he officially regarded as compensation but in fact used for public works projects, including the construction of a highway between Seoul and Pusan and major industrial plants such as the Pohang Iron and Steel Corporation and the North Han River Hydroelectricity Generation Plant. The Japanese government, in contrast, demanded that the funds be recognized for what they were: economic development aid.[18]

Not until a decade later, in 1975, did the Park government forward any of this money to Korean war victims as compensation for wartime losses, and then used only about 9.7 percent of the $300 million grant to make a token one-time payment of 300,000 *won* ($622) per person to a mere 9,546 Korean victims. Former forced laborers, comfort women, injured war veterans, atomic bomb victims, unrepatriated Koreans, and Koreans who died after 15 August 1945 were all excluded from the pool of eligible victims. The Japanese government, for its part, in 1971 followed up on its promise to hand over the remains and documentation of Koreans who died during their mobilization for Japan's war efforts, but this was also no more than a token gesture: it sent a list of 21,699 names of Korean soldiers and civilian employees of the Japanese military, excluding any information about forced laborers. That list, moreover, quickly disappeared into the Korean National Archives in Pusan without being made available to the public.[19] All this suggested to citizens of both countries that reconciliation was not a true goal in the normalization of relations on the state level.

The intense domestic protests against the basic treaty in both countries in the mid-1960s and the formation of Korean citizen groups to press for compensation in the early 1970s must be understood against this background.[20] In South Korea, massive student demonstrations against the treaty broke out in the major cities in the spring of 1964. The protesters linked demands for Japanese apologies and adequate compensation for its colonization of Korea with severe criticism of the Park government, calling for his resignation and the establishment of democracy. In Japan, meanwhile, the established left—the Socialist and Communist parties, the General Council of Trade Unions, and a host of opposition groups—protested against the Japanese government's treaty diplomacy precisely for its lack of contrition and remorse, which it saw as an integral part of the LDP's nationalist agenda.

The conservative right in Japan tended to focus on the term "Asian nationalism," which linked the spatial reorientation toward Asia with the temporal expansion of the historical past to include not only the war and postwar but a century of Japan's international involvement. Nationalist sentiment, in Japan as in its former colonies, cut in various directions and revealed competing memories of a *shared* history against the equally shared background of the U.S. military presence in the region. It was "Asian" nationalism, however, particularly the Korean variety, that prompted the conceptualization of a "national memory" in Japanese debates on foreign policy issues. In the context of the Japan–South Korea Peace Treaty, which produced intense protest among the political opposition both in Japan and in South Korea (for different domestic reasons), the Japanese public was reminded that prewar Japan had "miscalculated the nature of nationalistic trends in other Asian countries."[21]

The Association of Shinto Shrines strongly criticized Korean resistance to normalizing relations with Japan as a continuation of its fierce nationalism, which now used memories of earlier conflicts to drum up anti-Japanese feelings, when its nationalism should have been directed toward the United States as the real culprit of the postwar order in Asia. An article in the Association's journal *Jinja shinpō* referred to commentaries in the Korean press that explicitly linked the 1965 treaty with the Treaty of Portsmouth (which made Korea a Japanese protectorate) 60 years earlier. Sixty years mark one complete cycle of the lunar calendar, reinforcing the sense of history repeating itself. This "laughable" analogy, the author sneered, obviously conjured up "deep memories" among Koreans but not among Japanese, who considered this an "extreme anti-Japan sentiment."[22] The argument advanced here and largely representative of the political right was twofold. On the one hand, "Asian nationalism" made sense vis-à-vis the United States, whose postwar political guidance and economic aid to its allies in East Asia (Japan, South Korea, and Taiwan) had built a "notoriously bad record" because Americans misunderstood the distinctiveness of "Asian modernity." In other words, it was not Japan's war conduct but the postwar American presence in Asia that caused friction within East Asia. On the other hand, inasmuch as "Asian nationalism" was directed *against* Japan (as was evident in Korea), it bespoke contemporary self-interests and invoked historical memories of the Asia-Pacific War for domestic as well as foreign political purposes. In this rendition, Japan was at the mercy of other Asian countries' national memories, which spoke directly to their respective postwar experiences and contemporary power-political agendas.

Writers in *Jinja shinpō*, for example, argued that the true reason for Korean opposition to the 1965 treaty lay in South Korea's dismal political and economic situation, for which not Japanese colonialism but American postwar policy was responsible. Moreover, Korean nationalist memory of the colonial period turned out to be as integral a part of domestic Korean political conflict—and a result of "irresponsible" postwar education—as Japanese war memory was in Japan. In South Korea, the formidable student opposition drummed up popular memories of Japanese colonialism with their slogan "Protect peace until death!" to discredit the Park Chung Hee regime, which, they argued, had sold Korea to Japanese interests for the second time. The Korean president, meanwhile, sought to appease both the students and the Japanese government with a vague statement to the effect that "the sincerity of patriotism differs in each country." In Japan, in turn, opposition to the treaty among the JSP and its affiliates aimed at discrediting Satō's foreign policy by claiming that the treaty with Korea only deepened the Cold War split in Asia by making the division of Korea permanent.[23] As political commentators in both countries pointed out at the time, South Korean and Japanese opposition to the treaty advanced fundamentally different arguments in the service of obvious domestic political purposes.

The Specter of Japanese Militarism

America's wars in Asia, from Korea to Vietnam and later the Gulf Wars, critically shaped Japanese thinking about World War II and its own involvement in Asia, both by structuring domestic conflict over memory and by providing opportunities to (re)negotiate Japan's foreign political role in the international community. "Fire across the sea" (meaning major conflicts affecting Japan indirectly) lent pacifist movements in Japan public prominence incommensurate with their otherwise weak power-political status; it sharpened conflict over Japan's postwar "order" and the prominence of the United States in it; and it fueled an ethnic nationalism that encouraged a sense of solidarity with other "Asians," as opposed to the American "Westerners."[24] The Vietnam War in particular, coinciding with (and consolidating) an unprecedented degree of economic prosperity in Japan, refocused memory of World War II as a "national" and not only "special" interest within an emerging Asian regionalism that brought into sharp view the inadequacy of Japan's relations with the PRC and the Koreas and revealed it as a product of specifically American interests. The Vietnam War created a "maze of puzzles" for Japan, at the center of which lay the question of how legacies of the wartime past informed the postwar system. In Thomas Havens's fitting words, the United States turned out to be a "pragmatic participant in world politics rather than the genial model of democracy and fairness" that many remembered from the occupation period. This brought up two conflicting memories:

Progressives and conservatives alike were haunted by memories of how the Japanese armies had bogged down in China during World War II as they watched the Americans fight Vietnamese guerrillas on TV.

For many Japanese with long memories, the specter of American violence against Vietnam probably helped lighten Japan's guilty conscience about its own behavior in a guerrilla war in China two decades earlier, [while] for others, . . . the war increased their sense of guilt.[25]

Few Japanese were convinced that the United States was fighting a "righteous" war against Communism in Vietnam, just as there was little acceptance of the American rhetoric casting Communist China in the role of a "cold war enemy."[26] On the contrary, America's war in Vietnam brought home the fact that waging war, and by extension judging war in retrospect, had everything to do with power and self-interest, whether this concerned domestic or international politics, special or national interests. Moreover, the significance of a Western superpower fighting a war in a poor Asian country riddled by the legacies of Western colonialism was hardly lost on the Japanese public, especially at a time when discourses of cultural and civilizational differences enjoyed academic as well as popular prestige. Pacifist and nationalist opposition to the war in Vietnam thus cut across political lines and mobilized tens of thousands of otherwise politically apathetic individuals.

Meanwhile, the government under Prime Minister Satō Eisaku pursued a deliberate foreign policy of protecting Japan's special relationship with the United States, reducing its inherent inequality, and boosting Japan's international stature. In this situation, the issue of war memory and Japan's postwar responsibility came to loom large as interest groups across the political spectrum in Japan (and public spokespersons in Korea and China) interpreted Satō's diplomacy in light of their own views of past military conflicts in Asia. Arguments made in this context tended to revolve around the terms (Japanese) militarism, (American) imperialism, and (Asian) nationalism. No matter how polemical their uses, these terms were clearly linked and their proponents overlapped in various ways that even cut across political lines. They each shaped memories and interpretations of a particular aspect of Japan's prewar and wartime military involvement in Asia in terms of Japan's national interests, as they were perceived in the contemporary international context.

At the forefront of those accusing the Satō government of resurrecting "Japanese militarism" were the Teachers' Union, the General Council of Trade Unions, and other affiliates of the JSP—that is to say, the established "Old Left" (as opposed to the citizens' movements referred to as the "New Left"). In its "Peace Appeal" of 7 May 1965, the JTU leadership raised the specter of America's "war of aggression" (*shinryaku sensō*) in Vietnam unleashing a "total war" (*zenmen sensō*) in the region by fully mobilizing Japanese resources, just as Japanese aggression in Asia in the 1930s had led to World War II through the total mobilization of the Japanese people. This was already evident, the appeal claimed, in the large and increasing numbers of Japanese people and goods involved in supporting the American war effort through economic aid, the dispatching of medical teams to South Vietnam, the transportation of troops, and the manufacture of military arms, which amounted to an aggressive use of the U.S.-Japan Security Treaty by the Satō government. Citing a slogan coined during the Korean War, "Never send our students to the battlefield again!" the JTU called on teachers to act upon their "loathsome" experience of the Pacific War, and their "relentless reflection" (*kibishii hansei*) on that experience, to help guard the peace.[27] The established opposition thus cast Japan's complicity in the Vietnam War as part of government efforts to unravel postwar democracy (evidenced by its disregard of popular opposition to the war) and once again mobilize Japanese society in support of aggressive policies abroad.

Public concern about the possibility of constitutional revision and especially an expanded role for the Self-Defense Forces (SDF) lent urgency to this agenda, especially in the aftermath of the so-called Three Arrows' Exercise (*Mitsuya kenkyū*) incident in February 1965. This referred to the discovery of a detailed plan to make the SDF "an integral part of the United States Far Eastern strategy, . . . supporting U. S. offensive action by serving as a reserve force in Japan as well as in Korea and Manchuria," and react to emergencies with "total mobilization." By that was meant establishing "necessary agencies to control and regulate industry, communications, transportation, information media and all economic activity, including the allocation of civilian and military material, and prices, banks and financial institutions." The socialist representative Okada Haruo, who made the plan public, interpreted this as a plotted *coup d'état*—an attempt to override the constitution and reestablish an authoritarian type of government. To emphasize his sense that the past was repeating itself, Okada likened the plan in intent and significance to the attempted coup by high military officers in 1936, the infamous February 26 incident.[28]

Although the plan was never carried out, concern over the proximity of war in Vietnam, the opportunity to renegotiate Japan's power position in the region, and fear of Communist China's nuclear capability converged around the issue of the military as a defining aspect of *postwar* Japan, combining and exemplifying the dynamic mix of war legacies and Cold War constraints that fueled postwar political conflict. Indeed, Tsukasa Matsueda and George Moore's assessment of Japanese attitudes toward the military in 1967 registered a clear shift in public opinion, which they summarized as "an improved image of the SDF, a planned increase in military size and armament, an admitted weakening of opposition, and increasing business voices in military matters."[29] Still, such critical aspects as budget control and direct access to the emperor remained unambiguously outside the SDF's reach, and although its public image may have improved, antiwar demonstrations demanded even more attention. Above all, the conflict over this issue put the spotlight on Japan's uneasy power position between the United States and Communist Asia and the ubiquity of memories of World War II and of the early postwar period.

American policies in Vietnam (and, by extension, Satō's support for the United States) had been labeled "imperialist" by organizations such as the Japan-China Friendship Association. This critique came into sharp view in the context of growing demands within Japan to normalize relations with PRC, even as these relations had cooled once again. For the Friendship Association, the specter of "American imperialism" and "Japanese militarism" joining hands reached a new level of urgency as the war in Vietnam escalated and pushed China into dangerous isolation, intensified by the enigma of Mao's Cultural Revolution.[30] In light of the Friendship Association's internal conflict over how to interpret and whether to support the Cultural Revolution, it seemed particularly expedient to invoke the past—namely, wartime Japanese imperialism— on which there was agreement. As much as America's bogged-down military operations in Vietnam recalled the crimes of Japan's invasion of China, the critical point for the Friendship Association revolved around discrediting the entire postwar system of "American imperialism" for having obscured Japan's responsibility and thereby perpetuated aggression against the Chinese people. The demand that East Asian relations become centered on Japanese-Chinese friendship instead of the U.S.-Japan alliance struck a cord at a time when American proclamations of "peace and democracy" had turned out to be morally hollow and thoroughly self-interested. To remind the public of Japan's own imperial past (and offset the government preparations for the Meiji centennial), the Japan-China Friendship Association sponsored numerous commemorative events nationwide throughout 1967 to mark the thirtieth anniversary of the Marco Polo Bridge incident (7 July 1937), the official beginning of Japan's war against China.[31]

Conservative proponents of a Japanese China policy that was more independent of the United States approached the lingering issue of Japanese wartime imperialism from a more pragmatic standpoint. It is well known that "traditional Pan-Asianists" outside the mainstream faction of the LDP, such as Matsumoto Kenzō (1883–1971) and Takasaki Tatsunosuke (1885–1964), who had been instrumental in negotiating informal relations with the PRC in the 1950s and 1960s, were motivated by a "strong sense of guilt towards China and a consciousness of Asian solidarity."[32] In early 1965, a group of younger, non-mainstream party members around Utsunomiya Tokuma (1906–) formed the Asia-Africa Problems Research Association (Ajia Afurika mondai kenkyūkai) within the LDP, in response to the establishment the previous month of the anti-communist, pro-Taiwan Asia Problems Research Association (Ajia mondai kenkyūkai) under the leadership of Kaya Okinori, the president of the Japan Association of War-bereaved Families. In contrast to Kaya's entirely unapologetic nationalism, Utsunomiya addressed Japan's imperial aggression in Asia straightforwardly because he understood that the war responsibility issue had to be settled in order to set Japanese foreign policy on a course independent from U.S. strategic interests. The Asia-Africa Problems Research Association did not consider American policy as imperialistic aggression, but it shared with the Japan-China Friendship Association the desire to build a new Asian regionalism on Japanese-Chinese cooperation rather than exclusively on Japan's alliance with the United States.

There is no doubt that the memory of Japanese imperialism and colonialism in Asia was filtered through the Cold War structure of regional relations as it became part of national interests on all sides. This again became strikingly clear in 1972, when President Nixon's rapprochement with Communist China paved the way for a rapid normalization of relations between Japan and China, followed, more slowly, by the conclusion of the Peace and Friendship Treaty between the two countries in 1978. China's need to break out of the relative isolation imposed by the Cold War and intensified by the Sino-Soviet split in the late 1960s constituted a major reason for Mao's keen interest in securing economic aid from Japan. In a bold move, incoming Prime Minister Tanaka Kakuei (1972–74) made a first official visit to Beijing in September 1972 at the invitation of Premier Zhou Enlai, which resulted in the Joint Communiqué of the Government of Japan and the Government of the People's Republic of China. This document included the most strongly worded Japanese acknowledgment of its war responsibility to date and was accepted by the Chinese as a sincere step toward reconciliation. In it, both parties stated:

The Japanese side is keenly conscious of the responsibility for the serious damage that Japan caused in the past to the Chinese people through war, and deeply reproaches itself. Further, the Japanese side reaffirms its position that it intends to realize the normalization of relations between the two countries from the stand of fully understanding "the three principles for the restoration of relations" put forward by the Government of the People's Republic of China. The Chinese side expresses its welcome for this.

In turn, China renounced demands for reparations: "The Government of the People's Republic of China declares that in the interest of the friendship between the Chinese and the Japanese peoples, it renounces its demand for war reparation from Japan."[33]

In striking contrast to the Japan–South Korea Peace Treaty seven years before, Tanaka's China diplomacy elicited no significant protests in either country. On the contrary, it ushered in a "China boom" in the Japanese public media and expanded Chinese-Japanese exchanges in various fields throughout the 1970s, which became known as the "honeymoon decade" of Sino-Japanese relations. In China, it must be kept in mind, foreign relations issues remained firmly in the hands of the Communist Party and therefore had little chance of becoming subject to genuine public debate, let alone popular demonstrations. Indeed, popular criticism of Japan appeared only in the later 1980s and 1990s, when China's developing market economy gave rise to an increasingly vibrant civil society and a less tightly controlled local press.

Public memory of Japan's war in China nevertheless always had a prominent place in the PRC's own legitimization profile. Peter Hays Gries asserts in his study of China's contemporary nationalism that

the 1931/1937–1945 "War of Resistance against Japan" was the birthplace of the People's Republic of China. By mobilizing and leading the peasantry in nationalist resistance against the invading Japanese, the Communist Party gained the mass following it later used to defeat the Nationalist Party during the Civil War of the late 1940s. For over half a century now, "defeating the Japanese and saving the nation" has been a dual legacy at the heart of Chinese Communist claims to nationalist legitimacy.[34]

State-sponsored national memory under the Chinese Communist Party (CCP) constructed a "victor narrative" of heroic Communist survivors liberating the country from foreign invaders and finally unifying it after the "century of humiliation" that had begun with the Opium War. This narrative had little room for Chinese victims of Japanese aggression, and Mao's personal aura was certainly more conducive to celebrating heroism and victory than to dwelling on war victimization *per se*. Furthermore, more Chinese peasants died during the Great Famine in the 1950s and the Cultural Revolution in the mid-1960s, as a direct result of Communist policies, than during the war at the hands of the Japanese. Whereas Korea's postwar struggles were easily blamed on the legacies of Japanese colonialism, in China such arguments meshed poorly with the CCP's claim to have made a fresh start in 1949.

In Japan, meanwhile, the establishment of official diplomatic relations with China found widespread—although far from unanimous—support across the political spectrum. As in the 1930s, when the call for imperialism on the Asian mainland served multiple and often conflicting interests at home, Sino-Japanese rapprochement was welcomed by a variety of political players, including liberals emphasizing atonement for war crimes, conservatives trying to counterbalance American hegemony in East Asia, and of course the business community. Newspapers, popular journals, and academic publications actively promoted a public debate about Sino-Japanese relations, past and present, within the context of such pressing issues as the war in Vietnam and the reversion of Okinawa.

The call for a more prominent international position for Japan, conceived in terms of greater independence from U.S. policy or, worse, of assuming some of America's strategic responsibilities in East Asia, ensured competing war memories a prominent place in national policy debates. Memories of the Greater East Asia Co-Prosperity Sphere were never far from the surface among the victim nations. In addition, the longer trajectory of Japanese advances into Asia since the late nineteenth century figured strongly in Japanese public debates in the late 1960s and early 1970s, which were replete with interpretations of the Meiji era as Japan's entry into the international community. Satō's forceful negotiations over Okinawa in the context of a Cold War standoff in Vietnam struck some critics as a contemporary example of Japan seeking to revise its "unequal treaties" with a Western power in order to advance its own strategic interests in the region, as in the time of Japan's first imperialist wars.

Suspicious of the new emphasis placed on Japan's role in Asia, commentator Gotō Motoo wrote in 1969:

The situation existing [in the 1890s]—the abrogation of unequal treaties, Japan's advance into Asia, and the repercussions of the clashing interests of the three major powers of Great Britain, Russia and the United States—has something in common with the present situation in Asia—the problem of Okinawa's return, the conflict between the spheres of influence of the United States and the Soviet Union and the foreign policy of China which has just succeeded in getting her Great Cultural Revolution under control.[35]

In contrast to Hayashi Fusao's defensive characterization of Japanese imperialism as a necessary reaction to Western colonialism, Goto drew attention specifically to the foreign-political entanglement with Western strategic interests in the region as a determining factor in Japan's own imperialist behavior. U.S.-occupied Okinawa illustrated the reality of this entanglement perfectly, both as a historical continuity and as a specific legacy of the wartime past.

The Debate over Okinawa's Reversion to Japan

Beginning his three-day visit to Okinawa in August 1965, the first by a Japanese head of state since 1945, Prime Minister Satō told a cheering crowd at Naha airport: "I strongly believe that as long as the reversion of Okinawa to the fatherland is not realized, our country's 'postwar' is not over."[36] That day, riots broke out in Naha. Demonstrators demanded Okinawa's reversion but protested against Satō's leadership. In the following seven years, Japan's southern periphery became the center of public debate and an important terrain on which meanings of a Japanese *national* memory clashed. The promise of active involvement by the government in negotiating the reversion of Okinawa not only fueled the already intensifying reversion movement on the islands but also tapped nationalist feelings among mainland Japanese, focused pacifist opposition to involvement in the Vietnam War, and contributed to a growing awareness of persisting social inequalities within Japan.

At once a local, national, and international issue characterized by multilevel political involvement, the "Okinawa question" illuminated what may be termed the "Asia within Japan." Okinawa was arguably Japan's first colony, having been annexed officially in 1879 and subjected to the imperial state's policies of assimilation and discrimination. It was the site of the fiercest battles at the end of World War II, and it remained under American occupation twenty years longer than did mainland Japan, until 1972. Although local movements campaigned for political independence, especially in the early postwar years, by the 1960s all sides understood Okinawa to be essentially Japanese territory serving the United States' strategic interests in the Cold War. Thus, "reversion to the homeland" became the only solution to a situation that had transformed the islands into a U.S. military bastion largely deprived of the political reforms and economic growth that characterized the rest of postwar Japan.

Decades of American military occupation had left Okinawans without citizenship and the benefits that usually come with it, from health care to social security. But the central problem concerned land. Okinawa covers 1 percent of Japan's landmass yet hosts 75 percent of all U.S. bases in Japan, which occupy a full 20 percent of the main island. Foreign occupation thus meant most immediately and urgently the loss of land, which had been essential to the largely agricultural economy. Two years into the occupation, in 1947, one-third of all arable land had already been confiscated and paved over or put behind barbed wire. In 1952, the U.S. military issued twenty-year leases on previously confiscated land to 57,000 landowners, offering pitifully small compensation. As a result, Okinawa's agricultural economy was reoriented toward the service industry around U.S. bases, where extremely low wages were the norm. Poverty, environmental degradation, and the physical dangers of military installations—traffic accidents, noise and other pollution, and crimes committed by U.S. servicemen—came to characterize everyday life in Okinawa.[37] To an extent, these problems were endemic to military bases, including those in Japan proper, but their concentration in Okinawa had overwhelming consequences and earned Okinawa a reputation as a playground of sorts for the U.S. military.

Against this background, a reversion movement had been brewing since the early 1950s and became instrumental in defining an Okinawan subjectivity and public culture.[38] Reversion provided a common ground on which issues ranging from public policy to residents' concerns were fought out and different languages of protest (those of political ideology, racial self-determination, and citizens' rights) competed with one another. Outside perceptions of Okinawa, primarily those of Americans and mainland Japanese, helped shape this public culture as much as contemporary events and historical experiences. Comments by American authorities suggesting that the Okinawans represented a racial minority and could therefore serve as a "bridge of understanding" between the United States and Japan—clearly aimed at justifying the U.S. control of the Ryukyus—fired Okinawan insistence on being an integral part of Japan.[39] But the discourse on unity (*ittaika*)—no matter what timetable or method was to be used to achieve it—served also to articulate and explain the very reality of difference as a historical legacy of Japan's prewar, wartime, and postwar state policies as well as U.S. military prerogatives in East Asia since 1945. Viewed from the angle of memory, these different strategies only highlighted the many ways of making sense of the contemporary present using selected aspects of varied past experiences.

On the national level, an engaged public consciousness of Okinawa's occupied status as a national problem (and a problem of national integrity) emerged slowly. Contacts between Okinawans and the mainlanders were limited. Okinawans were not permitted to visit Japan freely and most political organizations did not establish branch offices in Okinawa until many years later. Well-established civic organizations of the kind discussed here did not typically invest much energy in the Okinawa problem until the mid-1960s, when Satō moved it to the top of the political agenda—in fact, 1967 was named "Okinawa Year."[40] Japanese anxiety about involvement in the Vietnam War through the use of Okinawa's military bases—as well as news about an increasing number of military, even nuclear, accidents in the midst of escalating protests against the U.S. occupation authorities—lent particular urgency to the reversion movement as an item on the national agenda.

Okinawa became the symbol for what had gone wrong with "the postwar," whether that meant the loss of national cohesion and pride, subservience to the Americans, the persistence of social inequalities, or environmental disaster. The Association of War-bereaved Families embraced the Okinawans as Japan's most heroic sufferers at the end of the war, having patriotically defended the fatherland during the American invasion in the spring of 1945. The JTU supported the reversion movement in order to press for changes in the Japanese education system, which it argued was riddled by bureaucratic control and social discrimination, just as in prewar times. The Japan-China Friendship Association saw the settling of Okinawa's political status as pivotal to the course of East Asian relations: a full reversion and closing of all course of East Asian relations: a full reversion and closing of all American bases would clear the way to an East Asia centered on Chinese-Japanese peace and rapprochement, while Japan's consent to the continuation of U.S. bases would indicate that "Japanese militarism" was once again on the rise.

In addition to the involvement of established political interest groups, local residents and environmental and women's groups gained momentum in the late 1960s and broadened public interest in the Okinawa issue because they allowed for citizen solidarity based on contemporary concerns with quality-of-life issues—felt in many parts of Japan, but starkly amplified in Okinawa. Residents' grievances specific to Okinawa thus converged, on a general level, with raised popular awareness of pollution, prostitution, consumer issues, and more, all configured within the politically explosive framework of "war and peace." Controversial political events such as the Satō-Johnson communiqué in Washington in November 1967 bound old and new organizations together in their opposition to the government, which appeared to disregard popular demands, in both Okinawa and the mainland, for immediate, unconditional, and complete reversion and instead forged even closer military relations with the United States. The local reversion movement undoubtedly benefited from the political influence of established interest groups, who also provided a forum for debates about the meaning of Okinawa in the wider context of Japan's past and present.

Conversely, the proliferation of politically nonaligned citizens' movements altered the landscape of civic political activism and challenged large interest groups to look beyond entrenched political affiliations toward greater popular appeal. A closer look at the JTU's involvement in the reversion movement sheds some light on the ways in which older patterns of war and postwar memory as special interests appropriated contemporary concerns. The creation of new organizational ties with local movements, the critique of the Japanese government's unification (*ittaika*) policies, and the unexpectedly divisive role of war memory among Okinawans themselves illuminated both the desire for a national consensus on solving war legacies and the persistent challenges that prevented a unified national memory from emerging.

When the Teachers' Union first embraced the campaign for Okinawa's reintegration into Japan proper as part of its anti–Vietnam War and anti–Security Treaty activities in 1966, its own previous neglect of Okinawan affairs became painfully clear. The JTU had established no local chapter in Okinawa in 1947–48, when all the other prefectural unions were formed, and had reserved no special place for occupied Okinawa on its political platform during the 1950 protests against the Peace Treaty or the 1960 Anpo struggle for abolition of the Security Treaty. Rather than belatedly establishing a chapter in Okinawa before reversion, however, the JTU headquarters in Tokyo decided to forge close contacts and cooperation with the Okinawa Teachers' Association (OTA), founded in April 1952, whose long-term president, Yara Chōbyō (1902–1997), was a central figure in the local reversion movement.[41] The JTU pledged to support the OTA and recognize its position of leadership, while affirming their combined efforts as a "struggle for national independence" (*minzoku dokuritsu*) centered on the peace movement.[42]

Hoshino Yasusaburō, professor at Tokyo Gakugei University, urged in a special report in the union's prominent journal *Kyōiku hyōron* (*Education Review*) that Japan's teachers learn from their counterparts in Okinawa. Japanese teachers were expected "to fully participate in the struggle to end foreign rule of Okinawa and the Ogasawara Islands in order to realize Japan's full independence and unity" and "to advance education and create a correct understanding of the Okinawa and Ogasawara problem for the new generation of Japan as educational and cultural workers." Hoshino welcomed the closer relationship between the Teachers' Union and the OTA, which had produced important joint publications on Okinawa to be used in Japanese classrooms; and he admonished JTU leaders to reflect critically on the belatedness of this recent cooperation as well as the historical meaning of Okinawa for Japan in general.[43]

Indeed, *Kyōiku hyōron* became a prominent venue for Okinawans—leaders of the local reversion movement, intellectuals, teachers, and students—to voice their views and report on the current situation in Okinawa for Japanese audiences. Yet there remained a clear consciousness of those voices as distinct from "the mainland." Okinawans tended to foreground concrete problems involving local living conditions in the present and recent past to demand (1) immediate, unconditional, complete reversion based on the abolition of Article 3 of the Peace Treaty, (2) the removal of the nuclear bases and opposition to all military bases, (3) the prompt enactment of the Japanese constitution, and (4) complete equality with mainland prefectures. Although the JTU's demands for reversion essentially mirrored those of the Okinawan movement, the Teachers' Union clearly embedded them within a larger struggle against the conservative establishment. Speaking at a mass rally on the mainland centered on youth and women's groups as well as labor unions, JTU leaders focused on methods of mass protest and vowed to "study the Okinawa struggle" in order to learn important lessons for their own peace movement.[44]

The government's reversion policies came in for severe criticism by JTU chairman Miyanohara Sadamitsu, who accused Satō of using the Okinawa issue to drum up popular nationalism but in turn used the same issue himself to articulate his union's fundamental criticisms of postwar democracy in general and education in particular. Okinawa provided a showcase of a failed education system, indeed reminiscent of Japan's prewar assimilation policies (which had combined integration with discrimination), Miyanohara claimed. He cited repressive laws concerning public education employees in local areas (the so-called *kyokō nihō*) and textbooks with almost no information on local history. But the degree to which the Satō cabinet attempted to use education for ideological purposes, Miyanohara continued, was unprecedented in the postwar period.[45] A proposal by the ruling LDP to "inaugurate [educational] policies for the promotion of love for the fatherland based on nostalgia for the Meiji era, a national spirit (*minzoku seishin*), and a consciousness of national defense" showed how the government sought to use education to strengthen popular support for its policies on Okinawa and Vietnam.[46]

In contrast, the JTU embraced a version of *ittaika* that highlighted the danger of Japan's unconstitutional involvement in the Vietnam War via the military bases in Okinawa and spearheaded the democratization of mainland Japan by educating people about Japan's discriminatory prewar and militarist wartime policies that were still in place.[47] The renowned education scholar Munakata Seiya linked the mainland education system to the Security Treaty by coining the term "Anpo education system" (*Anpo kyōiku taisei*). To him, Okinawa's reversion entailed a fundamental change in the mainland system of bureaucratic control (a system that infringed on teachers' human rights by not letting them be political actors) instead of an annexation of Okinawa to the existing system.[48]

Ōta Masahide, a professor at Ryukyu University and a future governor of Okinawa Prefecture, insisted that the meaning of reversion as well as the reversion movement itself could not be adequately understood without considering Okinawa's colonial education. Contemporary nationalism in Okinawa should not be construed as condoning the mainland political system, he warned. Instead, he explained it in terms of a pattern of accommodation to Japanese assimilation policies that had developed in the prewar period and continued after the war, along with Japan's discriminatory policies. "The nationalism displayed by Okinawans demanding immediate reversion resembles the prewar nationalism of Okinawans in light of Japanese government policies. It is now necessary to break with those prewar policies, reflect on the colonial *kōminka* education, recognize responsibility for it, establish education in Okinawa on the basis of human dignity and democracy, and do away with discrimination once and for all."[49]

The subject of prewar and postwar discrimination against Okinawans, however, proved unexpectedly divisive. If most agreed that it was not blood or language but "history" that accounted for the difference between Okinawa and mainland Japan,[50] then that history could be interpreted in different ways, even among Okinawans themselves. In 1971, a controversy unfolded in Osaka over the publication of a supplementary reader for classroom use entitled *Mankind* (*Ningen*), which dealt predominantly with discrimination against the *burakumin* or Japanese outcasts. Compiled by an Osaka-based research organization focusing on the *burakumin* problem, the All-Japan Liberation Education Research Group (Zenkoku kaihō kyōiku kenkyūkai), it included a section on discrimination against Okinawans. "Questioning Okinawa" ("Okinawa no toikakeru mono") consisted of letters by a mainland teacher to his junior high school students about his summer trip to Okinawa. In these letters, the teacher reflected deeply on his own (and by extension mainland Japan's) lack of knowledge about and concern for Okinawa, which amounted to a disregard for one's "responsibility as a human being." Recognizing this as a conscious or unconscious "discrimination" against Okinawans, this teacher conceived of the "Okinawa problem" as a problem rooted in the Japanese past.[51]

The Association of Okinawans in Osaka objected strongly to the implicit likening in the text of discrimination against Okinawans to that against *burakumin*. While the Liberation Education Research Group argued that both types of discrimination shared the same basic characteristics despite historical and social differences, the Association of Okinawans in Osaka held that the two were fundamentally different and that the Okinawans no longer faced discrimination comparable with that of the prewar era. In a February 1971 pamphlet, the president of this organization distinguished between "emotional discrimination" (*shinjōteki sabetsu*) and "systemic discrimination" (*seidoteki sabetsu*). Discrimination against *burakumin* was deeply embedded in Japan's history and society and manifested itself even today in marriage choice and in the workplace. If one could speak of discrimination against Okinawans, by contrast, it was merely a result of defeat and the Peace Treaty that had separated Okinawa from the mainland.

Commenting on this debate, Ryukyu University professor Okamoto Shigenori was deeply troubled by the Okinawans' participation in the willful forgetting of prewar and wartime discrimination. While his colleague Ōta Masahide pointed directly to prewar patterns of accommodation to Japanese assimilation policies as the root of such amnesia, Okamoto held the American postwar colonization of Okinawa and the rhetoric of "democracy" responsible, which had gradually removed issues of past discrimination and repression from popular consciousness. But he agreed with Ōta when he concluded, "The discrimination against Okinawans as a result of the U.S. colonial rule there is the exception, whereas Japanese discrimination against Okinawans is the rule in Japanese society."[52]

In the years leading up to reversion to Japan, many Okinawans did not deem this memory convenient for their cause, fearing to "wake the sleeping child" and choosing instead to "brush off the ashes that have fallen." But the intensity of this reaction itself suggested that the historical experience of prewar discrimination was very real indeed and had hardly been forgotten. Ōta Masahide's book *The Ugly Japanese* (*Minikui Nihonjin*, 1969) became an immediate bestseller in Okinawa and clearly spoke to an Okinawan memory that could easily be activated. The JTU helped make this history a critical part of the contemporary "Okinawa question" by closely examining existing textbooks and sponsoring a discussion of "How to Teach Okinawa" as part of a larger campaign that included advice on how to teach Korea, Taiwan, and the Meiji Restoration, as well as the Sino-Japanese and Russo-Japanese wars.

Individual Action as Counter-memory

The complexity of war memory within the framework of the postwar Japanese nation-state appeared greater in the late 1960s than ever before. Questions of national identity, diplomatic relations with other Asian countries, and even national territory became important anchors for negotiating conflicting lessons and legacies of the past in addition to the perennial contention concerning the war dead, Shrine Shinto, and history education. Whether seen as national or special interests, however, such negotiations of war memory tended to embrace the terrain of postwar democracy as an institutionalized political system operating through a variety of state and civic organizations. But this was also a time of significant shifts, splits, and realignments among so-called established political organizations, especially on the opposition left, in the course of which the bureaucratized "system" itself—and the very *form* of organized war memory as special interest politics—became a target of protest.

New citizens' movements proliferating after 1965—the New Left—sought to create their own decentralized "participatory" democracy in opposition to both the government's "paternalistic" democracy and the Old Left's "democratic centralism."[53] In rendering problematic not specific meanings of the war but the way these meanings competed within set bureaucratic structures, these popular movements posited a Foucaultian "counter-memory."[54] According to the novelist and critic Oda Makoto (1932–), such a counter-memory hinged on the recognition that memory as special interest politics suffered from persisting "feelings of [wartime and postwar] victimization," against which a "personal sense of involvement and responsibility" needed to be fostered in order to "challenge the principle of ultimate state authority."[55]

Oda Makoto was a key figure in the Citizens' Federation for Peace in Vietnam, or Beheiren (Betonamu ni heiwa o! shimin rengō), an alliance of groups and individuals who rejected the collective ideology of political organizations for the diversity, spontaneity, voluntarism, and decentralization of a movement promoting "individual action" against the state on behalf of pacifist principles.[56] Between 1965 and 1975, Beheiren kept up an astonishing degree of public involvement via the mass and "mini" media (e.g., newsletters), demonstrations and teach-ins, and international networks, emphasizing the community of like-minded individuals regardless of the politics of nation-states. The positive energy and commitment radiating from Beheiren's activism as well as the personalities of its leaders had tremendous popular appeal (and elicited equally harsh criticism). They clearly challenged established interest groups, which faced declining membership numbers and even organizational splits. Still, the older organizations, such as the Teachers' Union, were also able to incorporate the shift in emphasis toward spontaneous citizen participation and local residents' concerns, especially on issues that highlighted governmental disregard for popular participation in public policy. Moreover, Beheiren was a special phenomenon rather than the new norm for citizens' movements, which remained highly diverse and in general closely tied to older, established political organizations.

From the writings especially of Oda Makoto, it is nevertheless clear that at least the ideal of spontaneous and principled individual activism constituted a type of postwar responsibility, one that sought to make amends for the generally negative, reactive, even defensive manner in which particular memories of the war assumed public space in postwar Japan. The question of transmitting the memories of those who experienced the war to younger generations was all but irrelevant in this newer context. Oda (who later became active in Wadatsumikai) loathed the term "wartime experience" as "synonymous with 'experience as victim'" and stressed that "this perspective . . . fails to come to grips with the central point, the interlacing and admixture—indeed the complementarity—between each individual's victimized and victimizing aspects."[57] The issue of a "national memory" officially represented by the state, however, remained a target against which individual consciousness needed to assert itself if democracy was to become a reality.

Another prominent figure who tapped into the political ferment of committed antiestablishment activism was Honda Katsuichi, star reporter for the *Asahi shinbun* from the 1960s through the 1980s and a pioneer of ethnographic journalism who specialized in travel and adventure writing in different areas of the world. He wrote about minority peoples such as the Inuit in Canada, the New Guinea Highlanders, the

Bedouins of the Middle East, as well as minorities in the United States and in Japan itself. But it was his reporting from the front in Vietnam and his subsequent journey to China that opened his eyes to the connections between structures of hegemony and the politics of memory. Just as witnessing American war atrocities against Vietnamese people exploded the myth of peace and justice as attributes of democratic America, Honda's research into the Nanjing massacre and other Japanese atrocities against Chinese people during the war challenged the notion of Japanese victimhood. Serialized in several Asahi newspapers in 1971, his interviews with Chinese survivors sparked heated debates, which took on added significance in the context of the normalization of Sino-Japanese relations and ongoing controversies over history textbooks. His work was later published in book form, including *Journey to China* (*Chūgoku no tabi*, 1972) and later *The Road to Nanjing* (*Nankin e no michi*, 1987).[58]

Honda's style of "counter-memory" embraced the voices of witnesses and survivors of Japanese atrocities and set them against the postwar structures of memory in Japan on the one hand (the Tokyo war crimes trial and U.S. Cold War policy) and the alleged victimization narratives of the pacifist left on the other (the atomic bombings of Hiroshima and Nagasaki). In John Lie's reading, Honda saw the issue of war responsibility primarily as an ethical problem, and he was deeply troubled by how "intimately intertwined with contemporary politics" this issue had become. Honda's investigations, which were certainly not free of sensationalism, elicited a wave of conservative criticism, ranging from simple denials to valuable contributions to the historical record, in various combinations. In the course of the debate it became clear, for example, that some of Honda's reports of killing competitions between soldiers in Nanjing in 1937 had no basis in fact.[59] This prompted the conservative journalist Suzuki Akira and the World War II veteran Yamamoto Shichihei to dismiss the Nanjing massacre as a whole as an "illusion."[60] In this way, a steady stream of new publications investigating explicitly Japanese wartime atrocities, including the abuse of Korean comfort women and forced laborers, began to focus more public attention on the contentious politics of war memory.

In the following two decades, however, the most intense battles over war memory centered on "official memory" and its default custodian, the state, in the highly public controversies about the status of Yasukuni Shrine and the contents of history textbooks. The considerable broadening of citizen political activism through movements such as these slowly altered the overly restricted place of memory in public discourse. Yet the ideal of the autonomous citizen or truth-seeking investigator did not entirely supplant existing forms of memory as special interests.

CHAPTER EIGHT

Patronizing the War Dead:
The Contested Rites of Official Memory

One of the enduring ironies of Japan's politics of memory lay in the government's refusal to take an explicit, representative, "official" stance on the meaning of the war—one that could be communicated internationally—while it nonetheless shaped the domestic negotiation of memories through bureaucratic and sometimes unconstitutional means. With some well-publicized exceptions, almost all of them recent, cabinet members publicly neither condoned Japan's war effort nor denied war atrocities directly. But statements of apology or remorse for the crimes of the imperial army also remained few and far between until the 1990s. Nor did state leaders take an explicit moral stance on the concrete responsibilities that the postwar state had inherited from its prewar predecessor. These issues instead guided the dynamics of a civic political sphere and engaged the state in selective—and therefore particularly controversial—ways.

Indirect gestures by the government toward an uncritical continuation of wartime nationalist ideology thus came to attract ever more public attention. From the mid-1970s on, few political issues fed public controversy over the state's involvement in war memory as reliably as prime ministers' visits to Yasukuni Shrine on the anniversary of defeat, 15 August. The protests began in earnest with Prime Minister Miki Takeo's Yasukuni visit in August 1975—even though he went as a private citizen. Opponents of this ritualistic commemoration of the war

Fig. 8.1 Christian groups protesting against Prime Minister Miki Takeo's visit to Yasukuni Shrine, 15 August 1975. Used by permission of Kyōdō News Agency.

dead interpreted it as a sign of support for the proliferating nationalist citizens' groups campaigning for state recognition of the shrine for the military dead. Religious organizations, especially Buddhist and Christian pacifist groups, protested fiercely against a revival of state-sanctioned Shinto rituals on the grounds of constitutional violation (Fig. 8.1). A few years later, in the spring of 1979, the secret enshrinement of Class A war criminals at Yasukuni in October 1978 belatedly came to public light. Because enshrinement required cooperation between shrine authorities and government ministries, opponents were now convinced that the government was pushing an official memory of the war in line with nationalist special interests. So great was public outrage at this matter-of-fact resurrection of convicted war criminals that Prime Minister Ōhira Masayoshi needed bodyguards for his protection when he paid his respects at Yasukuni that April (Fig. 8.2).

The Yasukuni problem was one of two specific issues that have been at the center of struggles over war memory throughout the postwar decades. The other concerned the state screening of history textbooks and their coverage of the war years. Both issues involved the central bureaucracy, which, in contrast to government leaders, had always actively participated in shaping public memory. The Ministry of Edu-

Fig. 8.2 Prime Minister Ōhira Masayoshi visits Yasukuni Shrine on 21 April 1979, surrounded by bodyguards, during the controversy over the secret enshrinement of Class A war criminals the previous October. Used by permission of Mainichi Shinbunsha.

cation was consistently involved in shaping the process by which public educational materials on Japanese history were evaluated and implemented, at times overstepping its authority. The Ministry of Health and Welfare determined war victims' eligibility for compensation in ways that clearly privileged military families while excluding non-Japanese who had been colonial subjects. Textbooks and Yasukuni Shrine became symbols for the fiercest postwar conflicts over the meanings of citizenship and nationhood, which could be understood only against the background of state ideologies cultivated before and during the war.

After defeat, occupation officials singled out the education system and institutionalized religion as the two key areas of Japanese public life that had perpetuated wartime militarism and needed to be transformed into carriers of democracy by decentralizing education and privatizing

Shinto. But as soon as the occupation ended, political leaders on both extremes of the political spectrum seized upon these reforms and made them tools for their respective interest politics from within as well as from outside the bureaucracies, which had already become bastions of conservative power. Against the push from the Teachers' Union (JTU) for further decentralization, the Ministry of Education successfully instituted new prerogatives: textbook screening in 1953, curbing the political activities of public school teachers the following year. The Japan Association of War-bereaved Families (Izokukai), meanwhile, used the issue of regaining state protection of Yasukuni Shrine to forge close ties with politicians from the Liberal Democratic Party (LDP) and bureaucrats in the Ministry of Health and Welfare.

From the early 1950s to the late 1990s and beyond, these two issues worked their way through every level of public life, from the Diet, the courts, and the academy to the mass media. They remained by far the most salient issues of war memory, not only because they centered on the state as the official representative of Japan as a nation, but also because of the changing composition of actors willing to keep them in the public light. The rise of the New Left in the later 1960s and of the New Right in the 1970s began to offset the monopoly of large political pressure groups in fighting these issues. More and more citizens' organizations campaigned against what they saw as state infringements on civil rights—either as private citizens entitled to free expression or as members of the national community entitled to appropriate state representation. Such negotiations of citizenship and nationhood were constituent parts of all democracies in the latter half of the twentieth century, as Laura Hein and Mark Selden show convincingly in their comparative volume on textbook controversies in Japan, Germany, and the United States.[1] Hein and Selden highlight textbooks as "particularly important 'sites of memory'" not only because they are imbued with an official authority to disseminate national narratives, but also because the public controversies they invite "signal challenges to hegemony."[2]

This was undoubtedly true for postwar Japan, where education served a critical role in the (re)creation of the all-important web of social relations anchored in cultural legacies as well as in political lessons learned from the past. Ienaga Saburō, history teacher and author of a textbook covering the Asia-Pacific War, spearheaded a prominent movement against official attempts to whitewash Japan's colonial and war conduct by suing the Ministry of Education for textbook censorship three times.[3] His lawsuits, which spanned three decades (1965–97) and received enormous support from citizens' groups, were never entirely successful or completely defeated, but they kept the issue of official control over textbooks on the political agenda. More important, the textbook issue cast the dynamics of public memory firmly in the mold of liberal, responsible citizens struggling against an undemocratic and (scandalously) unapologetic government.

The Yasukuni Shrine problem complicates this picture. First of all, it focuses attention on a different but equally critical "site of memory," one in which the performative or "incorporated" quality of memory takes precedence over the textual or "inscribed."[4] The physical space of the shrine precincts and the commemorative rituals performed there embodied aspects of Japan's prewar and wartime ideology in ways that school texts could not. More than debates over historical narratives, Yasukuni tapped the dynamics of "social memory as ritual practice," as John Nelson phrased it, by giving physical expression to the public values associated with the cult of the war dead.[5] Because the site and rite of honoring the war dead represented a quintessential modern tradition invented in the context of empire and war, the survival into the postwar era of the Yasukuni cult—however unofficial—provided fertile ground for conflicts over the nature of that continuity. Yasukuni, therefore, became a clearly overdetermined site of memory, where place, ritual form, institutional networks, constitutional law, and interest politics all overlapped and finally converged on the role of the state. The governing LDP, meanwhile, instead of embracing questions of official memory as a genuinely public matter to be decided on the state-political level, tended to throw them back into the arena of interest politics—and then manipulate them via their own constituents.

Site of Memory, Symbol of Nation

Yasukuni Shrine occupies an extensive piece of prime real estate at the top of Kudan hill in central Tokyo, close to the Imperial Palace.[6] It features at least twenty sites, including shrine sanctuaries, halls for worship, Shinto gates (*torii*), memorial statues, a Japanese garden with tea houses, a Sumo ring, a Noh theater, and Japan's first museum of war paraphernalia, the Yūshūkan. Cherry trees abound on the shrine grounds, making it a popular destination for cherry-blossom viewing in the spring. Emperor Meiji granted the land for the establishment of a new Shinto shrine to honor the loyalists who had died fighting for the imperial (recast as national) cause in the Meiji Restoration.[7] Founded in 1869 as the Tokyo Shrine for the Invocation of the Military Dead (Tōkyō shōkonsha), the shrine was funded by the state with amounts that far exceeded the requirements for maintenance and ceremonies and in fact made it second in wealth only to Ise Shrine, the ancestral shrine of the imperial family.[8] Indeed, the Shrine for the Military Dead was built in early Meiji as a modern public space featuring state-of-the-art architecture and technology, a landmark in the transition from Edo to Tokyo, a place immersed in contemporary public life.[9]

In 1879, again by imperial decree, the shrine was renamed Shrine of the Peaceful Country (Yasukuni jinja) and came under the jurisdiction of the ministries of the Army and Navy rather than the Ministry of Home Affairs, which supervised other shrines. Subsequently, a close relationship developed between the military, the emperor, and the shrine that established Yasukuni as a *de facto* arm of the state in public life, long before Shrine Shinto as a whole was organized into what later came to be called State Shinto. For example, the Meiji emperor appointed generals or admirals on active duty as organizers of special festivals. In the early 1890s, the spring and fall festivals at Yasukuni became elaborate public events complete with popular entertainment such as circuses, horse races, panoramas, and kabuki performances. School trips to Yasukuni became commonplace, and board games and popular songs suffused enshrinement at Yasukuni (and thus death in war) with positive meaning.[10] In 1901 the hundreds of local shrines and memorials to the war dead that had been established in the preceding decades were all designated as "spirit-invoking shrines" (*shōkonsha*) and made into local subsidiaries of Yasukuni, the one national shrine in which all deities, including those of the local shrines, were enshrined together. In this way a modern cult of honoring the military dead emerged as part of the process of defining civil morality in terms of loyalty to the emperor and the nation.

Yasukuni came to loom large in public consciousness because the cult of the war dead provided the opportunity for individual Japanese both to remember their lost relatives and friends as the people they knew *and* to give meaning to their deaths in the context of contemporary ideologies. For all its emphasis on the war dead as a "collective spirit," the shrine did (and does) meticulously preserve the name as well as the place and time of death of each enshrined soul on an individual tablet in the Main Hall. The connection between individual remembering and public commemoration became more important with the dramatic increase of war dead and their surviving families at the time of the Russo-Japanese War (1904–5).[11] Even before the conclusion of the peace treaty in September 1905, 88,429 spirits of war casualties had been enshrined at Yasukuni, a number that dwarfed earlier enshrinements and necessitated the replacement of the horizontal scroll previously used as a register of names with a ledger.[12] But it was not until 1911, shortly before Emperor Meiji's death, that the emperor himself went to Yasukuni Shrine and paid his respects to the collective dead, celebrating them for the first time as "departed heroes" (*eirei*). At no other shrine and in no other way did the emperor actually honor his subjects, and this imperial recognition of the military dead in turn counted as the highest honor for many a bereaved family.

The use of religious rituals for the nation's war dead symbolized, through a reinterpretation of the spirits of the dead, the unchanging "essence" of the national community, expressed in the unity of ritual and governance (*matsurigoto*) and culminating in the emperor. As Harry Harootunian has pointed out, this is not to be understood as a peculiarly Japanese rejection of modern, secular society. On the contrary, in Japan, as in modern Europe and America, "the re-articulation of a religious memory in institutional form" was a decidedly *modern* phenomenon, in that it served modern state-building purposes but also expressed modern sensibilities.[13] At Yasukuni, the human loss and sacrifice that accompanied Japan's modernization—defined in military terms—were given meaning and purpose by celebrating the service of soldiers killed on duty, rather than mourning their deaths. The link between mourning and celebrating was the belief, prominent in both Shinto and Buddhism, that the souls of those who met an untimely or violent death became "wandering spirits" without a home, locked into an undefined and ambiguous relationship with the living.[14] While such spirits were thought of in the medieval period as angry or vengeful ghosts (*onryō-gami*) who required rites to pacify and console them, those who were (re)interpreted in the Tokugawa period as the spirits of martyrs "were enshrined so that they would act as protectors of a locale and its inhabitants."[15]

According to Sugiyama Kyūshirō, Yasukuni Shrine carried on this Tokugawa tradition, reinventing it, one must add, to forge the collective identities (of both the military dead and the living) that stood at the heart of the new imperial ideology. A decidedly individualistic conception of those who gave their lives for a higher cause as heroes became, after 1879, the celebration of a collective body of military dead in the name of the "country" (*kuni*) and subsequently the modern emperor state. To this end, another Shinto concept was invoked—namely, the homogenization of the military dead into a "collective spirit" through the ritual of enshrinement and perpetual ceremonies of worship.

Right after death the spirit is all sharp edges; it still has a very strong individual personality. If you enshrine it, it slowly loses its rough edges till finally it's round and smooth like a marble; it's lost all its individuality. These featureless spirits gather together and form a kind of collective spirit. . . . The end of the memorial period means the spirit has become part of a collective spirit.[16]

This metaphor resonated deeply with the dominant rhetoric among Meiji ideologues, who espoused shared moral values and service to the nation as the basis for a cohesive national community. But to the extent that national homogeneity remained more an ideal to strive for than a reality achieved, it could at least be celebrated as a remembered reality through the cult of the war dead. The periodic performance of memorial ceremonies for the "collective spirit" of the war dead, therefore, served symbolically to smooth out the differences among those who performed them or in whose name they were performed. It was as if the "collective spirit" of the war dead communicated with, and even joined, the collective living—the imperial subjects. In this way, memory of the war dead became timeless, metaphysical, canonical, and dissociated from any specific historical context.

The political use of the Yasukuni cult, however, did not become fully institutionalized until 1939, when all shrines to the war dead were simultaneously renamed "nation-protecting shrines" (*gokoku jinja*) and their priests began to serve as public officials.[17] In the same year, the

war bereaved, a visible political constituency entitled to government
pensions, were accorded their own bureaucratic organ, the Military
Protection Agency. After decades of state-initiated restructuring of
the shrine world in the name of national security and imperial expansion, Shinto leaders and war-bereaved families now represented an
important channel for public support of the war effort directly linked
to the bureaucracy. As an organized special interest—whose public
presence increased as the number of war dead on the continent and
in the Pacific skyrocketed—they were entitled to a wide range of state
privileges, including financial assistance in the form of pensions and
state-sponsored enshrinement ceremonies for the war dead at Yasukuni
Shrine.

This official privileging of military families also connected with the
popular imagination of Yasukuni as a place of individual remembrance
and veneration. A famous song popular with men heading off to the
war front ran: "You and I are cherry blossoms of the same year / even
if we're far apart when our petals fall / we'll bloom again in the treetops
of the capital's Yasukuni Shrine."[18] But the nexus between individual
and collective remembering of the war dead remained complex. John
Nelson quotes interesting examples of subtle—and not so subtle—
protest against the state appropriation of the war dead, again in songs:
"Your spirit is settled in Yasukuni / but sometimes it returns home / in
your mother's dreams."[19]

Another source indicates that the collective cult of the war dead practiced at Yasukuni did not automatically supplant feelings of personal
intimacy with the enshrined spirits of fallen relatives. Yasukuni's head
priest, Suzuki Takao, complained in an article written for army officers
in 1941:

You really have to think about this [process of enshrinement] and understand
it. A person who has lost a son cannot think about him as separate and their
own; you have to make him understand that his son has become a *kami*. Bereaved families are wrong to feel intimacy to the shrine and behave in casual
and inappropriate ways. To equate the human spirits (*jinrei*) with the divine
spirits (*shinrei*) shows a false orientation: these spirits now belong to the nation-state. The only will that survives is that of the state.[20]

This conceptualization of the war dead was characteristic of the Yasukuni cult at its height between 1939 and 1945—that is, in the context

of total war. It marked the culmination of a unique process through which the shrine ceased to commemorate the "birth" of the modern nation, but instead came to symbolize—if not to legitimize—the definition of the nation-state in relation to military engagement at home and abroad. By continuing to enshrine those who died in Japan's wars, the shrine avoided becoming a relic of the past and remained at the center of Japanese nation building as long as (and to the degree that) the national community was linked to military service and sacrifice for the emperor. Yasukuni's modernity in prewar and wartime Japan was based on the periodic updating of memory by the addition of the newly fallen to the collective body of the enshrined, while relating this process to the same underlying constant—Japan's "national essence" (*kokutai*).

As a site of memory and a symbol of nation, Yasukuni Shrine developed and perpetuated the cult of the war dead through its institutional role as an organ of the state, the interpretation and performance of religious rituals by the Shinto community, and the creation of a political constituency of war-bereaved families. Each of these three support systems was targeted as a pillar of militarism by the occupation reforms, and all three were again at stake in the postwar political conflict about war memory in contemporary Japan.

The "Yasukuni Question"

From the perspective of Shrine Shinto and the nationalist right, the "Yasukuni question" stemmed from early postwar occupation policies that imposed "foreign values" on Japan—a defeated country—in an effort to erase its essential spiritual structure, which occupation officials deemed "militaristic." Indeed, MacArthur had no deep historical knowledge of Yasukuni Shrine, but he understood that the cult of the war dead as it was practiced at its wartime height rested on a network of political and institutional links controlled by the state and culminating in the emperor. MacArthur dismantled Shrine Shinto's stronghold in the central bureaucracy, declared Yasukuni Shrine a private religious institution, and then relegated it to the nonpublic sphere under the new constitutional separation of state and religion. Under the same sweeping reforms, the wartime network of "nation-protecting shrines" throughout Japan and the colonies ceased its political function. The site of the shrine itself, however, and the enshrinement rituals performed there were left untouched. Exactly how to officially commemorate the millions of war dead, too, remained unresolved. Consequently, for the priests and supporters of Yasukuni Shrine, these were truly "winter years," as shrine retrospectives liked to call the occupation period.

Japan's independence had barely been negotiated in 1951 when the Yasukuni question in the broadest sense (including its physical site and ritual uses) reappeared as a political issue—within the limits set by the postwar constitution. For a short time it appeared as if the shrine grounds themselves were up for grabs. On 1 September 1951, several months into the Korean War, the peace movement found the shrine precincts an appropriate central location to stage a massive peace festival organized by the People's League for Peace in Japan (Nihon heiwa kokumin kaigi) in conjunction with the General Council of Trade Unions. Ten thousand people were drawn to the shrine, many waving the Communist Party newspaper, *Akahata*, and singing workers' liberation songs (illustrated on the cover of this book).[21] The following month, on 18 October, Prime Minister Yoshida Shigeru visited Yasukuni Shrine for the first time since the end of the war—presumably with SCAP permission—to participate in its prominent fall festival and pay his personal respects to the enshrined war dead.[22] Less than a year later, 15 August 1952 marked Japan's first commemoration of the end of the war as an independent country and inaugurated an annual government-sponsored nonreligious ceremony that came to be held at the Nihon Budōkan (a large public hall located across the street from Yasukuni Shrine), and is attended by the imperial couple as well as thousands of war bereaved. The emperor, moreover, performed rites at Yasukuni for the first time after its change in status to a private religious institution during its fall festival on 16 October 1952; he would appear six times thereafter for special anniversary celebrations (Table 1).

The political and cultural meanings of honoring the Japanese war dead through an official ceremony, as well as the institutional constraints of doing so at Yasukuni Shrine, clearly became a concern as soon as the occupation ended. Yoshida Shigeru paid a visit *as prime minister* in May (and two more times in 1953 and in 1954), and Emperor Hirohito worshiped at Yasukuni during the fall festival in October. This represented a major victory for the newly established Izokukai, which tied its own political clout to winning support for revising the shrine's status.

Table 1
Postwar Visits to Yasukuni Shrine by Emperor Hirohito

Date	Occasion
16 October 1952	Yasukuni Shrine becomes private religious legal body under new constitution
19 December 1954	Fall festival; 85th anniversary of Yasukuni's establishment
23 April 1957	Spring festival
8 April 1959	Special festival commemorating the 90th anniversary of Yasukuni's establishment
19 October 1965	Special festival for the 20th anniversary of the end of World War II
20 October 1969	Yasukuni Shrine centennial
21 November 1975	30th anniversary of the end of World War II

SOURCE: Tanaka Nobumasa, *Yasukuni no sengoshi* (2003).

A number of proposals for alternative places and ceremonies were floated in government circles at the time, but none put the Yasukuni question to rest. The annual Budōkan ceremony was unsatisfactory, in the eyes of the nationalists, because it corresponded too closely to the "foreign values" imposed on Japan after defeat instead of reflecting the values for which Japan's war victims had actually died. The decision in December 1952 to build a Tomb of the Unknown Soldier in the general vicinity of Yasukuni was all but ignored by Yasukuni supporters, and when it was finally built at the end of the decade, Izokukai leaders were quick to assert that any site commemorating unknown soldiers ought to be located within the Yasukuni precinct, whereas this new site (named Chidorigafuchi senbotsusha hoen) certainly did not supplant or compete with Yasukuni Shrine in any way.[23] Other ideas included a 1956 proposal from the JSP to reconceive the shrine as "Yasukuni Peace Hall" (Yasukuni heiwadō) and an LDP delegate's suggestion to create a national holiday, Yasukuni Day (*Yasukuni no hi*), on 15 August.[24] Neither was ever seriously considered.

The obvious availability of alternatives notwithstanding, the so-called Yasukuni question revolved around the uncompromising campaign by the organized war bereaved and Shrine Shintoists to bring the shrine once again under state management—that is, to make it the official site and symbol of Japan's war dead and thereby reproduce the prewar relationship between the state and the people. The logic behind this effort was deceptively simple and unyielding: because the war dead represented a collective, indeed official, entity that had served the state, their sacrifice required a collective, official response by the state. This "natural" reciprocal relationship, however, had been undercut and declared illegal by the Allied occupation forces, who insisted on the constitutional separation of state and religion and forced Yasukuni Shrine into an "unnatural" situation as a private religious body. A petition signed by the Association of Shinto Shrines, the All-Japan Committee of Shinto Youth, and the Tokyo Prefecture Association of Shinto Youth put it emotionally: "Can we silently endure this indifference by the state toward those who sacrificed their lives for the country?"[25] Concretely, state management or protection (*goji*) meant dissolving Yasukuni as a "religious juridical person" (*shūkyō hōjin*) and creating a special legal category, thereby shifting the expenses for commemorative rituals and festivals to the national government and incorporating visits to the shrine into the duties of state officials.

Conservative politicians recognized early on that the memory of the war dead generated political capital. War-bereaved Diet members from the LDP were organized into special leagues in the Lower House as early as March 1950 and in the Upper House in February 1951, providing a ready-made political network for Izokukai in its transition to a full-fledged political interest group. The issue of state protection of Yasukuni Shrine came to occupy a central place in the forging of close and powerful ties between the Association and the LDP, granting the Association representation of its interests at the highest level while guaranteeing the LDP a stable pool of votes.[26] In turn, many LDP politicians felt that visiting Yasukuni Shrine on the occasion of its annual festivals was the least they could do for public relations. It is fair to say that the movement for state protection of Yasukuni Shrine cemented the political relationship between the Association and the LDP, a relationship that defied generational change (the gradual dwindling in numbers of war bereaved as well as the fading of war memories) by ossifying a particular memory into a political structure that remains strong even today.

The hallmark of the close political relationship between the LDP and the Izokukai was the Yasukuni Shrine Bill (Yasukuni jinja hōan), championed by LDP representatives and the legal office of the Lower

House from 1956 on and finally presented to the Sixty-first Diet for deliberation on 30 June 1969, Yasukuni Shrine's centennial anniversary. The bill proposed to bring under the prime minister's direct supervision decisions concerning whose spirits qualified to be enshrined at Yasukuni, based on the recommendation of the shrine as well as "legal criteria." The purpose of the shrine, according to the bill, was "to express the people's feeling of reverence for the souls of those who died in war and those who gave their lives for their country, to commemorate their lasting services, to console them, and to perform ceremonies, rites, etc., to honor their deeds, and thereby keep their high merits forever in the memory of later generations."[27] It further stated that the name Yasukuni "Shrine" merely reflected the history of its establishment in the wake of the Meiji Restoration without signifying a religious institution, and it stipulated that Yasukuni could not represent a religious belief or sponsor religious activities such as teaching or caring for believers.

From the perspective of the popular progressive opposition, organized around Christian and Buddhist as well as peace groups, it was not occupation reforms but the introduction of this Yasukuni Shrine Bill to the Diet in 1969 that represented the beginning of the Yasukuni question. It certainly marked a turning-point insofar as the bill initiated a broadly public debate about war memory and responsibility linked to the official meaning and use of the shrine. Public opposition grew strong when the hegemonic qualities of this proposed government-sponsored "official memory" became apparent. It was seen as pushing the limits of the postwar constitution, which was widely considered to guard against renewed state domination of public life. The JSP interpreted the Yasukuni Shrine Bill as evidence of the LDP's intention to "extinguish Japanese feelings of guilt and war responsibility" and "reconfigure popular consciousness to serve the 'atomic security pact.'"[28] This came on the heels of the successful revival of National Foundation Day (*kenkoku kinen no hi*) in 1967 and the government's elaborate commemoration of the Meiji Centennial in 1968 and was paralleled by trends in education policy and commercial journalism. The confluence of these developments suggested to the left in general that these events were part of an effort to extend the state's reach further into public life.

The pacifist Wadatsumikai posed the problem succinctly by invoking the postwar constitution in response to the historical experience of wartime state coercion, of which Yasukuni Shrine was an important symbol. Explicating the opposition movement's point that Yasukuni represented Japanese militarism, and that reviving state management would amount to a denial of constitutional pacifism, Mitsui Taketomo wrote:

The constitution is a reflection on the conduct of the state during the war, putting in place a structure that will make it impossible for the state to wage war again and control the minds of the people. We can't let this be reversed. The problem is not so much that people desire militarism again, but that they become indifferent to how much power the state wields. . . . [Allowing Yasukuni Shrine to be managed by the state] is a matter of letting the state interpret history. . . . [Yasukuni] is a historical problem turned into a political one, and as such, it is of concern to all of us.[29]

The real thrust of the opposition's resistance to Shinto's infringement on other religions' rights and interests, however, centered on its wider social implications—namely, the resulting infringement on civil rights in general. The JSP stated this clearly in its response to the LDP's Yasukuni Shrine Bill proposal in 1969:

Freedom of religion does not exist by itself but is closely tied to other freedoms, that of thought and conscience (Article 19) and of congregation, organization, speech, press, etc. (Article 21). That they are connected is a historical experience of the Japanese people. The Meiji Constitution also proclaimed freedom of religion but practiced violation of many civil liberties, covering up the contradictions inherent in State Shinto by proclaiming it a non-religion.[30]

In other words, democracy itself, defined as the protection of individual rights and civil liberties from state intrusion, was at stake. Success for the Yasukuni Shrine Bill, it was feared, would set an important precedent for other items on the ultraconservative agenda geared toward overturning occupation reforms and strengthening the power of the state. For example, once Yasukuni Shrine became a state institution, nothing would prevent the many prefectural and local shrines to the war dead from also receiving state protection. And if Ise Shrine and Atsuta Shrine followed suit, both of which housed imperial insignia, the result would be the *de facto* revival of State Shinto, the openly proclaimed goal of the Association of Shinto Shrines.[31] The number of local lawsuits connected with the Yasukuni question beginning in the mid-1960s (five had become nationally prominent by the mid-1970s)[32] would suggest, however, that this controversy intersected with a whole field of social, political, and legal issues related to freedom of expression. It is no coincidence that those vehemently opposed to the Yasukuni Shrine Bill were also active in the labor union movement and the controversy over textbook authorization, as well as issues of minority rights.[33]

The Yasukuni Shrine Bill was presented to the Diet five times between 1969 and 1974 and finally failed in an Upper House vote. The early 1970s represented a particularly volatile time for the governing LDP. Party members turned out to be far from united in their assessment of whether the Yasukuni issue represented an asset or a liability. Clearly, the desire to gain considerable control over the nation's official memory was tempered by wariness about a constitutional quagmire and public opposition. Even before the Yasukuni Shrine Bill was first presented in the Diet, pragmatists criticized its timing, citing the priority of such issues as the student movement, the renewal of the Security Treaty, and the return of Okinawa. LDP representative Kusunoki Masatoshi, for example, argued in the Upper House on 12 March 1969: "It is of grave concern for our party that religious circles, which so far have supported our conservative agenda, are disappointed that we support such a bill. With 1970 ahead of us, we can't afford to polarize public opinion and confuse the people. Given the circumstances, we should carefully weigh if it is wise to put this bill on the agenda."[34]

In 1972 Nakasone Yasuhiro, then head of the LDP and a later prime minister, proposed to abandon the movement to change the legal status of Yasukuni Shrine and instead use state funds to erect a new memorial hall to the war dead (*senbotsusha no ireitō*). He went so far as to suggest that the denial of Yasukuni's religious nature amounted to a "fabrication" by the authors of the bill. Not surprisingly, Nakasone's plan, which he revealed at a mass meeting at Hibiya Hall in the presence of the media, drew sharp criticism from spokesmen for the Association of War-bereaved Families[35] and especially from Shrine Shintoists. *Jinja shinpō* dismissed Nakasone's idea as solving nothing but instead further complicating the issue by failing to recognize the historical significance of Yasukuni Shrine.[36]

Table 2

Postwar Visits to Yasukuni Shrine by Prime Ministers, 1951–2005

Prime Minister	Number of visits and occasion	Dates
Yoshida Shigeru (1948–54)	7 visits (3 by proxy), spring or fall festivals, other times	10/18/51, 5/5/52 (prox.), 10/17/52, 4/23/53, 10/24/53 (prox.), 4/25/54 (prox.), 10/20/54
Hatoyama Ichirō (1954–56)	No visits	none
Ishibashi Tanzan (1956–57)	No visits	none
Kishi Nobusuke (1957–60)	2 visits, spring or fall festivals only	4/25/57, 10/21/58
Ikeda Hayato (1960–64)	5 visits, fall festival and other times	10/18/60, 5/18/61, 11/15/61 11/4/62, 9/22/63
Satō Eisaku (1964–72)	11 visits, annually, spring or fall festivals only	4/21/65, 4/21/66, 4/22/67, 4/23/68, 4/22/69, 10/18/69, 4/22/70, 10/17/70, 4/22/71, 10/18/71, 4/22/72
Tanaka Kakuei (1972–74)	6 visits, twice annually, usually spring or fall festivals	7/8/72, 10/17/72, 4/23/73, 10/18/73, 4/23/74, 10/19/74
Miki Takeo (1974–76)	3 visits, annually, spring or fall festivals, Aug. 15	4/22/75, 8/15/75, 10/18/76
Fukuda Takeo (1976–78)	4 visits, annually, spring or fall festivals, Aug. 15	4/21/77, 4/21/78, 8/15/78, 10/18/78
Ōhira Masayoshi (1978–80)	3 visits, annually, spring or fall festivals only	4/21/79, 10/18/79, 4/21/80

Suzuki Zenkō (1980–82)	8 visits, annually, spring or fall festivals, Aug. 15	*8/15/80*, 10/18/80, 4/21/81, *8/15/81*, 10/17/81, 4/21/82, *8/15/82*, 10/18/82
Nakasone Yasuhiro (1982–87)	10 visits (once as P.M.), annually until 1985, spring or fall festivals, Aug. 15, New Year's	4/21/83, *8/15/83*, 10/18/83, 1/5/84, 4/21/84, *8/15/84*, 10/18/84 1/21/85, 4/22/85, *8/15/1985* (as P.M)
Takeshita Noboru (1987–89)	No visits	none
Uno Sōsuke (1989)	No visits	none
Kaifu Toshiki (1989–91)	No visits	none
Miyazawa Kiichi (1991–93)	No visits	none
Hosokawa Morihiro (1993–94)	No visits	none
Hata Tsutomu (1994)	No visits	none
Murayama Tomiichi (1994–96)	No visits, strongly encouraged cabinet to follow suit	none
Hashimoto Ryūtarō (1996–98)	1 visit, on his birthday	7/29/96
Obuchi Keizō (1998–2000)	No visits	none
Mori Yoshirō (2000–01)	No visits	none
Koizumi Jun'ichirō (2001–06)	4 visits, consciously avoiding Aug. 15	8/13/02, 4/21/02, 1/14/03, 1/14/04

NOTE: Italicized dates denote visits on the anniversary of Japan's defeat in World War II.
SOURCE: Tanaka Nobumasa, *Yasukuni no sengoshi* (2003).

From the mid-1970s on, leaders of Izokukai and the Association of Shinto Shrines, with their supporters in the LDP, worked out a less contentious arrangement. Instead of attempting to resolve the Yasukuni question through institutional change or even constitutional amendment, for which Diet approval was necessary, it became "customary" for prime ministers to attend not only the official commemoration ceremony at the Budōkan on 15 August, but to also worship at Yasukuni Shrine that day. As Table 2 shows, most prime ministers, beginning with Yoshida Shigeru in 1951, regularly visited the shrine, but they did so during the spring and fall festivals in honor of the war dead rather than on 15 August. This changed in 1975, when Miki Takeo visited the shrine on the thirtieth anniversary of Japan's defeat, honoring the Japanese war dead explicitly as a private citizen.[37] Nonetheless, Miki faced severe criticism from the JSP and the opposition in general.

Perhaps the decisive turning-point came in 1978, when Chief Cabinet Secretary Abe Shintarō laid out what would become the new rules for prime ministers' Yasukuni visits in a question-and-answer session in the Diet. Prime ministers were free to visit the shrine as private citizens, he asserted, use a government vehicle for security and identification purposes, allow cabinet members to accompany them, and even add their title to their signatures in the visitors' book.[38] Between 1975 and 1985, every prime minister except Ōhira Masayoshi visited Yasukuni on 15 August, following these new rules as they saw fit. Fukuda Takeo in 1978 used public funds to pay his respects at Yasukuni Shrine, and Suzuki Zenkō visited Yasukuni accompanied by his whole cabinet in 1981. At the fortieth anniversary of the war's end, in 1985, however, Nakasone's announcement that he was visiting Yasukuni Shrine officially as prime minister elicited a storm of protest (especially from other Asian countries) that in effect halted the practice.[39] Since then, both the domestic and the foreign press have sought to infer the state of Japan's official memory from what goes on at Yasukuni Shrine on 15 August.

Ōhira's abstention in 1979 from Yasukuni visits on the mid-August anniversary was surely calculated, for it was during his term in office that the secret enshrinement of fourteen convicted Class A war criminals at the 1978 Yasukuni fall festival came to light. On 17 October, the spirits of war leaders found guilty by the Tokyo war crimes tribunal of crimes

against peace and major crimes against humanity were quietly apotheo-
sized in a private ceremony that added them to the collective body of
the "heroic war dead." Those honored included wartime prime minister
Tōjō Hideki and General Matsui Iwane (in charge of the Kwantung
Army during the Nanjing massacre). When Suzuki Zenkō and Nakasone
Yasuhiro visited the shrine in subsequent years, they were thus honoring
not only the "ordinary" military victims of World War II but also those
who bore a great deal of responsibility for the war in the first place.
Records from the Health and Welfare Ministry show that the ministry
itself was centrally involved in supplying the necessary data on the war
criminals while Izokukai officials managed the cooperation between the
families of these war criminals, the shrine, and the government. The media, moreover, reported this event six months after the fact, on 19 April
1979, and in a matter-of-fact style that belied the extraordinary boldness
of this move and especially the undemocratic manner in which it was
decided, carried out, and kept from public view.[40] For many, the
enshrinement of top war criminals amounted to a Japanese verdict on
the "victor's justice" of the Tokyo war crimes tribunal more than a full-
fledged rehabilitation of war criminals. As *Jinja shinpō* editorialized on
30 April 1979, "to allow the spirits of the Class A war criminals to be
the only ones not enshrined [at Yasukuni] places a heavy responsibility
on the shrine for accepting the one-sided judgment of the Tokyo war
crimes trial by foreign hands."

The nationalist right has always contested Japan's official acceptance
of the Tokyo trial verdict, but the connection between the verdict and
the Yasukuni enshrinements is problematic. On the one hand, the *imperial* dimension of Yasukuni Shrine is indeed critical to understanding
the central meaning of the shrine. Yasukuni is dedicated to the spirits of
military men who died for the emperor, whether in a civil war (the
Boshin War, the Satsuma rebellion) or the imperial wars fought abroad.
By that logic, no one died as heroically for the emperor as the Class A
war criminals, who throughout the Tokyo war crimes trial remained silent on Hirohito's war responsibility as supreme commander-in-chief
and instead were themselves convicted of crimes against peace. In
many ways, they died quite literally as the "emperor's shield."[41] On the
other hand, how could one accept the war criminals' conduct during
the trial as shielding the emperor and then reject the trial's overall le-

gitimacy as "victor's justice"? No matter how one looked at it, the Allied war crimes trials complicated the issue of enshrinement.

For the nationalist right, the 1978 enshrinement and the annual Yasukuni visits by government officials were a step toward resolving the Yasukuni question. On 6 June 1979, the Association of Shinto Shrines won another victory when the use of imperial reign names to structure the Japanese calendar was formally written into law (*gengōhō*).[42] To trace these events exclusively on the state-political level, however, ignores their wider repercussions for the emergence of a broadly public debate on the meaning and function of the war dead and the rituals associated with their remembrance. On the surface, the outrage over the Yasukuni Shrine Bill in the Diet focused squarely on the pork-barrel politics of the LDP, thereby perpetuating the assumption that the Yasukuni question was essentially an institutional one. But it also spurred a broader discussion about war memory and the central place that the war dead occupied for Japanese of different political or even religious convictions. No less significantly, the competition over the memory of the war dead came to involve a wide variety of citizen activists, including those of nationalist persuasion, and thereby began to refocus war memory on a popular level of discourse. The 1970s turned out to be a critical decade in which the dynamics of the public contest over the past changed.

The Contested Memory of the War Dead

It was not inevitable that Yasukuni Shrine should become synonymous with the nationalist far right in Japanese politics. Yasukuni remained in the political limelight in part also because of efforts on the liberal left to tame the nationalistic flavor of the shrine, to rescue it from its prewar history, and to grant it positive relevance in the context of a peaceful postwar Japan. There was, after all, wide agreement both on the need to remember those who died in World War II and on the preservation of the shrine itself as a historical and cultural site. The JSP, for example, argued that "commemorating the souls of the victims of World War II should not be a privilege of Yasukuni Shrine but should instead be the task of the people as a whole by thinking deeply about the imperialistic wars and its victims from the standpoint of love for peace."[43] The Socialist and especially pacifist and left-leaning intellectual groups keen on exploring Japan's war responsibility sharply criticized Yasukuni's attempt to canonize war memory instead of opening it up to critical examination. They recognized early on that as long as the performance of established rituals dominated official memory of the war, there would be no debate about the state's war responsibility.

Resistance from various religious organizations, which formed the core of the opposition movement, hinged on the attempt by the proponents of the Yasukuni Shrine Bill to elevate Shinto rituals over other ceremonies of commemoration. The Japanese Religionists Council for Peace (Nihon shūkyōsha heiwa kyōgikai) and the peace organizations within various religions were the first to register their opposition to state management of Yasukuni for constitutional reasons.[44] The Japan Religion League (Nihon shūkyō renmei), an umbrella organization of various Buddhist sects, Christian churches, Sect Shinto, and several new religions issued a statement of protest on 22 January 1968, declaring that the Yasukuni Shrine Bill violated the constitutional guarantee of religious freedom (Article 20) and violated the rights and interests of religious organizations under the Religious Corporations Law.[45]

Because of Yasukuni's status as a private religious corporation, however, such alternative visions for the shrine's presence in Japanese public life were easily held at bay by the Shinto officials. To Shrine Shintoists as well as their war-bereaved supporters, it was of the utmost importance that Yasukuni not be reinterpreted and that the rituals performed there retain their exact prewar form. Precisely because so many aspects of Japanese society had been reinvented after 1945, the rites for the war dead—especially when conducted by or in the presence of the emperor—embodied the very continuity of the Japanese polity that the occupation had attempted to erase.[46] The Association of Shinto Shrines invoked the same argument put forth by the Meiji state in support of Shinto's nonreligious status and claimed that the performance of rites for the war dead at Yasukuni was merely Japanese "custom" and not a religion covered by the constitution. In participating in the rites, individuals were free to believe anything they wanted, and, in any case, among those who presently worshiped at Yasukuni, believing Shintoists made up only a small minority.[47] Moreover, Yasukuni owed its contemporary status as a private religious institution to the mistaken views of the occupation, which did not represent its "true characteristics."[48]

By far the most interesting debate from the perspective of memory centered on the war dead and those who claimed to speak for them. This ideological field was complex. Here the source of controversy was Izokukai's attempt to monopolize and homogenize the popular memory of the war dead, just as the Association of Shinto Shrines insisted on its monopoly in defining ritual purity. Against Izokukai's claim to speak for all war-bereaved families, the Teachers' Union mobilized 600,000 protesters by identifying the Yasukuni Shrine problem as an educational issue and a matter for the people as a whole to decide. Wadatsumikai collected numerous personal opinion essays by its own war-bereaved members in 1968.[49] And in June 1969 the Association of Christian War-bereaved (Kirisutosha izoku no kai) was organized, three months after Christians distanced themselves sharply from Izokukai's claim to represent all war bereaved as well as its effort to control how the intentions of the war dead should be interpreted.[50]

Popular protest centered on Izokukai's insistence, once again, on designating those enshrined at Yasukuni as "departed heroes" (*eirei*) instead of using the more neutral postwar term "people who died in war" (*senbotsusha*). The term *eirei* conveyed empathy with the war dead, which rested on the conflation of state objectives and soldiers' perceptions of national crisis. As such it clashed directly with other interpretations of the war dead. The voices of the fallen student-soldiers as constructed by Wadatsumikai, for example, did not reflect the country's crisis but their own personal sense of crisis, which resulted from the incompatibility of their longing for peace with their country's commitment to war.

While both versions defined contemporary national identity by reconstructing the imagined intentions of the war dead through commemoration, they differed sharply in the way they understood both the living and the dead as collectivities. The Izokukai perpetuated the prewar and wartime ideology of a collective spirit of the war dead, which, through ceremonies of celebration, forged among the living a collective sense of nationhood centered on the state. Wadatsumikai and other war-bereaved groups, in contrast, uncovered the individual experiences of those who died in the war and linked them to the individual, personal commitment to peace that they saw as the basis of postwar democracy. And yet, in collecting student testimonies into a book while favoring those that expressed pacifist thoughts, Wadatsumikai, too, gave the student dead a collective identity. The group's 20 May 1974 statement of protest against state management of Yasukuni Shrine concluded with the following words:

We are a group of people who have come together to keep alive the will of the dead student-soldiers as seen in *Kike Wadatsumi no koe* [*Listen to the Voices from the Deep*]. While these student-soldiers watched Japan plunge into disaster with open eyes and deep sorrow, they had no intention to become martyrs for their country. We firmly believe that they earnestly wished for Japan's rebirth as a peaceful state, that is, that fundamental human rights would be honored, that state rights would originate in the people, and that a democratic state based on the wish for eternal peace would be realized. The student-soldiers are actually worshipped at Yasukuni Shrine, but if the shrine's ultrareligious form of the predefeat era was restored through state-sponsored ceremonies, their spirits would lose their peace of mind. That is the reason why our organization Wadatsumikai sternly opposes the promulgation of this evil law.[51]

The attempt by Izokukai leaders and its supporters in the LDP not only to make Yasukuni Shrine the center of official commemorations but also to unify popular memories into a national memory clearly polarized the public along ideological lines. But it also revealed, thanks to the public debates it generated, the existence of multiple viewpoints and the need to subject Yasukuni, past and present, to a critique that took different meanings into account. Among the war-bereaved members of Wadatsumikai alone, there was a considerable range of personal perspectives, from insistence on viewing Yasukuni solely in terms of its historical (public) significance to an emphasis on deeply private relationships with dead relatives. President Nakamura Katsurō, whose older brother's testament had provided the inspiration for collecting the letters of fallen student-soldiers in the late 1940s, viewed Yasukuni Shrine as the embodiment of the prewar and wartime state's criminal nature and called the bill an "oracle bird of fascism."[52] Similarly, Iizaka Yoshiaki, professor at Gakushūin University, found Yasukuni's fascist essence alive and well within Japanese democracy, specifically in its continuing symbolism of victimhood and disregard for Japan's war crimes:

Our consciousness of ourselves as victims is strong, but we can't think of ourselves as perpetrators. You only have to go to Southeast Asia or to Korea to see the other side, that of Japanese killing Asians. And we go to these countries and erect memorial stones to honor these Japanese killers. We Japanese trample on the feelings of Asians, and that is what represents the essence of Yasukuni—namely, insensitivity toward others.[53]

But many war-bereaved members of Wadatsumikai, while clearly denouncing the Yasukuni Shrine Bill, emphasized that "Yasukuni represents something different for everyone, and there is no substitute for Yasukuni for the Japanese."[54] Hoshino Yasusaburō, professor of constitutional law at Tokyo Gakugei University, told about his brother's enshrinement at the *gokoku jinja* in Nikkō after his death in China in 1938, and again at Yasukuni after the war. Although his parents were long-term members of the Nikkō branch of Izokukai and worshiped at Yasukuni, he could not bring himself to go. The shock of the death of his brother, whom he loved and respected, left an emptiness in his memory that he refused to let others—especially the state—fill with their ideas. It would be as if "a third party inserted itself between the dead and the bereaved without reflecting either the will of the dead or the opinion of the bereaved."[55] Hoshino felt no public obligation for what he considered a deeply personal matter. Seventy-nine-year-old Ikeda Takei summed up this viewpoint, reclaiming the individuality of each of the fallen and each of the bereaved, saving personal memory from a homogeneous national memory: "The bill erases the individuality of the war dead, makes them into one unrecognizable lump, remains vague on how to worship them, and makes them into a political object. But Yasukuni Shrine concerns everybody individually and thus there cannot be a common feeling of the people [toward the war dead]."[56]

Those who recognized and resisted the bill's intended effect of manipulating and monopolizing national memory had various reasons: political orientation, religious conviction (for example, many Christians felt that Shinto rites violated their religious freedom), or direct personal memories of the war. By the same token, the bill was predicated on the majority's susceptibility to ready-made interpretations and its unwillingness to think through public meanings of the war on personal terms.

Organizing Popular Nationalism

The democratization, as it were, of the Yasukuni Shrine issue and the resulting broader public interest in matters of war memory had much to do with the changing dynamics of civic political activism in the late

1960s and 1970s. The bulk of the opposition movement operated on a level of spontaneous, issue-based, and often local citizen organization and relied on a high degree of personal motivation stemming from religious belief, political conviction, professional integrity, or historical experience. Few of the newly formed groups established themselves as viable organizations; a noteworthy exception was the Association of Christian War-bereaved founded in 1969. Most committees, leagues, discussion groups, and other anti-Yasukuni activity forums proved short-lived and disbanded when the bill repeatedly failed in the Diet. But they made the headlines in the mass media and found vocal support for their protests among the editors of the national press.[57]

An important new feature of Japan's protest culture that significantly shaped the course of the Yasukuni issue in public life was the filing of lawsuits by private citizens and their support networks against town mayors, prefectural civil servants, and other local officials. Most of these cases did not directly address the legal status of Yasukuni Shrine in Tokyo and thus cannot be seen as explicit strategies by the opposition movement against the bill in the Diet; moreover, most of these lawsuits were filed after the bill's failure in 1974. Rather, they protested against state involvement in perpetuating official Shinto rites on the local level of government and thereby provided immediate, practical examples for the theoretical debates about the constitutional ambiguity of the Yasukuni question in the Diet. The first such lawsuit, initiated in 1965 in the city of Tsu in Mie Prefecture, focused on the constitutional legality of using public funds for Shinto-style ground-purification ceremonies (*jichinsai*) for the construction of public buildings.[58]

Two other famous cases included the so-called Self-Defense Force Apotheosis case, filed in 1973 in Yamaguchi Prefecture, and the Mino Memorial case, filed two years later close to Osaka. In the former case, Nakaya Yasuko, the Christian widow of an SDF serviceman, sued the SDF Friendship Association over its enshrinement against her will of her late husband, who had died in a traffic accident while on duty.[59] In the latter, Satoshi and Reiko Kamisaka sued the mayor of Mino City for having used public funds to relocate and conduct ceremonies at the Mino *chūkonhi* memorial, where 298 World War II soldiers were enshrined.[60] These and other cases like them made state practices of official ritual memory a concrete local issue while engaging the national public through legal appeals that eventually reached the Supreme Court. They involved individual citizens taking on the state on behalf of their personal beliefs, but at the same time they represented a cross-section of public opinion challenging the domination of national memory by well-established organizations such as Izokukai.

Meanwhile, the conservative initiators of the movement for state protection of Yasukuni Shrine found their government-centered strategies ineffective and changed tactics. Although Izokukai had initiated several signature campaigns (it gathered 23.5 million signatures in 1966) and held large meetings as campaign events,[61] its activities had in fact focused squarely on the state level. In mid-March 1975, however, *Izoku tsūshin* announced the switch to a "gradualist approach," to be worked out with the LDP in a "Yasukuni Shrine Discussion Group" (Yasukuni jinja ni kansuru kondankai). Without retreating from the ultimate goal of bringing Yasukuni under state protection[62]—Izokukai leaders repeatedly pointed to the LDP's responsibility in this matter—they recognized that opinion regarding Yasukuni had grown more divided within the governing party, and that they could no longer rely on the LDP alone. Instead, as an article in *Izoku tsūshin* declared, "We need a popular consensus."[63] That summer, newspapers, television programs, and meeting halls were indeed filled with public debates about "Yasukuni," especially after the LDP announced that both Prime Minister Miki Takeo and the emperor would visit the shrine on 15 August, albeit as private persons.[64] Christian organizations and others responded with protest strikes all over Tokyo on that day, while Yasukuni-kyō, a league of organizations supporting Yasukuni's nationalization, placed a one-page ad entitled "Giving Thanks to the Heroic War Dead" in the conservative *Sankei shinbun*.[65]

In fact, a national opinion poll about attitudes toward Yasukuni Shrine taken by the advertising company Dentsū in late April 1975 had revealed overwhelming popular support for state-sponsored ceremonies for the war dead, even at Yasukuni Shrine: 79 percent of the 10,000 people questioned thought state "mourning" for the war dead was a matter of course, and 84 percent answered that all people should mourn those who died for the country regardless of their individual religion. When asked specifically whether these celebrations should take place on the precincts of Yasukuni Shrine, 57 percent agreed. These results were qualified, however, by the demographics of those who participated in the poll, their knowledge of the basic facts of the controversy, and the way the questions were formulated. The largest demographic group targeted in this poll consisted of housewives with a high school education or less and no income. Students made up only one percent of those questioned. Further, 61 percent of those questioned did not know that Yasukuni Shrine had become a private institution in 1945, and 56 percent were not aware of the constitutional separation of state and religion.[66] More important, the questions were, as much as possible, formulated as neutral or commonsensical (e.g., "Do you think that those who died for their country [not *for the state* or *the emperor*] should be mourned?"), and they avoided *eirei* and other controversial terms specific to the pro-Yasukuni movement.

Turning this latent popular approval into an active support movement became Izokukai's new strategy. To this end, leaders announced plans on 15 November to establish a nationwide organization for the manifestation of the departed heroes, eventually named the Association to Answer the Departed War Heroes (Eirei ni kotaeru kai) and officially inaugurated on 22 June 1976. The 46 founding member organizations included various subsections of Izokukai, the Association of Shinto Shrines and several Shinto groups, associations of veterans and the war injured, women's groups, and conservative educational and cultural groups, including one from Okinawa. Among the 59 individual promoters, about half were academics or university administrators, a third were presidents of other organizations, and the rest were writers, critics, musicians, and artists. Ishida Kazuto, a retired Supreme Court justice, was elected president; Uno Seiichi, a distinguished professor at Tokyo University, became vice-president; and the head of the board of directors simultaneously served on the board of Association of War-bereaved Families.[67] This new organization replaced the People's Assembly to Achieve State Management of Yasukuni Shrine (Yasukuni jinja kokka goji kantetsu kokumin kyōgikai) and was to function as a grassroots movement: issue-based, focused on a particular "spirit" rather than on politics, and organized by popular consent. There can be no question, however, that the "grassroots" assembled here were already well-organized and clearly represented the far right among LDP supporters in an effort to mobilize popular nationalism for party-political purposes.

Reminiscent of the Higashikuni cabinet's postsurrender appeal for "one hundred million to repent together,"[68] the new group adopted as its central slogan "Let's join one hundred million hearts together to answer the departed heroes!" Concretely, this meant:

1. to preserve our country's traditions and peace by praying for the souls of the dead (*mitama*)
2. to celebrate publicly the spirits of the glorious war dead
3. to bring home the remains of the war dead still scattered in the hills and on the fields.[69]

In his inaugural speech, President Ishida spoke of the deep emotional resonance that the term *eirei* had for him as a person who, like everybody else, hoped for world peace and the prosperity of the Japanese. Although he was intellectually or ideologically "impartial," he could not deny his emotions as a Japanese person. The "cruel" reforms introduced by the occupation after the war were not able to change him, and he had kept his Japanese spirit centered on the emperor.[70] The Association of Shinto Shrines powerfully endorsed this change of course, with its explicit emphasis on the spiritual sentiment underlying national celebrations of the war dead, in a *Jinja shinpō* article of 17 January 1977:

With the new organization Association to Answer the Departed Heroes, the [Yasukuni Shrine] movement has shifted its former emphasis on legal issues to the spiritual aspects of a popular movement. Reflecting on the movement's Tokyo-centeredness in the past, we now aim to widen it to include the whole nation, and the participation of the Shinto world in this is extremely important. Also, through this popular movement, we disengage ourselves from the LDP's policies in the Diet and aim at participating more widely in the policies of the governing parties.[71]

Itagaki Tadashi, chief of the board of directors, outlined the political goals of the new organization more clearly. He identified three problem areas in the movement for state protection of Yasukuni Shrine that the new organization was to remedy, starting with the nation's war bereaved and expanding into a large-scale citizens' movement. First, it represented an alteration in their former strategy of focusing on the Yasukuni Shrine Bill in the Diet. Second, although 80 percent of the general population (he claimed) understood and supported the Yasukuni issue, this was not reflected in the mass media and politics. Therefore, the new movement had to begin with a fundamental investigation of previous strategies. Third, the central problem was that the issue of the "heroic war dead" had been made a political tool in postwar society, centered as it was on party and religious factions and dominated by an "ideologically empty opposition."[72]

To correct this postwar atmosphere, the movement had to abandon its reliance on the LDP and government politics and instead remake itself into a citizens' movement based on a popular embrace of the manifestation of the departed heroes. Itagaki's criticism targeted not so much the LDP but the opposition movement, whose leadership came predominantly from citizens' organizations rather than the established left. The anti-Yasukuni coalition and the mass media had successfully portrayed efforts to bring Yasukuni Shrine under state protection as a matter of the state abusing its power and curbing the civil rights of ordinary citizens. In the public eye, the Yasukuni question represented a crisis of democracy in everyday life—not a dispute based on political ideology, in which conservative forces would have been able to attack the opposition as "communist." With the establishment of the Eirei ni kotaeru kai, the Izokukai and its ultraconservative supporters attempted to create a new public image for themselves while still reaping the political benefits of a close relationship with the governing LDP. By formally abandoning the bill in the Diet and accepting Yasukuni's legal status while inviting the emperor and prime minister to worship as private persons, Izokukai leaders aimed at taking the wind out of the opposition's sails.[73]

This change in conservative strategy was actually part of a larger phenomenon. Liberal scholars analyzed it as an important step in the development and institutionalization of a "reactionary ideology" in the 1970s[74] through the organization of popular nationalism around issues such as the revival of prewar national holidays (especially National Foundation Day), the nationalization of Yasukuni Shrine, and the legal anchoring of the Japanese calendar by imperial reign name. According to Nakashima Michio, the politicization of religious groups not only played an important role in the flourishing of reactionism in the 1960s and 1970s but can be seen as one of its foremost characteristics.[75] Whereas established religions such as the Buddhist sects Nishi and Higashi honganji and Tenrikyō were politically strong in the early postwar period, with representatives elected into the Diet, their influence steadily declined from the late

1950s on and was gradually replaced by so-called new religions, especially Sōkagakkai, which explicitly stressed politics over religion.

From the early 1970s on, the established religions no longer played a visible part in elections; instead, conservative—that is, anti-communist, anti-progressive, LDP-supporting—religious groups steadily expanded their power base in the Diet. The Truth of Life Movement (Seichō no ie) was a nationalist group with a concrete political agenda: hoisting the national flag, teaching the national anthem in schools, revising the constitution, and bringing Yasukuni Shrine under state management. It saw its first representatives elected in 1965. The Association of Shinto Shrines, interestingly, campaigned successfully in national elections only beginning in 1971, and on a clearly issue-based ticket alongside Izokukai and Seichō no ie, rather than as an "established" religion. In the late 1960s, the Yasukuni question contributed greatly to the political visibility of the Association of Shinto Shrines; in the following decade, Shrine Shinto's increasing political clout in turn helped to popularize Yasukuni and boost the LDP. By the end of the decade, conservative religious organizations constituted one of the LDP's four main supports, along with big business, the bureaucracy, and farmers.

In other words, the conservative religious, war-bereaved, women's, and youth groups that formed the Association to Answer the Departed War Heroes became part of a more expansive effort to strengthen popular support for the LDP by presenting nationalist sentiment as "democratic" and thus socially acceptable. The new association employed many of the same methods to arouse public attention as had its progressive counterparts. In November 1977 it started a massive signature campaign aiming at ten million supporters; a year later it cooperated with Izokukai in releasing the movie *The Thirty-Year Path of the Japan Association of War-bereaved Families* (*Nihon izokukai sanjūnen no ayumi*) and a book entitled *Thirty Years with the Departed Heroes* (*Eirei to tomo ni sanjūnen*).[76]

Public protest against Yasukuni appeared to mellow in the second half of the 1970s, only to flare up again in 1982. The context was international criticism of government attempts to whitewash Japan's war conduct in history textbooks. Instead of organizing public demonstrations, however, some opposition war-bereaved and intellectual groups such as Wadatsumikai incorporated the Yasukuni Shrine problem into their own overall agendas, not as a temporary issue, but as part of a larger sociopolitical structure whose corruption they tried to reveal through systematic research. The movement to "answer the heroic spirits of the war dead" directly challenged Wadatsumikai's dictum to "listen to the voices of the *wadatsumi* student-soldiers," who had died in agony over what they saw on the battlefields instead of with proud heroism. Both groups, in their different ways, endorsed communication with the war dead as a continuing process of legitimizing their respective interests. Throughout the 1970s, Wadatsumikai concentrated its efforts almost exclusively on the historical and contemporary dimensions of the emperor system (*tennōsei*), for which the Yasukuni Shrine was a powerful symbol. By the 1980s, when China and Korea had gained enough political strength to make Japanese war responsibility a matter of international relations, historical research had progressed significantly, and organized war memory was no longer tied exclusively to established political interests operating on the state level.

Conservative special interests had put Yasukuni Shrine on the political agenda in the early 1950s with the aim of organizing and defining an *official* memory through prewar commemorative rituals. During the second half of the 1960s and into the 1970s, a progressive opposition movement, backed by progressive special interests as well as the mass media, successfully resisted the legalization of a state-dominated official memory. But in the course of the 1970s, the real competition turned out to lie elsewhere: in vastly different personal and public relationships with the war dead that served as the dominant metaphor for an eclectically construed public memory of war and defeat. The government clearly took advantage of the withdrawal of the Yasukuni issue from Diet deliberations and got away with what were, strictly speaking, illegal acts. The enshrinement of Class A war criminals in 1978 caused a huge public controversy, but the constitutional structures governing postwar democracy remained unchanged. To some, this signaled a gradual undermining of the constitution by the LDP in power. To many more, the spectacle of politicians worshiping at Yasukuni was easy enough to tune out as long as constitutional revision was not involved. More importantly, however, by making Yasukuni Shrine a local as well as popular issue, the conservative right and the liberal left both contributed to loosening its ties to state politics and aiding the creation of a popular basis from which a genuine public debate on war memory would eventually emerge.

PART III

Changing Geographies of Memory

CHAPTER NINE

The Politics of Apology

Shifts in international relations, domestic politics, and an increasingly global public culture in the late 1980s provided the context in which war memory and postwar responsibility changed from being concerns of special interests to being topics of a broad public debate. One important catalyst of this process was the gradual coming together of Asia and especially East Asia as a world region with both a past and a future of consequence to the forces of globalization. No longer conceived solely in economic terms but also in political and cultural ones, relations between and among Asian countries became the critical space for building connections between national and global circuits of production and consumption. In the 1980s and 1990s, the dominant culture flows no longer connected Japan first and foremost to the United States, as had been the case in earlier postwar decades; instead they passed through and circled within a region loosely defined as Asia. Unresolved legacies of a shared past joined by legacies of severed relations during the Cold War became the terrain on which Japan and its Asian neighbors renegotiated regional relations within the context of globalization.

Roughly half a century after the end of the largest military conflict in the area, indeed the world, this shared past made itself apparent most powerfully (because belatedly and finally) in the life experiences of individuals brutally exposed to the conflict. Korean girls serving Japanese soldiers as sex slaves, and Chinese communists used as guinea pigs in the biological experiments of Japanese scientists, were only the most prominent examples. For decades, such experiences and their lingering consequences for individuals and communities had remained fragmented between and within national contexts. They had been overshadowed by the postwar hardships and terror of political turmoil (in China, Korea, Indonesia, and other Asian countries) and the ironic contrast to a comparatively peaceful and prosperous Japan. What made the eventual emergence of a lively national, cross-national, and international debate about the war possible was the recognition, and purposeful rediscovery, of the charged bonds between victims of past crimes and their victimizers, whether those roles were conceived in individual, social, gender, ethnic, or national terms. This process depended on greater political and economic stability in China, Korea, and Taiwan, a reorientation of Japan toward Asia, and an organizational network providing individuals and social groups with international connections.

The 1990s saw an explosion of memory productions that engaged with questions of war responsibility in various ways, but the political issues connected with them closely followed earlier patterns of remembering. There were some deep continuities throughout the postwar decades, including the perceived need to define responsibility intellectually; the framing of the issues in terms of contested ideas about "the postwar system"; and the apparent lack of a national or at least official consensus on the meaning of the war. But memory was no longer a special interest organized along earlier political lines. Large political pressure groups had to reposition themselves on a shifting terrain. The LDP had lost its hegemony but remained the *de facto* party in power; the JSP had all but ceased to exist; and nongovernmental organizations (NGOs) with international connections were proliferating to an unprecedented extent. Under international pressure, the Japanese government emerged as a more active player in national and international negotiations concerning the legacies of war. One by one, prime ministers in the 1990s offered apologies to Asian countries for Japan's wartime aggression. Prime Minister Murayama's speech on the fiftieth anniversary of Japan's defeat in 1995 attracted the most attention (Fig. 9.1, left). None of this made memory any less controversial or the nationalist right any less active, as Prime Minister Koizumi's continued visits to Yasukuni Shrine leading up to the sixtieth anniversary demonstrated (Fig. 9.1, right). But it did encourage greater public information and the

Fig. 9.1 (*left*) Prime Minister Murayama Tomiichi delivering a statement of apology on 15 August 1995, the fiftieth anniversary of Japan's defeat. (*right*) Prime Minister Koizumi Jun'ichirō paying his respects to the Japanese war dead at Yasukuni Shrine on 14 January 2004. Both photos used by permission of Mainichi Shinbunsha.

discourse of the past decade began to transform the intensely national ("one country"), victimization-focused, and moralistic understanding of peace and pacifism in postwar Japan.

Comparing Postwar Responsibilities

As the politics of memory became a phenomenon of global public culture, Japanese reassessments of the postwar in relation to the wartime past were increasingly guided by comparisons. Paradoxically, perhaps, the more other Asian nations made war responsibility an issue in their relations with Japan, the more public discourse within Japan looked to (West) Germany in an effort to define and qualify what was politically and conceptually at stake. While earlier comparisons between Japan and West Germany had focused on the course of modernization or the characterization of wartime militarism, the public debate in the late 1980s and 1990s centered on the management of the legacies of war in the postwar period.

At the time of the 1982 textbook scandal, Japanese audiences had already been exposed to sweeping comparisons of the West German and Japanese education systems with respect to treatments of their wartime pasts. In 1986 Japanese and West German grassroots organizations formed the Japanese-German Peace Forum (Nichidoku heiwa fōramu), which was closely associated with Wadatsumikai and represented efforts in both countries to locate the initiative for articulating the public memory of the war among citizens instead of the government.[1] Another four years later, in 1990, Japanese and South Korean historians organized the Japan–South Korean Joint Study Group on History Textbooks (Nikkan rekishi kyōkasho kenkyūkai), reviving a similar effort first proposed by UNESCO headquarters in the late 1960s but now modcled after German-Polish exchanges on textbook development. (The earlier South Korean–Japanese dialogue collapsed soon after its establishment in the context of Ienaga Saburō's textbook trail.)[2] In August 1995 Japanese NGOs invited former West German president Richard von Weizsäcker to Japan for extensive television interviews on the issue of taking responsibility for the past. These were aired live on the eve of the fiftieth anniversary of the war's end.

The practical as well as conceptual engagement with (West) German experiences of postwar memory intensified noticeably after the address given in 1985 by then-president von Weizsäcker to the German parliament.[3] In the widely covered speech, he had linked the war with the Holocaust, commemorated various groups of victims of German aggression, and spelled out the individual and collective (political) responsibilities of the present in relation to the past. Four months after the 8 May speech and only weeks after then-Prime Minister Nakasone's official visit to Yasukuni Shrine on 15 August, the well-known critic Hidaka Rokurō published excerpts of von Weizsäcker's speech in Japanese in the monthly journal *Sekai*.[4] An annotated translation of the full text by Nagai Kiyohiko appeared in the Iwanami booklet series the following year.[5] To a public outraged by Nakasone's official endorsement of the Japanese war dead (and war criminals) as national heroes, von Weizsäcker seemed to be everything Japanese leaders were not but needed the most to be: honest about what the war had been, earnest about the responsibilities left as a legacy of that war, and willing to join in a national consensus that made it look good in the world.

Germans were the first to admit that von Weizsäcker's internationally acclaimed speech owed more to rhetoric than to reality, and it unleashed some harsh criticism within Germany.[6] On the governmental level, the

Bundestag speech was preceded by West Germany's own scandalous analogue to Nakasone's Yasukuni shrine trip—namely, Chancellor Kohl and President Reagan's joint visit to Bitburg.[7] Within a year of these events, a public "battle of historians" (*Historikerstreit*) preoccupied the media in a display of national contention and divisiveness that should have erased the (international and particularly Japanese) illusion that Germans had reached a consensus on war culpability. Yet von Weizsäcker's speech was invoked over and over in the Japanese media for at least a decade because it spoke directly to what was lacking in the Japanese war responsibility debate and had recently emerged as a highly visible issue in domestic and international politics: a genuine public recognition of Japan's role as an aggressor in the war and a call for government policies to compensate the victims of this aggression.

The initial reaction to the Bundestag speech in the Japanese press gave little indication that it was to develop a life of its own in Japan. Newspaper articles at first flatly dismissed the need to speak such "earnest words" 40 years "after"—indeed, it reflected a "sad state of affairs," probably due to the "intense self-consciousness" of the Germans.[8] Beginning in 1987, however, comparisons not only broadened in scope but also delved into more detail as Japan's Germany experts joined the debate. By then, von Weizsäcker's speech had begun to be refracted through the *Historikerstreit*, proving German memory to be highly public and dynamic rather than simply a product of government policies. Popular critics Oda Makoto and Honda Katsuichi visited West Germany and wrote about their impressions, and scholars of modern Germany compared the two countries' modernities, postwar histories, and war legacies.[9] Meanwhile, the ultraconservative writers Nishio Kanji and Nishi Yoshiyuki conveyed a sense of betrayal by a wartime ally.[10] Above all, these writers introduced into the Japanese discourse on war responsibility (*sensō sekininron*) a new term: "facing the past" (*kako no kokufuku*), a translation of the German *Vergangenheitsbewältigung*.

Coined by high school teacher Nagai Kiyohiko while translating von Weizsäcker's speech, the phrase *kako no kokufuku* appeared in the national press for the first time in 1992 in an *Asahi shinbun* editorial entitled "A Time to Tackle 'Facing the Past'" ("'Kako no kokufuku' ni torikumu toki").[11] Linguistically, the use of the word *kokufuku* as opposed to other terms meaning "overcoming" was significant. *Kokufuku* means "making an effort to overcome difficulties," with the emphasis on "effort." The more usual *uchikatsu*, in contrast, means "succeeding in dealing with a difficulty," with the stress on "succeeding." *Kako ni uchikatsu* therefore rendered the past "water under the bridge." Nagai's use of *kokufuku*, in contrast, aimed at public recognition of the need to make Japan's wartime past a central issue in contemporary politics. The new phrase designated a broad political task in addition to the narrower intellectual and philosophical discourse (the "war responsibility debate") that had characterized earlier efforts to deal with the legacies of the war. In Nagai's definition, "'coming to terms with the past' means understanding the past internally and completely and making it one's own. . . . From 'bringing about trust and reflection,' it extends broadly to 'compensation and reparations' on both spiritual and material levels, and is not limited to one specific activity."[12]

Although Nagai and other specialists in German history, notably Satō Kensei, were well aware of the elusiveness of the German term *Vergangenheitsbewältigung* within different political contexts, importing it into Japanese was less an exercise in historical specificity than a political statement. That this term became the title of an editorial in the *Asahi shinbun* suggested, as Mochida Yukio pointed out, that "apology and compensation" had been recognized as contemporary problems to be faced squarely in politics as in society at large.[13] The comparison was designed to characterize and criticize postwar Japanese memory on the political, intellectual, and popular levels. It pointed to missed opportunities and to the incompleteness of the postwar project.[14]

In almost all accounts Germany possessed the better postwar, even if Japan, for a good number of conservatives, laid claim to the better war. Nishio Kanji, a crusader against what he and others termed "Japan-bashing" (*Nihon dameron*), devoted an entire book to the incomparability of the two countries, beginning with the different nature of their wars and ending with the evil intentions of a Germany newly unified, economically powerful, and ethically corrupted by the legacy of the East German *Stasi*.[15] On the center-left, the appropriateness of the comparison itself was never questioned. Japan and Germany's parallel histories of wartime fascism, defeat, occupation, and war crimes trials, followed by democratization and economic high growth, rendered the basis of the comparison self-evident. Typically, late postwar Japan appeared to be a latecomer to "facing the past," as prewar Japan had been a latecomer to modernization and early postwar Japan to modernity. Now, however, Germany, which for much of the past century had been viewed as Japan's partner in overcoming "backwardness" (to use Alexander Gerschenkron's phrase), had become the standard against which Japan was "late." This, in fact, was the root of the feeling of betrayal on the right.

And yet precisely *what* had gone wrong in Japan, in spite of the contextual similarity, seemed to interest people less than *why* things had gone wrong. The list of Japanese failures—lack of compensation payments to non-Japanese war victims, peace treaties without real rapprochement with other Asian countries, textbooks hiding the truth about Japanese war crimes, embarrassing blunders by politicians, and above all deep-seated victims' consciousness—soon became a familiar litany. It was the attempt to explain what conditioned these failures that revealed both the historical consciousness and the political stance of those who made these comparisons. In the writings of Mochida Yukio, Satō Kensei, Katō Shūichi, Yamaguchi Yasushi, Hirowatari Seigo, and others, as well as in the national press, Japan (compared with Germany) was at once disadvantaged by history and geography and ambiguous in its political and moral consciousness, but also exemplary in its pacifist and antinuclear convictions.

Most writers singled out obvious historical and geopolitical circumstances, often beyond Japan's control, to explain why that country never developed the kind of war responsibility debate that served Germany so well. Mochida Yukio, for example, pointed out that Germany's geopolitical situation after the war required an early rapprochement with former enemy countries (by acknowledging its wartime aggression) for the sake of economic recovery, whereas Japan's one-sided dependence on the United States made apologies to Asian countries unnecessary.[16] Others located the roots of Japan's missed opportunity in the occupation policies of the United States and especially the Tokyo war crimes trial in contrast to its Nuremberg counterpart. The fact that both West and East Germany had continued to conduct trials against Nazi war criminals on their own throughout the postwar period while Japan had not pursued its wartime leaders' legal responsibility could also be traced back to occupation policies, which had discouraged such

Japanese efforts early on.[17] Even the widespread feeling of victimization among the Japanese populace could be explained by pointing to
the blatant unfairness with which Allied prosecutors convicted the "little" war criminals in the Class B and C war crimes trials while shielding
some "big fish," foremost among them the emperor.[18]

A second trope found society and culture at fault. The Japanese, the
argument went, lacked the political and moral backbone necessary to
face their own responsibility. Katō Shūichi was perhaps the most
prominent representative of this line of thought. For Katō, European
or American ideas imported after the war never managed to change the
old Japanese way of thinking but were merely a veneer. "The war and
wartime crimes live on in the social structure, economic conditions, cultural tradition and mental attitudes in postwar Japan . . . and this concerns the Japanese people as a whole."[19] The Japanese failure to conduct their own war crimes trials in particular suggested a tendency to
keep the location of responsibility vague, while Germans demonstrated
a "high moral sense."[20]

Other comparative writings, however, endorsed Japanese ambiguity
toward war memory as more inclusive, tolerant, and truthful than German dogmatism—and turned Katō's argument on its head. A newspaper series in the liberal *Asahi shinbun* in January 1995—entitled "Beyond
the Abyss: Germany versus Japan"[21]—portrayed Germany as a less
complicated place than Japan with respect to war responsibility, not
because of a lack of controversy, but because of clear governmental
leadership. Japan's ambiguity, in contrast, on the one hand revealed a
lamentable lack of such leadership, and on the other appeared more
truthful to a problem that was best recognized as inherently insoluble.
The Japanese were sensitive to different views of the past, the argument
went, and would not trample on people's unique feelings, such as those
of the bereaved families. Furthermore, as international relations in Asia
were messy and unpredictable, it made sense to stay aloof from this
issue rather than get too deeply involved.

The third line of argument focused not on failure but on success, and
one of Japanese making: the people's deep pacifist and antinuclear convictions. Inasmuch as Japan was plagued by disadvantageous circumstances and an ambiguous social structure, pacifism was a rod of stability. Oda Makoto characterized this pacifism as the "moral backbone"

of postwar Japanese society, comparable with Christianity in Europe.[22] Indeed, popular opposition had until then thwarted all conservative attempts to revise Article 9 of the constitution, which renounces war. Pride in this "indigenous" pacifism (the American origins of the constitution were rarely mentioned in this context) permeated almost every center-left contribution to the debate and was used in part to deflect the loud accusation from the political right of engaging in "Japan-bashing." Satō Kensei and Mochida Yukio both interpreted pacifism, even if it was centered only on Japan ("one-country pacifism" or *ikkoku heiwashugi*), as the most important lesson drawn from the war experience.

Germans, by comparison, wavered on this issue and instead focused on "democracy" or "human dignity" as the central lesson of the war. Yet both Satō and Mochida rendered the lack of specificity to the meaning of "peace," and the victims' consciousness inherent in it, problematic. Japanese pacifism needed to be qualified by democracy. By placing the dignity of each human being at the center, Mochida concluded, Japan could live up to the challenge of facing the past.[23] In Satō's words, it was imperative for Japan today to reconsider peace education and at the same time deepen its training in democracy. In this effort, Tokyo would do well to consider "what Bonn had learned from Weimar," meaning the dangers of an incomplete or deeply flawed democratic system.[24]

The comparison with Germany thus demonstrated a sense of urgency in grappling with what had essentially become a problem of international relations, a willingness to reexamine critically the postwar discourse about war responsibility in its political, popular, and epistemological manifestations, and a recognition of the force of memory in power relations as a universal problem with particular—usually national—characteristics. Triggered more often by international than domestic events, the comparison introduced new terminology to signify a departure from the earlier discourse. *Kako no kokufuku*, a translation of the German word for "facing the past," stressed the honest need to acknowledge Japan's wartime acts of aggression as well as the human dignity of those who fell victim to these war crimes, regardless of nationality. The comparison with Germany also served to identify the political stakes in contemporary as well as future Japan. Above all, it became a vehicle for explaining how the legacies of the war came to linger unresolved for 50 years. A variety of answers singled out geopolitical circumstances, occupation policies, the persistence of prewar, even wartime, social and cultural attitudes among the people, and an unqualified though strong pacifism.

The Apology Conundrum

In the mid-1990s, many foreign observers of contemporary Japanese affairs were fascinated, almost obsessed, with the apparent inability, or at least unwillingness, of the Japanese to remember World War II except in terms of their own victimhood. It became common to portray Japanese youth drawing a blank on simple historical facts concerning the war, government ministers publicly denying Japanese war atrocities, and atomic bomb survivors describing their experiences as if the bomb had been dropped out of the blue.[25] The Japanese, it appeared, had much work to do, and other Asians demanded that they do it. Some of the economically rising and politically democratizing countries that Japan called its neighbors were demanding apologies and compensation for wartime wrongs before they were prepared to accept Japanese leadership in the regional integration desired by many. Under pressure from abroad, the Japanese government would belatedly embrace issues of war responsibility in order to move beyond "the long postwar"[26] and become a "normal" country no longer constrained by contested legacies of the war.[27]

1982

The summer of 1982 marked the first time that a domestic controversy over historical narratives of the Asia-Pacific War became a serious problem in international diplomacy and was resolved at the highest governmental level. The so-called Textbook Issue revolved around the alleged "distortion and beautification" of the terminology used in government-approved textbooks to describe Japan's wartime invasion of China.[28] The specific allegations, which were first reported in the Japanese press and then eagerly taken up by China and other Asian countries to launch formal protests against the Japanese government, turned out to be unfounded and were relatively quickly resolved. The political repercussions, however, were enormous.[29] "Asia" (specifically China and Korea but increasingly also Southeast Asia) emerged in the

1980s as a political region with both a past and a future of serious consequence for Japan, right at the time when trade conflicts with the United States intensified. Against this background, the longstanding struggle over Japan's textbook approval process, and indeed Japanese war responsibility in general, found a ready international audience who validated, by and large, the stance of the established political opposition against the conservative government on the terrain of war memory.[30]

1985

Prime Minister Nakasone's visit to Yasukuni Shrine in August to honor Japan's war dead, the first unequivocally *official* visit by a cabinet head, spurred the next wave of heated international as well as domestic protest against the Japanese government's unapologetic attitude toward World War II. Like the Textbook Issue three years earlier, this incident propelled a longstanding domestic political controversy into the international arena, where it reemerged as an annual media event for years to come. This time the protests were launched in the Chinese and Korean press, which registered outrage particularly in light of the co-enshrinement of fourteen convicted and executed Class A war criminals (Tōjō Hideki included) enshrined at Yasukuni since 1978. In Japan, Nakasone's bold gesture led religious and citizen groups to file a number of "Yasukuni lawsuits" in local courts, eventually ending with a full-bench declaration of the unconstitutionality of such visits by the Supreme Court in 1997.[31] But even this ruling has not put an end to the controversial mid-August ritual, as Prime Minister Koizumi's pledge to visit the shrine annually has shown.

Of perhaps equal importance, in this context, was the proliferation of new citizens' groups in the aftermath of Nakasone's Yasukuni visit, some of which produced leading activists in the debate about war memory in the 1990s. On 7 July 1986 (the forty-ninth anniversary of Japan's invasion of China), dissenting members of the Japan Association of War-bereaved Families, who had been organizing in Hokkaido since 1982 in opposition to its leadership's politics, formed a new peace group, the Association of War-bereaved Families for Peace (Heiwa izokukai zenkoku renrakukai, or Heiwa izokukai for short). This rapidly growing organization clearly linked the suffering of Japanese war victims to their role in a system that inflicted even greater pain on other

Asians. It called for an international alliance of the war bereaved to address the problem of war and postwar responsibility in an international context and played a leading role in the promotion of the compensation issue in the 1990s.[32]

1989

Emperor Hirohito's death from cancer on 7 January at age 87 generated a whole spectrum of public remembering, from the official Shinto rituals performed at his funeral and Akihito's inauguration as new emperor to an avalanche of personal reminiscences of the long Shōwa era (the duration of Hirohito's reign, 1926–89) and the heated debate about Japanese war crimes and Hirohito's responsibility. Coinciding, as it did, with the end of the Cold War in Europe, 1989 came to represent an important turning-point in Japan's postwar history, symbolized by the beginning of a new imperial era named Heisei, which means "the attainment of peace at home and abroad, in heaven and on earth." In political terms, this change came to be characterized by the dissolution, however incomplete, of the postwar "system." The official funeral events—carefully choreographed for international consumption—were undoubtedly meant to show the Japanese in collective mourning for the emperor as the symbol of their national community.

It soon became apparent, however, that the events had mainly fired public conflict about what constituted such a community and its imperial "symbol," and how this related to World War II on the one hand and the end of the Cold War on the other. The undemocratic manner in which the decisions about funeral and inauguration rites and the new reign name were made elicited its own share of protest. Only the highest levels of government were involved, and the decision was made quickly so as to avoid demands for public participation. Not surprisingly, social and political organizations, large and small, all responded to the emperor's final days—more generally conceived as the end of the Shōwa period—from their respective positions. Equally predictably, their responses reflected familiar political divisions.

The emperor and the imperial household, after all, represented an institutionalized continuity across 1945. All special interests organized around particular interpretations of the prewar and wartime past had to contend with this reality. Like a "ghost at the historical feast," to borrow

Carol Gluck's phrase, the emperor was an integral part of war memory, however differently opposing groups might construct it.[33] Embraced as the ultimate locus of Japanese tradition and national unity, rejected as the root of Japanese fascism, domesticated in popular discourse as *"Ten-chan"* ("Empy"), or ignored as a historical anachronism, the emperor served many purposes even while open public criticism remained unfashionable. Hirohito's demise provided the Association of Shinto Shrines with an unprecedented opportunity to declare the unity of the Japanese people (in mourning their emperor) and the successful preservation of Japanese culture and tradition on the basis of official adherence to Shinto ritual.[34] The Izokukai reaffirmed the close ties between the war bereaved and the emperor, bound by their common goal of securing their nation's integrity and their wishes for peace, and equally molded by the upheavals of Shōwa.[35] The Japan-China Friendship Association, on the other hand, all but ignored the emperor's death in its newspaper's mid-January issue and instead printed a scheduled report on various local meetings that had taken place a month before entitled "Pursuing the Emperor's War Responsibility."[36]

Wadatsumikai, in a more demonstrative move, issued a public statement on 9 February entitled "Hearkening to the Voices of Millions of War Victims" in protest against the late Shōwa emperor's state funeral. The declaration, a rejoinder to one issued the preceding November, clearly stated that the emperor bore ultimate responsibility for Japan's war of aggression in Asia and the Pacific, and that there had been insufficient recognition of the emperor's, the government's, and the people's responsibility in the postwar period. But the urgency of the February statement derived specifically from the official rites of mourning adopted by the government, which, for Wadatsumikai, pointed to a continuation of the politics of irresponsibility:

We inflicted much harm and damage, spiritually and physically, on peoples in Asia and the Pacific area, and have not as yet sufficiently atoned or compensated for that. We fear that for the government to recompense the late *Tennō*, the person who himself bore the above-mentioned responsibility, with a national funeral would appear to exonerate not only him of his war responsibility but also Japan itself. That would not only be contrary to the spirit of the constitution but also debase the persons who died as victims of the war, and trample upon the feelings of tens of millions of people who still suffer heavily from the hurt.[37]

Hirohito's war responsibility and the emperor system in general had long been a topic of discussion in left-wing, especially Marxist circles, but in the wake of the emperor's death this formerly marginalized critique exploded into a public debate of unprecedented proportions—what came to be known as the lifting of the "Chrysanthemum taboo." Beginning in 1989 and reaching a peak in 1991, a host of historical materials became publicly available that documented the Shōwa emperor's orchestrated transformation from Japan's supreme military leader to a symbol of postwar pacifism, as well as SCAP's critical role in safeguarding that transformation in the face of public demands to indict Hirohito as a war criminal. Perhaps no other document caught the public's attention as much as Hirohito's own dictated "Monologue," which was found in a private collection in the United States and published in the December 1990 issue of the monthly magazine *Bungei shunjū*.[38] In this carefully crafted personal statement, delivered by Hirohito to his closest advisors in the spring of 1946, the emperor portrayed himself as politically impotent when it came to major war decisions (other than surrendering on 15 August 1945) and resisted any admission of personal responsibility. But, in fact, a plethora of inconsistencies and contradictions in this text concerning his political and military role suggested quite the opposite and threw open a host of new questions concerning the foundation of Japan's postwar order.

Writing a new history of Shōwa was not only the business of professional historians in 1989. Many men and women also joined the fast-growing movement for personal history-writing (*jibunshi undō*). In the wake of the emperor's death, volumes of personal stories on the theme "My Shōwa" appeared on the market, often collected from newspaper or magazine writing contests, some complete with templates to provide guidelines on the appropriate form of such writings. At the same time, a whole network of commercial services developed to provide ordinary people with assistance in publishing their own stories, increasingly aided by the internet.[39] Petra Buchholz's study revealed that in the late 1980s, the majority of the authors were retirees, particularly men who had fought in World War II but had previously been too involved in their careers to reflect on that central experience in their lives. Their contribution to the emerging discourse on war memory was the public recovery of the ordinary, individual Japanese as an active participant in the war effort rather than a passive sufferer. As the emperor's war responsibility was publicly investigated, many participants in that war tried to reclaim for themselves a formidable part of their lives. Others opened long-concealed "boxes" of memories, such as the one Haruko and Theodore Cook discovered when they compiled their oral history of the war.[40] Some of these writings became testimonies in public controversies over particular Japanese war atrocities.

1991

In August, Kim Hak-sun, a Korean "comfort woman" forced to serve Japanese troops during World War II, came forth with the first public testimony about the comfort station system. She and 34 other former comfort women, sponsored by Korean women's and war-bereaved groups, in December filed a suit against the Japanese government in the Tokyo District Court, demanding formal recognition and compensation.[41] In January 1992, following the historian Yoshimi Yoshiaki's publication of documentary evidence that implicated the government in the comfort station system,[42] Prime Minister Miyazawa Kiichi issued an official apology during his visit to Seoul. Thus began a cross-national grassroots campaign that framed the issue of war memory in terms of the government's legal and moral responsibility to apologize to and compensate individual victims of war. Indeed, the "comfort women issue," as it came to be known, represented a paradigmatic shift in the debate about war responsibility toward the public recognition of formerly neglected war victims as individuals, as non-Japanese, and as women. This in turn led to a more direct acknowledgment of Japanese as war and colonial aggressors.

1993

A confluence of developments on both the governmental and non-governmental levels in 1993 confirmed the political salience of war memory in its new guise. The July elections marked the end of the long (38-year) conservative hegemony, resulting in a seven-party coalition cabinet headed by Hosokawa Morihiro. Hosokawa also became the first prime minister to refer publicly to Japan's war in Asia as an "aggressive war" and offer "condolences to the victims of war and their families in Asia and the world over" as part of the 15 August commemorative ceremonies.

At the same time, the Japanese government finally acknowledged in a report the coercive nature of the comfort women system but remained steadfast in refusing individual compensation payments. A national opinion poll taken by the *Asahi shinbun* shortly thereafter showed more than half of those questioned in favor of government compensation, with that trend on a steep rise in the following years. Among the 20- and 30-year-olds polled in 1993, 59 percent affirmed compensating former "comfort women," 78 percent felt that victims of Japanese colonialism were entitled to compensation for their suffering, and 78 percent wanted to see the government pay compensation to countries in which Japanese forces had committed atrocities.[43]

Perhaps most significantly, Japanese scholars, lawyers, and activists established in 1993 the country's first War Responsibility Data Center (Sensō sekinin shiryō sentaa), modeled after Germany's Zentralstelle zur Erforschung der Kriegsschuldfrage. This nongovernmental institute has since then served as a center for the collection of war and postwar materials on the question of Japan's war responsibility, published an important quarterly journal *Sensō sekinin kenkyū* (War Responsibility Research), and supported plaintiffs in lawsuits against the Japanese government.

Toward Reconciliation

1995

The fiftieth year of the postwar era was, in many ways, a year of disasters for Japan. The Hanshin earthquake in January and the Aum Shinrikyō sarin gas attack on the Tokyo subway system in March rocked public confidence. Politically, the failure of governmental and parliamentary politicians to formulate an unequivocal statement on the meaning of the fiftieth anniversary of defeat in World War II proved damaging, especially in the eyes of the international community. The furor over the drafting of this document, officially entitled "Resolution to Renew the Determination for Peace on the Basis of Lessons Learned from History," but popularly known as the Diet Resolution, consumed parliamentarians of all parties and their various leagues as well as the public media from June 1994 to its eventual adoption on 9 June 1995.

In large part this outcome was determined by the peculiar circumstances of a political alliance in which Socialist Prime Minister Murayama Tomiichi presided over a coalition of archrivals: the LDP and the JSP. This in turn had been made possible by the willingness of the JSP to give up almost the entire ideological platform that had defined it as the permanent opposition since at least the mid-1950s. Indeed, when Murayama took over on 18 June 1994, he announced the end of Socialist opposition to the U.S.-Japan Security Treaty and vowed to recognize the SDF as constitutional and to authorize their dispatch overseas to participate in UN Peace Keeping Operations. He even acknowledged the national flag and anthem as legitimate national symbols.[44] In accordance with this change, large JSP-affiliated interest organizations, such as the Japanese Trade Union Confederation (Rengō) and the Japan Teachers' Union (JTU), also abandoned their more extreme positions.

The ill-fated Diet Resolution may have represented above all a desperate effort to galvanize support for the JSP around its last remaining ideological principle: an official apology for Japan's wartime aggression.[45] If so, this strategy clearly backfired, inasmuch as it showed that while the special interest politics of the old left no longer worked (the JTU, astonishingly, could not bring itself to support Murayama's proposal because of internal divisions), they remained rather effective on the old right. Longstanding nationalist interest groups such as the Izokukai and the Association of Shinto Shrines and their various spinoffs organized themselves into the National Committee, brought prominent business figures on board as advisors,[46] and rallied conservative Diet representatives from the LDP and the New Frontier Party (Shinshintō) to oppose any resolution of remorse and apology that "unilaterally incriminated" Japan.[47] The spokesman for this far right opposition, Okuno Seisuke, an 81-year-old former director of the National Land Agency and a government technocrat during the war, articulated this position in familiar language: "Japan should no longer apologize for the war. . . . Adoption of such a resolution would not only desecrate the honor of Japanese soldiers killed in action but also erode pride in the nation among youths."[48] Okuno represented one of several notorious deniers of war crimes in official positions who created diplomatic difficulties for the government with their "insensitive blunders," a euphemism of the highest order. Justice Minister Nagano

Shigeto had to resign in May 1994 for alleging that the Nanjing Massacre had never taken place, while Environmental Minister Sakurai Shin asserted two days before the forty-ninth anniversary of defeat that Japan had never intended to wage an aggressive war against Asian countries.

Such pronouncements, however, were perhaps no less anachronistic in the context of the mid-1990s than some of the policy positions the JSP had just relinquished, such as refusal to recognize the SDF. Although the old ideological divisions had by no means vanished, the government's involvement in addressing pressing issues pertaining to Japan's wartime past had more to do with clearing away obstacles to future actions than settling the longstanding ideological disputes of the past. Indeed, one wonders with Norma Field exactly what an apology can accomplish more than 50 years after the crimes were committed.[49] Apart from Okuno and his Izokukai supporters, LDP dissenters to the Diet Resolution revealed a kaleidoscope of opinions, all marked in the first place by political pragmatism. Chūma Kōki took issue with the very idea of a Diet resolution, given that it was bound to be a product of compromise, unconvincing both at home and abroad. He argued that a more self-critical history curriculum or the secularization of Yasukuni Shrine was a more appropriate avenue for winning Asian nations' trust. In turn, Noda Seiko, a female junior LDP Diet member, considered a broad public debate about the memory of the war as essential for resolving the current impasse but warned against raising false hopes among Asian victims looking for government compensation.[50] In the end, the resolution did pass, a face-saver for Murayama, but it could not mask the utter lack of consensus in the Diet and thus was predictably met with cold scorn by the Japanese public and hot criticism in China and Korea. The full final text read:

The House of Representative resolves as follows:

On the occasion of the 50th anniversary of the end of World War II, this House offers its sincere condolences to those who fell in action and victims of wars and similar actions all over the world.

Solemnly reflecting upon many instances of colonial rule and acts of aggression in the modern history of the world, and recognizing that Japan carried out those acts in the past, inflicting pain and suffering upon the peoples of other countries, especially in Asia, the Members of this House express a sense of deep remorse.

We must transcend the differences over historical views of the past war and learn humbly the lessons of history so as to build a peaceful international society.

This House expresses its resolve, under the banner of eternal peace enshrined in the constitution of Japan, to join hands with other nations of the world and to pave the way for a future that allows all human beings to live together.[51]

Other fiftieth anniversary projects on the governmental level were only slightly more successful. In July, Murayama announced the inauguration of the so-called Asian Women's Fund (Josei no tame no Ajia heiwa kokumin kikin), for which he had secured the advice and cooperation of progressive scholars such as Wada Haruki and Ōnuma Yasuaki, both professors at Tokyo University. Consisting primarily of donations from private citizens, this fund was to offer each victim of the comfort women system from South Korea, Taiwan, and the Philippines an official letter of apology (eventually written by Murayama's successor, Hashimoto Ryūtarō, in 1996), medical and welfare funds paid by the government, "atonement money," and the guarantee of government support for further historical research.[52] This time the criticism came predominantly from the side of the victims and their supporters as well as the South Korean and Taiwanese governments, who expressed outrage at this circumvention of direct government compensation payments and the government's continued denial of its legal responsibility.

Ōnuma Yasuaki, a scholar of international law, defended the fund's intentions against this overwhelming public criticism, arguing that the joint governmental and private initiative represented a way for Japan as a whole to take responsibility, for "it was not only the Japanese government, but also the Japanese people, who gave birth to the abominable institution of 'comfort women'; it was not only the Japanese government, but also the Japanese people who failed to confront the problem for almost half a century after the war."[53] The Asian Women's Fund remained in place until 2002, with Murayama Tomiichi as president, and paid out ¥564 million raised by private donations to 285 former comfort women from the Philippines, Korea, and Taiwan. In addition, 79 Dutch victims received health and welfare payments from the government, and similar payments were ongoing (projected until 2007) to an unspecified number of Indonesian women.[54]

On 15 August, ten years after Nakasone Yasuhiro's widely criticized trip to Yasukuni Shrine, Prime Minister Murayama strongly discouraged his cabinet from worshiping at Yasukuni on the fiftieth anniversary of defeat and delivered a long-awaited apology for Japan's war crimes in Asia that included the following statement:

During a certain period in the not too distant past, Japan, following a mistaken national policy, advanced along the road to war, only to ensnare the Japanese people in a fateful crisis, and, through its colonial rule and aggression, caused tremendous damage and suffering to the people of many countries, particularly to those of Asian nations. In the hope that no such mistake be made in the future, I regard, in a spirit of humility, these irrefutable facts of history, and express here once again my feelings of deep remorse and state my heartfelt apology. Allow me also to express my feelings of profound mourning for all victims, both at home and abroad, of that history.[55]

The generally favorable reception of Murayama's speech abroad could not, however, repair the enormous damage done by the preceding political controversies. Most commentators in Asia understood it to reflect the socialist premier's own personal views rather than those of the Japanese public, a view apparently shared by some LDP cabinet members, who accused Murayama of using this public commemorative opportunity to espouse private opinions. For decades the divisiveness over the interpretation of Japan's role in the Asia-Pacific War had been taken for granted as part of domestic politics. Now the international community demanded a consensus and a measure of contrition that fit with contemporary concerns regarding long-neglected historical in-justices in many parts of the world. This is how Ozawa Ichirō, the leader of the New Frontier Party (founded in 1993), put it in his bestselling book *Blueprint for a New Japan* (*Nihon kaizō keikaku*, 1994): "We cannot deny the part aggression has played in our history in Asia. The issue is not that we have never discussed the question of our wartime respon-sibility, but that we did so only at home: we did not face the Asia-Pacific nations we had invaded. We have to admit that our government has not made much effort to settle the past."[56]

The Japanese government had no choice but to embrace "postwar resolution measures" (*sengo shori*) and "postwar responsibility" (*sengo sekinin*) as key issues in foreign as well as domestic politics in the 1990s. Even Hashimoto Ryūtarō, the LDP politician and former president of the Izokukai who succeeded Murayama as prime minister in 1996, be-latedly agreed with Murayama's 1995 apology—but nonetheless revived official visits to Yasukuni Shrine. Indeed, the following years brought no new departures in the government's handling of this issue: the government did accept *moral* responsibility for Japanese war atrocities, issuing apologies to victims and their descendants and supporting historical research, but it consistently denied *legal* responsibility.

1998

Two major summit meetings in Tokyo in the fall of 1998 provided historic opportunities for reconciliation and a redefinition of relations between Japan and its neighbors Communist China and South Korea. Chinese Premier Jiang Zemin's visit had originally been scheduled for September, and expectations for a resolution to the festering "history problem" were high on the Japanese side, given that relations between the two countries had generally been amicable since 1972 and Japanese apologies to China had been well received (in 1972 and during Emperor Akihito's visit in 1992). Circumstances in China forced Jiang to postpone his trip, however, and so the Japan–South Korea summit took place first, in early October. The ferocity of anti-Japanese sentiment in Korea, past and present, was well known in Japan, inflamed most recently by the comfort women issue and the comparative inadequacy, in the Korean view, of Japanese apologies for colonization. Contrary to expectation, however, Prime Minister Obuchi Keizō's talks with South Korean President Kim Dae Jung turned out to be an unprecedented success, whereas talks with Jiang Zemin the following month failed to produce mutual agreement.[57]

The Japan–South Korea summit produced agreements not only on such issues as fishing zones, joint naval exercises, and the joint action plan,[58] but also on historical responsibilities. The Joint Declaration signed by Obuchi and Kim included the following apology:

Looking back on the relations between Japan and the Republic of Korea during this century, Prime Minister Obuchi regarded in a spirit of humility the fact of history that Japan caused, during a certain period in the past, tremendous damage and suffering to the people of the Republic of Korea through its colonial rule, and expressed his deep remorse and heartfelt apology for this fact.[59]

Kim, for his part, accepted Obuchi's apology and stated his own conviction that "the present calls upon both countries to overcome their unfortunate history and to build a future-oriented relationship based on reconciliation as well as good-neighborly and friendly cooperation."[60] The Obuchi-Jiang summit in late November, in stark contrast, bogged down over Chinese demands—and Japanese resistance in response—that an apology be given not only orally but also in written form, and without assurances from Jiang that China would agree to lay the past to rest. In the end, the two summits rather confirmed what the nationalist right in Japan had been arguing: that China's and Korea's respective domestic political objectives played a huge role in this process, so much so that Japan was placed largely at the mercy of its neighbors in a regional power struggle. But it also proved the importance of personality and clear leadership, benefits of a self-critical stance in both offering and accepting apologies for historical injustices, and the very real reciprocity involved in the dynamics of apology.[61]

2005

The first few years of the new millennium, up to the sixtieth anniversary of Japan's defeat, focused public attention on the problem of reconciliation in East Asia more intensely than ever before. Prime Minister Koizumi continued the (recent) diplomatic etiquette of apologizing for Japan's war conduct when abroad, offering "heartfelt apologies" on 8 October 2001 after visiting the Memorial Museum of the Chinese People's Anti-Japanese War near the Marco Polo Bridge outside Beijing, where the second Sino-Japanese War began in 1937.[62] He then visited South Korea, where he also paid his respects at a museum commemorating Japanese atrocities and made an almost identical statement. But these international gestures did not, in Koizumi's eyes, require a revoking of domestic gestures he considered appropriate, such as commemorating the Japanese war dead as "departed heroes" (including Class A war criminals) at Yasukuni Shrine. To many Chinese and Koreans, this seemed proof of the Japanese government's insincerity. To LDP leaders it was political common sense, because special interest groups supporting Yasukuni Shrine (including the Association of War-bereaved Families) represented important electoral constituencies for the LDP. When Japanese foreign relations with China sharply deteriorated, however, public criticism of Koizumi's stance came forth from unexpected quarters. The president of the Izokukai, Koga Makoto, suggested in May

2005 that Koizumi's visits to Yasukuni disturbed the peace of the spirits of the war dead enshrined there because of the tensions such ceremonies had created in foreign relations.[63]

The spring of 2005 saw popular Chinese protests against Japan on an unprecedented scale. Ostensibly the demonstrators were demanding more apologies and an end to Yasukuni visits and nationalist textbooks. The latter two demands represented perhaps the oldest and most enduring domestic controversies in Japan, having colored political contests since the 1950s. But in the context of 2005, many Chinese and Koreans interpreted them as evidence of a recent Japanese return to a muscular sense of dominance in Asia built upon an unapologetic view of its wartime past. The protests involved huge demonstrations in China's major cities, the vandalizing of Japanese businesses in Shanghai and elsewhere, and a wave of internet hacking and anti-Japanese hate mail. In April 2005 newspapers were full of speculation as to how "spontaneous" or "scripted" by the Chinese Communist Party these protests were.[64] Some Chinese voices abroad calmly reminded readers how Chinese textbooks and government actions glossed over postwar crimes by the Communist Party that had left many more Chinese people dead than the Japanese victimized during their wartime invasion.[65]

There is no doubt that Japan's push for a seat on the UN Security Council, and the LDP's proposal for a constitutional revision that would abandon Article 9 and allow military operations, have played a significant role in provoking Chinese concerns about regional security. But the *popular* outrage among ordinary Chinese and Koreans had other roots as well. It arose in two increasingly open, more democratic civil societies that had only recently begun to reckon with their own postwar history— or the lack thereof. In contrast to Japan, where war memory was negotiated predominantly on the level of civic political activism, in China and Korea these issues had clearly been the prerogative of authoritarian states. The combination of a militarily and economically powerful China *and* a more robust civil society set the stage for the kinds of internal political conflicts about history that Japan has experienced for more than 50 years. The collective focus on Japan's culpability (not only for perpetrating war crimes but, more importantly, for neglecting its postwar responsibility) may lend a measure of national cohesion to Chinese society, but this is likely to be temporary. East Asian reconciliation now depends

not only on state-level diplomacy and leadership but on the mutual recognition and understanding of the *domestic* histories of war memory
in each of these countries.

On 15 August 2005, the sixtieth anniversary of Japan's defeat, Prime
Minister Koizumi did not visit Yasukuni Shrine but instead offered
perhaps the most concrete interpretation of Japan's war and postwar
responsibility by any Japanese head of state to this date. He recognized
and apologized for Japan's wartime aggression, but he also clearly presented Japan's postwar history *as a whole* to have "manifested remorse."
A provisional translation of the full text of his speech is posted on the
prime minister's website and reproduced in its entirety below.

On the 60th anniversary of the end of the war, I reaffirm my determination
that Japan must never again take the path to war, reflecting that the peace
and prosperity we enjoy today are founded on the ultimate sacrifices of those
who lost their lives for the war against their will.

More than three million compatriots died in the war—in the battlefield thinking
about their homeland and worrying about their families, while others perished
amidst the destruction of war, or after the war in remote foreign countries.

In the past, Japan, through its colonial rule and aggression, caused tremendous
damage and suffering to the people of many countries, particularly to those
of Asian nations. Sincerely facing these facts of history, I once again express
my feelings of deep remorse and heartfelt apology, and also express the feelings
of mourning for all victims, both at home and abroad, in the war. I am determined not to allow the lessons of that horrible war to erode, and to contribute
to the peace and prosperity of the world without ever again waging a war.

After the war, Japan rebuilt itself from a devastated land owing to the ceaseless
efforts of its people and the assistance extended by many countries, and accepted the San Francisco Peace Treaty, being the first step of its reversion to
the international community. Japan has resolutely maintained its principle of
resolving all matters by peaceful means and not by force, and proactively
extended material and personnel assistance for the sake of the peace and prosperity of the world through official development assistance (ODA) and United
Nations peace keeping operations.

*Japan's postwar history has indeed been six decades of manifesting its remorse on the
war through actions.* [emphasis added]

The post war generations now exceed 70% of Japan's population. Each and
every Japanese, through his or her own experience and peace-oriented education, sincerely seeks international peace. Today, many Japanese are actively

engaged in activities for peace and humanitarian assistance around the world, through such organizations as the Japan Overseas Cooperation Volunteers, and have been receiving much trust and high appreciation from the local people. Exchange with Asian countries in a wide variety of areas, such as economy and culture, has also increased on an unprecedented scale. I believe it is necessary to work hand in hand with other Asian countries, especially with China and the Republic of Korea, which are Japan's neighboring countries separated only by a strip of water, to maintain peace and pursue the development of the region. Through squarely facing the past and rightly recognizing the history, I intend to build a future-oriented cooperative relationship based on mutual understanding and trust with Asian countries.

The international community is now faced with more complex and difficult challenges than ever imagined before: progress of the developing countries, alleviation of poverty, conservation of the global environment, nonproliferation of weapons of mass destruction, and the prevention and eradication of terrorism. In order to contribute to world peace, Japan will proactively fulfill its role as a responsible member of the international community, upholding its pledge not to engage in war and based on its experience as the only nation to have suffered from the atomic bombings and the path it has followed over the 60 years after war.

On this occasion marking the 60th anniversary of the war's end, Japan, as a peace-loving nation, expresses here again that it will work to achieve peace and prosperity of all humankind with all its resources, together with all the nations of shared aspiration.[66]

Parts of this speech reflected routine statements by the emperor and prime minister at the annual Budōkan commemorative ceremonies: the mourning of three million Japanese war dead, the recognition of Japan's postwar prosperity as rooted in the war's devastation, Japan's unique atomic bomb experience, and the pledge never to let such a war happen again. Others made use of newly "standard" phrases of apology such as "deep remorse" and "heartfelt apology" and thereby continued an official practice that began a decade earlier with the fiftieth anniversary. But never had a prime minister's speech so clearly portrayed Japan's postwar history as one of *remorse for the war*, beginning with the San Francisco Peace Treaty, which forced Japan to accept the verdict of the Allied war crimes trials and thus remained a thorn in the side of the political right (Koizumi's allies). Koizumi clearly sought to establish Japan's long *positive* record in coming to terms with its wartime past—for example, through peace education and official development aid (ODA)—and to link it to Japan's current *right* and *duty* to assume a leadership role in regional and global affairs.

At the same time, he responded to domestic and foreign criticism of recent constitutional revision proposals by unambiguously committing himself to honor the pacifist spirit of the constitution and exercise "responsibility" in the international community. Looking forward to national elections the following month, this speech accentuated the concerns of the opposition and Japan's Asian neighbors rather than those of the nationalist right. But Koizumi also refuted more forcefully than any prime minister before him the well-established claim that Japan had scandalously "failed" to live up to its postwar responsibility.

The public attention focused on the government's handling of war memory during the decade between the fiftieth and the sixtieth anniversaries of Japan's defeat still showed no signs of waning. Moreover, it was matched by cultural and intellectual responses by a host of different actors. These proliferated on various levels of public life, in national and international settings. The changing spatial and sociopolitical topography of memory manifested itself in intellectual debates and public criticism (for which the mass media as well as a booming *mini-komi* or specialized publishing market were the conduits), in community-centered activities, in commemorative projects for popular consumption, and in public trials. Many of the old interest groups became actively involved by serving as sponsors or coordinators, but the creative energy most often came from individuals and citizens' organizations newly formed around a specific aspect of war memory.

CHAPTER TEN

Cultures of Commemoration at Century's End

By the end of the century, the fascination with historical memory had become part of a *global* public culture. Whether in South Africa, Argentina, the United States, or Japan, confronting historical injustices—whether as victim or as victimizer—spurred new government policies, legal procedures, intellectual thought, theoretical work, and cultural productions. At the same time, nationalist reactions to this type of global discourse erupted with impressive force. In Japan, this intense environment produced a context in which a wealth of commemorative productions came to fruition—some of which had long been in the making. A critical reading of a few prominent examples documents what was new, and what was not, on the public memory scene in the 1990s.

The choral work *The Devil's Gluttony (Akuma no hōshoku)* was a critical reflection on Japanese war crimes in China, specifically the human experiments conducted by the doctors of the biological warfare research Unit 731 in Manchuria. The poster advertising a performance of this work represents the research facilities in Pinfang with a smokestack from the ovens in which the victims of these experiments were burned (Fig. 10.1, left). The choral music was composed in 1983, but performances of it gained national and international recognition in the early 1990s, and it was still being staged in different locations in Japan and China at the sixtieth anniversary in 2005. Through this work, the composer and the performers hoped to bring Japanese and Chinese people together to think through the memory of this atrocity. In contrast, the

Fig. 10.1 (*left*) Poster for the choral work *The Devil's Gluttony (Akuma no hōshoku)*, a reflection on the crimes of Unit 731. Promotional material for the Kobe Municipal Choir. (*right*) Brochure for the Shōwa-kan, opened in 1999 in Kudanshita, Tokyo. Courtesy of the Shōwa-kan.

Hall of Shōwa (Shōwa-kan), a Tokyo museum of everyday life in Japan during the war and the early postwar years, reasserted the need to remember the Japanese people's sacrifices in a national framework, virtually deprived of international context (Fig. 10.1, right). This project originated in the late 1970s and finally opened to the public in 1999, delayed for four years because of public protest.

Confronting Silences: The Devil's Gluttony

Nothing substantiated the conceptual theorizing about postwar responsibility as much as new, or newly public, information about real wartime events. Indeed, a long-overdue examination of Japanese war atrocities in Asia—as well as their vehement denial by a few right-wing politicians and their supporters—informed and characterized the politics of memory from the late 1980s on, complicating Japan's "victims' consciousness" (*higaisha ishiki*) by stressing "victimizer consciousness" (*kagaisha ishiki*). The public recognized formerly neglected groups of victims as well as bearers of responsibility and linked the two in newly important ways. The wartime government system of sexual slavery (the "comfort women" system), the biological warfare facilities of Unit 731 in Manchuria, and the Nanjing Massacre of 1937–38 stood at the center of a genuinely public attempt to grapple with the criminal aspects of Japan's war conduct in Asia.

The real issue at stake, however, was the long postwar silence that appeared to have shrouded these events—the willful forgetting of both the victims and the political structures that had made this possible. This meant that rather than identifiable wartime perpetrators (with the exception of the emperor), it was postwar society *in toto* that stood accused. Strategies for disseminating knowledge and rousing public consciousness characterized this new phase of public memory, propelled by innovative forms of citizen activism that both inspired and took inspiration from such activism elsewhere in the world. Tapping into as well as creating new networks of domestic and international nongovernmental organizations, these voices became a critical force in the rights-based, cosmopolitan, and multilateral activism, political as well as legal, that has come to define an emerging global public culture.[1]

A trilogy of bestselling books both ignited public soul-searching and evoked a flat denial of the need for such self-examination. In the early 1980s Morimura Seiichi excavated for popular audiences the gruesome experiments conducted on human subjects under the auspices of Unit 731 in Pinfang, Manchuria. *The Devil's Gluttony* was neither the first nor the last historical reconstruction of the work of Unit 731, and it did not yet incorporate the government documents Japanese and American historians unearthed in the following years. But Morimura was able to expose with brutal clarity the "devilish work" of the inhuman treatment of Chinese, Russian, Korean, and even some American prisoners of war, used as guinea pigs in Japan's wartime program of researching, developing, producing, and testing biological weapons.[2] In the context of the international textbook controversy in the summer of 1982, Morimura's book became a "million seller" and later spurred an unusual citizens' movement devoted to deepening a collective sense of war responsibility. Indeed, *The Devil's Gluttony* offers a window onto the changing landscape of public memory between the early 1980s and the fiftieth anniversary of defeat in 1995.

Morimura's phenomenal success bore upon the emerging debate about Japanese war and postwar responsibility in multilayered ways.

The crimes themselves pointed to an institutionalized machinery of abuse and killing not unlike the crimes committed by the infamous Doctor Mengele; they simply could not be explained by the emotional terror of warfare alone.[3] Their victimizers were Japan's best doctors and scientists, not soldiers at the front trying to protect their own lives. But unlike Mengele, whose crimes came into full public view at the Nuremberg war crimes trials, the head of the Japanese biological weapons program, Ishii Shirō, never stood trial. Instead, he went underground after the war, while the data he and his team collected was quietly absorbed by U.S. intelligence through an arrangement made at the Tokyo war crimes trial. The entire facility at Pinfang was destroyed by Japanese troops on the night of 8 August 1945. Furthermore, efforts by a Russian war crimes tribunal in the late 1940s to convict those responsible for the atrocities of Unit 731 were immediately branded as communist propaganda by Washington and failed to attract international attention.[4] Meanwhile, an unknown number of Chinese, Japanese, Korean, Russian, and other workers, farmers, businessmen, journalists, refugees, and repatriates died in early postwar epidemics in the Pinfang area. The leading doctors and scientists of Unit 731, however, returned to Japan, changed their identities, and began new lives, a number of them once again rising to influential positions in the medical sciences.

Years later, the prize-winning novelist Morimura Seiichi contacted surviving members of the Unit 731 staff while researching his short story "Death Tool" (Shi no utsuwa) for serialization in the Sunday edition of the Japan Communist Party organ Akahata. At that time Japanese scholars had just begun to research the unit's activities, using documents from the Russian war crimes trial; school textbooks made no mention of it. What interested Morimura was the stark contrast between the international preservation of the knowledge produced by Unit 731 and the utter obscurity in postwar Japan of the people responsible for it.[5] Using his interviews with 31 former members of the unit, most of whom lived in remote areas of Japan, Morimura meticulously reconstructed their activities in Pinfang, complete with detailed maps and photographs of the facilities as well as its staff, taking care not to reveal the present identities of his interviewees. Publishers at first hesitated to take on the project because of the inherent sensitivity of the material and threats by right-wing groups. Indeed, less than a year after

Kodansha's publication of the first volume of the trilogy, some of the photographs Morimura had received from relatives of Ishii Shirō were revealed to be unrelated to Unit 731, dating instead to an outbreak of the plague in Manchuria in 1910–11. This revelation in the fall of 1982 not only brought the names of several former members of Unit 731 to light but fueled protests and death threats by right-wing extremists.[6]

Such tactics convinced Morimura that freedom of expression, despite its constitutional guarantee in Japan, was being undermined not by the state but by citizens themselves, and that it was also the citizens' responsibility to safeguard it.[7] That year, at an event billed as "Music and Performance Evening with Mr. Morimura to Think about Peace" in Kobe's International Hall (Kōbe kokusai kaikan), Morimura met the distinguished contemporary composer Ikebe Shin'ichirō. The evening so inspired Ikebe that he envisioned a new project for the Kobe Municipal Choir: to convey Morimura's message, and to confront Japanese war crimes individually and collectively, through music. Ikebe later admitted that it was the professional challenge that made him embark on this project rather than a desire to memorialize something he would rather forget.[8] The resulting cooperation between the writer Morimura and the composer Ikebe produced a cantata for a mixed chorus, using an abridged version of a poem Morimura wrote based on his book.

The piece represents a three-way conversation between contemporary humanity demanding the admission of guilt for the crimes committed, the victimizers, and the victims, who are called by the same dehumanizing term, "log" (*maruta*), that had rendered them mere objects of experimentation. Divided into seven distinct but structurally and musically uneven parts, the piece hinges on the gradual recovery of the human subjectivity of all three parties through the collective activity of facing the crimes, in this case through the medium of choral singing. The first two parts establish the unacknowledged guilt of the victimizers, first through weighty moral questions ("The Heavy Chains of 731"), then by supplying bitingly cynical answers ("We Deliver Live Subjects"):

> What happened in Unit 731? . . .
> Why did you give up your humanity? . . .
> Who killed the *maruta*? Who chopped up the youth?
> Why did you not refuse? . . .
> What happened in Unit 731? Ask yourself, Japan.

> Take your pick, we've got them all
> Men, women, young and old. . . .
> Chinese, Russians, Mongolians, Koreans.
> Subjects for your experiments.
> Welcome to 731. How about some sicknesses?
> Any experiment you desire. . . .
> Doctors with no conscience. Come to 731.

The next two parts recover the humanity, subjectivity, and agency of the victims. Part 3, "Red Chinese Shoes," portrays the emotional pain of families ripped apart; Part 4, "Rebellion," shows the *maruta* stand up to their victimizers in an effort to find in death the human dignity they were denied as "logs." Part 5, "A Wake in the Thirty-seventh Year," is the dramatic high point of the piece, musically the most dissonant and challenging, and marked by a narrator's brief interruption. In it, one of the scientists revisits his crime as an individual, facing his victims (a mother and child) and pushing the button on a stopwatch to release the poison gas that killed them.

> Why could you press the stopwatch?
> Why could you not disobey? . . .
> Why were you able to open your eyes and watch?
> I killed the Russian mother and child *maruta*. . . .
> Thirty-seven years later,
> I mourn, but my tears are too late.

The remaining two parts, "Friends, Bring White Flowers" and "You Shall Watch," reunite the dead and the living through a common bond of humanity restored by remembering, acknowledging, and telling (or singing). This section is musically the fullest and most harmonious, making up for the earlier tension. The *maruta* could forget their pain and wish for revenge if only their deaths could became "a lesson of history" that made people "pledge to end war forever." But the only way to do this is to face the past:

> You shall watch.
> Even if you want to turn away, you must not.
> You shall watch. . . .
> You shall listen.
> Even if you want to cover your ears, you must not.
> You shall listen.

The first public performance took place in Kobe in 1984 amid protests by right-wing groups, and beginning in 1990 *Akuma* received wide publicity, with performances at large concert halls in major cities around the country as well as in New Zealand and China. To what degree the musical event itself moved mass audiences is difficult to know. Ikebe and Morimura both worried about its initial reception among audiences likely to favor "easy listening." Instead, Ikebe characterized the piece as involving a kind of three-way struggle among the directors, the choir, and the listeners that required a willingness to stretch one's mental capabilities rather than indulging in a pleasurable listening experience. This wrestling would produce the individual and collective consciousness of responsibility that the piece was designed to evoke.[9] Quite clearly, it served its purpose well with respect to its creators as well as its performers. Neither Morimura (in researching and writing the book) nor Ikebe (in composing the music) started out with a particular interest in issues of war responsibility, political or otherwise, but both experienced the work itself as personally transforming. Ikebe admitted that he, like most people, had once preferred to forget— "naturally."[10] Short writings by members of the performing choirs similarly suggested that the intense experience of rehearsing and performing awakened a commitment to face the wartime past as victimizers that they had not felt when they auditioned for the choir "because they liked to sing and wanted to do something for peace."[11]

In launching a "singing movement" (*utagoe undō*) in 1990, Morimura, Ikebe, and producer Mochinaga Noriko resurrected a labor movement tradition from the 1950s, when workers forged solidarity by singing resistance songs together.[12] Mochinaga's chorus project *Akuma no hōshoku* was very much a middle-class undertaking, a formal choir led by Ikebe that performed in large concert halls, often in conjunction with classical music concerts. But the idea behind this movement was clearly to build awareness among the many local promoters who produced concerts in various cities, rather than simply to make an impression on passive audiences.[13] For rather than organizing a grand national tour by one choir, the movement worked through local networks and trained amateur choirs in many areas of the country, each time bringing together a new group of people to share their love for singing and experience a new level of commitment to peace. People from all walks of life would join these local choirs, men and women from 20 to 75 years old, and often a smaller, more experienced group from one city would join a group in another location for a performance.

Furthermore, the movement was neither masterminded nor sponsored by a single special interest organization, although the Japan-China Friendship Association promoted it through coverage in its newspaper and by making the concert a central event at its fortieth anniversary celebrations in 1990.[14] Instead, the movement relied predominantly on local grassroots networks, labor unions, law firms, citizen committees, and local businesses, transforming its public relations work into a public awareness campaign that fed into emerging movements demanding government recognition of and compensation for Asian victims of Japanese wartime aggression.

As Morimura stressed in a joint interview with Ikebe that was serialized in *Nitchū yūkō shinbun* (*Japan-China Friendship News*) in the fall of 1990, *Akuma* came to loom large in public life because it connected with contemporary political issues and thus presented an incentive for collective learning. He even likened *Akuma* (the book, a 1985 television documentary, and the concert) to Ienaga Saburō's textbook trials, which, through lengthy legal procedures and the appearance of witnesses, had kept Japan's wartime past in public view. In the context of the early 1990s, when the Cold War structures of international and domestic politics began to break up and new definitions of Japan's role as a global power became pressing, *Akuma* embodied important changes in the geography of memory. It confronted the individual and collective silence that had enveloped a particularly gruesome set of Japanese war atrocities with a clear focus on Japanese as victimizers rather than as victims and China as the target and site of this aggression.

Clearly aimed at challenging what many saw as the conservative monopoly on memory, *Akuma* also sought to break with the dominant pattern of left-wing pacifism, which was centered on a collective consciousness of victimhood. Furthermore, the concert production represented a shift in the organizational practices of memory in that it relied relatively little on the institutionalized channels of special interests and emphasized numerous local productions more than mass consumption. As the postwar "management" of the war's legacies became a politically pertinent and potentially explosive issue in the 1990s, *Akuma* proved meaningful to a growing segment of the Japanese public that came to see "memory" as instrumental in solving the lingering problems of "the postwar." Among the many different memory projects that Japan's public culture produced from the 1980s on, *Akuma no hōshoku* represented, in Ikebe's words, "one stone in the memorial pyramid of Japanese pacifism and democracy," and an urgently needed one at that.[15]

Galvanizing Popular Audiences: Last Friends

More conventional commemorative projects in the mid- to late 1990s included films and museum exhibitions playing to vast public audiences. These were intended less to educate than to forge a broad public consensus on the meaning of the war, and they tended to reflect the changes that memory was undergoing in the global public culture of the 1990s. In part these projects fit the expanded parameters in which particular memories were now framed—for example, by including Asian victims and Japanese perpetrators of the war—even though most did so without fundamentally changing long established narratives. At the same time, the commemorative films and exhibits put on display in the context of the fiftieth anniversary of the war's end were themselves products of compromises, often hard fought, to accommodate competing, even contentious, public sensibilities. Many of these projects were not entirely new but rather had their own postwar histories to wrestle with—and by extension the very real issue of 50 years of postwar memory. Two telling examples are Wadatsumikai's 1995 remake of its 1950 pacifist movie *Kike wadatsumi no koe* (dubbed *Last Friends* in 1995) and the Shōwa-kan, a new museum of everyday life during the war, which finally opened in 1999 after twenty years of preparation and is managed by the Japan Association of War-bereaved Families.

Last Friends opened in movie theaters in Tokyo and elsewhere in Japan on 3 June 1995. This was only days after the conclusion of lengthy negotiations between Tōei, the large commercial company that produced the film, and Wadatsumikai, which holds the copyright to the title *Kike wadatsumi no koe* and is well known in Japan as the representative of the student war dead of World War II. For 40 years, first Wadatsumikai and later Tōei had tried to remake the 1950 film, responding both to its contemporary popularity and to the criticism it had attracted at the time. In 1955–56 Tōei turned down the project on the grounds that pacifist war combat films no longer caught the public's imagination. In 1986 Wadatsumikai rejected Tōei's proposal to seek the sponsorship of the conservative media giants Fuji TV and *Sankei shinbun* for a new film. Only in 1994 did cooperation begin in earnest to produce a "fifti-eth anniversary" movie. Tōei chose the director (Deme Masanobu), screenwriter (Hayasaka Akira, known for his soap-opera scripts), cast, and staff, but it had to negotiate critical aspects of the content with Wadatsumikai. The result was an emotionally draining film whose mood stemmed from its oscillation between tough, action-packed war scenes and the heroes' desperate, melodramatic reflections on the absurdity of war and their desire for peace. It explicitly invited identification with the student-soldiers as both pathetic victims of militarism and war and as critically thinking yet despairingly powerless individuals whose war-time failures were in the end sublimated through the empathetic remem-bering of later generations.

The film's biggest claim to fame undoubtedly lay in Tōei's ability to attract popular television stars for the roles of the six "friends." These main characters represented four student-soldiers modeled on wartime testaments from the book *Kike wadatsumi no koe,* as well as a nurse and an irregular soldier from Taiwan, who supplied ammunition and Korean comfort women to Japanese units in the Philippines.[16] The film begins with an appeal to the audience's sympathetic imagination, presenting the student-soldiers as normal young people who wanted nothing more than to enjoy sports, studies, and friends—just like contemporary university students—but were deprived of these simple pleasures by war. A rugby player in the Shinjuku stadium sees phan-toms of wartime rugby players, who join in his game and then take him back into their world of 50 years ago, introducing themselves as students from Tokyo, Waseda, and Meiji universities. Thoroughly be-wildered, he has to learn the stark realities of Japan's militarist society in the closing years of the war (about which he appears to know noth-ing), when students from elite universities were forced to quit their studies and leave their families, friends, and young brides behind to join the troops at the front, swept up in the patriotic fever of the times.

Two of the four student-soldiers, former classmates at Meiji Uni-versity, meet again on a navy ship heading for the Philippines, bound by their friendship as classmates in Tokyo as well as by the brutality they endure from higher officers. When the ship is torpedoed, they become part of a small group of survivors who seek refuge on an island, which is promptly bombarded by American fighter planes, leaving them alive only by chance. Another one of the recruited students is sent to Okinawa and becomes a *kamikaze* or suicide pilot during the American invasion in the spring of 1945. These three characters live out the familiar story of Japan's gradual military defeat under the horrible conditions of jungle warfare, joined by the token female sufferer, a kind, courageous nurse caring tirelessly for the wounded at a Red Cross station. In contrast to both their violently brutal troop commanders and the bomb-dropping but otherwise invisible enemy, the student-soldiers are three-dimensional human beings. They suffer physically but especially spiritually and morally in their inability to stop the brutality of their own units against local villages, which is shown in vivid detail. They also attempt to interpret the horror around them with the intellectual tools at their disposal: private conversations with comrades, and sharing smuggled books, for example the classical poetry collection *Man'yōshū*, and especially a translated collection of letters by German student-soldiers in World War I, on which Wadatsumikai's bestselling book *Listen to the Voices from the Deep* was originally modeled.

The fourth friend, however, unconvinced by the official propaganda, dodges the draft by hiding in his parents' village, thereby causing much hardship for his family, who are ostracized as "noncitizens" (*hikokumin*) by neighbors and local officials. The film's narrative periodically swings back to Japan to follow this war resister's equally painful story, which Wadatsumikai admits is not based on a particular testament but rather represents the spirit of doubt and resistance found in many of the collected letters. The inclusion of this character was one of Wadatsumikai's conditions for making the film, and it is this resister, executed at the moment of the atomic bomb's explosion, who rises from the ashes and summons the spirits of his comrades back to life.

The two colonial subjects, the Taiwanese soldier and the Korean girl, were only loosely attached to the troops. Although they, too, became victims of war, they were not equally subjugated by Japanese militarists in this story but actually enjoyed an unusual measure of freedom to move about on their motorbike, joining the troops as comrades. The

Korean "comfort woman" proudly revealed her identity by using her Korean name and entertaining the troops with Korean folk songs. In one scene, however, she was shown enduring customer after customer as the troops' paid provider of sexual services, while the men who took advantage of her were left faceless. She herself appeared to harbor no hard feelings against the troops as she cheerfully helped with their evacuation. In the end, she and the Taiwanese soldier die by an American bomb while riding their motorcycle, independent of the Japanese unit.

On the eve of the fiftieth anniversary of the war's end, *Last Friends* provided Japanese audiences with the chance to relive their country's defeat in personal terms through some of the most enduring pacifist icons of the postwar period: the student-soldiers paired with the atomic bomb. Stylistically and in terms of narrative it was an unremarkable film. Technically and artistically, reviewers found it decent but not spectacular, and although the film did relatively well at the box office and was nominated for best film of the year, it did not win any great distinction. More importantly, it failed to challenge the dominant narrative of Japanese wartime suffering, despite the politically correct inclusion of scenes depicting Japanese aggression. The student-soldiers' (forced) participation in raiding a Philippine village and killing innocent women and children, and the presence of the Korean "comfort woman," rounded out the picture in only the most tangential ways— a bow toward Wadatsumikai's demand for a multidimensional sense of the war on whose stage the student-soldiers learned to love peace. The biggest point of conflict lay in Tōei's insistence on setting the film in the Philippines and Okinawa rather than in China, as Wadatsumikai had envisioned with the explicit goal of bringing Japanese aggression into sharper view. As it turned out, *Last Friends* engaged with none of the controversial aspects of the war and, it could be argued, even denigrated Korean women's claims for belated justice by depicting them as valued comrades rather than as sex slaves.

As with all products designed for mass consumption and thus competition in the capitalist marketplace, Tōei's 1995 production of *Kike wadatsumi no koe* involved compromises that clearly played off the huge public concern with war memory. Rather than simply sanitizing history to circumvent conflicting meanings, however, this film simulated a

largely inclusive view of multiple levels of responsibility and victimization. It did so by tapping into the long-established trope of youth's
pacifist humanism in the context of everyday life, both then (brutally
distorted by war) and now. In effect, this strategy capitalized on Wadatsumikai's message since the early 1950s but divorced it from the organization's radical leftist politics. In its negotiations with Tōei, Wadatsumikai had demanded that the war be treated explicitly as a war of
aggression against all of Asia, that the *wadatsumi* student-soldiers' experience not be exclusively portrayed as one of tragedy but also one of
responsibility, that their action be understood against the background
of Japanese wartime coercion and thought control, and that various
forms of resistance against militarism be shown. To the extent that
Tōei satisfied most of these points without dramatically altering the
popular narrative of Japanese victimization, Wadatsumikai suddenly
appeared to be representing mainstream public opinion—supported by
none other than the Ministry of Education, who highly recommended
Last Friends to high school and college students.

Wadatsumikai no doubt welcomed the publicity generated by the
movie and used it, in turn, to promote the latest edition of *Kike wadatsumi no koe*, published that year. Tellingly, the postscript to this new
edition clearly acknowledged its own shortcomings and those of both
earlier editions in excluding an Asian perspective on the student-soldiers'
torment. Although the 1995 edition did strive to restore the original
letters and include formerly abridged passages revealing the students
not only as victims but also as victimizers, it did not go so far as to
include letters by Korean and Taiwanese student-soldiers who were
forcibly conscripted and died under even more brutal conditions.[17] In
explaining the group's development since 1970 from the perspective of
the mid-1990s, the postscript asserted: "In preparation for a later date
if and when China, Korea, and other Asian nations should voice harsh
criticism of what they consider Japan's distortion of history, the society
has gradually but steadily been building toward a position that is sufficiently independent for the framing of a sincere response."[18]

Indeed, the organization's biannual journal carried forth this commitment to examine Japanese war responsibility, including that of student-soldiers, and remained at the forefront of the contemporary critical discourse that enveloped public life in Japan.

Tōei, meanwhile, produced another movie that engaged war memory but from an unapologetically nationalistic standpoint: *Pride: The Fateful Moment (Puraido)*, released in 1998, which sought to rehabilitate the wartime leader and executed war criminal Tōjō Hideki. This time, it cooperated with a notorious group of neo-revisionist intellectuals led by Fujioka Nobukatsu and Nishio Kanji, who had founded the Japanese Society for History Textbook Reform (Atarashii rekishi kyōkasho o tsukurukai, or Tsukurukai) in 1996 in protest over the inclusion of the comfort women issue in official textbooks. Insofar as film production gives any indication of current popular sensibilities, issues of war memory continued to capture the public imagination in Japan throughout the decade—but the context appeared to have changed once again in critical ways. By the end of the decade public consumption of memory became inundated with political messages indicating a renewed interest in neo-nationalist interpretations of the past, no doubt in response to the substantial challenges posed by the global dynamics of memory politics. Film was but one small area in which this made itself apparent; other public "sites of memory" included history textbooks, a perennial source of conflict, and, new in the late 1990s, Japan's first state-sponsored war museum, the Shōwa-kan.

The Izokukai's Last Hurrah? The Shōwa-kan

The Shōwa-kan opened in the spring of 1999 after twenty years of preparation and public conflict. The contestants included the Japan Association of War-bereaved Families, who proposed the project in 1979 and now manage it; the Ministry of Health and Welfare, the museum's official sponsor; and a host of citizen groups and individuals, some of whom supported the project while most challenged it from a variety of standpoints. In contrast to the enormous controversy surrounding the planning process in the first half of the 1990s, the years following the museum's opening to the public generated little fanfare.[19] In fact, judging from the heavy and increasing volume of advertising for the museum in schools, newspapers, and on television, the Shōwa-kan has hardly become a household word even in Tokyo. In part this had to do with a general lack of name recognition. The project had been known by various names, the most prominent of which was the "War Dead Peace Memorial Hall" (Senbotsusha tsuitō heiwa kinenkan). It acquired the name "Shōwa-kan" shortly before its opening, as a last-minute compromise.

More importantly, the museum excluded any provocative interpretation of Japan's war effort and instead displayed a variety of objects pertaining to the everyday home life of Japanese—overwhelmingly belonging to women and children—within a trans-war framework between 1935 and 1955.[20] The Shōwa-kan invited viewers to re(dis)cover the material hardships of those decades (whether painfully or nostalgically) without references to the Japanese military, the war in Asia, and even the war dead. In contrast to the openly nationalistic museum at Yasukuni Shrine, the Yūshūkan, the heroes of the Shōwa-kan were the survivors, not the dead. While this decision no doubt served to mute much explosive criticism, public voices of various convictions clearly recognized political messages in such a "sanitized" framework. The conservative writer Kamisaka Fuyuko, who once served as advisor to the project but resigned in protest in 1995, commented on the final design:

Shōwa-kan? What is that supposed to mean? "Shōwa" and "war" have come to stand for almost the same thing. Can anything meaningful be said about "Shōwa" if Japan's military ventures, which established the context for the hard work and sacrifice of Japanese citizens, aren't at all represented? You can't just leave out the single most significant aspect of that time. What's the point of having just pots and pans? These aren't exhibits about the Stone Age, after all. After twenty years and a tremendous amount of money, after such big talk about war orphans and praying for peace, in the end this turned out to be a big flop, for no logical connection is made between the items on display and the era as such. It is a symbol of an apologetic Japan with no will of its own.[21]

Rightist critiques of contemporary Japan as spineless and unsure of both its present place and its future direction underline in important ways the subtler messages of the Shōwa kan. These, in Kerry Smith's words, sharply contrast current social realities with those of the era of reconstruction, idealized as "one of shared purpose and hard-won gratification."[22] These were also precisely the ideals around which the Izokukai had built its nationwide network in the first postwar decades, and they were still at stake in the 1990s, when the Association of War-bereaved Families found itself confronted by a radically changed and changing environment in which war memories seemed up for grabs.

Indeed, the Shōwa-kan controversy instructively represented the status of contemporary nationalism in Japan with important parallels to similarly controversial museum exhibitions in the United States (e.g., the 1995 Smithsonian Enola Gay exhibit) and Germany (e.g., the 1999 Wehrmacht exhibit). That it was built at all surely testified to the continued strength of the Association's close ties to the LDP and bureaucracy, a connection that itself became the explicit target of protests in 1993–95.

Despite this structural continuity, however, a comparison of the Shōwa-kan in 1999 with earlier plans reveals that contemporary nationalism no longer relied on its most cherished symbols, the emperor and the "manifestation of the heroic deeds of the war dead" (*eirei no kenshō*). Instead, the Shōwa-kan was reduced to what was essentially a nationalistic interpretation of a common theme in the 1990s: that ordinary people were victims of war, whether children or adults, men or women, Japanese or other Asians. Moreover, in the final outcome the Shōwa-kan was situated on the commemorative landscape just as the rest of Japan's museums had been throughout the postwar period, representing particular interests, ideologies, and memories. Rather than towering over all other war/peace museums as Japan's first national museum of World War II, the Shōwa-kan in effect ended up in its rightful place as a museum of the historical roots of the Association of War-bereaved Families, despite the troubling issue of state funding.

A closer look at the language used to describe the Shōwa-kan and its previously planned incarnations as part of the longer history of the Association makes this clear. At the brief 30-minute opening ceremony on 27 March 1999, four high-profile speakers gave addresses: Prime Minister Obuchi Keizō, Welfare Minister Miyashita Sōhei, Izokukai president Nakai Sumiko, and a delegate of the former prime minister and former Izokukai president Hashimoto Ryūtarō (who did not appear). Prime Minister Obuchi steadfastly stuck to a narrative of suffering in his address:

In the half-century that has passed since the end of the last world war, we have built, by the people's efforts, today's peaceful and affluent Japan.

But when I think of the hardships defying both pen and tongue that you war bereaved have endured, the loss of your loved ones in war and the painful struggle of life in the midst of the confusion and upheaval after the war, I am overcome by a flood of emotions. . . . *The need to collect, preserve, and pass on to the next generation historical documents and information of this experience and reality now looms large* [emphasis added].

After the war, the country extended various support measures to the war bereaved and war injured in the form of state compensation. The opening of the "Shōwa-kan," which transmits to younger generations the hardships of the people's daily lives during and after the war, has an immensely deep meaning and achieves its stated goal completely by connecting broadly with the people of today. We expect that it will make great contributions to the twenty-first century.[23]

Hashimoto Ryūtarō, in contrast, acknowledged that the project originated in the Association's desire to have the state build a Commemoration Hall for the War-bereaved Children to *console* the war orphans and function as an added support measure for the war bereaved. Suehiro Sakae, spokesman for the Association in 1996, asserted in an interview that the organization considered this project (termed alternately "commemoration hall" and "prayer hall")[24] a way for the state to make restitution to the war bereaved, who had been forced to rebuild their lives without the appropriate compensation and state-sponsored ceremonies for the war dead that they were entitled to. Neither this sense of entitlement nor the ritual aspect of "consolation" and "prayer" were present in the final version of the project. Instead, the outcome represented a long-resisted compromise, intended to appease critics both on the left, who protested against the violation of the constitutional separation of state and religion, and on the right, led by Yasukuni Shrine, who insisted that there could be no legitimate place for ritual remembering except Yasukuni itself. In the final outcome, the Shōwa-kan was defined simply as "an institution that collects, preserves, and displays historical documents and information about the hardship of the people's everyday life that the war-bereaved families, beginning with the orphans, experienced during and after the war (1935–55), and that gives later generations the opportunity to learn about these hardships."[25]

This no doubt represented a significant failure for Nihon izokukai. The name "Shōwa-kan" could not speak fully to its ideological concerns. The briefest of explanations asserted that "the emblem of the Shōwa era was the last great war, and the hardship of people who suffered in it became the cornerstone of the prosperity of postwar society."[26] Indeed, the clear linkage of wartime and early postwar material suffering with later postwar affluence placed the memory of material and social conditions at the center of the reconstruction of the national community. Under the occupation, when all references to a *political* community of war bereaved had to be avoided, these material and social hardships had served to legitimize an organization called, at that time, the Japan League for the Welfare of the War-bereaved. Moreover, SCAP had required that the organization not be limited to military families but also include the war bereaved with no connection to the military. Now, at the end of the century, it was as if the language of the Shōwa-kan reconnected with the earliest incarnation of the Association of War-bereaved Families as a social welfare group rather than the political pressure group into which it had evolved with the end of the occupation.

A consideration of the Shōwa-kan's opening as a moment in the Association's history reveals a long-established special interest group at the crossroads. The opening ceremony actually had a twin, smaller in scale but worthy of the front page of the Association's newspaper, whereas the museum opening was covered on page two. On the eve of the opening, the former youth section (now the middle-age section, or *sōnenbu*), which stood at the center of the Shōwa-kan project, formally dissolved itself. It was a ceremony of closure, of reflection and remembering an almost 40-year history of activism. The youth section had formed in 1960, when the war orphans were becoming the new focal point of war-bereaved activism. Generational change and the importance of transmitting a "correct" memory of the war and contemporary patriotism to those without concrete war experience had then become a critical objective of the organization. The youth section was a tool to control this transfer of correct national sentiment rather than a result of youth organizing on its own behalf.

At the end of the century, these "youths" were of course past their prime. It was as if the museum, which remembered their suffering and honored their strength in rebuilding the country, would take their place in society—"displayed memory" replacing lived experiences, so to speak. From the coverage in *Izoku tsūshin*, it was clear that this dissolution marked a turning point in the Association's history, one that had been pondered in general terms over the past years. It indicated not only the reality of generational turnover, which war-bereaved associations inescapably face over time, but also the need to relocate long-established special interests on a shifting and much widened terrain of civic political activism.

The Discourse about War Responsibility at the Turn of the Millennium

Sixty years after Japan's defeat in World War II, issues of memory remain important precisely because they are at once politically useful, personally meaningful, intellectually stimulating, and perennially interesting to the public, whether at the box office or in the bookstore. In contrast to the first half of the 1990s, however, when long-neglected war victims fueled the global public "discovery" of Japanese war atrocities, today the viability of contentious memory claims has become an unmistakable fact of public life. Indeed, laying claim to the past—however recent that past may be, and whether one is victim, perpetrator, bystander, or cooperator—is a hallmark of contemporary society, in Japan as elsewhere in the world. Today the abiding public interest in memory is perhaps less tied to the war victims themselves than to the "imaginative power" of their experiences.[27] This has raised a host of questions about "restorative justice" for past atrocities[28] and about what one may call the culture of war writ large—namely, the conditions that spur the recurrence of atrocities against civilians all over the globe, most recently in Bosnia, Rwanda, and Iraq. Concurrently, the public focus on particularly Japanese characteristics of dealing with war responsibility has also brought to the fore academic debates about the larger political and epistemological structures of war memory in postwar Japan and the degree to which they may be overcome.

At the turn of the millennium, debates about Japanese culpability still had not been resolved but instead dovetailed with a wider global discourse on repairing historical injustices.[29] This development centered on the problem of compensation and redress for long-neglected war victims, especially former military comfort women and forced laborers from various Asian and Allied countries. Initially, the compensation debate owed much of its significance to the recognition by all who participated in it that it took place "belatedly" in biological time (potential recipients were nearing the end of their lives or had already died) and in world time (compared with other countries facing similar issues). Public hearings and other testimonies as well as oral histories assumed a now-or-never urgency, sustained by a new realization of the political consequences of half a century of silences and silencings. Of course Japan was not alone in this but in the good company of most of its Asian neighbors, who were only now beginning to complicate and negotiate the politics of memory and restitution in their own countries and internationally. Moreover, the worldwide attention summoned by this intra Asian memory debate suggested that war memory and responsibility were acute issues in other world regions as well.

The more than 50 redress lawsuits filed in Japanese and in American courts against the Japanese government or Japanese corporations had important political, legal, and organizational implications that fuel the debate today. The lawsuits spurred new activist alliances that are decidedly international in scope and use the internet to publicize their work and network with others. The Korean Council for the Women Drafted for Sexual Slavery by Japan formed in 1990 as the first of several internationally visible groups to support lawsuits against the Japanese government. In 1993, the Japan War Responsibility Center (JWRC) was established in Tokyo as the foremost archive of historical materials on issues of Japanese war responsibility; it publishes the most recent research in its quarterly journal.[30] The JWRC also serves as a liaison office for academics, lawyers, and activists supporting redress lawsuits in the Tokyo District Court. The North American coalition of mainly Chinese-born activists, the Global Alliance for Preserving the History of World War II in Asia, was founded in 1994 to remedy the dearth of information on Japanese war crimes in American public life and around the world through museum exhibitions and web-based virtual exhibits.[31] A particularly dynamic link in this kind of activism grew out of Asian feminist networks involved in conferences sponsored by the United Nations Commission on Human Rights in the mid-1990s and led to the establishment of the Violence Against Women in War–Network Japan (VAWW–NET Japan) in 1998.[32]

VAWW–NET Japan, under the leadership of Matsui Yayori, a well-known journalist and activist against the international trafficking of women, was the principal organizer of a seminal event held in Tokyo in December 2000. The Women's International War Crimes Tribunal 2000 for the Trial of Japanese Military Sexual Slavery was a people's tribunal, organized by Asian women and human rights organizations, staffed by prosecution teams from nine countries across the Asia-Pacific region, presided over by four judges of international reputation, and attended by over a thousand spectators and three hundred media anchors every day for four days. It placed on trial both Emperor Hirohito and the state of Japan "for the crimes of rape and sexual slavery as crimes against humanity" during World War II.[33] The testimony of 64 survivors and two Japanese veterans formed the core of the proceedings, accompanied by the statements by academic historians, specialists in international law, and psychologists who contextualized the testimonies with respect to the Japanese wartime state, especially the role of the emperor, the structure of the Japanese army, and the psychological mechanisms of trauma. The final judgment, delivered to the United Nations Human Rights Commission in The Hague one year later, established a clear historical record of the institutional structure and practical functioning of the comfort women system as an integral part of military policy. It found Emperor Hirohito guilty and called on the Japanese government to acknowledge and provide compensation to the victims of this atrocity.[34]

The Women's Tribunal 2000 stands as a major signpost in the history of Japanese war memory. First, it was the crowning event of a decade-long struggle in Japan and Asia to make the Japanese system of sexual slavery in World War II internationally known, publicly validate the survivors' pain and thereby restore their personal dignity, and establish the Japanese government's political responsibility. The tribunal dramatized the paradigm shift that had taken place in the discourse on memory, now centered on crimes against women within the ethnic and social hierarchies of Japanese colonialism and war. In Itō Ruri's interpretation, treating violence against women in an explicitly public and international framework "signifies a redefinition of the relationship between domestic and international law, as well as . . . the division between public and private." She continues:

Because of this, the Tribunal itself, involving women as citizens, became an agent in the process of realizing law, not only criticizing the "common sense" of international law, or the right to trial of the state, but also embodying an actual practice of legal reconstruction while transcending national boundaries. . . . Herein lies a critique of the very framework that rigidly distinguishes between internal/domestic and external/international relations and that takes the sovereign state to be the basic component in that structure.[35]

Clearly, the tribunal embodied a particular vision for redirecting the dynamics of memory and justice that was also borne out by the demonstrated viability of cross-national and international citizens' networks and NGOs.

Second, as a public event, the Women's Tribunal participated in current efforts around the world to design new and case-specific forms of "restorative justice," which Martha Minow defines as seeking "to repair the injustice, to make up for it, and to effect corrective changes in the record, in relationships, and in future behavior."[36] The tribunal combined the prosecution-oriented nature of a war crimes trial with the therapeutic and reconciliatory aspects of a truth commission. The restorative justice sought here had an ulterior motive from its inception— namely, to make an explicit connection between the Japanese system of sexual slavery during World War II and contemporary violence against women in war all over the world, most blatantly demonstrated in the mass rapes of Muslim women in Bosnia in 1993.[37] Here the tribunal made an original and pathbreaking contribution to international justice, for it was the first war crimes trial to focus exclusively on crimes against women. More importantly, its findings persuaded the UN Human Rights Commission to declare systematic rape not just a war crime but a crime against humanity. The comfort women issue also brought the Japanese and Asian historical record and its scholars into the global discourse on negotiating historical injustices to an unprecedented degree. These kinds of links across time and across space now define the terrain on which issues of historical memory are being understood in terms of their contemporary relevance in global society.

Third, while encapsulating new developments in the memory debate, the Women's Tribunal also advertised the real constraints facing those who attempt to change the political dynamics and conceptual parameters of war memory. As a so-called people's tribunal, it lacked legal authority and thus could not force the Japanese government to acknowledge its responsibility and compensate the former comfort women. Indeed, media coverage in Japan was sparse, while an NHK documentary about the Tribunal showed obvious signs of backdoor censorship, as Tessa Morris-Suzuki has suggested.[38] In terms of the political goals of eliciting government compensation for the survivors, therefore, the tribunal accomplished little. Furthermore, the comfort women issue as a whole mobilized the neo-nationalist right around campaigns to rescue Japan's national identity and pride from foreign outrage over war crimes, which some extremists actually denied. Vocal groups like the Japanese Society for History Textbook Reform (Atarashii rekishi kyōkasho o tsukurukai), commonly known as Tsukurukai, used populist strategies and targeted familiar locales of public struggles over war memory, demanding the removal from school texts of recently added references to comfort women and Japanese war crimes.[39] Popular cartoons, such as Kobayashi Yoshinori's *Sensōron* (*On War*), and films (for example, *Puraido*) focused much public attention on nationalist resistance to the new perpetrator-memory driven by the feminist left.

Laura Hein concluded in the context of the comfort women debate that "information about specific aspects of the war . . . simply found its place within [the] two Japanese versions of the past"—that is, the war "as a morally bankrupt disaster and as a noble, although failed, enterprise."[40] More precisely, perhaps, the enduring pattern of appropriating memory for specific political purposes has itself now become the subject of academic debates in Japan. The leftist promoters of compensation for former military comfort women have issued a heavy indictment not only of the Japanese government but of the postwar political system that entrenched the long neglect of this issue. Their strategy has been to summon international support, to make connections to other human rights violations, to argue in effect that the public should care because systemic sexual abuse is not history but very much a contemporary reality. The reactionary right in Japan, meanwhile, focused attention away from the actual atrocities and instead on the problem of accusation and judgment, especially when they came from abroad. Domestically, this strategy fed into neo-nationalist agendas by validating what many on the conservative right saw as the injustice of American occupation reforms—which smacked of "victor's justice"—as well as their enduring political legacy through the end of the century. Both the right and the left thus identified, in their different ways, specific legacies of the war that had led to systemic problems in the postwar political status quo.

In today's post–Cold War context, in which the global renegotiation of international relations failed to lift the constraints of the past from Japan's foreign policy but arguably intensified them, the nationalist critique has appeal. It decries what many Japanese have come to see as a "global double standard" in the politics of apology, which singles out Japan while allowing other aggressor countries to evade responsibility for similar war atrocities and human rights violations. Ōnuma Yasuaki, a prominent scholar of international law and human rights activist who has written voluminously on issues of Japan's postwar responsibility, regretted Asian war victims' eagerness to accept American support for their litigation, given that Americans have refused to examine their own military conduct abroad. In his view, this kind of globalization of the issue of Japan's war responsibility has lent the neo-nationalist agenda in Japan an air of moral credibility.[41]

The political and legal challenges of the war responsibility issue thus raised important questions about the political dynamics of memory. By the end of the 1990s, war memory (*sensō no kioku*) had become an important interdisciplinary topic among Japanese academics, as reflected in the many published collections of essays and journal articles that continue to appear on the market. Two strands of this new discourse stood out: the feminist critique of war memory on the one hand, and the debate about a Japanese historical subjectivity (*shutaisei ronsō*) on the other.

Feminist scholars Ueno Chizuko, Ōgoshi Aiko, and Suzuki Yūko were among the first to propose a gendered reading of war responsibility in which an established patriarchal paradigm was being challenged and contested by feminist perspectives. The comfort women debate, which relied in good part on survivors' testimonial evidence presented half a century after the war, was no doubt the main catalyst for a critique that had been curiously absent even among feminist historians until the 1990s. For Ueno, who directly took issue with the neo-nationalist revisionists, the important difference between a positivist and a feminist analysis lay in historical methodology, specifically in source material. Against the privileging of "objective" historical facts established on the basis of print documents, she argued for the equal validity of victims' testimonies as historical evidence. Precisely because feminist historiography was about "making silenced voices speak," oral

testimonies were central to the project of dislocating established paradigms. The Women's Tribunal 2000 thus became a pivotal event.[42]

Ōgoshi Aiko took a historical approach. She first established that the
crime of sexual slavery was constitutive of imperialism, colonialism, and
nationalism as deeply patriarchal political systems before 1945. Then she
went on to show how the patriarchal nature of politics had not ended
in 1945 but in fact had become the hallmark of postwar democracy
(evident, for example, in special interest politics), which explained
why sexual war crimes had not registered as crimes in postwar Japan.
Ōgoshi tried to make sense of the fact that the "coming-out" of the
former comfort women in the 1990s, which should have constituted
a crucial turning-point in Japanese memory, did not (in her view) result
in a paradigmatic shift in the political and philosophical discourse on
war responsibility, which continued to be male-centered.[43] Applied to
revisionists like Fujioka Nobukatsu and the Tsukurukai, this point was
obvious enough; Ōgoshi, however, directed her critique more toward
the participants in the other prominent memory debate of the late
1990s: the controversy over Katō Norihiro's essay "Haisengoron" (On
the Post-defeat Era) and the search for a unified Japanese subjectivity.[44]

The so-called historical subjectivity debate (*rekishi shutaisei ronsō*) revolved around intellectual, even psychohistorical, efforts to overcome
the deep political divisions that characterized postwar Japan, and thereby facilitate a unified, collective, uncontested way of facing and resolving
Japan's colonial and wartime past. The literary critic Katō Norihiro had
inaugurated this debate in a series of essays, three of which were collected in the volume *Haisengoron* (1995), the book that lay at the center of
the discussion. Katō's critique represented a sustained scrutiny not of the
meaning of the war, but of the postwar political dynamics that had guaranteed war memory a public space. He allowed himself to imagine what
it would take to eliminate the seemingly inevitable political struggle associated with memory of the war. First, he proposed, Japanese must recognize that their postwar history exhibited a "Jekyll and Hyde" type of
schizophrenia that was the legacy of defeat, incomplete mourning, and
the bitter ironies of democratization under the American military occupation. The imposition of a "peace" constitution by a foreign military
power that had just demonstrated the capability of nuclear destruction
seemed to him particularly fundamental. Second, the deeply ingrained

ambivalence of the Japanese toward both their wartime past and their postwar alliance with the United States had to be overcome in order to take appropriate responsibility for their colonial past. Third, this might be done by honestly mourning Japan's own war dead while fully recognizing their complicity in the war and without glorifying them, which would then lead to mourning the twenty million Asian war dead.

Katō sought to reconcile the two most prominent uses of the war dead (nationalist and pacifist) as a fundamental aspect of Japanese war memory by recognizing the validity of both and rejecting the politicization of the dead themselves. A national consensus on the war as unjust could be established, Katō argued, in turn clearing the way for a true apology to the Asian victims of Japanese aggression. Finally, the process of mourning would free the Japanese to discard the U.S.-imposed constitution and adopt a peace constitution of their own making.[45]

As if to prove Katō's point about Japan's split psyche, his essays ignited a controversy over precisely where he fit into the political spectrum of memory. His straightforward acknowledgment of Japanese war crimes and especially the emperor's responsibility put him in the liberal camp, but his proposal to grieve first for Japan's own war dead and only then to move on to Asian victims revealed nationalist sympathies. His idea of constructing a unified national subject, moreover, came close to replicating fascist tendencies (or patriarchal hegemony). The liberal philosopher Takahashi Tetsuya led the counterattack; for him, resurrecting the right-wing use of the Japanese war dead was anathema. Instead, he demanded that the Japanese of today embrace the Asian war dead, insisting that this was the only way to face their criminal past. Critical readers of this exchange have pointed out the fundamental similarities of these two positions, for both assumed the need for a collective national consensus and neither was ready to look beyond the centrality of the war dead, Japanese or Asian. Historians of memory, meanwhile, cringed at Katō's nonchalant way of extrapolating psychological mechanisms from individuals to nations, as if this extension were common sense. The work of memory, and the reason for its enduring contestation, lies rather at the intersection of different processes, which Tessa Morris-Suzuki put in a nutshell in her critique of Katō:

The legacy of the Pacific War in Japan is just one point at which issues of public political action, group identity and responsibility, and personal memory and emotion meet, and it is a legacy that can only be dealt with by working through the intersection between these dimensions of human experience. This intersection is fraught with difficulties: problems of responding to political demands for apologies and compensation, without allowing the response itself to become a release from the continuing task of remembering; problems of distinguishing the responsibility of citizens to remember national pasts from the responsibilities of people to remember the human history of an increasingly globalizing world; problems of relating historical truth seeking to sentiments of nostalgia, regret or grief about the past.[46]

To try to reduce this multidimensional field of memory to a particular event, reason, or solution is to overdetermine that selection, which is exactly where the use of memory as interest politics originates. Few Japanese intellectuals have attempted to formulate a comprehensive vision of what remembering the war as a public, social process would entail, except perhaps in the first postwar decade and again at the end of the century, framed by two very different contexts. These respective contexts matter enormously, of course, but so do the patterns and dynamics of selective remembering that developed in the intervening decades. War memory and postwar responsibility have become entirely intertwined over the past half-century, and the patterns of that interaction form a critical part of the political dynamic that determines the public negotiation of conflicting memories. Indeed, even though Katō Norihiro's *Haisengoron* claimed to overcome the selective politicization of postwar memory, he, too, participated in a specific intellectual tradition, so to speak, one that may be linked to the political philosopher Maruyama Masao, as Yoshikuni Igarashi has suggested. Maruyama in the 1940s, like Katō in the 1990s, attempted to explain what had gone wrong with Japan in terms of a pathological split in society rooted in a particular historical moment. For Maruyama, the prewar modernization process in Japan was never able to overcome the stark division between public and private that was created in the Tokugawa era and that ultimately prevented Japan from becoming a true democracy. The particular—and undoubtedly modernist—analytical strategy that Maruyama developed rooted this fundamental binary opposition in what Igarashi calls an "originary event," thus explaining a contemporary political and social phenomenon by its historical point of origins while ignoring the historical process of its development since then. Katō implicitly (and unacknowledged by the participants in the debate) replicated that strategy, Igarashi argues, by reducing the political division over war memory so obvious in the 1990s to the originary event of defeat after World War II.[47]

These recent debates among public intellectuals may exhibit the same kind of self-reflexivity that characterized the early postwar discourse on war responsibility. But the current concern with questioning engrained political and intellectual strategies in dealing with the question of war legacies in postwar politics is new and exciting. It is no doubt easier to recognize changes in a contemporary context than it is to isolate and critique habits of mind, whether in political terms such as special interest politics, or in intellectual terms, such as the tendency to return to defined points of origin to explain contemporary problems. In the case of Japanese memory at the turn of the millennium, the political demands inaugurated by the end of the Cold War, and the economic and cultural challenges of what has come to be known as globalization, have opened up unprecedented possibilities—indeed the necessity—for reform, in turn conjuring up earlier attempts to change the postwar status quo. To frame these attempts in terms of "remembering and forgetting issues," Gerrit Gong's awkward term, is simply too narrow and cannot capture what was and is at stake—namely, the continuous and complicated process of negotiating the different demands placed upon remembering and forgetting the wartime past.[48] Clearly, there is urgency behind current quests to understand patterns of memory established earlier in the postwar era from various angles, in Japan, outside Japan, and comparatively. The possibilities for historical work are vast, for even if we have a clear picture of the contemporary politics of memory, the multiple ways in which it engages older, less visible strategies of negotiating the past has today become a terrain of public contention in its own right.

CONCLUSION

The salience of memory as a lens through which to interpret the post–Cold War present in light of the postwar past was symptomatic of a more general quest for political reorientation in the late twentieth century. It may be, to paraphrase Walter Benjamin, that in order to anticipate what is new in the future we must recover a past that has been suppressed. The international public debate in the 1990s about previously neglected Asian victims of Japanese colonialism and war certainly served as a means for envisioning greater East Asian integration after the end of the Cold War. Indeed, belated efforts at reconciliation through official apologies and individual compensation may well turn out to be a gateway to the future in a globally organized world.

Perhaps, as Pierre Nora observed, the speed of (post)modern life and our own advanced stage of amnesia call for a more urgent grip on the past. Japan's recent proliferation of museums and commemoration halls of different political persuasions indeed represents a global trend. For example, in 1995, Okinawa Prefecture opened its new Okinawa Peace Museum and the adjacent Cornerstone for Peace, where the names of Japanese, Korean, Taiwanese, American, and British soldiers and civilians who died in the Battle of Okinawa are commemorated together on large stone plates that zigzag around a peace flame. The Shōwa-kan in Tokyo in 1999 fulfilled the long-term desire of the war bereaved to make their suffering and their contributions to postwar prosperity known to the public at large. In August 2005, the Women's Active Museum on War and Peace (WAM), Japan's first resource center on sexual slavery during World War II, opened in Tokyo. That same year the cities of Hiroshima and Nagasaki added commemoration halls to their respective peace parks, the oldest and best known in Japan.

Beyond phenomenological treatments of the widespread interest in issues of memory, this concrete historical analysis of Japan's contemporary memory culture in light of half a century of civic debate and activism reveals an interesting dynamic between two philosophically different yet practically complementary conceptions of public memory. On one side is the ideal of a unified memory as a form of atonement, whether in the name of nationalism or pacifism—that is, memory as an ethical problem detached from self-interest. Katō Norihiro made a case for this conception of memory in his controversial book *Haisengoron*. On the other side is the notion of a fragmented memory built around special interests and therefore by definition self-interested. Japan's overall history of war memory suggests a closer correspondence to the latter idea of memory and a comparative neglect of the former. In reality, however, people drew on both and negotiated them differently within changing contexts. Each of the civic groups surveyed here conducted its political activism through a combination of defining political principles of universal value on the terrain of the past, and negotiating these principles selectively according to their political expedience within a specific contemporary context. At times the defined lessons of the war and their presentability coalesced in ways that enhanced an organization's public profile; at other times they did not. In other words, war memory was characterized by an inherent tension between the ideal of memory guiding postwar politics, and the politics of "the postwar" guiding what was remembered.

This dynamic had an important parallel on the terrain of public culture, as Benjamin Lee observed in the public-sphere debates of the early 1990s. Lee called attention to the tension between the ideal of a rational and universally valid public, famously analyzed by Jürgen Habermas in the 1960s, and a mass-mediated public built around the notion of interest.[1] Placing the problem of memory within the larger context of public culture—a public culture clearly parochial yet also interacting with the global—sheds light on this interplay between the ideal of a principled society and the changing processes of producing, transmitting, and consuming different knowledges publicly. It is not a matter of posing the ethics of remembering against the politics of forgetting. Rather, the making of memory is best observed in a space informed by both, just as everything "public" was governed by both the principles of liberal democracy and the forces of the mass market. This space may be conceived as a zone of cultural debate shaped by changing political and social relations, material conditions, and media of communication, both domestic and international in scope. It is a zone of political relations that bridges the gap between state and society, official and popular discourse, elite and mass culture, arenas that at least on the terrain of memory tend to blur into each other. In this account, civic organizations, with their respective formulation of principled memories and political networks, through which they negotiate their principles in search of public space, serve as vehicles for articulating public culture in Japan.

Global and comparative perspectives on public memory are likely to confirm this dynamic as characteristic of democratic and specifically late-capitalist societies. But the question remains why war responsibility did not become more explicitly a matter of state policy in Japan, as it was in Germany. Recent work on German memory also focuses on a multiplicity of agents on the middle level of political life,[2] but the state led the way in articulating a German consensus on its culpability for the Holocaust to the international community—and this primacy undeniably colored its history of memory for many decades. Much public discourse has focused on (West) Germany, either as the nation with the most obvious need to deal with its criminal past or as a model for how to do so successfully. That "success" has been measured primarily in international terms—political reconciliation with former enemy nations and the people who suffered large-scale war atrocities. Japan's "failure" in this regard has been so routinely invoked, especially in the American media, as to be a cliché. More often than not, cultural explanations have taken precedence over historical analysis, ranging from "Oriental" mentality to political immaturity.

A broadly comparative look at the key historical factors that influenced the place of war memory in postwar politics in Japan and Germany provides some answers. Certainly one important factor for Japan lay in the striking continuities between the wartime and postwar political elites, despite the new democratic constitution. Emperor Hirohito, who had been the supreme commander of all Japanese military forces during the war, weathered the transition largely unscathed; he neither abdicated nor faced any criminal prosecution but instead was declared the symbolic cornerstone of Japan's new peace constitution. This effectively placed him beyond public criticism, and indeed it was not until after his death in 1989 that inquiries into his war responsibility became widely acceptable. Further, although occupation authorities ordered the closing of some wartime ministries, large parts of the social and economic bureaucracy remained intact and regained their position of power in the postwar political structure. In the early 1950s, when SCAP revoked the military purge, many a wartime politician or bureaucrat recovered his government position.[3]

In Germany, some continuities with the Nazi state certainly existed, especially on the nongovernmental level, but the political leadership that emerged in both West and East predominantly reconnected with the Weimar (prewar) political elite, as Jeffrey Herf has shown.[4] Both postwar German states, however different their ideologies, developed their "legitimization profiles"[5] by defining themselves in direct opposition to the Nazi regime and by declaring Nazi sympathies illegal. In Japan, prewar socialist politicians entered politics on the side of the opposition or as leaders of civic organizations, making criticism of the wartime regime part of their political agenda, while the governing elites remained largely silent on this subject. One could even argue that the legitimization profile of the Japanese state hinged on sheer bureaucratic competence, and the most competent postwar politicians and bureaucrats tended to have gained their expertise during the war.

The U.S. occupation bears a fair amount of responsibility for this outcome. The decision to keep the emperor came as early as 1942, as part of occupation planning. In fact, given that the United States had already decided to meet Japan's condition of protecting the emperor, Truman's insistence on unconditional surrender in the Potsdam Declaration may have unnecessarily postponed Japan's surrender until after the atomic bombings.[6] The Allied war crimes trials, which exempted the emperor from prosecution even though he was the military commander-in-chief, moreover left the Japanese public with a deep cynicism and distrust of legal measures in dealing with war responsibility. The Nuremberg Trials, in contrast, are generally credited with a positive, even pathbreaking legacy, and indeed encouraged Germans to seek resolution of outstanding issues of war responsibility through public trials throughout the postwar decades. The emphasis on the postwar West German state as a "legal state" in contrast to the declared illegality of the Nazi state (and of postwar Nazi sympathies) certainly added positive significance to legal measures for dealing with the past. In Japan, the wartime state was never declared *illegal* (it had certainly been constitutional) but instead *undemocratic*, and postwar efforts to pursue issues of war responsibility became part and parcel of defining and defending *democracy*.

The occupation's "reverse course" policies convinced many progressives in Japan that "democracy" was less a matter of state structure than of civic political participation. SCAP's decreased tolerance of Communist and left-wing activities in Japan, the heightened emphasis on economic recovery, and official encouragement of Japanese military buildup in the deepening Cold War may not have registered as a significant change of policy from a U.S. perspective. But a significant number of Japanese who had embraced the earlier emphasis on demilitarization and democratization concluded that under the circumstances it was up to "the people" (as opposed to the state) to bring about a democratic revolution. Indeed, the ideological differences that emerged in the early 1950s split the national public almost the way the thirty-eighth parallel divided Korea, according to a famous remark by Prime Minister Yoshida Shigeru.

In Germany, the onset of the Cold War bore different consequences, for it divided the country into two ideologically opposed states. Marxist interpretations of wartime fascism were thereby largely exiled to the socialist regime in the East, which embraced "antifascism" as its legitimization profile, while the West German government celebrated American-style democracy as having triumphed over the Nazi dictatorship. German memory of World War II and the Holocaust on both sides of the Iron Curtain was therefore always bound up with the contemporary reality of a divided Germany, which was itself a legacy of the war. In Japan, however, different interpretations of the Asia-Pacific War became the tools for ideologically charged domestic conflict, in which Marxist and Communist interpretations of the war carried much weight in the early postwar years. Yet the discourse espoused by the Japanese left was not simply comparable to East Germany's socialist rhetoric, because it was not state-sanctioned. Although the vocabulary overlapped, the Japanese left used war memory to define itself in op-position to the conservatives in power, whereas in East Germany it functioned as official doctrine.

Of equally far-reaching consequence for the institutionalization of memory in Japan and Germany were the respective world regional con-texts, which dictated—or allowed for—very different interactions with their neighbors and former enemy countries. In Peter Katzenstein and Takashi Shiraishi's formulation, "Japan and Germany engage Asia and Europe differently"— -whether in terms of foreign policy or trade.[7] Here, too, the United States assumed an instrumental role. The bilateral U.S.-Japan alliance under the San Francisco system (established in 1952) set the parameters—political as well as economic—in which Japan rebuilt its place in the international community as "economic giant and political dwarf" and eventually negotiated its war debts with other countries.[8] Under the "partial" peace treaty of 1952, Indonesia and a few other Southeast Asian countries demanded and received reparations for war damages, and they benefited for decades from substantial amounts of Japanese overseas development aid (ODA). The People's Republic of China and the two Koreas were excluded from the treaty and received economic aid only much later and in place of reparations. More gen-erally, one could argue that Japan's place in the *Pax Americana* reposi-tioned it from a nation whose economic and security needs pivoted on East Asia to a nation that had little political incentive to make amends for its past involvement there.

In comparison, American involvement in the reconstruction of Ger-many (and Western Europe in general) after the war, while hugely sig-nificant, was not marked by the same *exclusiveness* as the U.S.-Japan bilateral relationship. To begin with, Germany was divided into four occupation zones (the American, British, French, and Soviet sectors), of which the United States came to rule three while the Soviet Union kept its own sector. As the two sectors grew into separate German states, both quickly came to see their future in Europe, East and West respectively. Shaping separate interpretations of their shared Nazi past (in part through apology and compensation) became a useful tool in German-German rivalry, but it also formed a central part of their respective European identities. In the West, the reconstruction of mainland Europe hinged on the coal supplies of the border region with Belgium and France and thus forced Germany's Chancellor Konrad Adenauer to make reconciliation with France a priority. Furthermore, and in sharp contrast to the U.S. marginalization of China after the Communist Revolution in 1949, American backing of the new state of Israel set the context in which West Germany began its massive compensation payment program to that country in 1953. Under the circumstances Germany had little choice but to make amends with its neighbors, while Japan was effectively cut off from the Asian mainland and forced to seek its future in the alliance with the United States.

In the 1950s, war memory in West Germany was colored by state efforts to "settle the past" through social integration policies designed to de-criminalize former Nazis while settling national debts with countries in the Western alliance. In Japan, in contrast, different and incompatible memories of war and defeat competed for public space as important tools of domestic politics and precluded even the pretense of a state-led consensus on war memory. This pattern was challenged in both countries in the 1960s and early 1970s in the context of the Vietnam War, the radical student movement, and the easing of Cold War tensions. West Germany achieved a lasting breakthrough in its history of memory when the issue of *Vergangenheitsbewältigung* finally began to engage the public at large, starting with high-profile Nazi trials, fired by a significant generational conflict in 1968, and championed by the new Social Democratic government under Willy Brandt. Brandt's famous gesture of atonement, his *Kniefall* in front of the Warsaw Ghetto memorial in 1970, symbolically swept the heretofore policy-oriented notion of state responsibility into the public sphere, where people from all walks of life—and in particular educators, writers, and artists—made the Holocaust a subject of public discussion. The immediate political context here was an opportunity to seek reconciliation across the Iron Curtain, and more specifically to lay the foundation for an eventual reunification with East Germany. Japan, too, sought territorial integration and successfully negotiated the return of U.S.-occupied Okinawa in 1972, the same year Japan and China normalized official relations. Issues of war responsibility were recognized on the government level at that juncture and also began to be debated more broadly in public life, thanks to a "China boom" in Japanese publications. But the opportunity for a substantive change in the dynamics of war memory was not fully used, in part perhaps because neither China nor Korea was in a position to press for such a change, given domestic political instability and dependence on large amounts of economic aid from Japan.

At the beginning of the twenty-first century, the structural differences in Japan's and Germany's respective histories of memory have closed to a remarkable degree. The Japanese government has embraced the politics of apology (although perhaps too late to be convincing to many critics). In unified Germany, domestic interest struggles over aspects of the past—now complicated by the addition of the East German past— have made themselves apparent. Neo-nationalist organizations, publications, and websites, too, are in evidence in both countries, and elsewhere in the world. But the public media judge them differently, as if official acts of memory were somehow reflective of national morality. In this vein, memory issues (especially those related to World War II) tended to be treated symptomatically rather than historically, as a topic of state policy rather than as a complex process with its own dynamics. There is in fact no self-evident formula for how nations should come to terms with their criminal past, nor is it obvious that a national framework is automatically the most appropriate. But as long as crimes are committed in the name of the nation and under the auspices of a nation-state, the question of memory and responsibility for these crimes on behalf of the successor state is politically and ethically inescapable.

The tendency of the Japanese state under LDP leadership to push substantive debates about the war and its postwar legacies onto the level of civic political activism and to influence the outcome indirectly through pork-barrel politics is thus clearly problematic. It nonetheless forces the observer to consider the political dynamics of war memory not as a contained topic but as a structural feature of postwar public life with a history—not a history entirely of its own, but a history shared with other "deep issues" of postwar politics. To the extent that war memory was bound up with very real institutional, intellectual, and social legacies of the past, the obvious selectivity and malleability of that memory became an integral part of Japan's postwar history. This was hardly an abstract process. On the contrary, it derived from the dynamism of the Japanese people in weaving different and conflicting strands of memory into the fiber of postwar democracy, understood

as guaranteeing various interests public space through political participation. It certainly allowed for an honest recognition of Japanese war
crimes, for atonement, apology, and justice for the victims as part of
this diverse landscape. But such a self-critical memory did not form an
ethical, political, or legal imperative on which to found serious *official*
efforts of reconciliation with people who suffered great personal and
collective injustices under Japanese rule. Rather, the struggle over war
memory and postwar responsibility created a variety of political relationships, both domestic and international, which in turn fed into other
political struggles. The fact that Japan's historical injustices are still
hotly debated today speaks less to the severity of the atrocities or the
"silences" of some abstract "Japanese" memory, and more to the complex process by which the past is absorbed into the ever-changing present as experienced by people themselves—on all sides of the spectrum
and beyond Japan as well.

Reference Matter

Notes

Introduction

1. For an analysis of this concept of war responsibility, see Hosaka, *Haisen zengo no Nihonjin*, and especially "Ichioku sōzange to iū katarushisu," pp. 167–84.

2. Koschmann, "Intellectuals and Politics"; Kersten, *Democracy in Postwar Japan*.

3. Oral testimonies and final judgments of the tribunal are available at the website of VAWW–NET Japan at http://www1.jca.apc.org/vaww-net-japan/english/womenstribunal2000/judgement.html. Accessed 16 July 2006.

4. Justice Radhabinod Pal from India wrote a strong dissenting opinion of the final verdict in which he criticized the Tokyo trial as politically motivated and therefore unjust. In the 1960s, the concept of "victor's justice" received an unequivocal endorsement by a scholar on the American left, Richard Minear, in his study of the Tokyo war crimes trial, *Victors' Justice*. In Japan, however, this critique has been most firmly embraced by the political right; for example, a bust of Justice Pal has long graced the front of the Yūshūkan, the military museum attached to Yasukuni Shrine.

5. Harris, *Factories of Death*.

6. Hosoya et al., eds., *The Tokyo War Crimes Trial*.

7. Norgren, *Abortion before Birth Control*, p. 15.

8. An excellent recent survey of the state of civil society in Japan from a historical and political science perspective is Schwartz and Pharr, eds., *The State of Civil Society in Japan*.

9. Pempel, "Prerequisites for Democracy: Political and Social Institutions," pp. 27–28.

10. The 1995 edition was translated by Yamanouchi and Quinn, eds., *Listen to the Voices from the Sea*.

11. Wilson, "The Past in the Present: War in Narratives of Modernity in the 1920s and 1930s," p. 173.

12. See Ōnuma, "Tōkyō saiban, sensō sekinin, sengo sekinin."

13. Veterans of the war responsibility debate Ōkuma Nobuyuki, Mashita Shin'ichi, Maruyama Masao, and the conservative critic Fukuda Tsuneari were joined by Tsurumi Shunsuke, Hidaka Rokurō, Murakami Hyōe, and Ienaga Saburō, all scholars of roughly the same generation.

14. Seraphim, "The Debate about War Responsibility in Early Postwar Japan."

15. Two such publications attracted huge attention at the time: Hayashi Fusao, *Daitōa sensō kōteiron*, and Ueyama Shunpei, *Daitōa sensō no imi*.

16. Excellent recent studies include Hein and Selden, eds., *Living with the Bomb: American and Japanese Cultural Conflicts in the Nuclear Age*; Yoneyama, *Hiroshima Traces*; and Orr, *The Victim as Hero*, especially Chap. 3.

17. See for example Ōnuma, *Sensō sekininron josetsu*.

18. For example Takahashi Hikohiro, *Minshū no gawa no sensō sekinin*.

19. For an interesting analysis see Yamaguchi, "The Gulf War and the Transformation of Japanese Constitutional Politics."

20. Laura Hein, "Citizens, Foreigners, and the State in the United States and Japan since 9/11," *ZNet Japan* (4 Dec. 2003), http://www.zmag.org/content/showarticle.cfm?SectionID=17&ItemID=4614. Accessed 16 July 2006.

21. Boyd and Samuels, *Nine Lives?*

Chapter One

1. Jinja honchō kenshūjo, *Jinja honchō shikō*, pp. 7–8.

2. Jinja honchō, *Jinja honchō jūnenshi*, p. 51. Also quoted in Creemers, *Shrine Shinto after World War II*, p. 66.

3. This photograph appears in Yasukuni jinja Yasukuni no inori henshū iinkai, ed., *Yasukuni no inori*, p. 167.

4. The term "State Shinto" has been employed differently by Shinto scholars and historians. In emphasizing the organizational structure of prewar Shrine Shinto as a state institution, I refer to State Shinto for the period from 1900 to 1945, when it was formally represented by a Shrine Office (*jinja kyoku*) in the Home Ministry. See Hardacre, *Shinto and the State*, pp. 4–7.

5. For an English translation of this text, see Creemers, *Shrine Shinto after World War II*, appendix E.

6. This law originated in The Hague Convention of 1907.

7. Teeuwen, "Jinja Honcho and Shrine Shinto Policy," pp. 177–88.

8. *Jinja honchō shikō*, p. 4.

9. For a discussion of Shinto's precarious path between politics and religion before 1945, see Creemers, *Shrine Shinto after World War II*, Chap. 1; Hardacre, *Shinto and the State*, pp. 34–36.

10. Hardacre, *Shinto and the State*, p. 25.

11. Finn, *Winners in Peace*, p. 49.

12. *Jinja honchō shikō*, pp. 13–15.

13. For a comprehensive discussion of MacArthur's relationship with Hirohito and SCAP's policies toward the imperial institution, see Dower, *Embracing Defeat*, Chap. 9. The popular dimension of this relationship as "foundational myth" is discussed in Igarashi, *Bodies of Memory*, Chap. 1.

14. General Headquarters Daily Intelligence Summary, no. 50-1298, Oct. 1945. Courtesy of General Douglas MacArthur Foundation, Norfolk, VA.

15. General Headquarters Daily Intelligence Summary, no. 73-1321, 16 Nov. 1945.

16. At that time executive director of the Kōtenkōkyūsho, not to be confused with the postwar prime minister of the same name.

17. A record of the interview between Bunce and Yoshida is included in *Jinja honchō jūnenshi*, pp. 60–65. For comments on this meeting, see Creemers, *Shrine Shinto after World War II*, pp. 68–70; Woodard, *The Allied Occupation of Japan 1945–1952 and Japanese Religion*, pp. 190–91.

18. Creemers, *Shrine Shinto after World War II*, pp. 48–49, nn. 22–24.

19. Kokugakuin University in Tokyo, a private institution, and the formerly public Kōgakukan University in Ise, which became private in January 1946.

20. A section of SCAP, headed by Ken R. Dyke, which handled educational and religious issues.

21. Teeuwen, "Jinja Honcho and Shrine Shinto Policy," p. 186.

22. Quoted in Creemers, *Shrine Shinto after World War II*, pp. 219–22.

23. This ordinance was especially adapted in February 1946 to include the shrines. See Teeuwen, "Jinja Honcho and Shrine Shinto Policy," pp. 178–81.

24. Ashizu, "Shinpō kiji no sakuseishatachi," pp. 32–40.

25. In contrast to the shrines, the priests were nationally organized. See Woodard, *The Allied Occupation of Japan 1945–1952 and Japanese Religion*, p. 57.

26. "Shintō seishin undō to kyōka iin no ninmu," *Jinja shinpō*, 30 June 1947.

27. Foreign Affairs Association Japan, *Japan Year Book*, 1946–48 and 1949–52.

28. "Shintō seishin undō to kyōka iin no ninmu," *Jinja shinpō*, 30 June 1947.

29. Creemers, *Shrine Shinto after World War II*, pp. 199–200.

30. Shibukawa, "Jinja shinpō haigo no hitobito," p. 18.

31. Ibid., p. 9.

32. "Tennō heika to Tōkyō saiban no hanketsu," *Jinja shinpō*, 29 Nov. 1948.

33. "Jinja shinpō no hokori to hansei," in *Jinja shinpō senshū hoi*, pp. 9–16.

34. "Shin Nihon koku kenpō no seitei ni saishite," *Jinja shinpō*, 14 Oct. 1946.

35. "Jinja shinpō no hokori to hansei," p. 11.

36. Ise Shrine is customarily reconstructed every twenty years, and until 1945 this was done with government funds. The sixtieth reconstruction was scheduled to be completed in 1949 but was postponed by the Imperial House until 1953. The Association of Shinto Shrines was able to raise the money for the reconstruction from private contributions.

37. "Rekishi kyōiku ni shintō teki tachiba o," *Jinja shinpō*, 21 Sept. 1953.

38. "Gyaku kōsu no gen sesō to kigensetsu fukkatsu no ugoki," *Jinja shinpō*, 4 Feb. 1952.

39. Ibid.

40. Ibid.

41. *Jinja honchō jūnenshi*, pp. 220–21, 244. See also Creemers, *Shrine Shinto after World War II*, pp. 83–84.

42. "Nihon saibusō mondai to shūkyōjin no sekinin," *Jinja shinpō*, 22 Jan. 1951.

43. Ibid.

44. "Saigunbiron to jinseikan," *Jinja shinpō*, 18 Feb. 1952.

45. Ashizu, "Dokuritsu Nihon to shintō seishin," *Jinja shinpō*, 17 Sept. 1951.

46. See Chapter 4 below on the Japan-China Friendship Association.

47. "Nihon no shōrai to Ajia no minzoku shugi," *Jinja shinpō*, 8 Jan. 1951.

48. Ibid.

Chapter Two

1. These figures are based on Dower, *Embracing Defeat*, pp. 45–48.

2. Military rank had a great influence on pension payments, both before 1946 and after 1953.

3. Garon, *Molding Japanese Minds*, p. 50.

4. In January 1938, the social welfare section covering the military injured and bereaved moved from the Home Ministry to the Ministry of Welfare.

5. Shakai kyoku rinji gunji engo bu, *Shōi gunjin oyobi gunjin izoku no hogo seido gaiyō*, pp. 25–31. I thank Lee Pennington for providing me a copy of this document.

6. See Lee Pennington's doctoral dissertation, "Wartorn Japan: Disabled Veterans and Society, 1931–1952."

7. Tanaka et al., *Izoku to sengo*, pp. 36–38.

8. See also Dower, "Sensational Rumors, Seditious Graffiti, and the Nightmares of the Thought Police," in *Japan in War and Peace*.

9. Quoted in Nelson, "Social Memory as Ritual Practice," p. 453.

10. General Headquarters Daily Intelligence Summary, no. 18-1266, 22 Sept. 1945.

11. General Headquarters Daily Intelligence Summary, no. 50-1298, 24 Oct. 1945.

12. Quoted in General Headquarters Daily Intelligence Summary, no. 104-1352, 17 Dec. 1945.

13. In the case of the disabled, their compensation was to be removed unless their disabilities had originated from an incident unrelated to the military.

14. Tanaka et al., *Izoku to sengo*, pp. 83–84.

15. Shakai hoshō kenkyūjo, *Nihon shakai hoshō shiryō*. Quoted in Tanaka et al., *Izoku to sengo*, p. 86.

16. Tanaka et al., *Izoku to sengo*, p. 85.

17. See ibid., p. 40.

18. *Nippon Times*, 29 Nov. 1945. Cited in General Headquarters Daily Intelligence Summary, no. 88-1336, 1 Dec. 1945.

19. This film is briefly discussed in Hirano, *Mr. Smith Goes to Tokyo*, pp. 172–73. See also Dower, "Japanese Cinema Goes to War," in *Japan in War and Peace*.

20. This first issue is discussed in detail in Kitagawa, *Sengo no shuppatsu*, pp. 144–47.

21. Ibid., pp. 146–47.

22. Tanaka et al., *Izoku to sengo*, pp. 41–45.

23. Nihon izokukai, *Nihon izokukai jūgonenshi*, p. 22.

24. Quoted in Tanaka et al., *Izoku to sengo*, p. 42.

25. Ibid.

26. Ibid.

27. *Nihon izoku kōsei renmei kaihō* (hereafter *Kaihō*), 10 Feb. 1949.

28. Kawaguchi, *Sensō mibōjin*, p. 10.

29. Ibid., pp. 11–12.

30. Garon, *Molding Japanese Minds*, p. 181

31. This included, for the first time, old-age pensions and unemployment insurance among other provisions.

32. A videotape in the section of the Shōwa-kan (National Shōwa Memorial Museum) devoted to the war-bereaved quotes a 1946 survey of 237 war widows and their diverse ways of trying to make a living in Tokyo: 7 cleaned up rubble from war destruction; 13 peddled small commodities, shined shoes, etc.; 27 did manual work in industry; 48 were employed in banks and small companies; 53 did in-home work, often sewing; and 89 held no job. The museum displays useful graphs showing the discrepancy between war widows' meager income and their expenses, which were all the more severe for larger families.

33. *Nihon izokukai no jūgonenshi*, p. 16.

34. Kitagawa, *Sengo no shuppatsu*, pp. 143–46.

35. Kawaguchi, *Sensō mibōjin*, p. 116.

36. Kitagawa, *Sengo no shuppatsu*, p. 9.

37. Garon, *Molding Japanese Minds*, 180–81.

38. Kitagawa, *Sengo no shuppatsu*, pp. 178–79.

39. Ibid., pp. 182–83.

40. In 1958, the Izokukai established the National Orphans' Research Group (*Zenkoku iji kenkyūkai*).

41. "Namida ni uttaeru tsurasa; kibō wa waga ko no seichō ni," *Kaihō*, 15 April 1949.

42. "Mibōjin kokoro-e, Saga-ken de," *Kaihō*, 15 April 1949.

43. Morita, "Nihon izoku kōsei renmei no ninmu ni tsuite," *Kaihō*, 10 Feb. 1949.

44. Numbered consecutively starting with the first issue of *Kaihō*, 471 issues in all (1949–90) were reprinted and published in two large volumes with a foreword, afterword, index, and a chronological table of Izokukai's history.

45. For example, Nissan Fire and Maritime Insurance and Taiyō Products Stock Company placed ads in *Kaihō*.

46. "Izoku mondai no kokusaisei," *Nihon izoku tsūshin* (hereafter *Izoku tsūshin*), 25 April 1950.

47. Ikeda, "Baku suru 'Izoku mondai no kokusaisei'," *Izoku tsūshin*, 15 June 1950.

48. Nihon izokukai, *Nihon izokukai no jūgonenshi*, pp. 26–31.

49. Here the official sources differ slightly. The history of the Izokukai Women's Section reports a total of 28 representatives having participated in the sit-in. *Nihon izokukai fujinbu yonjūnen*, p. 7. The fifteen-year history of the main organization claims a total of 35. *Nihon izokukai jūgonenshi*, p. 135. Both agree that ten women participated.

50. Tōkyōto fukushikyoku seikatsu fukushibu engo fukushika, *Engo to irei no ayumi*, pp. 131–38 and statistics on pp. 219–20, 222–23.

51. Tanaka et al., *Izoku to sengo*, p. 94.

52. Tanaka, *Yasukuni no sengoshi*, pp. 39–40, and 154–55.

53. *Engo to irei no ayumi*, p. 123 and statistics on pp. 218, 221.

54. Tanaka et al., *Izoku to sengo*, pp. 55–56.

55. Ibid., pp. 63–64.

56. Murakami, *Irei to shōkon*, pp. 151–52.

57. "Eirei seishin to wa nani ka: 'Kihon mondai chōsa bu' de tōshin," *Izoku tsūshin*, 30 June 1961.

58. Tanaka et al., *Izoku to sengo*, p. 79.

Chapter Three

1. Thurston, *Teachers and Politics in Japan*, p. 43.

2. Nishi, *Unconditional Democracy*, p. 167.

3. Ibid., p. 172.

4. Ibid., pp. 56–57.

5. In his study of the early union movement, Thurston found no evidence of significant participation by teachers on the political right.

6. Nishi, *Unconditional Democracy*, p. 164.

7. Document no. 16, "Suspension of Courses in Morals, Japanese History, and Geography," in Beauchamp and Vardamon, eds., *Japanese Education since 1945*, pp. 74–75.

8. Thurston, *Teachers and Politics in Japan*, pp. 31–39.

9. Gordon, *The Evolution of Labor Relations in Japan*, p. 332.

10. Garon, *The State and Labor in Modern Japan*, p. 236.

11. Just as the establishment of the JTU in 1947 represented a merger of earlier teachers' unions, both communist and anticommunist in political orientation, so various labor unions combined in 1950 to form Japan's largest national labor federation, the General Council of Trade Unions (Sōhyō) of which the JTU became a member. Sōhyō strongly supported the left wing of the Socialist Party and retained close ties to the Communist Party, especially with the establishment in 1964 of another focal organization for organized labor, the All Japan General Federation of Labor (Zen Nihon rōdō sōdōmei, or Dōmei), which was anticommunist and supported the right wing of the Socialist Party. The JTU remained a member of Sōhyō and also joined the International Labor Organization (ILO).

12. Thurston, *Teachers and Politics in Japan*, p. 50.

13. Nishi, *Unconditional Democracy*, pp. 62–64.

14. *Asahi shinbun*, 21 Dec. 1945, quoted in Nishi, *Unconditional Democracy*, p. 64.

15. Thurston, *Teachers and Politics in Japan*, p. 15.

16. Nihon kyōshokuin kumiai, *Nikkyōso jūnen shiryō hen*, p. 4.

17. Ibid., p. 8.

18. "Hakkan no kotoba," *Atarashii kyōiku to bunka* (Nov. 1947): 1.

19. Naka, "Kyōin kumiai to kyōikukai no minshuka."

20. Thurston, *Teachers and Politics in Japan*, pp. 13–22.

21. Hani, "Kanryōshugi hihan."

22. Maruyama, "Theory and Psychology of Ultra-Nationalism."

23. Mashita, "Seijiteki mukanshin koso neofashizumu no kanshō," *Bunka shinbun*, 25 Nov. 1946.

24. Koschmann, *Revolution and Subjectivity in Postwar Japan*.

25. "Kyōiku mondai no seijiteki shori," *Atarashii kyōiku to bunka* (Jan. 1948): 1.

26. Thurston, *Teachers and Politics in Japan*, p. 259 and Chap. 5.

27. See Gluck, *Japan's Modern Myths*, pp. 154–55.

28. Quoted in Nishi, *Unconditional Democracy*, pp. 147, 150.

29. Katsuta, "Kyōiku no fukko to fukkō."

30. The founder of this conservative union was the well-known prewar social activist and Christian Kagawa Toyohiko, a member of the prewar proto-labor union, the Yūaikai. See Thurston, *Teachers and Politics in Japan*, pp. 56–57.

31. Ibid., pp. 111–12.

32. This was done through the Law Concerning the Organization and Management of Local Educational Administration. See, in a nutshell, Dower, *Empire and Aftermath*, pp. 351–52; in detail Nishi, *Unconditional Democracy*, pp. 210–19.

33. Nikkyōso has published several periodicals: a weekly newspaper, *Kyōiku shinbun* (*Education Newspaper*), since 1946; a monthly journal entitled *Kyōiku hyōron* (*Education Commentary*) since 1951, predated by *Atarashii kyōiku to bunka* (*New Education and Culture*) from 1947 to 1949; an annual report of Union conferences entitled *Nihon no kyōiku* (Japanese Education) since 1951; and, since 1972, an occasional English-language newsletter, *Nikkyōso News*, which summarized important points raised at annual meetings. Among these periodicals, the monthly journal *Kyōiku hyōron* served as the Union's primary forum for intellectual exchange on a wide range of topics relating to education in the context of domestic and foreign policy issues. In 1966 the JTU opened to its members a central educational library (Kyōiku toshokan) in Tokyo, now with its own newsletter and an estimated collection of 50,000 monographs related to education and an additional 62,000 newspapers, journals, and pamphlets.

34. "Kyōin ni nani o nozomu ka," *Atarashii kyōiku to bunka* (July 1948): 30–31.

35. Kawada, "Kyōin kumiai ron," p. 8.

36. The Red Purge in education is discussed in Smethurst, "The Origins and Policies of the Japan Teachers' Union 1945–56," p. 144. It was carried out indirectly. By officially lowering the number of teachers needed in public schools, the Ministry of Education weeded out teachers suspected of communist affiliation without admitting that it was engaged in a purge.

37. Dower, *Empire and Aftermath*, pp. 369–72.

38. This was a basic argument of Maruyama Masao and the Peace Problem Discussion Group (*Heiwa mondai danwa kai*). See Kersten, *Democracy in Postwar Japan*, p. 189.

39. On the influence of the Chinese Communist Revolution on the Japanese left, see Koschmann, "Mao Zedong and the Postwar Japanese Left."

40. The most extensive discussion in English on this subject is Kersten, *Democracy in Postwar Japan*.

41. Nihon kyōshokuin kumiai, *Nikkyōso jūnenshi*, pp. 770–79.

42. Barshay, "Postwar Social and Political Thought, 1945–90," p. 301.

43. Habermas, *The Structural Transformation of the Public Sphere*, introduction.

44. Maruyama, "Sensō sekinin ni tsuite (zadankai)," pp. 205–6. Also see Maruyama, "Theory and Psychology of Ultra-Nationalism."

Chapter Four

1. "Tōmen no mokuhyō nitsuite." *Nihon to Chūgoku*, 20 February 1950. This journal, *Japan and China*, was inaugurated in February 1950 under the auspices of the Japan-China Friendship Association Preparatory Committee and grew into the Friendship Association's main organ after its formal establishment in October 1950.

2. Ibid.

3. Fogel, "The Other Japanese Community," pp. 44–47.

4. Fogel, ed., *Life along the South Manchurian Railway*, p. 203.

5. Ibid., introduction, p. xxvi.

6. Shakai undō chōsakai, *Sayoku dantai jiten*, pp. 586–90.

7. See especially Ōnuma, *Saharin kimin: sengo sekinin no tenkei.*

8. Okamoto Kōichi, "Imaginary Settings," p. 183.

9. Ibid., p. 198.

10. Ibid., pp. 184–86, 191.

11. "Kōwa ni kan suru seimeisho," *Nikkyōso gojūnenshi*, p. 596.

12. "Tōmen no mokuhyō ni tsuite," *Nihon to Chūgoku*, 20 Feb. 1950.

13. Olson, "Takeuchi Yoshimi and the Vision of a Protest Society in Japan," in *Ambivalent Moderns*, p. 58.

14. Ibid., p. 45.

15. Mishima Hajime, "'Shina' to 'Chūgoku.'"

16. "Shinchūgoku to Nihon," *Nihon to Chūgoku*, 11 Dec. 1953.

17. Nihon Chūgoku yūkō kyōkai zenkoku honbu, *Nihon Chūgoku yūkō kyōkai undō shi* (hereafter *Nitchū yūkō undō shi*), p. 58.

18. Shimizu Ikutarō, "Atarashiku moeru minshushugi," quoted in Kersten, *Democracy in Postwar Japan*, pp. 173–74.

19. Koschmann, "Asianism's Ambivalent Legacy," p. 103.

20. I am here adopting Akira Iriye's translation. See Iriye, "Chinese-Japanese Relations, 1945–1990."

21. The concept and practice of "people's diplomacy" has been treated in depth in Cho, *Die Volksdiplomatie in Ostasien.*

22. *Nitchū yukō undō shi*, p. 35.

23. "8.15 o mezashite: Chūgoku ni aisatsu o okurō!" *Nihon to Chūgoku*, 10 July 1951.

24. See Scalapino, *The Japanese Communist Movement, 1920–1966*; Koschmann, "Mao Zedong and the Postwar Japanese Left," pp. 349, 351.

25. "Nihon Chūgoku yūko kyōkai," *Sayoku dantai jiten*, pp. 586–88.

26. "Seimeisho: Nihon Chūgoku yūkō kyōkai ni kan suru Mainichi shinbun no kiji ni tsuite," *Nihon to Chūgoku*, 1 Aug. 1950.

27. *Nitchū yūkō undō shi*, pp. 42–50.

28. "Yoshida shokan ni tsuite no seimei," *Nihon to Chūgoku*, 15 Feb. 1952.

29. They were: Families of Japanese Living in China (Zaika hōjin kazoku kai), Friends of the Chinese Language (Chūgokugo tomo no kai), Meeting Group of the Japanese-Chinese Translation Publishing Company (Nitchū hon'yaku shuppan konwakai), National Student League for Chinese Studies (Chūgoku kenkyū zenkoku gakusei rengōkai), the Chinese Music Studies Organization (Chūgoku ongaku kenkyūkai), and the Chinese Literature and Art Studies Organization (Chūgoku bungaku geijitsu kenkyūkai).

30. The Liberal Democratic Party, Progressive Party, Japan Socialist Party (right and left wings), Japan Communist Party, and Labor-Farmer Party.

31. "Nitchū yūkō kankei dantai," *Nihon to Chūgoku*, 15 April 1953.

32. *Nitchū yūkō undō shi*, p. 60.

33. This organization was newly founded in preparation for the Asia-Pacific Peace Conference.

34. Hirano, "Kikokusha no minasan e."

35. "Chūgoku seifu no shori hōshin," *Nihon to Chūgoku*, 21 July 1956.

36. "Shiroto banare no engi," *Nihon to Chūgoku*, 21 Oct. 1956.

37. Kasahara Chizu, "Sensō hanzai to sensō sekinin."

38. This speech was reprinted in *Nihon to Chūgoku*, 1 Sep. 1950. Katsumata, "Nitchū yūkō kaigi keizai bumon hōkoku."

39. This was the opinion of Mamoru Shigemitsu, vice-president of the conservative Democratic Party and former president of the Progressive Party. See "Views on China," *Japan Quarterly* 2, no. 1 (Jan.-Mar. 1955).

40. Letter by Murata Shōzō and Ikeda Masanosuke to Lei Ren-min (chair of the PRC trade delegation) on 4 May 1955. Quoted in Cho, *Die Volksdiplomatie in Ostasien*, pp. 109–10.

41. Ibid., p. 115.

42. On cultural internationalism, see Iriye, *Cultural Internationalism and World Order* and Abel, "Warring Internationalisms."

43. Cho, *Die Volksdiplomatie in Ostasien*, p. 149.

44. "Yūkō wa bunka kōryū kara," *Nihon to Chūgoku*, 1 March 1952.

45. These statistics and a useful map specifying all locations of wartime incidents involving the death of Chinese laborers are included in the guide accompanying the three-part documentary video featuring interviews with labor camp survivors made by the Japan-China Friendship Association between 1991 and 2001. Nitchū yūkō kyōkai, *Shōgen: Chūgokujin kyōsei renkō*, pp. 78–83.

46. Nihon Chūgoku yūkō kyōkai, ed., *Nitchū yūkō undō no hanseiki*, pp. 26–27.

47. Author's translation based on a photograph of the memorial to the victims of the Hanaoka massacre in Odate City, Akita Prefecture, inaugurated on 22 May 1966. Courtesy of Yazaki Mitsuharu of the Japan-China Friendship Association.

48. *China Daily*, 19 May 2005.

49. Giordano, *Die Zweite Schuld, oder: Von der Last Deutscher zu sein*.

Chapter Five

1. Jean Tardieu, "Glory of a Poet" in *Editions de Minuit*, 1943. Translation by Midori Yamanouchi and Joseph L. Quinn. http://www.geocities.com/wadatsumikai/index2.html. Accessed 16 July 2006.

2. "Prospectus," 11 Mar. 1950. Reprinted in "Shiryō ni yoru Wadatsumikai no rekishi," *Wadatsumi no koe* (hereafter *Koe*), no. 3 (1960): 58–60. The numbered issues of *Koe* refer to Wadatsumikai's semiannual journal inaugurated in 1959. The dated issues of *Koe* refer to Wadatsumikai's newspaper published between 1950 and 1958 and reproduced in a reprint edition in 1991.

3. "Nihon senbotsu gakusei kinenzō kansei," *Koe*, 10 Oct. 1950.

4. According to Nakamura Katsurō, who chose this term, *wada* came from the Korean word for "sea," *tsu* signified the preposition *no* ("of"), and *mi* meant "spirits." Nakamura, *Ani no kage o otte—takasareta "Wadatsumi no koe."*

5. Quoted in Hosaka, *"Kike Wadatsumi no koe" no sengoshi*, pp. 38–39.

6. Dower, *Embracing Defeat*, Chap. 16.

7. Ibid., p. 486.

8. The All-Japan Student Self-government General Committee (Zen Nihon gakusei jichikai sōrengō), founded in 1948, formed the center of the postwar student movement. As a cell of the JCP, it waged a national struggle against university and other educational policies at both public and private institutions, participated in the peace movement, and became notorious for its involvement in the 1960 and 1970 struggles against the Security Treaty.

9. From the group's "Prospectus," 11 Mar. 1950.

10. An English translation, including a dedication by Nanbara Shigeru, was published in 2005. See Quinn and Yamanouchi, *In the Faraway Mountains and Rivers*.

11. Yamashita et al., "Senryō jidai to 'Wadatsumi no koe.'" in *Koe*, no. 35 (1966): 1–20.

12. Ibid., pp. 8–11.

13. See Hartman, "Introduction: Darkness Visible," p. 5.

14. Odagiri, postscript to the first edition of *Kike wadatsumi no koe* (1949), quoted in Dower, *Embracing Defeat*, p. 502. This postscript is not included in

Yamanouchi, *Listen to the Voices From the Sea* (2000), but Odagiri's postscript to the 1959 Japanese edition expresses the same sentiment. See Yamanouchi pp. 302–8.

15. Dower, *Embracing Defeat*, p. 502.

16. "Prospectus," 11 Mar. 1950.

17. Ibid.

18. The economist Ōuchi Hyōe and the philosopher Mashita Shin'ichi were arrested in 1938 in connection with the Jinmin sensen incident; the Marxist historian Hani Gorō was arrested twice under the Peace Preservation Law for antifascist activities; the Marxist philosopher Hirano Yoshitarō was purged from his academic position at Tokyo Imperial University and arrested in 1936; Nakano Shigeharu was arrested in 1932 and renounced his communist beliefs (*tenkō*). For an intellectual biography of Ōuchi Hyōe, see Hein, *Reasonable Men, Powerful Words*.

19. The philosopher Abe Yoshishige became president of Gakushūin University in 1947; Ōuchi Hyōe became president of Hōsei University in 1950; the critic Odagiri Hideo founded the literary magazine *Kindai bungaku* in 1946 and became professor at Hōsei University; Mashita Shin'ichi became professor at Nagoya University in 1948; Watanabe Kazuo became professor at Tokyo University in 1947; Hani Gorō was elected into the Lower House in 1947 and greatly influenced the establishment of the National Diet Library; the journalist and publicist Yoshino Genzaburō founded the monthly journal *Sekai* in 1946 and became head of the Japan Journalists' Society; Nakano Shigeharu served as Lower House member from 1947 to 1950; the sociologist Shimizu Ikutarō became a professor at Gakushūin University in 1949; the sculptor Hongō Arata helped establish the Japan Arts Society in 1945; Mori Arimasa, an authority on French philosophy, became assistant professor at Tokyo University in 1945; and Ōyama Ikuo was elected to the Lower House in 1950 and received the Stalin Peace Prize in 1951.

20. "'Shinryaku no kyōi wa aru ka'—Doitsu to kyōsō suru saigunbi," *Koe*, 15 Oct. 1951.

21. "Shōwa nijūgonendo jigyō keikakusho sōan," *Koe*, no. 2 (1960): 10.

22. "Zenkokumin no shiteika ni daini wadatsumi seisaku susumu," *Koe*, 10 Oct. 1950. Also see Mashita, "Shinario 'Kike Wadatsumi no koe' o yonde kansō," in the booklet *Kike Wadatsumi no koe* (hereafter *Booklet*).

23. Hosaka, *"Kike Wadatsumi no koe" no sengoshi*, p. 45.

24. In a short comment on the movie in *Booklet*, Wadatsumikai addressed the responsibility of the survivors, who all carried individual visible or invisible wounds, to open their ears to the plea of the dead and dedicate themselves—as intellectuals—to open resistance against a renewed call to arms.

25. "'Kike wadatsumi no koe' gekiba kyakuhon kansei jōen semaru," *Koe*, 10 Oct. 1950.

26. "Shutsuensha no kotoba," in *Booklet*.

27. "Wadatsumi no koe ni kotaete: sensō no kawari ni kinenzō o," *Koe*, 22 Jun. 1951.

28. "'Tama no furusato ni': kinenzō wa itsu tatsu," *Koe*, 15 Jan. 1951.

29. "Tōdai ni hinan shūchū: kinenzo mondai o megutte," *Koe*, 15 Jan. 1950.

30. Quoted in Hosaka, *"Kike Wadatsumi no koe" no sengoshi*, p. 52.

31. "Wadatsumi no zō: furusato e kaeru," *Koe*, 7 June 1951.

32. Hosaka, *"Kike Wadatsumi no koe" no sengoshi*, p. 52.

33. Suekawa, "Wadatsumizō no oshieru mono," *Koe*, 13 June 1953.

34. Hosoka, *"Kike Wadatsumi no koe" no sengoshi*, p. 50.

35. Yanagida, "Sensō wa fukahi de wa nai: 1951 nen o koete," *Koe*, 15 Jan. 1951.

36. *Koe* special issue, Spring 1951.

37. "Heiwa undō no kokusaiteki rentaisei o! 'Heiwa kondankai' kessei," *Koe*, 25 Feb. 1951.

38. For example, see the images accompanying Odagiri, "Nihon no wakaku atarashii sedai ni," and Uchida Kowashi, "Seinen yo riseiteki yūki no moto ni kesshū seyo," *Koe*, 25 Nov. 1951. See also "Zenkoku shokun ni uttaeru," *Koe*, 25 Jan. 1952.

39. *Koe*, 15 Aug. 1952.

40. *Koe*, 15 Sept. 1952.

41. Nihon senbotsu gakusei kinenkai, "Chōsen sensō no isshūnen ni atari hitobito ni uttaeru," *Koe*, 10 July 1951.

42. "Ajiajin no sakebi: kodomo made ga korosareta," *Koe*, 25 June 1951.

43. "Te o tsunagō Chūgoku no tomo: zō ni takusu fusen no chikai," and "Nitchū yūkō wa Ajia heiwa no hoshō: Chūgoku kara atatakai heiwa no okurimono," *Koe*, 21 Nov. 1954.

44. For example, Toyoda, "Nihon gunkokushugi no fukkatsu," *Koe*, 20 April 1956.

45. Okada, "Shōshi: Wadatsumi kai no undō 1950–58," in Nihon senbotsu gakusei kinenkai, *Wadatsumi no koe 1950–1958*.

46. Yamanouchi and Quinn, eds., *Listen to the Voices from the Sea*.

Chapter Six

1. "Chūgoku no genbaku jikken ni tsuite no Nihon Chūgoku yūkō kyōkai seimei," 27 Oct. 1964, in Nihon Chūgoku yūkō kyōkai zenkoku honbu, *Nihon Chūgoku yūkō undō shi*, pp. 261–62.

2. See Orr, *The Victim as Hero*, Chap. 6.

3. See especially Yoshida Yutaka, *Nihonjin no sensōkan*.

4. "Minshu kyōikusha hansei seyo: shōnen no aida ni moeagaru uyoku," *Jinja shinpō*, 11 Feb. 1961.

5. For a discussion of the theme of war memory in literary, film, and television productions over the postwar decades, see Shimazu, "Popular Representations of the Past."

6. "'Rekishi būmu' o kangaeru," *Asahi shinbun*, 8 Aug. 1965.

7. Mitscherlich and Mitscherlich, *The Inability to Mourn*.

8. Kelly, "Finding a Place in Metropolitan Japan."

9. Winter, *Sites of Memory, Sites of Mourning*.

10. "Hitotsu no kunō to hitotsu no kōmyō to: Doi Yoshiko-san to hachiju man no iji," *Izoku tsushin*, 1 Jan. 1951.

11. Takahashi Ryūtarō, "Wakai sedai no ikusei o kyōka."

12. Tanaka Tadao, "Eirei seishin no keishō o: 'kyō no seishōnen mondai.'"

13. Ibid.

14. "Sensō no nai heiwa na sekai o," *Izoku tsūshin*, 31 Aug. 1958.

15. "Wadatsumikai jimukyoku no kyōsei heisa o kaijo seyo," *Wadatsumi no koe* (hereafter *Koe)*, 11 March 1955.

16. "Watashitachi wa nani ga sabakeba ii? Hiroshima dai 'Kike Wadatsumi no koe' dokushokai," *Koe*, 15 Feb. 1956.

17. "Wadatsumi no koe kyūkan ni atatte," *Koe*, 22 Oct. 1958.

18. Odagiri Hideo, "For the New Reader of This Book" (preface), in *Kike wadatsumi no koe* (1959). Translation based on the English version included in Yamanouchi and Quinn, eds., *Listen to the Voices from the Sea*, pp. 302–9.

19. Ibid.

20. Sasaki-Uemura, *Organizing the Spontaneous*.

21. See in particular Barshay, "Imagining Democracy in Postwar Japan."

22. Tsurumi Shunsuke, for example, was a member of Wadatsumikai's board of directors but led the spontaneous citizens' group Voiceless Voices (Koe naki koe no kai) in demonstrations against the treaty.

23. Yamashita, "Kai no undō no kihon hōshin ni tsuite"; Ueda, "Bokutachi no sanka."

24. The annual symposium on some aspect of "*Wadatsumi* thought" was the center of the second phase of Wadatsumikai's activism between 1960 and 1969. The topics illuminate the trajectory of intellectual activity during this period: "An Intellectual Pursuit of the War Experience" (Sensō taiken no shisōka, 1960); "How to Revive the *Wadatsumi* Thought" (Wadatsumi shisō o dō ikasu ka, 1961); "The Meaning of the War Experience Today" (Kyō ni okeru sensō taiken no imi, 1962); "The Fifteen-year War and the Present" (Jūgonen sensō to gendai, 1963); "Ethnicity and the War Experience" (Minzoku to sensō taiken, 1964); "The Twenty Postwar Years from the Standpoint of Peace" (Heiwa no tachiba

kara sengo nijūnen, 1965); "The People's Foundation for Peace" (Heiwa no tame no kokuminteki kiban, 1966); "Ethnicity and Peace" (Minzoku to heiwa, 1967); "Thinking about August 15" (8.15 o kangaeru, 1968).

25. Yamada, " 'Sensō taiken no shisōka' ni tsuite."

26. Hidaka, "Sensō taiken to sensō sekinin."

27. Wadatsumikai president Abe Tomoji and board member Sugi Toshio delivered eulogies at a public memorial for Kanba on 24 June. See *Koe*, no. 4, 1960.

28. Koyama, "Anpo hantai undō no naka de."

29. A term Maruyama Masao coined for progressive intellectuals concerned with their own war responsibility in the early years following Japan's defeat.

30. "Daigokai gakusei seminaa no kiroku," *Koe*, no. 4, Aug. 1960.

31. Mutō Mitsurō, "Minshushugi teki jiyū o mamoru michi," *Izoku tsūshin*, 31 May 1960.

32. "Tsuyoi heiwa e no ishi: zenkoku kenshūkai sankasha no kansō," *Izoku tsūshin*, 30 Sept. 1959.

33. Ibid.

34. "Nihon izokukai seinenbu sengen," *Izoku tsūshin*, 30 Oct. 1960.

35. Nihon izokukai seinenbu, *Nihon izokukai seinenbu jūgonen no ayumi*, p. 5.

36. Ibid., pp. 7–8.

37. On Peleliu, there appear to be two monuments erected by the Japanese government in cooperation with the Republic of Palau. One is a monument in the village cemetery of Ngerchol estimated to date back to 1978, which features a simple inscription, "A memorial for all the Japanese who died here." The other is the newer Peleliu Peace Memorial Park located at the far southwest corner of the island dated to March 1985 and the only monument that provides its text in Japanese, English, and Palauan. The English text reads, "In memory of all those who sacrificed their lives in the islands and seas of the West Pacific during World War II and in dedication to world peace." I am indebted to Stephen C. Murray at the University of California Santa Barbara for sharing this information with me. See his doctoral dissertation entitled "War and Remembrance on Peleliu: Islander, Japanese, and American Memories of a Battle in the Pacific War" (2006).

38. Japan Youth Memorial Association (JYMA), *Ima, nani o kataran*.

39. Nihon izokukai, *Nihon izokukai jūgonenshi* and *Ishizue: senbotsusha izoku no taiken kiroku*, respectively.

40. Nihon izokukai, *Ishizue*, preface.

41. Nihon izokukai, *Ishizue*, postscript.

42. *Nihon izokukai jūgonenshi*.

43. Ibid., pp. 207–9.

44. Ibid., p. 211.

45. Kaya, "Seinenbu ni kitai suru."

46. See, for example, *Koe*, no. 17, 1963.

47. "Wadatsumikai e no kibō," *Koe*, no. 7, 1961.

48. Hashikawa, "Ankeeto o yonde."

49. Hosaka Masayasu discusses this incident and its relevance in the history of *Wadatsumi no koe* in his chapter "Taoreta 'Wadatsumi-zō'" in *"Kike Wadatsumi no koe" no sengoshi.*

50. "Gakusei wadatsumikai: zenkoku kyōgikai yori no seimei," *Koe*, no. 47, 1969.

51. Nihon senbotsu gakusei kinenkai produced two collections of essays based on this research: *Tennōsei o toitsuzukeru* (1978) and *Ima koso tou tennōsei* (1989).

52. "Chichi to ko: sensō, sengo no taiken o keishō sareru ka," *Sekai*, Aug. 1969. See especially Kamono Hidehiko, a 21-year-old student in Tokyo: "Sensō nanka shiranai yo: aru senmuha no gigen" (I don't know anything like war: the joke of a so-called war-less generation), pp. 239–41.

Chapter Seven

1. For the explosion of academic studies about Japan in the vein of modernization theory by scholars based in the United States, see Dower, "Sizing Up (and Breaking Down) Japan."

2. The key word in Japanese was *minzoku*, which is usually rendered as "ethnic community" in a sense closest to the German *Volk*.

3. Barshay, "Postwar Social and Political Thought," pp. 329–37.

4. Igarashi, *Bodies of Memory*, p. 145.

5. Yoneyama, *Hiroshima Traces*.

6. Hayashi, "Daitōa sensō kōteiron."

7. Morris-Suzuki, *Re-Inventing Japan*.

8. See Gluck, "The Past in the Present."

9. "Shokuzai ishiki to jikoku sadizumu," *Jinja shinpō*, 9 Sept. 1969.

10. Sakamoto, "Meiji hyakunen ni omou."

11. Hall, "Reflections on a Centennial."

12. Welfield, *An Empire in Eclipse*, Chap. 8.

13. Ibid., p. 209.

14. *Sankei shinbun*, 14 May 1966, quoted in Welfield, *An Empire in Eclipse*, p. 209.

15. Quoted in Wakamiya, *The Postwar Conservative View of Asia*, p. 236.

16. Ibid.

17. Ibid., p. 208.

18. "1965 Japan–South Korea Normalization Talks" *Asahi shinbun*, 18 Jan. 2005.

19. Park Soon-Won, "The Politics of Remembrance," unpublished manuscript. Cited with the author's permission.

20. The first such organization was the Repatriates' Comrade Society (Kwihwan tongchihoe), founded in 1948, and reorganized in April 1973 under the name Society for Pacific War Victims and Surviving Families (T'aep 'yongyang chonchaeng hisaengcha yuzokhoe). Park, "The Politics of Remembrance."

21. Wakamiya, *The Postwar Conservative View of Asia*, p. 391.

22. "Nihonjin no taibei chūkoku," *Jinja shinpō*, 2 Jan. 1965.

23. "Kankoku gakusei no jii undō," *Jinja shinpō*, 4 April 1964. See also Kim Sam-kyu, "A Korean View of Ratification," and Mobius, "The Japan-Korea Normalization Process and Korean Anti-Americanism."

24. See especially Havens, *Fire across the Sea.*

25. Ibid., pp. 5–6.

26. Ogata, "Japanese Attitude toward China."

27. Nihon kyōshokuin kumiai, "Heiwa apiiru."

28. For quotations and a careful analysis of this incident, see Matsueda and Moore, "Japan's Shifting Attitudes toward the Military."

29. Ibid., p. 622.

30. See, for example, "Nitchū yūkō kyōkai to Chūnichi yūkō kyōkai kyōdō seimei," *Nihon to Chūgoku*, 31 Oct. 1966; Nihon Chūgoku yūkō kyōkai, "Dai jūrokukai taikai sengen: rekishitekina shōri osameru," ibid., 13 March 1967.

31. Nihon Chūgoku yūkō kyōkai, "Kōhan na kakukai ni yobikake: 7.7; sanjūsshūnen kinen gyōji," *Nihon to chūgoku*, 24 April 1967.

32. Ogata, "Japanese Attitude toward China," p. 394. See also Johnson, "The Patterns of Japanese Relations with China, 1952–1982."

33. An unofficial English translation by Japan's Foreign Ministry is available from the "The World and Japan" Database Project at the following URL: http://avatoli.ioc.u-tokyo.ac.jp/~worldjpn/documents/texts/docs/19720929. D1E.html. Accessed 16 July 2006.

34. Gries, *China's New Nationalism*, p. 69.

35. Gotō, "Japan in Asia," p. 388.

36. Nanpō dōhō engokai, *Okinawa fukki no kiroku*, p. 668.

37. The *Wall Street Journal* revealed in a 18 July 1969 front-page article that chemical and biological weapons were stored on Okinawa.

38. Higa, "The Okinawan Reversion Movement," in Hosoya, ed., *Okinawa Reversion.*

39. Beginning with Douglas MacArthur's comment in 1946 that the people of Okinawa were not Japanese but a racial minority suffering under Japanese

oppression, many other American utterances suggested that the United States viewed Okinawa as separate from Japan. High Commissioner Albert Watson II, for example, said in the mid-1960s that "Okinawa should serve as a bridge between the United States and Japan," and Representative Melvin Price commented that "Okinawa is located quite a distance from Japan and is a region that has its own individual culture." Sakanaka, "The Present Status of the Okinawa Reversion Movement."

40. Omori, "Controversy between Government and Opposition Parties."

41. On 10 November 1968, Yara Chōbyō was elected the first chief executive of the Ryukyuan government. See Havens, *Fire across the Sea*, p. 195.

42. Rōdō kyōiku sentaa, *Nikkyōso yonjūnenshi shiryō hen*, pp. 1152–56, 1162–65.

43. Hoshino, "Okinawa wa Nihon no kyōshi ni futatsu no sekinin o yōsei suru."

44. " 'Okinawa shūkai' no seikō o mezashite," *Kyōiku hyōron* (Feb. 1968): 22–24.

45. For a statement on the meaning of unification (*ittaika*) in education by the government-sponsored Okinawa Problem Discussion Group (Okinawa mondai kondankai), see Yamano, *Okinawa henkan hitorigoto*, pp. 291–308.

46. Ibid.

47. Saito, "Nikkyōso no Okinawa tōsō"; Ōta, "Okinawa no shiseiken henkan to 'Nihonjin kyōiku.' "

48. Munakata, "Watashi wa iwayuru 'Anpo kyōiku taisei' ni tsuite," *Kyōiku hyōron* (Jan. 1969): 14–19.

49. Ōta, "Okinawa no shiseiken henkan to 'Nihonjin kyōiku,' " p. 17.

50. Muramatsu, "Okinawa henkan o dō toraeru ka." By "same blood," Muramatsu meant that the Japanese and the Okinawans were both a mixed race with Japanese, Chinese, and Korean elements. Ōta explained that the historical difference was construed in the prewar period in terms of modernization—with Okinawa "centuries behind" Japan.

51. Okamoto Shigenori, " 'Sabetsu' no mondai o tsūjite kangaeru Okinawa."

52. See ibid., pp. 31–33, for all quotations.

53. Takabatake, "Citizens' Movements: Organizing the Spontaneous." Also see Ellis Krauss's thorough review essay in *Journal of Japanese Studies* 7, no. 1 (1981): 165–80.

54. Foucault, *Language, Counter-Memory, Practice.*

55. Oda, "The Ethics of Peace."

56. For an excellent analysis of Beheiren as a movement, see Havens, *Fire across the Sea*, Chap. 2.

57. Ibid., pp. 158–59.

58. See John Lie's introduction to Honda Katsuichi, *The Impoverished Spirit in Contemporary Japan.*

59. See Wakabayashi, "The Nanking 100-Man Killing Contest Debate."

60. Monographs resulting from this criticism include Suzuki Akira, "*Nankin daigyakusatsu" no maboroshi* (1973) and Yamamoto Shichihei, *Watakushi no naka no Nihongun* (1975), both quoted in Yoshida, "A Battle over History," pp. 79–84.

Chapter Eight

1. Hein and Selden, eds., *Censoring History.*

2. Ibid., p. 4.

3. For a useful historical overview of the textbook lawsuits in English, see Nozaki and Inokuchi, "Japanese Education, Nationalism, and Ienaga Saburo's Textbook Lawsuits." See also Ienaga, *Japan's Past, Japan's Future.*

4. See Connerton, *How Societies Remember.*

5. Nelson, "Social Memory as Ritual Practice."

6. The precinct covers an impressive 93,356 square meters, of which 10,585 square meters are used for buildings. Kokuritsu kokkai toshokan chōsa rippō kōsa kyoku, *Yasukuni jinja mondai shiryōshū* (hereafter *Shiryōshū*), p. 1.

7. See, for example, Nelson, *Enduring Identities.* A more precise chronology traces the origin of Yasukuni Shrine to 1862, when Chōshū leaders asked the Kōmei emperor to sponsor a ceremony to honor those who had died fighting against the Tokugawa shogunate. This first ritual for the military dead (*irei no saiki*) was performed at Kyoto higashiyama ryōzan in December 1862, by both Shinto and Buddhist priests. See *Shiryōshū*, p. 359.

8. Murakami, *Japanese Religion in the Modern Century*, p. 113.

9. Tsubouchi, *Yasukuni*, Chap. 3.

10. Hardacre, *Shinto and the State*, p. 91.

11. The Sino-Japanese War of 1894–95 had produced 13,619 war dead spirits. *Shiryōshū*, p. 129.

12. Ibid., pp. 362–63.

13. Harootunian, "Memory, Mourning, and National Morality," p. 148.

14. A fascinating "heretical interpretation" of the war dead as spirits *to be pacified* rather than *pacifying* the country can be found in Antoni, "Yasukuni-Jinja and Folk Religion," in *Religion and Society in Modern Japan*, pp. 121–32. See also Chap. 5.2.3.1: "Die häretische Interpretation der Yasukuni-Götter," in Antoni, *Shinto und die Konzeption des japanischen Nationalwesens.*

15. Sugiyama, "Facts and Fallacies about Yasukuni Shrine."

16. Hirō and Yamamoto, "Yasukuni Shrine and the Japanese Spirit World," pp. 76–77.

17. Hardacre, *Shinto and the State*, p. 92.

18. Quoted in Tsubouchi and Yoshida, "Yasukuni Shrine as a Symbol of Japan's Modernization."

19. Quoted in Nelson, "Social Memory as Ritual Practice," p. 453, and referenced in Tsunoda, *Yasukuni to chinkon*.

20. 'Ōe Shinobu, *Yasukuni jinja*, p. 136. Also quoted in Nelson, "Social Memory as Ritual Practice," pp. 451–52.

21. *Shiryōshū*, p. 372.

22. Tanaka Nobumasa, *Yasukuni no sengoshi*, pp. 25–28.

23. "Yasukuni jinja to tairitsu mono de nai: Mumei senbotsusha no haka de kōshō ga tōben," *Izoku tsūshin*, 1 Dec. 1956.

24. LDP politician Namiki Yoshio in the Lower House Education Commission on 29 February 1956, in *Shiryōshū*, p. 43. For LDP and JSP proposals, see "Jimintō: Yasukunisha hō sōan yōkō" (Liberal Democratic Party: Yasukuni law draft proposal), 14 Mar. 1956, in *Shiryōshū*, pp. 120–21, and "Shakaitō: Yasukuni heiwadō ni kan suru hōritsu sōan yōkō" (Socialist Party: draft proposal for Legislation pertaining to Yasukuni Peace Hall), 22 Mar. 1956, in *Shiryōshū*, pp. 122–23. Both proposals avoid identifying Yasukuni Shrine as a shrine, that is, a religious institution.

25. In Lokowandt, *Zum Verhältnis von Staat und Shinto*, p. 193.

26. The Izokukai-LDP relationship is discussed in detail in Tanaka et al., *Izoku to sengo*, pp. 194–204. Illuminating examples of the Izokukai's local political connections can be found in O'Brien and Ohkoshi, *To Dream of Dreams*.

27. The entire bill (30 June 1969) is reprinted in *Shiryōshū*, pp. 145–54. A German translation of the bill can be found in Lokowandt, *Zum Verhältnis von Staat und Shinto*. For an in-depth discussion in Japanese, see Tanaka Nobumasa, "Nihon izokukai no gojūnen," and idem, *Yasukuni no sengoshi*, pp. 101–3. For brief introductions in English, see Hardacre, *Shinto and the State*, and Murakami, *Japanese Religion in the Modern Century*.

28. Lokowandt, *Zum Verhältnis von Staat und Shinto*, pp. 189–93.

29. Mitsui, "Mohaya damatte wa irarenai."

30. "The Socialist Party's Response to the Yasukuni Shrine Bill" (1969) in Lokowandt, *Zum Verhältnis von Staat und Shinto*, p. 189.

31. Discussed, for example, ibid., p. 21.

32. *Shiryōshū*, Chap. 6.

33. A comprehensive attempt to bring together various dimensions of these issues in postwar Japan is Beer, *Freedom of Expression in Japan*.

34. Translated in Lokowandt, *Zum Verhältnis von Staat und Shinto*, p. 182.

35. "Kotowari wa magerarenu: Nakasone hatsugen no mōten o tsuku," *Izoku tsūshin*, 15 March 1972.

36. "Nakasone kōsō ni hantai: Yasukuni mondai no kaiketsu ni naranai," *Jinja shinpō*, 8 Feb. 1972.

37. Miki Takeo stressed that he had paid this visit in a private capacity; he had used a private car to ride to the shrine precincts, offered cash from his own pocket, was not accompanied by government officials, and did not sign the books as prime minister.

38. "Yasukuni: Behind the Torii—Each Premier Has His Own Way," *Daily Yomiuri*, 15 June 2005.

39. Tanaka, *Yasukuni no sengoshi*, p. 113.

40. Ibid., pp. 152–55.

41. I owe this idea to John Dower.

42. For details on this campaign, see Ruoff, *The People's Emperor*.

43. "The Opinion of the Japan Socialist Party Regarding the Yasukuni Shrine Problem," in Lokowandt, *Zum Verhältnis von Staat und Shinto*, p. 192.

44. Murakami, *Japanese Religion in the Modern Century*, p. 166.

45. This statement was echoed by Kusunoki Masatoshi, an LDP Upper House representative and chair of the Committee for Religious Questions on 12 March 1969 in the Diet, reprinted in Lokowandt, *Zum Verhältnis von Staat und Shinto*, p. 182.

46. For example, "Kiki ni tatsu jinjakai: haisen ni yori kokutai wa horobita ka," *Jinja shinpō*, 4 June 1957.

47. "Appeal by the Association of Shinto Shrines for State Management of Yasukuni Shrine" (1969), in Lokowandt, *Zum Verhältnis von Staat und Shinto*, pp. 193–97.

48. Jinja honchō, "Yasukuni jinja hōan ankeeto ni tai suru kaitō," May 1975, in *Shiryōshū*, pp. 262–65.

49. "Mohaya damatte wa irarenai," in *Koe*, no. 44, 1968.

50. Tanaka et al., *Izoku to sengo*, pp. 155–56.

51. "Seimei: Yasukuni jinja hōan haizetsu o negau," in *Koe*, no. 58, 1974.

52. Nakamura Katsurō, "Yasukuni mondai o kangaeru," ibid., pp. 28–29.

53. Iizaka, "Yasukuni mondai to minshushugi," ibid., pp. 54–67.

54. Hoshino, "Yasukuni jinja hōan no ikensei," ibid., pp. 39–53.

55. Ibid.

56. Ikeda Takei, "Izoku no tachiba kara—ikan sanjūnen."

57. Lokowandt, *Zum Verhältnis von Staat und Shinto*, p. 19.

58. For a short narrative of this case, see Hardacre, *Shinto and the State*, pp. 149–50, and O'Brien and Ohkoshi, *To Dream of Dreams*, 84–85. Documents relating to the court decisions in this case are assembled in *Shiryōshū*, pp. 311–19, and in German translation in Lokowandt, *Zum Verhältnis von Staat und Shinto*, pp. 89–152.

59. This case became even more famous and is discussed in Hardacre, *Shinto and the State*, pp. 153–57; "Yamaguchi: An Ordinary Woman," in Field, *In the Realm of a Dying Emperor*, and O'Brien and Ohkoshi, *To Dream of Dreams*, Chap. 6.

60. This case is treated in detail in O'Brien and Ohkoshi, *To Dream of Dreams*.

61. On 14 April 1966, 3,300 people gathered on the grounds of Yasukuni Shrine. At this meeting, the Izokukai adopted the "Yasukuni Shrine Song" (*Yasukuni jinja no uta*) as its official song: *Shiryōshū*, pp. 380–81.

62. "Yasukuni hōan chikaku ketsuron e: kihon mokuteki wa fuhen honkai no taidō o kakunin," *Izoku tsūshin*, 15 March 1975.

63. "Yasukuni jinja mondai: shin kyokumen ni," *Izoku tsūshin*, 15 July 1975.

64. For a politician to worship at Yasukuni Shrine as a private person, he or she (1) had to announce in advance that the upcoming visit was to be undertaken in a private capacity, (2) could not use a public vehicle, (3) could not sign the visitors' book with an official title, (4) could not be accompanied by a public employee. After Miki's trip in 1975, these criteria were interpreted more and more loosely. As long as government money was not used to pay for the rite, prime ministerial visits to Yasukuni were still counted as "private," with "public visits" referring to worship as a "government activity" and "using government funds to pay for the *tamagushi* rite." See Tanaka, *Yasukuni no sengoshi*, p. 229.

65. *Shiryōshū*, p. 396.

66. Ibid., pp. 303–8.

67. A useful chart of all names and institutional affiliations of the founding members can be found in Nakashima, "Seiji handō ni okeru shūkyō kyōdan no yakuwari," pp. 158–59.

68. This meant that all Japanese were responsible for defeat.

69. Itagaki, "'Eirei ni kotaeru kai' hossoku ni saishite," *Izoku tsūshin*, 15 July 1976. The last line appears to invoke the notorious war song "Umi yukaba": "Across the sea, corpses soaking in the water. / Across the mountains, corpses heaped up on the grass. / We shall die by the side of our lord. / We shall never look back." I am indebted to John Dower for this reference.

70. "Ishida kaichō aisatsu yoshi," *Izoku tsūshin*, 15 July 1976.

71. *Jinja shinpō*, 17 Jan. 1977, quoted in Nakashima, "Seiji handō ni okeru shūkyō kyōdan no yakuwari," p. 162.

72. Itagaki, "'Eirei ni kotaeru kai' hossoku ni saishite," *Izoku tsūshin*, 15 July 1976.

73. Nakashima, "Seiji handō ni okeru shūkyō kyōdan no yakuwari," p. 161.

74. See, for example, Yamaguchi and Sōichi, eds., *Sengoshi to handō ideorogii.*

75. The following is based on Nakashima, "Seiji handō ni okeru shūkyō kyō-dan no yakuwari."

76. *Izoku tsūshin,* 15 Feb. and 15 Mar. 1978.

Chapter Nine

1. Taguchi Hiroshi, "'Nichidoku heiwa fōramu' ni sanka shite."

2. This movement is treated in some detail in Kimijima, "The Continuing Legacy of Japanese Colonialism." See note 1 for reference on the 1960s South Korean–Japanese textbook dialogue.

3. For an English translation, see Weizsäcker, "Speech by Richard von Weizsäcker," in Hartman, ed., *Bitburg in Moral and Political Perspective.*

4. Hidaka, "Mitsu no yonjūnenme."

5. Related publications by the same author include Nagai, "Waitsusekka enzetsu ni gyakufū tsunoru"; *Waitsusekka no seishin.*

6. Dieter, "Wadatsumikai no messēji."

7. For a collection of critical essays on this event, see Hartman, ed., *Bitburg in Moral and Political Perspective.*

8. Quoted in Nagai, "Waitsusekka enzetsu ni gyakufū tsunoru."

9. Oda, *Nishi-Berurin de mita koto, Nihon de kangaeta koto;* Honda, "The Burden of Being Japanese," in *The Impoverished Spirit in Contemporary Japan;* Mochida, *Futatsu no kindai;* Yamaguchi Yasushi, "Nihon, Doitsu, Itaria no sengo"; Satō Kensei, "Nihon to Doitsu no rekishi no kyōkun: watashitachi no nasubeki koto."

10. Nishi, *Han'ei Nishi-Doitsu ga ochita wana;* Nishio, "'Nihon no tomo.'"

11. See Mochida Yukio's introduction in Awaya et al., *Sensō sekinin, sengo sekinin.*

12. Quoted in Awaya, *Miketsu no sensō sekinin.* For a detailed discussion of the term *kako no kokufuku,* see Nagai, *Waitsusekka no seishin.*

13. In Awaya et al., *Sensō sekinin, sengo sekinin,* p. 6.

14. For example, Tōkyō shinbun, *Owari naki sengo: shōgen to kiroku* (Tokyo booklet, no. 8).

15. Nishio, *Kotonaru higeki.*

16. Mochida, *Sensō sekinin to sengo sekinin* (Kamogawa booklet, no. 77).

17. Nishio, *Kotonaru higeki,* p. 81.

18. Ōnuma, "Tōkyō saiban, sensō sekinin, sengo sekinin," in *Tōkyō saiban kara sengo sekinin no shisō e* (for an English translation of this article, see "The Tokyo War Crimes Trial, War Responsibility, and Postwar Responsibility," in Li et al., eds., *Nanking 1937*); Satō Kensei, "Sengo shori ni okeru Doitsu to Nihon," pp. 72–73.

19. Katō Shūichi, *Sensō sekinin no ukekata* (Bukuletto ikiru), pp. 8–9.

20. Mochida, *Sensō sekinin to sengo sekinin.*

21. "Fukaki fuchi yori: Doitsu hatsu Nihon," *Asahi shinbun,* 1–10 Jan. 1995.

22. Oda, "Rikaishi yurusuna."

23. Mochida, "Sensō sekinin, sengo sekinin ni miru Doitsu to Nihon."

24. Satō Kensei, "Nihon to Doitsu."

25. Arguments of this sort are too numerous to reference here. The more nuanced journalistic and scholarly works in this vein include Buruma, *The Wages of Guilt*; McCormack, *The Emptiness of Japanese Affluence*; Field, "War and Apology."

26. Gluck, "The 'Long Postwar': Japan and Germany in Common and in Contrast."

27. Johnson, "Japan in Search of a 'Normal' Role."

28. For example, Japan's invasion of China was allegedly downscaled to an "advance."

29. The most complete treatment of this incident is Rose, *Interpreting History in Sino-Japanese Relations.*

30. Both the Japan Teachers' Union and the Japan-China Friendship Association were at the forefront of intense domestic protests against the government's textbook screening and what they saw as a more general failure to acknowledge Japan's war responsibility.

31. Tanaka Nobumasa, "What Is the Yasukuni Problem?" *Japan in the World,* 24 May 2001. http://www.iwanami.co.jp/jpworld/text/yasukuni01.html. Accessed 16 July 2006.

32. Tanaka Nobumasa, "Nihon izokukai no gojūnen."

33. See Gluck, "The Past in the Present."

34. "Seijō hōgyo," *Jinja shinpō,* special issue, 8 Jan. 1989.

35. "Gekidō no Shōwa ni mananda mono," *Izoku tsūshin,* 15 Feb. 1989.

36. "Tennō no sensō sekinin o tou," *Nitchū yūkō shinbun,* 15 Jan. 1989.

37. This English translation was published along with the Japanese text by Nihon senbotsu gakusei kinenkai: "Hearkening to the Voices of Millions of War Victims: In Protest of the State Funeral for the Late Shōwa Tenno."

38. Months later, it was published as a book: Terasaki and Miller, eds., *Shōwa tennō dokuhakuroku—Terasaki Hidenari goyōgakari nikki.* For analyses in English, see especially Bix, "The Showa Emperor's 'Monologue' and the Problem of War Responsibility"; Awaya, "Emperor Shōwa's Accountability for War."

39. For a study of this phenomenon, see Buchholz, *Schreiben und Erinnern* and Figal, "How to '*Jibunshi.*'"

40. "Introduction to a Lost War," in Cook and Cook, *Japan at War.*

41. The most closely documented account of the early political development of this issue is Hicks, *The Comfort Women.* See also Yoshimi, *Comfort Women.*

Other useful sources include the special issue on "The Comfort Women: Colonialism, War, and Sex," *Positions* 5, no. 1 (1997).

42. Yoshimi, ed., *Jūgun ianfu shiryōshū.*

43. These percentages were decisively lower among those aged 50 and older, with 41 percent approving compensation for former comfort women, 68 percent in favor of compensating victims of Japan's colonial rule, and 64 percent affirming the need to compensate victims of Japanese war atrocities. Asahi shinbun sengo hoshō mondai shuzaihan, *Sengo hoshō to wa nani ka.*

44. See, for example, "The End of Socialism," *The Economist*, 30 July 1994.

45. Mukae, "Japan's Diet Resolution on World War Two."

46. For example the chairman of Nisshō (Japan Chamber of Commerce and Industry), Inaba Kōsaku; the chairman of Nikkeiren (Japan Federation of Employers' Association), Nagano Takeshi; and former Prime Minister Fukuda Takeo.

47. *Asahi shinbun*, 26 May 1995. Quoted in Mukae, "Japan's Diet Resolution on World War Two," p. 1020.

48. Quoted in "Debate Rages over Resolution to Apologize for Pacific War," *Japan Times*, 23 Feb. 1995.

49. Field, "War and Apology."

50. Ibid.

51. Translated by the Secretariat, House of Representatives; quoted in Mukae, "Japan's Diet Resolution on World War Two," p. 1012.

52. Ōnuma Yasuaki lists ¥2 millon per person as private atonement money regardless of residency, and government medical welfare programs ranging from ¥1.2 million for Filipino victims to ¥3 million for Taiwanese and Korean victims. These statistics are based on Ōnuma et al., eds., *'Ianfu' mondai to Ajia josei kikin*, p. 148.

53. Ōnuma, "Japanese War Guilt and the Postwar Responsibility of Japan," talk at Harvard University on 3 March 2002, published in Japanese as "Nihon no sensō sekinin to sengo sekinin."

54. "Ajia josei kikin no tsugunai jigyō e no hokin ni gokyōryoku kudasatta minasama e," *Asahi shinbun*, 20 Nov. 2002; press statement of Chief Cabinet Secretary Nakagawa Hidenao on 1 Sept. 2000. I am indebted to John Dower for providing me with a copy of the text.

55. "Statement by Prime Minister Tomiichi Murayama, 15 August 1995," *Japan Times*, 16 Aug. 1995.

56. Ozawa Ichirō, *Blueprint for a New Japan*, pp. 128–29.

57. See essays by Cha and Yang in Funabashi, *Reconciliation in the Asia-Pacific.*

58. *New York Times*, 8 Oct. 1998.

59. Japan–Republic of Korea Joint Declaration: A New Japan–Republic of Korea Partnership towards the Twenty-first Century, 8 October 1998, available in an unofficial translation at http://www.mofa.go.jp/region/asia-paci/korea/joint9810.html. Accessed 16 July 2006.

60. Ibid.

61. Yōichi Funabashi, an *Asahi shinbun* journalist who has covered the reconciliation efforts thoughtfully, points to the importance of implementing a reconciliation policy as a process and offers the following recommendations: (1) Human rights violations are a universal human experience; (2) "our" history is everyone's history; (3) reconciliation over the past is a process; (4) there is no universal formula; (5) reconciliation must be a joint effort by victimizers and victimized; (6) use a forward-looking, realistic approach; (7) cultivate democracy; (8) the approach should be based on multilateralism and regionalism; (9) political leadership is key; (10) individual initiative is essential; (11) our behavior should reflect the kind of nation we hope to build. Funabashi, *Reconciliation in the Asia-Pacific*, pp. 176–83.

62. "Visit to the People's Republic of China by Prime Minister Junichiro Koizumi, 8 October 2001," http://www.mofa.go.jp/region/asia-paci/china/pmv0110/meet-2.html. I thank Mike Mochizuki for this reference. Accessed 16 July 2006.

63. Wakamiya, "War-bereaved Families' Dilemma: Thoughts on Japan's War," *Japan Focus* (posted on 13 July 2005), http://japanfocus.org/products/details/1615. Accessed 16 July 2006.

64. Kahn, "China Is Pushing and Scripting Anti-Japanese Protests," *New York Times*, 15 April 2005.

65. For example, Pu, "China's Selective Memory," *New York Times*, 28 April 2005.

66. This translation is posted on the prime minister's website at http://www.kantei.go.jp/foreign/koizumispeech/2005/08/15danwa_e.html. Accessed 16 July 2006.

Chapter Ten

1. Examples of such activism around the world are too numerous to list here. The comfort women issue brought forth a multitude of legal, research, women's, and human rights organizations, focused renewed interest in the prosecution of war crimes specifically against women, and challenged the Japanese government for the first time to offer official apologies and change textbooks (the government has resisted—to this day—demands to financially compensate non-Japanese war victims).

2. The "objects" of the experiments were not ordinary prisoners of war but people who had come under Japanese suspicion for communist, resistance, or spying activities.

3. For a detailed account in English of the Japanese biological warfare program and its subsequent coverup, see Harris, *Factories of Death.*

4. Ibid., pp. 226–31.

5. Preface to *Akuma no hōshoku* (1981 ed.).

6. Morimura, "Goyō no keii."

7. Morimura and Ikebe, "Nihon Chūgoku yūkō kyōkai sōritsu yonjūnen kinen biggu taiwa (2)."

8. Morimura and Ikebe, "Nihon Chūgoku yūkō kyōkai sōritsu yonjūnen kinen biggu taiwa (1)."

9. Morimura and Ikebe, parts 1 and 2.

10. Ibid., part 1.

11. At least two volumes of one-page writings by *Akuma* chorus members have been collected by Mochinaga Noriko. The first was printed in 1993 and distributed to members without a title. The second, "Tomo yo shiroi hara o," was edited by Saitama Akuma no hōshoku o utau gasshōdan and printed in 1996.

12. The earlier singing movements are treated in Gordon, *The Wages of Affluence* and Yamamoto, *Grasroots Pacifism in Post-War Japan.*

13. Mochinaga is a long-time member of the Japan-China Friendship Association and editor in chief of *Nitchū yūkō shinbun.*

14. The Japan-China Friendship Association had included the Nanjing Massacre in its list of Japanese war crimes all along, presenting first-hand accounts, likening it to Hiroshima and Auschwitz, and criticizing the lack of public knowledge about it in postwar Japan. See, for example, Nagatomi, "Ikita rekishi o kataru." See also "Nankin, Hiroshima, Aushuwitsu: tairyō gyakusatsu unda honshitsu eguru," *Nitchū yūkō shinbun*, 10 Aug. 1974; "Zanninsei no kyokugen: Nanjing daigyakusatsu: kokumin ni wa nani o shirasazu ni," *Nitchū yūkō kyokai*, 17 April 1976. Unit 731 was not much discussed until 1976, and until the 1980s, in the context of *Akuma*, neither atrocity had received nearly as much attention from the Japan-China Friendship Association as had the Hanaoka massacre or the Marco Polo Bridge incident.

15. *Akuma no hōshoku*, "Goaisatsu" (performance program).

16. The student-soldiers were played by Oda Yūji, Kazama Tōru, Nakamura Tōru, and Ogata Naoto; the nurse by Tsuruta Mayu; and the irregular soldier by Matoba Kōji.

17. Postscript translated in Yamanouchi and Quinn, eds., *Listen to the Voices from the Sea.*

18. Ibid., p. 324.

19. Hammond, "Commemoration Controversies."

20. For a detailed and thoughtful analysis of the Shōwa-kan in 2001, see Smith, "The Showa Hall."

21. "Seishikimei 'Shōwa-kan'," *Asahi shinbun*, 16 Dec. 1998, quoted in Smith, "The Showa Hall," p. 48.

22. Ibid., pp. 63–64.

23. *Izoku tsūshin*, 15 April 1999.

24. Both are *kinenkan* in Japanese, but written with different characters: 記念館 (commemoration hall) and 祈念館 (prayer hall).

25. *Izoku tsushin*, 15 Feb. 1999.

26. Ibid.

27. Laura Hein, "Savage Irony: The Imaginative Power of the 'Military Comfort Women' in the 1990s."

28. The term comes from Martha Minow, *Between Vengeance and Forgiveness*.

29. A particularly useful recent collection of both conceptual and empirical essays on this topic is John Torpey, ed., *Politics and the Past*.

30. The table of contents of back issues is available at http://www.jca.apc.org/JWRC/center/english/E-conten.htm. Accessed 16 July 2006.

31. http://www.global-alliance.net/related.html. Accessed 16 July 2006.

32. http://www1.jca.apc.org/vaww-net-japan/english/index.html. Accessed 16 July 2006. A good overview of the development of war compensation lawsuits and the main issues at stake is Hein, "War Compensation."

33. The VAWW–NET website offers much valuable information and many documents about the Women's Tribunal. A summary of findings is available, and the full final judgment can be ordered at http://www1.jca.apc.org/vaww-net-japan/english/womenstribunal2000/whatstribunal.html. Accessed 16 June 2006.

34. An overview of the tribunal by one of its judges is Christine M. Chinkin, "Women's International Tribunal on Japanese Military Sexual Slavery."

35. Itō, "Engendering the Concept of Peace," *ZNet Japan Focus*, 3 April 2003. http://www.zmag.org/content/showarticle.cfm?SectionID=17&ItemID=3380. Accessed 16 June 2006.

36. Minow, *Between Vengeance and Forgiveness*, p. 91.

37. For context, see Desai, "From Vienna to Beijing."

38. Morris-Suzuki, "Free Speech—Silenced Voices," *ZNet Japan*, http://www.zmag.org/content/showarticle.cfm?SectionID=17%ItemID=8514. Accessed 16 July 2006.

39. On historical revisionism in contemporary Japan, see Saaler, *Politics, Memory and Public Opinion*.

40. Hein, "Savage Irony," p. 342.

41. Hein, "Citizens, Foreigners, and the State in the United States and Japan since 9/11," pp. 140–42. See also Kaneko et al., *Gurōbarizēshon to sensō sekinin*, Iwanami booklet, no. 530.

42. Ueno, "The Politics of Memory."

43. Ōgoshi, "Zange no neuchi mo nai."

44. Ōgoshi, " 'Rekishi shutai ronsō' o koeru—jendaaka shita shisō sen."

45. Katō, *Haisengoron*. For insightful discussions of *Haisengoron* in English, see Morris-Suzuki, "Unquiet Graves"; Okamoto, "Beyond Dichotomy"; Igarashi, "The Unfinished Business of Mourning."

46. Morris-Suzuki, "Unquiet Graves," p. 28.

47. Igarashi, "The Unfinished Business of Mourning," pp. 212–14.

48. Gong, "A Clash of Histories."

Conclusion

1. Lee, "Going Public."

2. For example, Frei, *Adenauer's Germany and the Nazi Past.*

3. Dower, "The Useful War."

4. Herf, *Divided Memory: The Nazi Past in the Two Germanies.*

5. I am borrowing Jeffrey Olick's term. Olick, "What Does It Mean to Normalize the Past?"

6. For documentary evidence on this thorny issue see Dower, "July 25, 1945: 'The Most Terrible Bomb in the History of the World,'" especially pp. 314–16.

7. Katzenstein and Shiraishi, "Conclusion: Regions in World Politics, Japan and Asia—Germany in Europe," p. 371.

8. Dower, "Occupied Japan and the Cold War in Asia."

Bibliography

Newspapers and Periodicals

Asahi shinbun (1879–)
Atarashii kyōiku to bunka (1947–49)
Japan Times (1956–)
Jinja shinpō shukusatsuban (1946–95)
Kyōiku hyōron (1951–)
Nihon izoku kōsei renmei kaihō (1949–50)
Nihon izoku tsūshin (1990–)
Nihon izoku tsūshin: Nihon izokukai kikanshi shukusatsuban, vols. 1–2 (1949–90)
Nihon to Chūgoku (1950–65)
Nitchū yūkō shinbun (1965–)
Wadatsumi no koe (1959–)
Wadatsumi no koe shukusatsuban (1950–58)

Other Published Materials

Abel, Jessamyn Riech. "Warring Internationalisms: Multilateral Thinking in Japan, 1933–1964." Ph.D. diss., Columbia University, 2004.

Abiko Kazuyoshi, Uozumi Yōichi, and Nakaoka Narifumi, eds. *Sensō sekinin to "wareware": "rekishi shutai ronsō" o megutte.* Kyoto: Nakanishiya shuppan, 1999.

Adorno, Theodor W. "What Does Coming to Terms with the Past Mean?" In *Bitburg in Moral and Political Perspective,* edited by Geoffrey Hartman, 114–29. Bloomington: Indiana University Press, 1986 (orig. 1959).

Ajia minshū hōtei junbikai. *Hakubutsukan to "hyōgen no fujiyū": "Senbotsusha tsuitō heiwa kinenkan" kōsō o kangaeru.* Tokyo: Kinohanasha, 1994.

————. *Jikō naki sensō sekinin: sabakareru tennō to Nihon.* Tokyo: Ryokufū shuppan, 1990.

————. *Tennō Hirohito no sensō sekinin, sengo sekinin.* Ajia minshū hōtei booklet, no. 4: *Renzoku "Shōhōtei" no kiroku.* Tokyo: Kinohanasha, 1995.

Amano Teiyū. "Bunka no honshitsu to kyōiku." *Atarashii kyōiku to bunka* (March 1948): 4–13.

Antoni, Klaus. *Shinto und die Konzeption des japanischen Nationalwesens (kokutai): Der religiöse Traditionalismus in Neuzeit und Moderne Japans.* Leiden: Brill, 1998.

————. "Yasukuni-Jinja and Folk Religion." In *Religion and Society in Modern Japan: Selected Readings,* edited by Shimazono Susumu, Mark R. Mullins, and Paul L. Swanson, 121–32. Berkeley: Asian Humanities Press, 1993.

Appadurai, Arjun, and Carol A. Breckenridge. "Why Public Culture?" *Public Culture* 1, no. 1 (1988): 5–16.

Arai Shin'ichi, ed. *Sensō hakubutsukan.* Iwanami booklet, no. 328. Tokyo: Iwanami shoten, 1994.

————. "Sensō sekinin to wa nani ka." *Sekai* (February 1994): 187–201.

————. *Sensō sekininron.* Tokyo: Iwanami shoten, 1995.

Asahi shinbun sengo hoshō mondai shuzaihan. *Sengo hoshō to wa nani ka.* Tokyo: Asahi shinbunsha, 1994.

Ashizu Uzuhiko. "Daitōa sensō no shisōteki seikaku." *Jinja shinpō,* 3 August 1963.

————. "Dokuritsu Nihon to shintō seishin." *Jinja shinpō,* 17 September 1951.

————. "Shinpō kiji no sakuseishatachi." In *Jinja shinpō hōi, yonjūnen kinen,* 32–40. Tokyo: Jinja shinpōsha, 1986.

Awaya Kentarō. "Controversies Surrounding the Asia-Pacific War: The Tokyo War Crimes Trial." In *America's War in Asia: A Cultural Approach to History and Memory,* edited by Philip West and Steven I. Levine, 221–32. Armonk, NY: M.E. Sharpe, 1998.

————. "Emperor Shōwa's Accountability for War." *Japan Quarterly* 38, no. 4 (1991): 386–89.

————. *Miketsu no sensō sekinin.* Tokyo: Kashiwa shobō, 1994.

————. "Tōkyō saiban kara nani o manabu ka." In *Kunin no kataru sensō to ningen,* edited by Miyake Akimasa and Wakakuwa Midori, 97–132. Tokyo: Ōtsuki shoten, 1991.

————. *Tōkyō saibanron.* Tokyo: Ōtsuki shoten, 1989.

Awaya Kentarō, Tanaka Hiroshi, Hirowatari Seigo, Mishima Ken'ichi, Mochida Yukio, and Yamaguchi Yasushi. *Sensō sekinin, sengo sekinin: Nihon to Doitsu wa dō chigau ka.* Tokyo: Asahi shinbunsha, 1994.

Barkan, Elazar. *The Guilt of Nations: Restitution and Negotiating Historical Injustices.* New York: W. W. Norton, 2000.

Barshay, Andrew E. "Imagining Democracy in Postwar Japan: Reflection on Maruyama Masao and Modernism." *Journal of Japanese Studies* 18, no. 2 (1992): 365–406.

———. "Postwar Social and Political Thought, 1945–90." In *Modern Japanese Thought*, edited by Bob Tadashi Wakabayashi, 273–356. Cambridge, UK: Cambridge University Press, 1998.

Beer, Lawrence Ward. *Freedom of Expression in Japan: A Study in Comparative Law, Politics, and Society.* Tokyo, New York: Kodansha International, 1984.

Berger, Thomas U. *Cultures of Antimilitarism: National Security in Germany and Japan.* Baltimore: Johns Hopkins University Press, 1998.

Bix, Herbert P. *Hirohito and the Making of Modern Japan.* New York: Harper-Collins, 2000.

———. "The Showa Emperor's 'Monologue' and the Problem of War Responsibility." *Journal of Japanese Studies* 18, no. 2 (1992): 295–363.

Boyd, J. Patrick, and Richard J. Samuels. *Nine Lives?: The Politics of Constitutional Reform in Japan.* Policy Studies 19. Washington, DC: East-West Center, 2005.

Buchholz, Petra. *Schreiben und Erinnern: Über Selbstzeugnisse japanischer Kriegsteilnehmer.* Munich: Iudicium Verlag, 2003.

Buruma, Ian. *The Wages of Guilt: Memories of War in Germany and Japan.* New York: Farrer, Straus and Giroux, 1994.

Chang, Iris. *The Rape of Nanking: The Forgotten Holocaust of World War II.* New York: Penguin Books, 1997.

Chinkin, Christine M. "Women's International Tribunal on Japanese Military Sexual Slavery." *American Journal of International Law* 95 (2001): 335–41.

Cho, M. Y. *Die Volksdiplomatie in Ostasien: Entstehung, Theorie und Praxis—Die Asienpolitik der Vereinigten Staaten und die Beziehungen zwischen der Volksrepublik China und Japan.* Wiesbaden: Otto Harrassowitz, 1971.

Christy, Alan S. "The Making of Imperial Subjects in Okinawa." *Positions* 1 (1993): 607–39.

Cohen, David. "Beyond Nuremberg: Individual Responsibility for War Crimes." In *Human Rights in Political Transitions: Gettysburg to Bosnia*, edited by Carla Hesse and Robert Post, 53–92. New York: Zone Books, 1999.

Confino, Alon. "Collective Memory and Cultural History: Problems of Method." *American Historical Review* 102, no. 5 (Dec. 1997): 1386–403.

Connerton, Paul. *How Societies Remember.* Cambridge, UK: Cambridge University Press, 1989.

Conrad, Sebastian. *Auf der Suche nach der verlorenen Nation: Geschichtsschreibung in Westdeutschland und Japan 1945–1960.* Göttingen: Vandenhoeck & Ruprecht, 1999.

————. "What Time Is Japan? Problems of Comparative (Intercultural) Historiography." *History and Theory* 38, no. 1 (1999): 67–83.

Cook, Haruko Taya, and Theodore F. Cook. *Japan at War: An Oral History*. New York: New Press, 1992.

Creemers, Wilhelmus H. M. *Shrine Shinto after World War II*. Leiden: Brill, 1968.

Crump, Thomas. *The Death of an Emperor: Japan at the Crossroads*. Oxford: Oxford University Press, 1991.

Desai, Manisha. "From Vienna to Beijing: Women's Human Rights Activism and the Human Rights Community." In *Debating Human Rights*, edited by Peter Van Ness, 184–98. London: Routledge, 1999.

Dierkes, Julian Beatus. "Teaching Portrayals of the Nation: Postwar History Education in Japan and the Germanys." Ph.D. diss., Princeton University, 2003.

Dieter, Wilfriede. "Wadatsumikai no messēji." *Wadatsumi no koe*, no. 89 (1989): 146–47.

Dower, John W. "'An Aptitude for Being Unloved': War and Memory in Japan." In *Crimes of War: Guilt and Denial in the Twentieth Century*, edited by Omar Bartov, Atina Grossmann, and Mary Nolan, 217–41. New York: New Press, 2002.

————. *Embracing Defeat: Japan in the Wake of World War II*. New York: W. W. Norton/New Press, 1999.

————. *Empire and Aftermath: Yoshida Shigeru and the Japanese Experience, 1978–1954*. 2d ed. Cambridge, MA: Harvard University Press, 1979.

————. "Japanese Cinema Goes to War." In *Japan in War and Peace: Selected Essays*, 33–54. New York: New Press, 1993.

————. "July 25, 1945: 'The Most Terrible Bomb in the History of the World,'" in *Days of Destiny: Crossroads in American History*, edited by David Rubel with James M. McPherson and Alan Brinkley as general editors, 309–34. New York: DK Publishing, 2001.

————. "Occupied Japan and the Cold War in Asia." In *Japan in War and Peace: Selected Essays*, 155–93. New York: New Press, 1993.

————. "Sizing Up (and Breaking Down) Japan." In *The Postwar Development of Japanese Studies in the United States*, edited by Helen Hardacre, 1–36. Leiden: Brill, 1998.

————. "The Useful War." In *Showa: The Japan of Hirohito*, edited by Carol Gluck and Stephen R. Graubard, 49–70. New York: W. W. Norton, 1992.

————. "Triumphal and Tragic Narratives of the War in Asia." In *Living with the Bomb: American and Japanese Cultural Conflicts in the Nuclear Age*, edited by Laura Hein and Mark Selden, 37–51. Armonk, NY: M.E. Sharpe, 1997.

Executive Committee International Public Hearing. *War Victimization and Japan: International Public Hearing Report.* Tokyo: Tōhō shuppan, 1993.

Field, Norma. *In the Realm of a Dying Emperor.* New York: Pantheon Books, 1991.

———. "War and Apology: Japan, Asia, the Fiftieth, and After." *Positions* 5, no. 1 (1997): 1–50.

Figal, Gerald. "How to '*Jibunshi*': Making and Marketing Self-histories of Shōwa among the Masses in Postwar Japan." *Journal of Asian Studies* 55, no. 4 (1996): 902–34.

Finn, Richard B. *Winners in Peace: MacArthur, Yoshida, and Postwar Japan.* Berkeley: University of California Press, 1992.

Fogel, Joshua A., ed. *Life Along the Manchurian Railway: The Memoirs of Itō Takeo.* Armonk, NY: M.E. Sharpe, 1988.

——— ed. *The Nanjing Massacre in History and Historiography.* Berkeley: University of California Press, 2000.

———. "The Other Japanese Community: Leftwing Japanese Activities in Wartime Shanghai." In *Wartime Shanghai,* edited by Wen-hsin Yeh, 43–61. London: Routledge, 1998.

Foreign Affairs Association Japan. *The Japan Year Book.* Tokyo: Foreign Affairs Association of Japan, 1946–52.

Foucault, Michel. *Language, Counter-Memory, Practice: Selected Essays and Interviews.* Edited by Donald F. Bouchard. Ithaca: Cornell University Press, 1977.

Frei, Norbert. *Adenauer's Germany and the Nazi Past: The Politics of Amnesty and Integration.* New York: Columbia University Press, 2002.

Fuhrt, Volker. *Erzwungene Reue: Vergangenheitsbewältigung und Kriegsschulddiskussion in Japan 1952–1998.* Hamburg: Verlag Dr. Kovač, 2002.

Fujitani Takashi. "Electronic Pageantry and Japan's 'Symbolic Emperor.'" *Journal of Asian Studies* 51 (1992): 824–50.

Fujitani Takashi, Geoffrey M. White, and Lisa Yoneyama, eds. *Perilous Memories: The Asia-Pacific War(s).* Durham: Duke University Press, 2001.

Fujiwara Akira, ed. *Nankin jiken o dō miru ka.* Tokyo: Aoki shoten, 1998.

Fujiwara Akira and Anzai Ikurō. *Sensō kara heiwa e: nijūisseiki no sentaku.* Kamogawa booklet, vol. 68. Kyōto: Kamogawa shuppan, 1994.

Fujiwara Akira and Arai Shin'ichi, eds. *Gendaishi ni okeru sensō sekinin.* Tokyo: Aoki shoten, 1990.

Fujiwara Akira, Awaya Kentarō, Yoshida Yutaka, and Yamada Akira, eds. *Tettei kenshō: Shōwa tennō "Dokuhakuroku."* Tokyo: Ōtsuki shoten, 1991.

Funabashi Yōichi, ed. *Reconciliaiton in the Asia-Pacific.* Washington, DC: Institute of Peace Press, 2003.

Fukashiro Junrō. "The New Left." *Japan Quarterly* 17, no. 1 (1970): 27–36.

Fukatsu Masumi. "A State Visit to Yasukuni Shrine." *Japan Quarterly* 33, no. 1 (1986): 19–24.

Fukuda Tsuneari. "Bungaku to sensō sekinin." In *Sengo Nihon shisō taikei*, edited by Hidaka Rokurō, 227–35. Tokyo: Chikuma shobō, 1968 (orig. 1946).

Garon, Sheldon. *Molding Japanese Minds: The State in Everyday Life*. Princeton: Princeton University Press, 1997.

———. *The State and Labor in Modern Japan*. Berkeley: California University Press, 1987.

George, Aurelia. *The Comparative Study of Interest Groups in Japan: An Institutional Framework*. Canberra: Research Committee of the Australia-Japan Research Center, 1982.

Gibney, Frank, ed. *Sensō: The Japanese Remember the Pacific War*. New York: M.E. Sharpe, 1995.

Giordano, Ralph. *Die Zweite Schuld, oder: Von der Last Deutscher zu sein*. Hamburg: Rasch und Röhring, 1987.

Gluck, Carol. "The 'End' of the Postwar: Japan at the Turn of the Millennium." *Public Culture* 10, no. 1 (1997): 1–23.

———. "Entangling Illusions: Japanese and American Views of the Occupation." In *New Frontiers in American–East Asian Relations: Essays Presented to Dorothy Borg*, edited by Warren I. Cohen, 169–236. New York: Columbia University Press, 1983.

———. "The Idea of Showa." In *Showa: The Japan of Hirohito*, edited by Carol Gluck and Stephen R. Graubard, 1–26. New York: W. W. Norton, 1992.

———. *Japan's Modern Myths: Ideology in the Late Meiji Period*. Princeton: Princeton University Press, 1985.

———. "The 'Long Postwar': Japan and Germany in Common and in Contrast." In *Legacies and Ambiguities: Postwar Fiction and Culture in West Germany and Japan*, edited by Ernestine Schlant and J. Thomas Rimer, 63–78. Washington and Baltimore: Woodrow Wilson Center Press and Johns Hopkins University Press, 1991.

———. "The Past in the Present." In *Postwar Japan as History*, edited by Andrew Gordon, 64–98. Berkeley: University of California Press, 1993.

Gong, Gerrit W. "A Clash of Histories: 'Remembering and Forgetting' Issues, Structures, and Strategic Implications." In *Memory and History in East and Southeast Asia: Issues of Identity in International Relations*, edited by Gerrit W. Gong, 26–43. Washington, DC: Center for Strategic and International Studies Press, 2001.

———, ed. *Remembering and Forgetting: The Legacy of War and Peace in East Asia*. Washington, DC: Center for Strategic and International Studies, 1996.

Gordon, Andrew. *The Evolution of Labor Relations in Japan: Heavy Industry, 1853–1955.* Cambridge, MA: Harvard University Press, 1985.

———. *The Wages of Affluence: Labor and Management in Postwar Japan.* Cambridge, MA: Harvard University Press, 1998.

Gotō Motoo. "Japan in Asia." *Japan Quarterly* 16, no. 4 (1969): 387–96.

———. "Political Awareness among the Japanese: On the *Asahi Shinbun* Public Opinion Survey." *Japan Quarterly* 14, no. 2 (1967): 165–74.

Grass, Günter, and Kenzaburo Ōe. *Gestern, vor 50 Jahren: Ein deutsch-japanischer Briefwechsel.* Goettingen: Steidl Verlag, 1995.

Gries, Peter Hays. *China's New Nationalism: Pride, Politics, and Diplomacy.* Berkeley: University of California Press, 2004.

Habermas, Jürgen. *The Structural Transformation of the Public Sphere: An Inquiry into a Category of Bourgeois Society.* Translated by Thomas Burger with the assistance of Frederick Lawrence. Cambridge, MA: MIT Press, 1989.

Halbwachs, Maurice. *On Collective Memory.* Translated by Lewis Coser. Chicago: University of Chicago Press, 1992.

Hall, John Whitney. "Reflections on a Centennial." *Journal of Asian Studies* 27, no. 4 (1968): 711–20.

Hammond, Ellen H. "Commemoration Controversies: The War, the Peace, and Democracy in Japan." In *Living with the Bomb: American and Japanese Cultural Conflicts in the Nuclear Age,* edited by Laura Hein and Mark Selden, 100–21. Armonk, NY: M.E. Sharpe, 1997.

"Handobukku sengo hoshō" henshū iinkai. *Handobukku: Sengo hoshō.* Tokyo: Nashinokisha, 1994.

Hani Gorō. "Kanryōshugi hihan." *Nihon hyōron* (October 1946): 24–40.

Hardacre, Helen. *Shinto and the State 1868–1988.* Princeton: Princeton University Press, 1989.

Harootunian, Harry. "Memory, Mourning, and National Morality: Yasukuni Shrine and the Reunion of State and Religion in Postwar Japan." In *Nation and Religion: Perspectives on Europe and Asia,* edited by Peter van der Veer and Hartmut Lehmann, 144–60. Princeton: Princeton University Press, 1999.

Harries, Meirion, and Susie Harries. *Sheathing the Sword: The Demilitarisation of Japan.* London: Hamish Hamilton, 1987.

Harris, Sheldon H. *Factories of Death: Japanese Biological Warfare, 1932–45, and the American Cover-Up.* London and New York: Routledge, 1994.

Hartman, Geoffrey. "Introduction: Darkness Visible." In *Holocaust Remembrance: The Shapes of Memory,* edited by Geoffrey Hartman, 1–22. Oxford, UK: Blackwell, 1994.

———, ed. *Bitburg in Moral and Political Perspective.* Bloomington: Indiana University Press, 1986.

Hasegawa, Michiko. "A Postwar View of the Greater East Asia War." *Japan Echo* 11 (special issue, 1984): 29–37.

Hashikawa Bunzō. "Ankēto o yonde." *Wadatsumi no koe*, no. 7 (1961): 23–25.

Hashimoto, Akiko. "Japanese and German Projects of Moral Recovery: Toward a New Understanding of War Memories in Defeated Nations." Cambridge, MA: Edwin O. Reischauer Institute for Japanese Studies Occasional Papers, Harvard University, 1999.

Hata Ikuhiko. "The Postwar Period in Retrospect." *Japan Echo* 11 (special issue, 1984): 12–21.

———. "When Ideologues Rewrite History." *Japan Echo* 13, no. 4 (1986): 73–78.

Havens, Thomas R. H. *Fire across the Sea: The Vietnam War and Japan, 1965–1975.* Princeton: Princeton University Press, 1987.

Hayasaka Akira. "Kike wadatsumi no koe." *Shinario*, no. 7 (1995): 124–55.

Hayashi Fusao. *Daitōa sensō kōteiron.* Tokyo: Banchō shobō, 1964.

———. *Zoku daitōa sensō kōteiron.* Tokyo: Banchō shobō, 1965.

Hein, Laura. "Citizens, Foreigners, and the State in the United States and Japan since 9/11." *ZNet Japan Focus*, 4 December 2003, http://www.zmag.org/content/showarticle.cfm?SectionID=17&ItemID=4614.

———. *Reasonable Men, Powerful Words: Political Culture and Expertise in Twentieth-Century Japan.* Berkeley: University of California Press, 2004.

———. "Savage Irony: The Imaginative Power of the 'Military Comfort Women' in the 1990s." *Gender and History* 11 (1999): 336–72.

———. "War Compensation: Claims against the Japanese Government and Japanese Corporations for War Crimes." In *Politics and the Past: On Repairing Historical Injustices*, edited by John Torpey, 127–48. Lanham: Rowman & Littlefield, 2003.

Hein, Laura, and Mark Selden, eds. *Censoring History: Citizenship and Memory in Japan, Germany, and the United States.* Armonk, NY: M.E. Sharpe, 2000.

———. *Islands of Discontent: Okinawan Responses to Japanese and American Power.* Lanham, MD: Rowman & Littlefield, 2003.

———. *Living with the Bomb: American and Japanese Cultural Conflicts in the Nuclear Age.* Armonk, NY: M.E. Sharpe, 1997.

Heiwa hakubutsukan o hajimeru kai. *Heiwa hakubutsukan o kangaeru.* Tokyo: Heiwa no atorie, 1994.

Herf, Jeffrey. *Divided Memory: The Nazi Past in the Two Germanies.* Cambridge, MA: Harvard University Press, 1997.

Hicks, George. *The Comfort Women: Japan's Brutal Regime of Enforced Prostitution in the Second World War.* New York: W. W. Norton, 1994.

———. *Japan's War Memories: Amnesia or Concealment?* Aldershot: Ashgate, 1997.

Hidaka Rokurō. "Mitsu no yonjūnenme: 'kioku o iki-iki to tamotsu koto' no imi." *Sekai* (September 1985): 37–46.

———. "Okinawa, senryaku taisei no naka no sabetsu." *Sekai* (August 1967): 10–17.

———. *Sengo Nihon o kangaeru.* Tokyo: Chikuma shobō, 1986.

———. "Sensō taiken to sensō sekinin." (orig. 13 Aug. 1956). Reprinted in *Gendai ideorogii*, 371–75. Tokyo: Keisō shobō, 1960.

———, ed. *Sengo Nihon shisō taikei.* Vol. 1: *Sengo shisō no shuppatsu.* Tokyo: Chikuma shobō, 1968.

Hielscher, Gebhard, and Kanji Nishio. "Nichiyō ronsō: Hidoku no sengo shori." *Mainichi shinbun*, 21 August 1994.

Higa Mikio. "The Okinawan Reversion Movement." In *Okinawa Reversion*, edited by Hosoya Chihiro, 1–24. Pittsburgh: International Studies Association, 1977.

Higaki Takashi and Tanaka Nobumasa. "'Rekishi' to 'shinwa' no aida." *Sekai* (May 1995): 155–69.

Higuchi Yōichi. "'When Society Is Itself the Tyrant.'" *Japan Quarterly* 35, no. 4 (1988): 350–56.

Hirai Hiroyuki. *Aru sengo: Wadatsumi daigaku kyōshi no yonjūnen.* Tokyo: Chikuma shobō, 1983.

Hirano, Kyoko. *Mr. Smith Goes to Tokyo: Japanese Cinema under the American Occupation, 1945–1952.* Washington, DC: Smithsonian Institution Press, 1992.

Hirano Yoshitarō. "Kikokusha no minasan e." *Nihon to Chūgoku*, 1 April 1953.

Hirō Sachiya and Yamamoto Shichihei. "Yasukuni Shrine and the Japanese Spirit World." *Japan Echo* 13, no. 2 (1986): 73–80.

Hiroshima heiwa kyōiku kenkyūjo. *Heiwa kyōiku jissen jiten.* Tokyo: Rōdō junpōsha, 1981.

Hogan, Michael J., ed. *Hiroshima in History and Memory.* Cambridge, UK: Cambridge University Press, 1996.

Honda Katsuichi. *The Impoverished Spirit in Contemporary Japan: Selected Essays of Honda Katsuichi.* Edited by John Lie. New York: Monthly Review Press, 1993.

———. *The Nanjing Massacre: A Japanese Journalist Confronts Japan's National Shame.* Translated by Karen Sandness. Edited by Frank Gibney. Armonk, NY: M.E. Sharpe, 2000.

Horikiri Kazumasa. *Sanjūdai ga yonda "wadatsumi."* Tokyo: Tsukiji shokan, 1993.

Horio Teruhisa. *Educational Thought and Ideology in Modern Japan: State Authority and Intellectual Freedom.* Translated by Steven Platzer. Tokyo: University of Tokyo Press, 1988.

———. *Kyōkasho mondai: Ienaga soshō ni takusu mono.* Iwanami booklet, no. 211. Tokyo: Iwanami shoten, 1992.

Hosaka Masayasu. *Haisen zengo no Nihonjin.* Tokyo: Asahi shinbunsha, 1985.

———. *"Kike wadatsumi no koe"no sengoshi.* Tokyo: Bungei shunjū, 1999.

Hoshino Yasusaburō. "Okinawa wa Nihon no kyōshi ni futatsu no sekinin o yōsei suru." *Kyōiku hyōron* (March 1967): 23–27.

———. "Yasukuni jinja hōan no ikensei." *Wadatsumi no koe,* no. 58 (1974): 39–53.

Hosoya Chihiro, ed. *Okinawa Reversion.* International Studies Occasional Paper no. 12. Pittsburgh: International Studies Association, 1977.

Hosoya Chihiro, Ando Nisuke, Ōnuma Yasuaki, and Richard Minear, eds. *The Tokyo War Crimes Trial: An International Symposium.* Tokyo, New York, San Francisco: Kodansha International, 1986.

Hosoya Chihiro and Ide Magoroku. "Sensō o kioku suru to iu koto, rekishi o kiroku suru to iu koto." *Sekai* (April 1995): 22–37.

Huyssen, Andreas. "Present Pasts: Media, Politics, Amnesia." *Public Culture* 12, no. 1 (2000): 21–38.

I Sune. *Sengo sedai no sensō sekininron: haisengoron o megutte.* Iwanami booklet, no. 467. Tokyo: Iwanami shoten, 1998.

Ienaga, Saburo. *Japan's Past, Japan's Future: One Historian's Odyssey.* Translated by Richard H. Minear. Lanham, Boulder, New York, Oxford: Rowman & Littlefield, 2001.

Igarashi, Yoshikuni. *Bodies of Memory: Narratives of War in Postwar Japanese Culture, 1945–1970.* Princeton: Princeton University Press, 2000.

———. "The Unfinished Business of Mourning: Maruyama Masao and Postwar Japan's Struggles with the Wartime Past." *Positions* 10, no. 1 (2002): 195–218.

Iida Momo. "Nihonjin no Okinawa ninshiki." *Sekai* (August 1967): 33–48.

Iizaka Ryōmei. "Yasukuni mondai to minshushugi." *Wadatsumi no koe,* no. 58 (1974): 54–67.

Ikeda Heiji. "Baku suru 'Izoku mondai no kokusaisei.'" *Nihon izoku tsūshin,* 15 June 1950.

Ikeda Hiroshi. *Sensō sekinin to sengo sekinin.* Tokyo: Shakai hyōronsha, 1994.

Ikeda Kiyohiko. *Tennō no sensō sekinin saikō.* Tokyo: Yōsensha, 2003.

Ikeda Takei. "Izoku no tachiba kara—ikon sanjūnen." *Wadatsumi no koe,* no. 58 (1974): 30–38.

Inoguchi Takashi. "Japan's Response to the Gulf Crisis: An Analytic Overview." *Journal of Japanese Studies* 17, no. 2 (1991): 257–73.

Inoki Masamichi and Kitaoka Shin'ichi. "The Gulf War and Pacifist Japan." *Japan Echo* 18, no. 2 (1991): 20–26.

Inoue Kiyoshi. *Tennō no sensō sekinin.* Tokyo: Gendai hyōronsha, 1975.

Irei Takashi. *Okinawajin ni totte no sengo.* Asahi sensho 201. Tokyo: Asahi shinbunsha, 1982.

Irie Takanori. "The Lingering Impact of Misguided Occupation Policies." *Japan Echo* 11 (special issue, 1984): 22–28.

Iriye, Akira. "Chinese-Japanese Relations, 1945–1990." *China Quarterly* 124 (Dec. 1990): 624–38.

———. *Cultural Internationalism and World Order*. Baltimore: Johns Hopkins University Press, 1997.

Irokawa Daikichi, ed. *1945 nen haisen kara nani o mananda ka*. Tokyo: Shōgakukan, 1995.

Ishida Takeshi. "The Development of Interest Groups and the Pattern of Political Modernization in Japan." In *Political Development in Modern Japan*, edited by Robert E. Ward, 293–336. Princeton: Princeton University Press, 1968.

Ishikawa Itsuko. *Chidorigafuchi e ikimashita ka*. Tokyo: Kashinsha, 1995.

———. *Mumei senbotsusha tachi no koe*. Iwanami booklet, no. 176. Tokyo: Iwanami shoten, 1989.

Ishizaka Kōichi. " 'Fusen ketsugi' to wa nani ka." *Sekai* (May 1995): 181–86.

Itagaki Tadashi. " 'Eirei ni kotaeru kai' hossoku ni saishite." *Nihon izoku tsūshin*, 15 July 1976.

Itō Ruri. "Engendering the Concept of Peace: On Violence against Women." *ZNet Japan Focus*, 3 April 2003, http://www.zmag.org/content/showarticle.cfm?SectionID=17&ItemID=3380.

Itō Takashi. "Higai joseitachi no koe o kike: Moto 'jūgun ianfu' wa nani ni kurushinde iru ka." *Sekai* (October 1994): 247–53.

Itō Takashi and Satō Seizaburō. "Ano sensō to wa nan datta no ka." *Chūō kōron* (January 1995): 26–43.

Iwamatsu Shigetoshi. *Hankaku to sensō sekinin*. Tokyo: San'ichi shobō, 1982.

Japan Youth Memorial Association (JYMA). *Ima, nani o kataran: Heisei jūgonendo haken hōkokusho*. Tokyo: JYMA, 2004.

Jinja honchō. *Jinja honchō jūnenshi*. Jinja honchōshi kenkyū sōsho 1. 2d ed. Tokyo: Jinja honchō, 1956.

———. *Jinja honchō jūgonenshi*. Tokyo: Jinja honchō, 1961.

———. *Jinja honchō nijūgonenshi*. Tokyo: Jinja honchō, 1971.

———. *Jinja honchō sanjūnenshi*. Tokyo: Jinja honchō, 1976.

———. *Jinja shinpō senshū hōi*. Tokyo: Jinja shinpōsha, 1986.

Jinja honchō kenshūjo. *Jinja honchō shikō*. Tokyo: Jinja honchō, 1989.

Johnson, Chalmers. "Japan in Search of a 'Normal' Role." *Daedalus* (Fall 1992): 1–33.

———. *MITI and the Japanese Miracle: The Growth of Industrial Policy, 1925–1975*. Stanford: Stanford University Press, 1982.

————. "The Patterns of Japanese Relations with China, 1952–1982." *Pacific Affairs* 59, no. 3 (1986): 402–28.

————, ed. *Okinawa: Cold War Island*. Albuquerque: Japan Policy Research Institute, 1999.

Kamata Satoshi. "Ima nao sensō." In *Dokyumento: Gendai*, 5–122. Tokyo: Chikuma shobō, 1989.

Kamisaka Fuyuko. *Rekishi wa nejimagerarenai*. Tokyo: Kodansha, 1997.

Kaneko Masaru, Takahashi Tetsurō, and Yamaguchi Jirō. *Gurōbarizēshon to sensō sekinin*. Iwanami booklet, no. 530. Tokyo: Iwanami shoten, 2001.

Kanki Haruo, ed. *Sankō: Nihonjin no Chūgoku ni okeru sensō hanzai no kokuhaku*. Tokyo: Kōbunsha, 1957.

Kasahara Chizu. "Sensō hanzai to sensō sekinin." *Nihon to Chūgoku*, 11 November 1956.

Kasahara Tokushi. *Nankin jiken*. Iwanami shinsho 530. Tokyo: Iwanami shoten, 1997.

————. *Nankin jiken to Nihonjin: Sensō no kioku o meguru nashonarizumu to gurōbarizumu*. Tokyo: Kashiwa shobō, 2002.

Kataoka Tetsuya. "The Revisionists and Their Vision." In *The Price of a Constitution: The Origin of Japan's Postwar Politics*, 129–63. New York: Russak, 1991.

Katō Norihiro. *Haisengoron*. Tokyo: Kōdansha, 1997.

Katō Norihiro, Hashizume Daisaburō, and Takeda Seiji. *Tennō no sensō sekinin*. Tokyo: Komichi shobō, 2000.

Katō Shūichi. *Sengo sedai no sensō sekinin*. Kamogawa booklet. Kyōto: Kamogawa shuppan, 1994.

————. *Sensō sekinin no ukekata: Doitsu to Nihon*. Bukkuretto ikiru. Tokyo: Adobanteiji sābā, 1993.

Katsumata Seiichi. "Nitchū yūkō kaigi keizai bumon hōkoku." *Nihon to Chūgoku*, 1 September 1950.

Katsuta Shūichi. "Kyōiku no fukko to fukkō." *Kyōiku hyōron* (October 1952): 5–7.

Katzenstein, Peter J., and Takashi Shiraishi. "Conclusion: Regions in World Politics: Japan and Asia—Germany in Europe." In *Network Power: Japan and Asia*, edited by Peter J. Katzenstein and Takashi Shiraishi, 341–82. Ithaca and London: Cornell University Press, 1997.

Kawada Hisashi. "Kyōin kumiai ron." *Atarashii kyōiku to bunka* (January 1949): 4–11.

Kawaguchi Emiko. *Sensō mibōjin: higai to kagai no hazama de*. Tokyo: Domesu shuppan, 2003.

Kawai, Kazuo. *Japan's American Interlude*. Chicago: University of Chicago Press, 1960; Chicago: Midway Reprints, 1979.

Kaya Okinori. "Seinenbu ni kitai suru." *Nihon izoku tsūshin*, 1 Mar. 1968.

Kelly, William W. "Finding a Place in Metropolitan Japan." In *Postwar Japan as History*, edited by Andrew Gordon, 189–238. Berkeley: University of California Press, 1993.

Kersten, Rikki. *Democracy in Postwar Japan: Maruyama Masao and the Search for Autonomy*. New York: Routledge, 1996.

Kike wadatsumi no koe henshū iinkai. *Kike wadatsumi no koe: Nihon senbotsu gakusei no tegami*. Tokyo: Tōdai kyōdō kumiai shuppanbu, 1949.

Kim Hyun Sook. "History and Memory: The 'Comfort Women' Controversy." *Positions* 5, no. 1 (1997): 73–106.

Kim Sam-kyu. "A Korean View of Ratification." *Japan Quarterly* 12, no. 4 (1965): 445–543.

Kimijima Kazuhiko. "The Continuing Legacy of Japanese Colonialism: The Japan–South Korea Joint Study Group on History Textbooks." In *Censoring History: Citizenship and Memory in Japan, Germany, and the United States*, edited by Laura Hein and Mark Selden, 203–25. Armonk, NY: M.E. Sharpe, 2000.

Kinoshita Junji. *Between God and Man: A Judgment on War Crimes*. Translated by Eric J. Gangloff. Tokyo: University of Tokyo Press, 1979.

Kisa Yoshio. *"Sensō sekinin" to wa nani ka*. Tokyo: Chūō kōron shinsha, 2001.

Kitagawa Kenzō. "Haisengo no izoku undō to sensō mibōjin." In *Senryōki no genron: shuppan to bunka*, edited by Purange bunko ten kirokushū henshū iinkai, 126–45. Tokyo: Waseda daigaku, Ritsumeikan daigaku, 2000.

———. *Sengo no shuppatsu: Bunka dantai, seinendan, sensō mibōjin*. Tokyo: Aoki shoten, 2000.

Kobayashi Yoshinori. *Sensō*. Tokyo: Gentosha, 1998.

Kobori Keiichiro. "A Letter of Gratitude to the War Dead." *Japan Echo* 11 (special issue, 1984): 38–45.

Kojima Noboru. *Tennō to sensō sekinin*. Tokyo: Bungei shunjūsha, 1988.

Kokuritsu kokkai toshokan chōsa rippō kōsa kyoku. *Yasukuni jinja mondai shiryōshū*, vol. 76-2. Research Material Series. Tokyo: Research and Legislative Reference Department, National Diet Library, 1976.

Kokusai fōramu jikkō iinkai. *Sengo hoshō o kangaeru*, vol. 6: *Ajia no koe*. Tokyo: Tōhō shuppan, 1992.

"Kokusai shinpojiumu no kiroku" henshū iinkai. *"Kako no kokufuku" to shinsō kyūmei: Nichibeikan de susumu rekishi jijitsu chōsa*. Tokyo: Kinohanasha, 2002.

Komatsu Setsurō. "Bunkashugi no kokufuku." *Atarashii kyōiku to bunka* (June 1948): 2–7.

Komori Yōichi and Takahashi Tetsuya, eds. *Nashonaru hisutorii o koete*. Tokyo: Tōkyō daigaku shuppankai, 1998.

Kōriyama Yuki. "Iyana Nihon." *Nihon izoku kōsei renmei kaihō*, 25 December 1949.

Koschmann, J. Victor. "Asianism's Ambivalent Legacy." In *Network Power: Japan and Asia*, edited by Peter J. Katzenstein and Takashi Shiraishi, 83–110. Ithaca: Cornell University Press, 1997.

———. "Intellectuals and Politics." In *Postwar Japan as History*, edited by Andrew Gordon, 395–423. Berkeley: University of California Press, 1993.

———. "Mao Zedong and the Postwar Japanese Left." In *Critical Perspectives on Mao Zedong's Thought*, edited by Paul Healy, Arif Dirlik, and Nick Knight, 342–64. Atlantic Highlands: Humanities Press International, 1997.

———. "Maruyama Masao and the Incomplete Project of Modernity." In *Postmodernism and Japan*, edited by Masao Miyoshi and H. D. Harootunian, 123–42. Durham: Duke University Press, 1989.

———. *Revolution and Subjectivity in Postwar Japan*. Chicago: University of Chicago Press, 1996.

———, ed. *Authority and the Individual in Japan: Citizen Protest in Historical Perspective*. Tokyo: University of Tokyo Press, 1978.

Kōseishō shakai engo kyoku. *Engo gojūnenshi*. Tokyo: Gyōsei, 1997.

Koyama Hiromitsu. "Anpo hantai undō no naka de." *Wadatsumi no koe*, no. 4 (1960): 11–15.

Krauss, Ellis S. "Review Essay: Authority and the Individual in Japan." *Journal of Japanese Studies* 7, no. 1 (1981): 165–80.

Kurahashi Masanao. *Jūgun ianfu mondai no rekishiteki kenkyū*. Tokyo: Kyōei shobō, 1994.

Kyōkasho kenkyū kyōgikai jimukyoku. "Iwayuru 'Nikkyōso no kyōkasho' o megutte." *Atarashii kyōiku to bunka* (August 1948): 36–41.

Lee, Benjamin. "Going Public." *Public Culture* 5 (1993): 165–78.

Li, Fei Fei, Robert Sabella, and David Liu, eds. *Nanking 1937: Memory and Healing*. Armonk, NY: M.E. Sharpe, 2002.

Lie, John, ed. *The Impoverished Spirit in Contemporary Japan: Selected Essays of Honda Katsuichi*. New York: Monthly Review Press, 1993.

Lokowandt, Ernst. *Zum Verhältnis von Staat und Shinto im heutigen Japan*. Wiesbaden: Otto Harrassowitz, 1981.

Maeda Tetsuo. *PKO: Sono sōzōteki kanōsei*. Iwanami booklet, no. 221. Tokyo: Iwanami shoten, 1991.

Maier, Charles S. *The Unmasterable Past: History, Holocaust, and German National Identity*. Cambridge, MA: Harvard University Press, 1988.

Mainichi shinbunsha. *Sengo gojūnen: Postwar 50 Years*. Tokyo: Mainichi shinbunsha, 1995.

Maruyama Hisashi. *Minikomi sengoshi: jānarizumu no genten o motomete*. Tokyo: San'ichi shobō, 1985.

Maruyama Masao. "Sensō sekinin nitsuite (zadankai)." *Shisō no kagaku kaihō* 17 (March 1957): 205–6.

———. "Theory and Psychology of Ultra-Nationalism." In *Thought and Behaviour in Modern Japanese Politics*, edited by Ivan Morris, 84–134. London: Oxford University Press, 1963 (orig. 1949).

Masamura Kimihiro. "Writing Finis to the Postwar Period." *Japan Quarterly* 32, no. 3 (1985): 261–65.

Mashita Shin'ichi. "Shinario 'Kike wadatsumi no koe' o yonda kansō." In *Kike wadatsumi no koe* (booklet). Tokyo: Nihon senbotsu gakusei kinenkai, 1986 (orig. 1950).

Mason, Robert J. "Whither Japan's Environmental Movement? An Assessment of Problems and Prospects at the National Level." *Pacific Affairs* 72, no. 2 (1999): 187–207.

Matsueda, Tsukasa, and George E. Moore. "Japan's Shifting Attitudes toward the Military: *Mitsuya kenkyū* and the Self-Defense Force." *Asian Survey* 7 (1967): 614–25.

Matsui Yayori. "The Aims of the Women's International War Crimes Tribunal on Japan's Military Sexual Slavery 2000." Paper presented at the Conference on "Contested Historiography: Feminist Perspectives on World War II," German Institute for Japanese Studies, Tokyo, 14 April 2000.

Matsushita Keichi. "Citizen Participation in Historical Perspective." In *Authority and the Individual in Japan: Citizen Protest in Historical Perspective*, edited by J. Victor Koschmann, 171–88. Tokyo: University of Tokyo Press, 1978 (orig. 1971).

McCormack, Gavan. *The Emptiness of Japanese Affluence*. Armonk, NY: M.E. Sharpe, 1996.

———. "The Japanese Movement to 'Correct' History." In *Censoring History: Citizenship and Memory in Japan, Germany, and the United States*, edited by Laura Hein and Mark Selden, 53–73. Armonk, NY: M.E. Sharpe, 2000.

McKean, Margaret A. *Environmental Protest and Citizen Politics in Japan*. Berkeley, CA: University of California Press, 1981.

Minear, Richard H. *Victors' Justice: The Tokyo War Crimes Trial*. Rutland and Tokyo: Tuttle Books, 1971.

Minow, Martha. *Between Vengeance and Forgiveness: Facing History after Genocide and Mass Violence*. Boston: Beacon Press, 1998.

Mishima Hajime. "'Shina' to 'Chūgoku.'" *Nihon to Chūgoku* (February 1950): 2.

Mishima Ken'ichi. "Nichidoku sengo gojūnen no sawagi no ato de." *Sekai* (February 1996): 22–33.

Mitscherlich, Alexander, and Margarete Mitscherlich. *The Inability to Mourn*. Translated by Beverly R. Placzek. Preface by Robert Jay Lifton. New York: Grove Press, 1975.

Mitsui Taketomo. "Mohaya damatte wa irarenai: Yasukuni jinja to Meiji hyakunen." *Wadatsumi no koe*, no. 44 (1968): 25–31.

Mitsuoka Kenjirō. *Nihon no rikujō bōei senryaku to sono tokusei.* Tokyo: Kyōikusha, 1979.

Miyahara Seiichi. "The Japan Teachers' Union and Its Code of Ethics." *Journal of Social and Political Ideas in Japan* 1, no. 3 (1963): 129–31.

Miyanohara Sadamitsu. "Heiwa no kyōiku no kiki ni saishite." *Kyōiku hyōron* (March 1968): 10–13.

Mobius, J. Mark. "The Japan-Korea Normalization Process and Korean Anti-Americanism." *Asian Survey* (April 1966): 241–48.

Mochida Yukio. *Futatsu no kindai.* Tokyo: Asahi sensho, 1988.

———. "Sensō sekinin, sengo sekinin ni miru Doitsu to Nihon." *Sensō sekinin kenkyū* 6 (Winter 1994): 2–7.

———. *Sensō sekinin to sengo sekinin: sofu no tsumi o mago ga tsugunau no ka.* Kamogawa booklet, no. 77. Kyoto: Kamogawa shuppan, 1994.

Molasky, Michael S. *The American Occupation of Japan and Okinawa: Literature and Memory.* London and New York: Routledge, 1999.

Morimura Seiichi. *Akuma no hōshoku.* Tokyo: Kōbunsha kappa bukkusu, 1981.

———. *Zoku akuma no hōshoku.* Tokyo: Kōbunsha kappa bukkusu, 1982.

Morimura Seiichi and Ikebe Shin'ichirō. "Nihon Chūgoku yūkō kyōkai sōritsu yonjūnen kinen biggu taiwa: Morimura Seiichi vs. Ikebe Shin'ichirō (1)." *Nitchū yūkō shinbun*, 25 August 1990.

———. "Nihon Chūgoku yūkō kyōkai sōritsu yonjūnen kinen biggu taiwa: Morimura Seiichi vs. Ikebe Shin'ichirō (2)." *Nitchū yūkō shinbun*, 5 September 1990.

Morita Shunsuke. "Nihon izoku kōsei renmei no ninmu nitsuite." *Nihon izoku kōsei renmei kaihō*, 10 February 1949.

Morris, Ivan I. *Nationalism and the Right Wing in Japan: A Study of Post-War Trends.* London: Oxford University Press, 1960.

Morris-Suzuki, Tessa. "Free Speech—Silenced Voices: The Japanese Media, the Comfort Women Tribunal, and the NHK Affair." *ZNet Japan Focus*, 15 August 2005, http://www.zmag.org/content/showarticle.cfm?SectionID=17&ItemID=8514.

———. *The Past Within Us: Media, Memory, History.* London: Verso, 2005.

———. *Re-Inventing Japan: Time, Space, Nation.* Armonk, NY: M.E. Sharpe, 1998.

———. "Unquiet Graves: Katō Norihiro and the Politics of Mourning." *Japanese Studies* 18, no. 1 (1998): 21–30.

Mukae, Ryuji. "Japan's Diet Resolution on World War Two: Keeping History at Bay." *Asian Survey* 36 (1996): 1011–30.

Munakata Seiya. "Watashi wa iwayuru 'Anpo kyōiku taisei' ni tsuite." *Kyōiku hyōron* (January 1969): 14–19.

Murakami Shigeyoshi. *Irei to shōkon: Yasukuni no shisō*. Tokyo: Iwanami shoten, 1974.

———. *Japanese Religion in the Modern Century*. Translated by H. Byron Earhart. Tokyo: University of Tokyo Press, 1980.

———. *Yasukuni jinja*. Iwanami booklet. Tokyo: Iwanami shoten, 1988.

Muramatsu Takashi. "Okinawa henkan o dō toraeru ka." *Kyōiku hyōron* (June 1971): 10–15.

Murray, Stephen C. "War and Remembrance on Peleliu: Islander, Japanese, and American Memories of a Battle in the Pacific War." Ph.D. diss., University of California at Santa Barbara, 2006.

Mutō Mitsurō. "Minshushugiteki jiyū o mamoru michi: sayū no dokusai shugi no keikai se yo." *Nihon izoku tsūshin*, 31 May 1960.

Nagai Kiyohiko. "Waitsusekka enzetsu ni gyakufū tsunoru." *Sekai* (July 1987): 15–18.

———. *Waitsusekka no seishin*. Tokyo: Iwanami shoten, 1991.

Nagatomi Hiroyuki. "Ikita rekishi o kataru: Akumu no Nankin daigyakusatsu." *Nitchū yūkō shinbun*, 31 July 1967.

Naka Torata. "Kyōin kumiai to kyōikukai no minshuka." *Atarashii kyōiku to bunka* (April 1949): 37–41.

Nakamura Katsurō. *Ani no kage o otte: takasareta "Wadatsumi no koe."* Iwanami booklet, no. 370. Tokyo: Iwanami shoten, 1995.

———. "Yasukuni mondai o kangaeru." *Wadatsumi no koe*, no. 58 (1974): 28–29.

Nakashima Michio. "Seiji handō ni okeru shūkyō kyōdan no yakuwari." In *Sengoshi to handō ideorogii*, edited by Yamaguchi Keiji and Matsuo Sōichi, 142–82. Tokyo: Shin Nihon shuppansha, 1981.

Nakayama Tarō. *Futatsu no haisen kokka: Nihon to Doitsu no gojūnen*. Tokyo: Yomiuri shinbunsha, 1995.

Nanbara Shigeru. "Taii no mondai." In *Nanbara Shigeru chosakushū*, vol. 9. Tokyo: Iwanami shoten, 1973 (orig. 16 Dec. 1946).

Nanpō dōhō engokai. *Okinawa fukki no kiroku*. Tokyo: Nanpō dōhō engokai, 1972.

Nelson, John. *Enduring Identities: The Guise of Shinto in Contemporary Japan*. Honolulu: University of Hawaii Press, 2000.

———. "Shifting Paradigms of Religion and the State: Implications of the 1997 Supreme Court Decision for Social, Religious and Political Change." *Modern Asian Studies* 33, no. 4 (1999): 797–814.

———. "Social Memory as Ritual Practice: Commemorating Spirits of the Military Dead at Yasukuni Shinto Shrine." *Journal of Asian Studies* 62, no. 2 (2003): 443–67.

Nihon chūgoku yūkō kyōkai. *Nitchū yūkō undō no hanseiki: sono ayumi to shashin.* Tokyo: Keyaki shuppan, 2000.

———. *Shōgen: Chūgokujin kyōsei renkō.* Video guidebook, 1995.

Nihon Chūgoku yūkō kyōkai zenkoku honbu. *Nihon Chūgoku yūkō kyōkai undōshi.* Tokyo: Shōnen shuppansha, 1980.

Nihon heiwa gakkai. *Shimin, NGO undō to heiwa.* Tokyo: Waseda daigaku shuppanbu, 1989.

Nihon izokukai. *Ishizue: senbotsusha izoku no taiken kiroku.* Tokyo: Nihon izokukai jimukyoku, 1963.

———. *Nihon izokukai fujinbu yonjūnen.* Tokyo: Nihon izokukai jimukyoku, 1995.

———. *Nihon izokukai jūgonenshi.* Tokyo: Nihon izokukai jimukyoku, 1962.

Nihon kirisutosha heiwa no kai. *Kirisutosha no senso sekinin to heiwa undō.* Kamogawa, no. 44. Kyoto: Kamogawa shuppan, 1991.

Nihon kyōshokuin kumiai. "Heiwa apiiru." *Kyōiku hyōron* (July 1965): 43.

———. *Nikkyōso jūnenshi.* Tokyo: Dai Nihonin kabushiki kaisha, 1958.

———. *Nikkyōso nijūnen shiryō.* Tokyo: Rōdō junpōsha, 1970.

———. *Nikkyōso sanjūnenshi.* Tokyo: Rōdō kyōiku sentā, 1977.

———. *Nikkyōso yonjūnen shiryōshū: 1970 nen–1985 nen.* Tokyo: Rōdō kyōiku sentā, 1988.

———. *Nikkyōso gojūnenshi.* Tokyo: Rōdō kyōiku sentā, 1997.

Nihon no sensō sekinin shiryō sentā jimukyoku. "Kaiin ni natte kudasai." Pamphlet. Nihon no sensō sekinin shiryō sentā, 1993.

Nihon o mamoru kokumin kaigi. *Manshū jihen, Shina jihen, Nichibei sensō o konponteki ni tōinaosu: Nihon wa shinryaku kokka de wa nai,* vol. 2: *Daitōa sensō.* Tokyo: Nihon o mamoru kokumin kaigi, 1994.

Nihon senbotsu gakusei kinenkai. "Dai gokai shinpojium hōsoku: minzoku to sensō taiken—dainiji taisen ka no kaku kokumin." *Wadatsumi no koe,* no. 24 (1964): 20–33.

———. *Gakutō shutsujin.* Tokyo: Iwanami shoten, 1993.

———. "Hearkening to the Voices of Millions of War Victims: In Protest of the State Funeral for the Late Showa Tenno." In *Ima koso tou tennōsei: ikusenman sensō giseisha no koe ni kikitsutsu,* edited by Nihon senbotsu gakusei kinenkai, 242–245. Tokyo: Chikuma shobō, 1989.

———. *Ima koso tou tennōsei.* Tokyo: Chikuma shobō, 1989.

———. *Kike wadatsumi no koe.* Tokyo: Iwanami shoten, 1988.

———. "'Kike wadatsumi no koe' ni tsuite (orig. 1950)." In *Kike wadatsumi no koe* (booklet), edited by Nihon senbotsu gakusei kinenkai. Tokyo: Nihon senbotsu gakusei kinenkai jigyōkyoku, 1986.

———. *"Kike, Wadatsumi no koe" Nihon senbotsu gakusei no shuki—eiga no tebiki.* Tokyo: Zenkoku daigaku seikatsu kyōdō kumiai rengōkai, 1995.

————. "Minzoku to heiwa: Meiji hyakunen to wareware no tachiba." *Wadatsumi no koe*, no. 41 (1967): 1–26.

————. "Nihon senbotsu gakusei no shuki: 'Kike wadatsumi no koe' shinario (orig. 1950)." In *Kike wadatsumi no koe* (booklet), edited by Nihon senbotsu gakusei kinenkai, 7–25. Tokyo: Nihon senbotsu gakusei kinenkai, 1986.

————. *Peace! Peace! Peace! Watashitachi ni senso sekinin wa nai no ka*. Tokyo: Jōkyō shuppan, 1995.

————. "Seimei: Yasukuni jinja hōan haizetsu o negau (20 May 1974)." *Wadatsumi no koe*, no. 58 (1974): 1–3.

————. *Tennōsei o toitsuzukeru*. Tokyo: Chikuma shobō, 1978.

Nishi Toshio. *Unconditional Democracy: Education and Politics in Occupied Japan 1945–1952*. Stanford: Hoover Institution Press, 1982.

Nishi Yoshiyuki. *Han'ei Nishi-Doitsu ga ochita wana: Nihon wa hontō ni daijōbu ka*. Tokyo: Kōbunsha, 1988.

Nishida Masaru et al. *Ajia kara mita Nagasaki higai to kagai*. Iwanami booklet, no. 157. Tokyo: Iwanami shoten, 1990.

Nishio Kanji. "Doitsu no shūsen kinenbi." *Voice* (Sep. 1995): 45–47.

————. *Kotonaru higeki: Nihon to Doitsu*. Tokyo: Bungei shunjūsha, 1994.

————. "'Nihon no tomo': Shumitto zen Nishidoku daitōryō ni hanmon suru." *Chūō kōron* (July 1988): 190–203.

Norgren, Tiana. *Abortion before Birth Control: The Politics of Reproduction in Postwar Japan*. Princeton: Princeton University Press, 2001.

Nozaki, Yoshiko, and Hiromitsu Inokuchi. "Japanese Education, Nationalism, and Ienaga Saburo's Textbook Lawsuits." In *Censoring History: Citizenship and Memory in Japan, Germany, and the United States*, edited by Laura Hein and Mark Selden, 96–126. Armonk, NY: M.E. Sharpe, 2000.

O'Brien, David M., and Yasuo Ohkoshi. *To Dream of Dreams: Religious Freedom and Constitutional Politics in Postwar Japan*. Honolulu: University of Hawai'i Press, 1996.

Oda Makoto. "The Ethics of Peace." In *Authority and the Individual in Japan: Citizen Protest in Historical Perspective*, edited by J. Victor Koschmann, 154–70. Tokyo: University of Tokyo Press, 1978.

————. *Nishi Berurin de mita koto, Nihon de kangaeta koto*. Tokyo: Mainichi shinbunsha, 1988.

————. "Rikaishi, yurusuna: Sengo gojūnen, rekishi no bunkiten ni tatte." *Wadatsumi no koe*, no. 99 (1994): 1–15.

Odagiri Hideo. "Nihon no wakaku atarashii sedai ni." *Wadatsumi no koe*, 25 November 1951.

Ōe Kenzaburō. "A Portrait of the Postwar Generation." *Japan Quarterly* 12, no. 3 (March 1965): 147–351.

Ōe Shinobu. *Yasukuni jinja.* Tokyo: Iwanami shoten, 1984.

Office of Intelligence Research. "Japanese Sentiment for Release of War Criminals." 1–4. Washington, DC: Department of State, 1956.

Ogata Sadako. "Japanese Attitude toward China." *Asian Survey* 5 (1965): 389–98.

Ōgoshi Aiko. "'Rekishi shutai ronsō' o koeru—jendāka shita shisō sen." In *Sensō sekinin to wareware: "Rekishi shutai ronsō" o megutte,* edited by Abiko Kazuyoshi and Uozumi Yōichi, 142–67. Kyoto: Nakanishiya shuppan, 1999.

———. "Zange no neuchi mo nai." In *Nashonaru historii o koete,* edited by Komori Yōichi and Takahashi Tetsuya, 123–40. Tokyo: Tōkyō daigaku shuppankai, 1998.

Oka Saburō. "Sōkan ni yosete." *Kyōiku hyōron* (December 1951): 5.

Okada Hiroyuki. "Shōshi: Wadatsumi kai no undō 1950–58." In *Wadatsumi no koe shukusatsuban* (1950–58). Tokyo: Nihon senbotsu gakusei kinenkai, 1991.

Okamoto, Kōichi. "Beyond Dichotomy: Kato Norihiro and Historical Discourse after the 50th Anniversary of the End of World War II." *Waseda Journal of Asian Studies* 23 (2002): 65–78.

———. "Changing Discourse: A Review of Yoshida Yutaka *Gendai rekishigaku to sensō sekinin* [Studies of Contemporary History and War Responsibility]." *Waseda Journal of Asian Studies* 19 (1999): 57–67.

———. "Imaginary Settings: Sino-Japanese-U.S. Relations during the Occupation Years." Ph.D. diss., Columbia University, 2000.

———. "Re-Contextualizing History: American Views of World War II and the Occupation of Japan." *Waseda Journal of Asian Studies* 21 (1999): 57–70.

———. "'Senshō gojusshūnen' to 'sengo gojūnen.'" *Sensō sekinin kenkyū* 11 (March 1996): 32–35, 87.

Okamoto Shigenori. "'Sabetsu' no mondai o tsūjite kangaeru Okinawa: fuku yomihon 'Ningen' o meguru mondai." *Kyōiku hyōron* (June 1971): 30–33.

Okazaki Hisahiko. "A Generation Lost in History." *The Japan Times,* 5 November 1996.

Okinawa Times. *Okinawa sengo shi 1945–1998: Shashin rikoku.* Naha: Okinawa Times, Ltd., 1998.

Ōkuma Nobuyuki. *Sensō sekininron.* Tokyo: Yuijinsha, 1948.

Olick, Jeffrey. In the *House of the Hangman: The Agonies of German Defeat, 1943–1949.* Chicago: University of Chicago Press, 2005.

———. "What Does It Mean to Normalize the Past?" *Social Science History* 22, no. 4 (1998): 547–71.

Olson, Lawrence. *Ambivalent Moderns: Portraits of Japanese Cultural Identity.* Savage: Rowman & Littlefield Publishers, 1992.

Omori Shigeo. "Controversy between Government and Opposition Parties." *Japan Quarterly* 15, no. 1 (1968): 22–29.

―――. "June 1970." *Japan Quarterly* 17, no. 4 (1970): 383–92.

Ōnuma Yasuaki. "Beyond Victors' Justice." *Japan Echo* 11 (special issue, 1984): 63–72.

―――. "Nihon no sensō sekinin to sengo sekinin." *Kokusai mondai* (December 2001): 62–81.

―――. *Saharin kimin: sengo sekinin no tenkei.* Tokyo: Chūkō shinsho, 1992.

―――. *Sensō sekininron josetsu.* Tokyo: Tōkyō daigaku shuppankai, 1975.

―――. "The Tokyo War Crimes Trial, War Responsibility, and Postwar Responsibility." In *Nanking 1937: Memory and Healing*, edited by Fei Fei Li, Robert Sabella, and David Liu, 205–235. Armonk, NY: M.E. Sharpe, 2002.

―――. "Tōkyō saiban, sensō sekinin, sengo sekinin." In *Tōkyō saiban kara sengo sekinin no shisō e*, 145–204. Tokyo: Tōshindō, 1987.

Ōnuma Yasuaki, Shimomura Mitsuko, and Wada Haruki, eds. *"Ianfu" mondai to Ajia josei kikin.* Tokyo: Toshindo, 2000.

Orr, James J. *The Victim as Hero: Ideologies of Peace and National Identity in Postwar Japan.* Honolulu: University of Hawai'i Press, 2001.

Osawa Masamichi. *Sengo ga sengo de nakunaru toki.* Tokyo: Chūō kōronsha, 1995.

Ōshio Seinosuke. *Yurusarete ikiru: sensō sekinin, kokuhaku no michi.* Tokyo: Nihon kirisutokyōdan shuppankyoku, 1989.

Osiel, Mark. *Mass Atrocity, Collective Memory, and the Law.* New Brunswick: Transaction Publishers, 1997.

Ōta Masahide. "Okinawa no shiseiken henkan to 'Nihonjin kyōiku.'" *Kyōiku hyōron* (April 1969): 12–17.

―――. "War Memories Die Hard in Okinawa." *Japan Quarterly* 35, no. 1 (1988): 9–16.

Ōta Masahide and Ikezawa Natsuki. *Okinawa kara hajimaru.* Tokyo: Shūeisha, 1998.

Ōtake Hideo. *Adenaua to Yoshida Shigeru.* Tokyo: Chūō kōronsha, 1986.

Ozawa Ichirō. *Blueprint for a New Japan.* Tokyo, New York: Kodansha International, 1994.

Park Soon-Won. "Japanese Reparations Policies and the 'Comfort Women' Question." *Positions* 5, no. 1 (1997): 107–34.

―――. "The Politics of Remembrance: The Case of Korean Forced Laborers in World War II." In *Rethinking Historical Injustice in Northeast Asia: The Korean Experience in Regional Perspective*, edited by Soon-Won Park et al. London and New York: Routledge, forthcoming.

Pearson, Richard. "The Place of Okinawa in Japanese Historical Identity." In *Multicultural Japan: Palaeolitic to Postmodern*, edited by Mark Hudson, Donald

Denoon, Gavan McCormack, and Tessa Morris-Suzuki, 95–116. Cambridge, UK: Cambridge University Press, 1996.

Pempel, T. J. "Prerequisites for Democracy: Political and Social Institutions." In *Democracy in Japan*, edited by Takeshi Ishida and Ellis S. Krauss, 17–38. Pittsburgh: University of Pittsburgh Press, 1989.

Pennington, Lee. "Wartorn Japan: Disabled Veterans and Society, 1931–1952." Ph.D. diss., Columbia University, 2005.

Platt, Kristin, and Mihran Dabag, eds. *Generation und Gedächtnis: Erinnerungen und kollektive Identitäten.* Opladen: Leske und Budrich, 1995.

Powles, Cyril. "Yasukuni Jinja Hoan: Religion and Politics in Contemporary Japan." *Pacific Affairs* 49 (1976): 491–505.

Rekishi kyōikusha kyōgikai. *Heiwa hakubutsukan sensō shiryōkan gaidobukku (shinpan).* Tokyo: Aoki shoten, 2000.

Rekishigaku kenkyūkai. *Sengo gojūnen o dō miru ka.* Tokyo: Aoki shoten, 1995.

———. *Sengo rekishigaku saikō.* Tokyo: Aoki shoten, 2000.

Rōdō kyōiku sentā. *Nikkyōso yonjūnenshi shiryō hen.* Tokyo: Rōdō junpōsha, 1989.

Rose, Caroline. *Interpreting History in Sino-Japanese Relations.* London and New York: Routledge, 1998.

Ruoff, Jeffrey, and Kenneth Ruoff. *The Emperor's Naked Army Marches On: Yukiyukite shingun.* Wiltshire: Flicks Books, 1998.

Ruoff, Kenneth J. *The People's Emperor: Democracy and the Japanese Monarchy, 1945–1995.* Cambridge, MA: Harvard University Asia Center, 2001.

Saaler, Sven. *Politics, Memory and Public Opinion: The History Textbook Controversy and Japanese Society.* Deutsches Institut für Japanstudien, vol. 39. Munich: Iudicium Verlag, 2005.

Saeki Shōichi. "Shintō fukkō wa kanō ka." *Jinja honchō kyōgaku kenkyūjo* 3 (20 Feb. 1998): 267–85.

Saito Masahiko. "Nikkyōso no Okinawa tōsō: sono keika to tenbō." *Kyōiku hyōron* (August 1968): 33–35.

Sakamoto Ken'ichi. "Meiji hyakunen ni omou." *Jinja shinpō*, 19 and 26 Mar. 1966.

Sakanaka Tomohisa. "The Present Status of the Okinawa Reversion Movement." *Japan Quarterly* 15, no. 1 (1968): 30–41.

Sasaki-Uemura, Wesley. *Organizing the Spontaneous: Citizen Protest in Postwar Japan.* Honolulu: Hawaii University Press, 2001.

Satō Kensei (Takeo). "Doitsu no sengo shori o megutte (1): Doitsu gendaishi ni okeru baishō to hoshō—futatsu no sekai taisen to Doitsu." *Sensō sekinin kenkyū* 1, no. 1 (1993): 40–46.

————. "Doitsu no sengo shori o megutte (2): 'Kokumin tsuitōbi' no rekishiteki imi—futatsu no sekai taisen to senbotsusha no tsuitō." *Sensō sekinin kenkyū* 1, no. 2 (1993): 68–75.

————. "Doitsu no sengo shori, Nihon no mohan ka?" *Sekai* (February 1991), 296–309.

————. "Nihon to Doitsu no rekishi no kyōkun: watashitachi no nasubeki koto." *Rekishi hyōron* (June 1992): 50–57.

————. "Nihon to Doitsu: 'kako' ni tsuite no aratana kyokumen." *Sekai* (November 1994): 97–104.

————. "Nishi-Doitsu ni okeru 'kako no kokufuku' mondai: sensō sekinin, sengo sekinin, soshite ima." *Rekishi hyōron* (August 1988): 26–39.

————. "Sengo shori ni okeru doitsu to Nihon: Nani ga konponteki ni chigau no ka." *Sensō sekinin kenkyū* 3 (Spring 1994): 69–74.

Satō Nobuo. *Rekishi kyōiku to sensō sekinin.* Tokyo: Azumino shobō, 1988.

Scalapino, Robert A. *The Japanese Communist Movement, 1920–1966.* Berkeley: University of California Press, 1967.

Schlant, Ernestine, and J. Thomas Rimer, eds. *Legacies and Ambiguities: Postwar Fiction and Culture in West Germany and Japan.* Washington and Baltimore: Woodrow Wilson Center Press and Johns Hopkins University Press, 1991.

Schwartz, Frank J., and Susan J. Pharr, eds. *The State of Civil Society in Japan.* Cambridge, UK: Cambridge University Press, 2003.

Seraphim, Franziska. "The Debate about War Responsibility in Early Postwar Japan." M.A. thesis, Columbia University, 1992.

————. "Der Zweite Weltkrieg im öffentlichen Gedächtnis Japans: Die Debatte zum fünfzigsten Jahrestag der Kapitulation." In *Überwindung der Moderne? Japan am Ende des zwanzigsten Jahrhunderts,* edited by Irmela Hijiya-Kirschnereit, 25–56. Frankfurt/M: Edition Suhrkamp, 1996.

————. "Im Dialog mit den Kriegstoten: Erinnerungspolitik zwischen Nationalismus und Pazifismus." *Periplus: Jahrbuch für aussereuropäische Geschichte* 11 (2001): 12–25.

————. "Kriegsverbrecherprozesse in Asien und globale Erinnerungskulturen." In Christoph Cornelissen, Lutz Klinkhammer, and Wolfgang Schwentker, eds. *Erinnerungskulturen: Deutschland, Italien, und Japan seit 1945.* Frankfurt am Main: Fischer Verlag, 2003.

Shakai hoshō kenkyūjo. *Nihon shakai hoshō shiryō,* vol. 1. Tokyo: Shiseidō, 1975.

Shakai kyoku rinji gunji engo bu. *Shōi gunjin oyobi gunjin izoku no hogo seido gaiyō.* Collection of Kizokuin jimukyoku chōsaka. Tokyo: Daiichi insatsujo, 1938.

Shakai shinri kenkyūjo. *Shōwa bunka 1945–1989.* 2 vols. Tokyo: Keiso shobō, 1990.

Shakai undō chosakai. *Sayoku dantai jiten.* Tokyo: Kyokutō shuppansha, 1966.

Shibukawa Ken'ichi. "Jinja shinpō haigo no hitobito." In *Jinja shinpō senshū hōi*, 17–31. Tokyo: Jinja shinpōsha, 1986.

Shimazu Naoko. "Popular Representations of the Past: The Case of Postwar Japan." *Journal of Contemporary History* 38, no. 1 (2003): 101–16.

Shimizu Hayao. "The War and Japan: Revisionist Views." *Japan Echo* 11 (special issue, 1984): 3–11.

Shinchōsha jiten henshūbu. *Shinchō Nihon jinmei jiten.* Tokyo: Shinchōsha, 1991.

Shintō seiji renmei. *Seisaku suishin no kadai o kangaeru.* Tokyo: Kabushiki gaisha bun'eisha, 1995.

———. *Shinjidai o koeta tenshitsu mondai no toraekata, Shinseiren katsudō taisaku shiriizu.* Tokyo: Kabushiki gaisha bun'eisha, 1993.

Shioda Shōbei, Hasegawa Masayasu, and Fujiwara Akira, eds. *Nihon sengoshi shiryō.* 2d ed. Tokyo: Shin Nihon shuppansha, 1995.

Smethurst, Richard J. "The Origins and Policies of the Japan Teachers' Union 1945–56." In *Studies in Japanese History and Politics*, edited by Richard K. Beardsley, 117–60. Ann Arbor: University of Michigan Press, 1967.

Smith, Kerry. "The Showa Hall: Memorializing Japan's War at Home." *Public Historian* 24, no. 4 (2002): 35–64.

Sodei Rinjirō. "Public History to wa nani ka: Smithsonian genbakuten to heiwa shinnenkan." *Sekai* (April 1995): 38–44.

Soh, Chunghee Sarah. "The Korean 'Comfort Women': Movement for Redress." *Asian Survey* 36 (1996): 1226–40.

Sone Yasunori. "Interest Groups and the Process of Political Decision-Making in Japan." In *Constructs for Understanding Japan*, edited by Yoshio Sugimoto and Ross E. Mouer, 259–95. London and New York: Kegan Paul International, 1989.

Suekawa Hiroshi. "Wadatsumizō no oshieru mono." *Wadatsumi no koe*, 13 June 1953.

Sugiyama Kyūshirō. "Facts and Fallacies about Yasukuni Shrine." *Japan Echo* 13, no. 2 (1986): 69–72.

Sumitani Takeshi et al., ed. *Tōkyō saiban handobukku.* Tokyo: Aoki shoten, 1989.

Suzuki Akira. *Nankin daigyakusatsu no maboroshi.* Tokyo: Bungei shunjū, 1973.

Suzuki Yūko. *Chōsenjin jūgun ianfu.* Iwanami booklet 229. Tokyo: Iwanami shoten, 1991.

———. *Jūgun ianfu naisen kekkon: sei no shinryaku, sengo sekinin o kangaeru.* Tokyo: Miraisha, 1992.

———. *Sensō sekinin to jendā: "Jiyū shugi shikan" to Nihongun "ianfu" mondai.* Tokyo: Miraisha, 1997.

Taguchi Hiroshi. "'Nichidoku heiwa fōramu' ni sanka shite." *Wadatsumi no koe*, no. 86 (1988): 42–45.

Taguchi Yasushi. "Kimura Hisao to BC kyū senpan saiban." *Wadatsumi no koe*, no. 94 (1992): 19–32.

Takabatake Michitoshi. "Citizens' Movements: Organizing the Spontaneous." In *Authority and the Individual in Japan: Citizen Protest in Historical Perspective*, edited by J. Victor Koschmann, 189–99. Tokyo: University of Tokyo Press, 1978.

Takagi Ken'ichi. *Jūgun ianfu to sengo hoshō: Nihon no sengo sekinin*. Tokyo: San'ichi shinsho, 1994.

———. *Saharin to Nihon no sengo sekinin*. Tokyo: Gaifusha, 1990.

———. *Saharin zanryū Chōsenjin mondai: Nihon no sengo sekinin*. Edited by Ōsaka jinken rekishi shiryōkan. Osaka: Ōsaka jinken rekishi shiryōkan, 1989.

Takagi Masayuki. "The Japanese Right Wing." *Japan Quarterly* 36, no. 3 (1989): 300–5.

———. "Right Wing Draws Public Attention." *Japan Quarterly* 27, no. 4 (1980): 479–86.

Takahashi Hikohiro. *Minshū no gawa no sensō sekinin*. Tokyo: Aoki shoten, 1989.

Takahashi Ryūtarō. "Wakai sedai no ikusei o kyōka." *Nihon izoku tsūshin*, 30 November 1958.

Takahashi Saburō. *'Senki mono' o yomu: sensō taiken to sengo Nihon shakai*. Tokyo: Akademia, 1988.

Takahashi Saburō et al. *Kyōdō kenkyū: Sen'yūkai*. Tokyo: Tabata shoten, 1983.

Takaishi Fumito, ed. *"Yasukuni" mondai kanren nenpyō*. Kyōto: Nagata bunshodō, 1990.

Takano Yūichi. "Okinawa no henkan to kyokutō no heiwa—sono hōteki chii o megutte." *Sekai* (August 1967): 18–32.

Takeyama Michio. "Questions on the Tokyo Trial." *Japan Echo* 11 (special issue, 1984): 55–62.

Tanabe Toshihiro, Ikeda Kōhei, and Miyano'o Bunpei. *Wadatsumi no shi, "Sensō to heiwa" shimin no kiroku 3*. Tokyo: Nihon tosho sentā, 1992.

Tanaka Hiroshi. "Nihon wa sensō sekinin ni dō taishite kita ka." *Sekai* (February 1994): 122–32.

Tanaka Nobumasa. "Nihon izokukai no gojūnen." *Sekai* (September 1994): 34–52.

———. "What Is the Yasukuni Problem?" *Japan in the World*, 24 May 2001. http://www.iwanami.co.jp/jpworld/text/yasukuni01.html.

———. *Yasukuni no sengoshi*. Tokyo: Iwanami shoten, 2003.

Tanaka Nobumasa, Tanaka Hiroshi, and Hata Nagami. *Izoku to sengo*. Tokyo: Iwanami shoten, 1995.

Tanaka Tadao. "Eirei seishin no keishō o: 'Kyō no seishōnen mondai.'" *Nihon izoku tsūshin*, 30 June 1959.

Tanaka, Yuki. *Hidden Horrors: Japanese War Crimes in World War II*. New York: Westview Press, 1996.

———. *Japan's Comfort Women: Sexual Slavery and Prostitution during World War II and the US Occupation*. London and New York: Routledge, 2002.

Teeuwen, Mark. "Jinja Honcho and Shrine Shinto Policy." *Japan Forum* 8, no. 2 (1996): 177–88.

Terasaki Hidenari and Mariko Terasaki Miller, eds. *Showa tennō dokuhakuroku— Terasaki Hidenari goyōgakari nikki*. Tokyo: Bungei shunjusha, 1991.

Thurston, Donald R. "The Decline of the Japan Teachers Union." *Journal of Contemporary Asia* 19, no. 2 (1989): 186–205.

———. *Teachers and Politics in Japan*. Princeton: Princeton University Press, 1973.

Tōdai yuibutsuron kenkyūkai and Gakusei shobō henshūbu. *Ikinokotta seinentachi no kiroku, "Sensō to heiwa" shimin no kiroku 20*. Tokyo: Nihon tosho sentā, 1992.

Tōei-Bandai sakuhin. *Kike wadatsumi no koe*. Booklet. Tokyo: Tōei eizōjigyōbu, 1995.

Tōkyō shinbun. *Owari naki sengo: shōgen to kiroku*. Tokyo booklet, no. 8. Tokyo: Tōkyō shinbun shuppankyoku, 1994.

Tōkyōto fukushikyoku seikatsu fukushibu engo fukushika. *Engo to irei no ayumi: sengo gojusshūnen kinen*. Tokyo: Gyōsei, 1995.

Tomiyama Taeko. *Sensō sekinin o uttaeru hitori tabi: London, Berlin, New York*. Iwanami booklet. Tokyo: Iwanami shoten, 1989.

Tomura Masahiro. *Nihonjin to Yasukuni mondai: Japanese People and the Question of Yasukuni*. Tokyo: Shinkyō shuppansha, 1971.

Torpey, John, ed. *Politics and the Past: On Repairing Historical Injustices*. Lanham, MD: Rowman & Littlefield, 2003.

Toyoda Shirō. "Nihon gunkokushugi no fukkatsu." *Wadatsumi no koe*, 20 April 1956.

Tsubouchi Yūzō. *Yasukuni*. Tokyo: Shinchōsha, 1999.

Tsubouchi Yūzō and Yoshida Tsukasa. "Yasukuni Shrine as a Symbol of Japan's Modernization." *Japan Echo* 26, no. 3 (1999): 48–51.

Tsuji Kunio, Tsutsumi Seiji, and Yasue Ryōsuke. *Sengo gojūnen o tou*. Nagano: Shinano mainichi shinbunsha, 1994.

Tsurumi Kazuko. "The War Tribunal: The Voice of the Dead." In *Social Change and the Individual: Japan before and after Defeat in World War II*, 138–79. Princeton: Princeton University Press, 1970.

Tsurumi Shunsuke. *A Cultural History of Postwar Japan 1945–1980*. London: KPI Ltd., 1984.

———. "Wadatsumi no sedai ni tsuite." *Wadatsumi no koe*, no. 3 (1960): 9–11.

Tsurumi Yoshiyuki. "Beheiren." *Japan Quarterly* 16, no. 4 (1969): 444–48.

Uchida Kowashi. "Seinen yo riseiteki yūki no moto ni kesshū seyo." *Wadatsumi no koe*, 25 November 1951.

Uchida Masatoshi. *"Sengo hoshō" o kangaeru*. Tokyo: Kodansha, 1994.

———. *Sengo no shikō: jinken, kenpō, sengo hoshō*. Tokyo: Renga shobō shinsha, 1994.

Ueda Yūji. "Bokutachi no sanka." *Wadatsumi no koe*, no. 1 (1959): 22–24.

Ueno Chizuko. "The Politics of Memory: Nation, Individual and Self." *History and Memory* 11, no. 2 (1999): 129–52.

Ueyama Shunpei. *Daitōa sensō no imi*. Tokyo: Chuō kōronsha, 1964.

Umehara Takeshi. "Shin 'Wadatsumikai' ni tai suru iken." *Wadatsumi no koe*, no. 2 (1960): 1–2.

Urano Masahiko. "Seinenbu ni kitai suru—risō wa takaku, kibō wa ōkiku, soshite kōdō wa daichi ni tsuite." *Nihon izoku tsūshin*, 1 September 1965.

Ushijima Kimiko. "Okinawa ni tsukai shite." *Nihon izoku tsūshin*, 1 September 1952.

Utsumi Aiko. "BC kyū senpan no sengo hoshō o megutte." *Gekkan Forum* 2 (1995): 14–19.

———. "Nihon no sensō sekinin to Ajia." *Rekishi hyōron* (August 1988): 40–50.

Utsumi Aiko et al., eds. *Handobukku sengo hoshō*. Tokyo: Nashi no kiseki, 1993.

Utsumi Aiko, Takagi Ken'ichi, and Tanaka Hiroshi. "Sensō, shokuminchi shihai hansei no kokkai ketsugi o." *Sekai* (March 1995): 160–67.

Wakabayashi, Bob Tadashi. "The Nanking 100-Man Killing Contest Debate." *Journal of Japanese Studies* 26, no. 2 (2000): 307–40.

Wakamiya Yoshibumi. *The Postwar Conservative View of Asia: How the Political Right Has Delayed Japan's Coming to Terms with Its History of Aggression in Asia*. Tokyo: LTCB International Library Foundation, 1999.

———. "War-bereaved Families' Dilemma: Thoughts on Japan's War." *Japan Focus*, 13 July 2005, http://japanfocus.org/products/details/1615.

Watanabe Akio. "The Roles of Non-Governmental Groups in the Reversion of Okinawa." In *Okinawa Reversion*, edited by Hosoya Chihiro, 43–66. Pittsburgh: International Studies Association, 1977.

Watanabe Kiyoshi. "Haigun shōnenhei no haisen taiken." *Shiryō Nihon gendaishi geppō*, no. 10 (1980): 1–7.

Watanabe Nobuo. *Sensō sekinin to sengo sekinin*. Tokyo: Shinkyō shuppansha, 1971.

Weizsäcker, Richard von. "Speech by Richard von Weizsäcker, President of the Federal Republic of Germany, in the Bundestag during the Ceremony Commemorating the 40th Anniversary of the End of the War in Europe and of National Socialist Tyranny, May 8, 1985." In *Bitburg in Moral and Political Perspective*, edited by Geoffrey Hartman, 262–73. Bloomington: Indiana University Press, 1986.

Welfield, John. *An Empire in Eclipse: Japan in the Postwar American Alliance System.* London and Atlantic Highlands, NJ: Athlone Press, 1988.

White, James W. "The Dynamics of Political Opposition." In *Postwar Japan as History*, edited by Andrew Gordon, 424–48. Berkeley, CA: University of California Press, 1993.

Wilson, Sandra. "The Past in the Present: War in Narratives of Modernity in the 1920s and 1930s." In *Being Modern in Japan: Culture and Society from the 1910s to the 1930s*, edited by Elise K. Tipton and John Clark, 170–84. Honolulu: University of Hawai'i Press, 2000.

————. "The Russo-Japanese War and Japan: Politics, Nationalism and Historical Memory." In *The Russo-Japanese War in Cultural Perspective, 1904–05*, edited by David and Sandra Wilson Wells, 160–93. New York: St. Martin's Press, 1999.

Winter, Jay. *Sites of Memory, Sites of Mourning.* Cambridge, UK: Cambridge University Press, 1995.

Wolfe, Robert, ed. *Americans as Proconsuls: United States Military Government in Germany and Japan, 1944–1952.* Carbondale and Edwardsville: Southern Illinois University Press, 1984.

Woodard, William P. *The Allied Occupation of Japan 1945–1952 and Japanese Religion.* Leiden: Brill, 1972.

Yamada Munemutsu. "'Sensō taiken no shisōka' ni tsuite." *Wadatsumi no koe*, no. 5 (1960): 15–20.

Yamaguchi Jiro. "The Gulf War and the Transformation of Japanese Constitutional Politics." *Journal of Japanese Studies* 18, no. 1 (1992): 155–72.

Yamaguchi Keiji and Matsuo Sōichi, eds. *Sengoshi to handō ideorogii.* Tokyo: Shin Nihon shuppansha, 1981.

Yamaguchi Yasushi. "Nihon, doitsu, itaria no sengo." In *Sekai no ima o kangaeru*, edited by Hidaka Rokurō, 35–61. Tokyo: Chikuma shobō, 1989.

————, ed. *Shimin jiritsu no seiji senryaku.* Tokyo: Asahi shinbunsha, 1992.

Yamaguchi Yasushi and Ronald Ruprecht, eds. *Rekishi to aidentitii: Nihon to Doitsu ni totte no 1945 nen (Geschichte und Identität).* Kyoto: Shibunkaku shuppan, 1993.

Yamamoto, Mari. *Grassroots Pacifism in Post-war Japan: The Rebirth of a Nation.* London: RoutledgeCurzon, 2004.

Yamamoto Shichihei. *Watakushi no naka no Nihongun.* Tokyo: Bungei shunjū, 1975.

Yamano Kokichi. *Okinawa henkan hitorigoto.* Tokyo: Gyōsei, 1982.

Yamanouchi, Midori, and Joseph Quinn, S. J., eds. *Listen to the Voices from the Sea.* Scranton: University of Scranton Press, 2000.

Yamashita Hajime. *Gakutō shutsujin gojūnen.* Iwanami booklet, no. 317. Tokyo: Iwanami shoten, 1993.

———. "Kai no undō no kihon hōshin ni tsuite." *Wadatsumi no koe,* no. 1 (November 1959): 4–9.

Yamashita Hajime, Odagiri Hideo, Nakamura Yoshirō, Bekki Tatsuo, Furuyama Hiromitsu, Yasuda Isamu, and Suzuki Hitoshi. "Senryō jidai to 'Wadatsumi no koe.'" *Wadatsumi no koe,* no. 35 (1966): 1–20.

Yamazaki Masakazu. "The Intellectual Community of the Showa Era." In *Showa: The Japan of Hirohito,* edited by Carol Gluck and Stephen R. Graubard, 245–64. New York: W. W. Norton, 1992.

Yamazaki Masato. "History Textbooks That Provoke an Asian Outcry." *Japan Quarterly* 34, no. 1 (1987): 51–55.

Yamazumi Masami. "Textbook Revision: The Swing to the Right." *Japan Quarterly* 29 (1981): 472–78.

Yanagida Kenjūrō. "Sensō wa fukahi de wa nai: 1951 nen o koete." *Wadatsumi no koe,* 15 January 1951.

Yasukawa Junosuke. *Nihon no kindaika to sensō sekinin: Wadatsumi gakutōhei to daigaku no sensō sekinin o tou.* Tokyo: Akashi shoten, 1997.

Yasukuni jinja Yasukuni no inori henshū iinkai, ed. *Yasukuni no inori.* Tokyo: Sankei shinbunsha, 1999.

Yokota Kisaburō. "Sensō hanzai to kokusaihō no kakumei." *Chūō kōron* (January 1946): 31–40.

Yoneyama, Lisa. *Hiroshima Traces: Time, Space, and the Dialectics of Memory.* Berkeley: University of California Press, 1999.

Yoshida, Takashi. "A Battle over History: The Nanjing Massacre in Japan." In *The Nanjing Massacre in History and Historiography,* edited by Joshua Fogel, 70–132. Berkeley: University of California Press, 2000.

———. *The Making of the "Rape of Nanking": History and Memory in Japan, China and the United States.* Oxford, UK: Oxford University Press, 2006.

Yoshida Yutaka. *Gendai rekishigaku to sensō sekinin.* Tokyo: Aoki shoten, 1997.

———. *Nihonjin no sensōkan.* Tokyo: Iwanami shoten, 1995.

———. "Senryōki ni okeru sensō sekininron." *Hitotsubashi ronsō* 105, no. 2 (1991): 121–38.

———. "Sensō no kioku". *Iwanami kōza: Sekai rekishi,* no. 25. Tokyo: Iwanami shoten, 1997.

————. "Sensō sekininron no konnichiteki shikaku." In *Jikō naki sensō sekinin: sabakareru tennō to Nihon*, edited by Ajia minshū hōritsu junbikai, 173–89. Tokyo: Ryōkufū shuppan, 1990.

————. *Shōwa tennō no shūsenshi.* Tokyo: Iwanami shoten, 1992.

Yoshimi Yoshiaki. *Comfort Women.* Translated by Suzanne O'Brien. New York: Columbia University Press, 2000.

————. *Kusa no ne no fashizumu: Nihon minshū no sensō taiken.* Tokyo: Tōkyō daigaku shuppankai, 1987.

————, ed. *Jūgun ianfu shiryōshū.* Tokyo: Ōtsuki shoten, 1992.

Yoshimoto Takaaki and Takei Akio. *Bungakusha no sensō sekinin.* Tokyo: Awaji shobō, 1956.

Index

Abe Shintarō, 244

Adenauer, Konrad, 321

Adorno, Theodor, 139

Aizawa Hiroshi, 180

Akahata (Communist newspaper), 236, 290

Akihito, emperor of Japan, 272

Akuma no hōshoku. See Devil's Gluttony, The (Akuma no hōshoku)

Allied countries, 305, 318

Allied Forces, 1, 17

Allied occupation. *See* occupation

All-Japan Committee of Shinto Youth, 238

All-Japan Liberation Education Research Group, (Zenkoku kaihō kyōiku kenkyūkai), 220

Amaterasu (sun goddess), 39

amnesia, 4. *See also* war memory

Anpo movement, 168, 173, 174–81, 187, 195, 218; intellectuals in, 177, 178; student radicals and, 175–76, 177, 178–79; Wadatsumikai and, 176–77, 178–79; war responsibility and, 175, 177–78

antimilitarism, 63, 104. *See also* pacifism

antinuclear movement, 150, 172, 173, 267, 268; Nils Bohr's participation in, 151; student movements and, 152–53

anti–Security Treaty movement. *See* Anpo movement

Antiterrorism Measures Special Law, 28

antiwar protests, 190, 194, 209. *See also* Anpo movement; pacifism; Wadatsumikai; Teachers' Union and, 217; Vietnam War, 14, 23, 190, 194, 214

apology, 4, 226, 261, 270, 322; to comfort women, 279; compensation and, 313; Diet Resolution, 276–79; to East Asia, 283–84; of Koizumi, 282, 284–85; of Murayama, 262–63, 279–80

"Appeal to the People" (JCP message), 89

Arai Shiroichi, 117

Arisugawa, Prince, 43

Harvard East Asian Monographs
(*out-of-print)

Harvard East Asian Monographs

Harvard East Asian Monographs

Harvard East Asian Monographs

Harvard East Asian Monographs

203. Robert S. Ross and Jiang Changbin, eds., *Re-examining the Cold War: U.S.-China Diplomacy, 1954–1973*

204. Guanhua Wang, *In Search of Justice: The 1905–1906 Chinese Anti-American Boycott*

205. David Schaberg, *A Patterned Past: Form and Thought in Early Chinese Historiography*

206. Christine Yano, *Tears of Longing: Nostalgia and the Nation in Japanese Popular Song*

207. Milena Doleželová-Velingerová and Oldřich Král, with Graham Sanders, eds., *The Appropriation of Cultural Capital: China's May Fourth Project*

208. Robert N. Huey, *The Making of 'Shinkokinshū'*

209. Lee Butler, *Emperor and Aristocracy in Japan, 1467–1680: Resilience and Renewal*

210. Suzanne Ogden, *Inklings of Democracy in China*

211. Kenneth J. Ruoff, *The People's Emperor: Democracy and the Japanese Monarchy, 1945–1995*

212. Haun Saussy, *Great Walls of Discourse and Other Adventures in Cultural China*

213. Aviad E. Raz, *Emotions at Work: Normative Control, Organizations, and Culture in Japan and America*

214. Rebecca E. Karl and Peter Zarrow, eds., *Rethinking the 1898 Reform Period: Political and Cultural Change in Late Qing China*

215. Kevin O'Rourke, *The Book of Korean Shijo*

216. Ezra F. Vogel, ed., *The Golden Age of the U.S.-China-Japan Triangle, 1972–1989*

217. Thomas A. Wilson, ed., *On Sacred Grounds: Culture, Society, Politics, and the Formation of the Cult of Confucius*

218. Donald S. Sutton, *Steps of Perfection: Exorcistic Performers and Chinese Religion in Twentieth-Century Taiwan*

219. Daqing Yang, *Technology of Empire: Telecommunications and Japanese Expansionism, 1895–1945*

220. Qianshen Bai, *Fu Shan's World: The Transformation of Chinese Calligraphy in the Seventeenth Century*

221. Paul Jakov Smith and Richard von Glahn, eds., *The Song-Yuan-Ming Transition in Chinese History*

222. Rania Huntington, *Alien Kind: Foxes and Late Imperial Chinese Narrative*

223. Jordan Sand, *House and Home in Modern Japan: Architecture, Domestic Space, and Bourgeois Culture, 1880–1930*

224. Karl Gerth, *China Made: Consumer Culture and the Creation of the Nation*

225. Xiaoshan Yang, *Metamorphosis of the Private Sphere: Gardens and Objects in Tang-Song Poetry*

226. Barbara Mittler, *A Newspaper for China? Power, Identity, and Change in Shanghai's News Media, 1872–1912*

227. Joyce A. Madancy, *The Troublesome Legacy of Commissioner Lin: The Opium Trade and Opium Suppression in Fujian Province, 1820s to 1920s*

Harvard East Asian Monographs

Harvard East Asian Monographs